4

edition

CAREER
Development & Planning

A
Comprehensive
Approach

Robert C. Reardon, Ph.D.

Janet G. Lenz, Ph.D.

Gary W. Peterson, Ph.D.

James P. Sampson, Jr., Ph.D.

FLORIDA STATE UNIVERSITY

Cover image © 2012, Shutterstock, Inc.

www.kendallhunt.com
Send all inquiries to:
4050 Westmark Drive
Dubuque, IA 52004-1840

Copyright © 2000, 2005 Wadsworth
Copyright © 2006, 2009 Cengage Learning

Copyright © 2012 by Kendall Hunt Publishing Company

ISBN 978-1-4652-0006-8

Printed in the United States of America
10 9 8 7 6 5 4 3 2

Contents

Preface to the Fourth Edition

The aim of *Career Development & Planning: A Comprehensive Approach* is to provide instructors and students with knowledge drawn from cognitive psychology that can be used to solve career problems and make career decisions. This text and related teaching materials provide a comprehensive, integrated system of career learning activities intended to improve instruction and enhance learning outcomes.

In order to meet college level general education requirements, the knowledge base of a textbook is of crucial importance. The three knowledge domains of this text are (a) cognitive and social foundations, (b) the occupational world and work behavior, and (c) career choice and development in individuals and organizations.

Learner Outcomes

As a result of using this text in a course, students will be able to:

1. Understand the multidisciplinary nature of information related to career and work behavior and how individuals differ in the use of that information;
2. Understand the acquisition of semantic and personal knowledge;
3. Understand how memory and cognitive information processing relate to human problem solving in general and career decision making more specifically;
4. Understand how the cognitive approach, including the Pyramid of Information-Processing Domains and the CASVE Cycle, are applied to individual career decision making and problem solving;
5. Identify unique, personal information, including self-knowledge, occupational knowledge, decision-making skills, and metacognitions, affecting career development;
6. Understand how interdisciplinary social and behavioral sciences inform persons about job acquisition and employment processes;
7. Formulate personal goals and action plans designed to proactively enhance one's career/life planning; and
8. Develop personal, employment-related skills and information.

Text Design

The text includes theoretical work in cognitive psychology and relevant knowledge from the applied behavioral sciences.

- Part I (Chapters 1–5) focuses on the theory base in cognitive information processing, with detailed, practical examples of the application of the theory in typical career situations, including self-knowledge, occupational knowledge, and decision making.
- Part II (Chapters 6–10) provides a multidisciplinary overlay of issues that affect career decisions, such as economic trends, organizational culture, new work styles, and dual careers.

- Part III (Chapters 11–15) focuses on concrete steps for executing a strategic career plan and seeking employment, including an examination of familiar topics such as interviewing, resume writing, negotiating, and work adjustment, from a cognitive and multidisciplinary perspective.

This text draws upon cognitive information processing theory (CIP; Peterson, Sampson, & Reardon, 1991; Sampson, Reardon, Peterson, & Lenz, 2004) and the applied behavioral sciences which can assist faculty in obtaining approvals for offering an undergraduate career course at the university level that merits credit for liberal studies or general education. This text integrates knowledge from several career theories judged to be the most influential in the practice of career services. In addition, it has been tested in practice through a variable credit, three semester hour, repeatable career course offered in a university since 1974. Finally, the text uses a learning theory model which means that each student will be expected to acquire cumulative knowledge about career development in addition to learning strategies for solving specific individual career problems.

Validation

Research based on this course has undergone peer review in nine journal articles (see citations at the end of this Preface). In addition, CIP theory and related materials have been peer reviewed, and client versions of the theory-based materials used in the text have appeared in more than a dozen academic journals disseminated worldwide.

The four authors have successfully collaborated on more than 100 occasions writing journal articles, chapters, books, or making professional presentations at national and international meetings. The authors have more than 100 years of combined professional experience in career theory and practice at the college level. The first author of this text has taught this course more than 75 times.

Fourth Edition

The cover shows a pathway or *course* through a forest. We selected this cover because "career" in the *Oxford English Dictionary* is defined as the general *course* or progression of one's working life and professional achievements. Carrière in Old French suggested a *road* for carts or wagons moving people and things. This book is about constructing a unique life *course* through space and time when considering options, which we believe this cover suggests. Career development and planning involves seeing the forest as well as the trees.

We had several goals in producing this fourth edition. First, we wanted to update sources and provide new information about occupations and employment. Several chapters were revised by describing new systems for the delivery of occupational information (3), research about employment (7), ways to work (8), work arrangements (9), work/life balance (10), and developments with the Internet (12). Chapter references and links were updated as needed.

Second, we removed material from some chapters because the book was simply too dense in places—there was just too much content for students to learn or instructors to teach in a three-hour semester class. So, we pruned content in Chapters 2, 3, 5, 6, 8, 10, 11, 14, and 15.

Finally, we updated the *Instructor's Manual* with more strategies based on principles of "active learning." Worksheets, assignments, and other learning tools for students can be found in the appendices of the text. This manual, of about 225 pages, includes teaching and learning activities for 28 classes, test items for each unit, and more than 370 PowerPoint slides.

Acknowledgments

Many of our past and present colleagues have provided ideas to help us produce this latest edition (more than 300 persons have taught this course on our campus). We are especially appreciative of the work of Karin Snider, the acquisitions editor who found us a publishing home and provided support throughout this process, and Michelle Bahr, the project coordinator who managed our work on this new edition for seven months. We look forward to producing future editions of this text and welcome the comments of instructors and students to that end.

Robert C. Reardon, Ph.D.
Janet G. Lenz, Ph.D.
James P. Sampson, Jr., Ph.D.
Gary W. Peterson, Ph.D.

July 2012
Tallahassee, Florida

References

Folsom, B., Peterson, G. W., Reardon, R. C., & Mann, B. (2004–2005). Impact of a career-planning course on academic performance and graduation. *Journal of College Retention, 6,* 461–473.

Gerken, D., Reardon, R. C., & Bash, R. (1988). Revitalizing a career course: The gender roles infusion. *Journal of Career Development, 14,* 269–278.

Lee, J., & Anthony, W. (1974). An innovative university career planning course. *Journal of College Placement, 35,* 59–60.

Reardon, R. C., Leierer, S. J., & Lee, D. (2007). Charting grades over 26 years to evaluate a career course. *Journal of Career Assessment, 15,* 483–498.

Reardon, R. C., Leierer, S. J., & Lee, D. (2012). Class meeting schedules in relation to students' grades and evaluations of teaching, *The Professional Counselor, 2*(1), 81–89.

Reardon, R. C., & Regan, K. (1981). Process evaluation of a career planning course. *Vocational Guidance Quarterly, 29,* 265–269.

Reardon, R. C., & Wright, L. (1999). The case of Mandy: Applying Holland's theory and cognitive information processing theory. *The Career Development Quarterly, 47,* 195–203.

Reed, C. A., Reardon, R. C., Lenz, J. G., & Leierer, S. J. (2001). A cognitive career course: From theory to practice. *The Career Development Quarterly, 50,* 158–167.

Vernick, S. H., Reardon, R. C., & Sampson, J. P., Jr. (2004). Process evaluation of a career course: A replication and extension. *Journal of Career Development, 30,* 201–213.

Chapter One

Introduction to Career Planning

Most of us who have grown up in the United States of America take for granted the idea of having a career. It is almost like a birthright. As the jingle goes, "It's as American as the 4th of July, baseball, apple pie, and Chevrolet." Parents, teachers, and friends expect us to have a career. Our success in life and our identities are often measured by our careers. We go to school and choose a field of study to prepare for our career. The "right" career, we are told, can lead to happy, successful, fulfilling lives.

These are some common ideas about career, and they are shared by important people in society who shape our attitudes and values. These ideas are instilled by teachers, parents, TV broadcasters, preachers, and politicians. These expectations put a lot of pressure on us to pick the right occupation and on society to ensure that good jobs are available to us.

But are good jobs and important careers still reasonable expectations for college students today? This book explores these ideas and examines some new ways of looking at the latest developments in career services, research, and theory. We will focus on things that are effective in helping students solve practical career problems and make career decisions.

A Historical Perspective

Before we explore this new approach to career planning, let's take a brief look at the past. Where did this career idea come from anyway? Has it always been there? What forces out there have contributed to our current thinking about career?

The whole concept of career is pretty new. Indeed, the practice of choosing an occupation was not the norm for most people until the beginning of the twentieth century. In other words, the principle of "having a career" is only about 100 years old. Before that, most people automatically adopted their parents' occupations. If you were a male and your father was a farmer or a shopkeeper, you would probably follow in his footsteps. If you were a female, you often did whatever your mother did. Career choice was almost nonexistent. Your career was what you were born into. There was no need to plan and make a decision yourself: you just followed the path laid down by your family's circumstances.

There were some exceptions. For example, if your family was very wealthy or of a privileged class, you could prepare for one of the professions. You could pursue positions like priest, physician, teacher, artist, or government official. This was especially true if you were male. Of course, all of these required college training, and at that time, college was generally restricted to white men.

Why did things change? Most of the changes were brought about by an external force—the industrial revolution—which in turn brought about other changes. In the

United States, the development of new, big industries such as oil, railroads, textiles, meat packing, shipping, automobiles, utilities, construction, timber, banking, and steel transformed the economy. The jobs created by these industries attracted workers from farms and rural areas who were eager to accumulate wealth and enjoy a higher standard of living. These positions were new; they had not been available to older generations. Suddenly, an enormous number of options were available.

There were also changes due to the freedom and the nature of the economic system in America. In the early 1900s, hundreds of thousands of Europeans uprooted their families, left their native homes, and emigrated to America, the land of opportunity. America wasn't only a place, it was an ideal, and a chance for a person to start over and be anything he or she wanted to be. A newcomer could go into a new trade, start a business, and develop new skills—and become rich and successful in the process. Of course, there were risks. One might fail, but the opportunity to be free of old ways of thinking and living was a powerful attraction. All of this newfound freedom was embodied in career choice and the responsibility to make a good career plan.

There were some problems. In the early 1900s, many of these new jobs were dangerous. Some employers in factories exploited children and recently arrived immigrants. Young people left school to get a factory job and help support their families. In some Eastern cities, the school dropout rate was 90%. Eventually, the federal government passed laws that protected the safety and education of children, enabled workers to organize into unions, and mandated safe working conditions. Many newly arrived immigrants did not speak English or know how to be citizens in this American democracy, and they were sometimes used and abused by dishonest politicians and businesspeople. In many ways, this all sounds like the United States now in the early 21st century.

Enter Vocational Guidance

To help both young people and adults sort out this increasingly complex process of choosing an occupation, a man named Frank Parsons created the Vocations Bureau in 1908 in a neighborhood settlement house in Boston. This new program guided job seekers (especially newly arrived immigrants) in examining their personal characteristics and local employment options and helped them select the best job available. This was the beginning of the career counseling process as we know it today.

Parsons' ideas were very popular, and his book, *Choosing a Vocation* (Parsons, 1909), explained his program to those interested in developing one in another city. Parsons' program defined three steps for making a wise vocational choice:

1. Careful self-assessment of one's interests, skills, values, goals, background, and resources,
2. study all of the available options for school, additional training, employment, and occupations, and
3. a careful reasoning of which choice was best in light of information uncovered in the first two steps.

Parsons' three-step model may strike you as a very logical, rational approach to solving career problems and making career decisions. Perhaps it reflects Parsons' early training as a lawyer, engineer, and professor. In any event, Parsons' ideas are still useful today, a major breakthrough in the way we think about career choice.

Since the early 1950s, career theorists have increasingly promoted the idea that career is not only an occupation or a job, but also a lifelong process of deciding how to live. In other words, Parsons' three-step process is used over and over as a person makes adjustments in his or her life roles. Examples of these life roles include worker, student, parent, and citizen. In this more recent view, vocational guidance is seen to involve more than just choosing and entering an occupation. We will explore these newer ideas later in this chapter.

Careers in the Present Day

This brings us to the present. How is career planning different now from 100 years ago? First, our lives are affected by global and rapid changes that strike at the heart of the career development process. The dramatic transformations that affect us all influence when, how, where, and why we work. This, in turn, affects how we plan and pursue our careers.

The basic nature of work is changing, just as it did a century ago. Gone are the days when one began his or her career at a company or organization and remained there as a loyal employee until retirement. That idea just does not fit the reality of life for many working people today. In addition, work and organizations have become international in scope, not simply bound to one country. Additionally, workers are viewed as a commodity, like fuel or electricity. An American worker is viewed in terms of costs and returns in comparison with a worker in countries like Mexico or China. Chapters 6 and 7 examine these ideas in more detail.

In addition to 40-hour work weeks with benefits, many employees' work schedules are part-time, flextime, temporary, on contingency, or involve telecommuting or other work arrangements, often without benefits. These new, flexible work schedules provide increased complexities for career building. Chapters 7 and 8 examine these ideas.

Diversity in the workplace has affected work and careers in dramatic ways. Organizations in America are now composed of a workforce that reflects the recent wave of immigrants from Central and South America and from Asia and Southeast Asia, surpassing the multitude that came ashore in the early 1900s.

The balance between gender and work is changing. This phenomenon is certainly related to current ideas about family life, but the fact that women are increasingly taking jobs outside the home has led to dramatic shifts in work organizations and in daily family life. The entry of women into the workforce has led to many changes in the way organizations now define job duties and make work-related decisions. This trend has also created pressures for more egalitarian views of male and female roles in the home. In some families today, Dad is expected to do his share of the cooking, housework, child care, and running the household now that Mom works outside the home.

Finally, the career materials and resources available to help people make career and job choices have expanded dramatically. Career professionals call these things career interventions, meaning the computer systems, inventories, books, multimedia and print materials, and professional and para-professional staff that can be used to help people in their career development. The array of potential interventions is much larger now than ever before, and it can be difficult for consumers to know which is best to use in any particular situation.

In summary, the dramatic, rapid changes in our social and economic lives have made career planning a much more challenging task. However, even with all the changes and new complexities, we believe that it is possible for you to learn how to formulate and execute an effective career plan.

Career Problems

The economic recession of 2007–2009 in the U.S. was the most severe since World War II and the Great Depression, with large, dramatic losses of jobs for millions of workers (Bruyere, Podgornik, & Spletzer, 2011). Moreover, Peck (2010) believes that "a whole generation of young adults is likely to see its life chances permanently diminished by this recession" (p. 6). This is a real problem for college students and it requires a strong response in the form of positive thinking, perseverance, adaptability, persistence, and humility.

Individuals often experience great trauma as a result of job loss, a change of career direction, or family-work conflicts. Organizations, however, also suffer great difficulties because of the career problems of workers. One of the most critical issues for any organization is to get the right person into the right position, because this greatly affects the organization's performance. Even nations are aware of the importance of career development. Both new, emerging nations and older, industrialized nations seek to develop educational and economic programs that will enable citizens to be engaged in meaningful career activities wherever possible.

Full employment is the goal of every nation in the world today. A nation's health and strength is often judged in terms of whether its people are working and whether it can produce more than it needs for itself. Nations get into trouble when people are unemployed or underemployed, because as citizens become restless, fearful, and angry at the nation's leaders, there is increased likelihood of revolution and strikes. Some international conflicts have involved one nation's efforts to keep jobs "at home." Individual career development is therefore directly tied to national and global political and economic forces that stimulate job growth.

Jim Clifton, the CEO of the Gallup organization, has conducted worldwide polls and found that "the primary *will of the world* is no longer about peace or freedom or even democracy; it is not about having a family, and it is neither about God nor about owning a home or land. The will of the world is first and foremost to have a good job. Everything else comes in after that" (Clifton, 2011, p. 185).

The quality of career life is important because increases in unemployment have been directly related to increases in individual health problems, domestic violence, and crime. For individuals, the loss of a job is sometimes a trigger for cardiovascular problems, stomach ulcers, emotional stress, and other health problems. Job loss is also associated with increases in child and spouse abuse, robbery, assault, and other forms of personal injury and loss of property. All of this means that when the quality of work life in a nation declines, the social and economic costs to the nation spiral upwards.

In recent years, large organizations such as Countrywide Financial, General Motors, Goldman Sachs, and the State of California have laid off thousands of employees, dramatically revamped jobs and positions, or even gone out of business. The trauma of the collapse or failure of such organizations has far-reaching effects on both individuals and communities. Your individual career development may be directly tied to the success and stability of an industry or an organization.

Career problems are important because of their magnitude. Every day millions of people move in and out of employment or move from one job to another; there is great instability in the job market. Sometimes these shifts can even be thought of as "careerquakes" (Bolles, 2012). Given the importance of full employment for individuals and nations, cataclysmic events such as an economic recession, where millions become unemployed in a short period of time, are profoundly important. To make matters worse, the system for getting people back into the workforce is very inefficient. The quality of your career will likely be affected by the economic health of your country, industry, and organization, as well as the methods you use to find jobs.

Career Development Terms

Familiar words like *career, vocation, work, employment, job, occupation, position,* and *industry* deserve special attention in this book because in the career development field they have different meanings from their ordinary, common usage in the news media or casual conversation. We will give other words such as *interest, value, skill, ability,* and *goal* special treatment in terms of definitions.

Why are these special definitions needed? One reason is that this is the way knowledge and facts in the career development field are organized and communicated. It is important for you in your career decision making to know the difference between occupational information, employment information, and career information, because the facts and data for each are different. When you seek assistance in solving a career problem, you need to ask for the right kind of information. Using the correct terms helps you more quickly get the right answers.

Another reason these special definitions are needed is that the tools of career development services, such as inventories and computer information systems, use this special terminology. To be an informed consumer of career services, you need to know and effectively use the terminology of this field.

Definitions

Here are several of the most important definitions in the career field. We will focus on other important terms that you need to know throughout the book. The following definitions are taken from an article in the *Vocational Guidance Quarterly* (Sears, 1982).

CAREER DEVELOPMENT. The total constellation of economic, sociological, psychological, educational, physical, and chance factors that combine to shape one's career.

Career development is a big concept, as this definition indicates. It is affected by money and financial resources, group membership and social class, mental health and personality, educational level and record, physical abilities and traits, and chance factors. All of these factors combine to influence how one's career path unfolds. It is important to note that no single one of them determines a person's career, but rather they combine in complex ways to shape it. Later on, we will look more closely at how one expert, Dr. Anne Roe, thought these factors might combine to shape a person's career.

CAREER. Time extended working out of a purposeful life pattern through work undertaken by the person.

This definition was developed by the National Career Development Association and is the one most widely used in the career field. There are some important ideas contained in this definition of career that have practical importance for persons engaged in career planning.

Time extended indicates that career is not something that happens as the result of one event or choice. A career is not time limited or tied to one particular job or occupation. Rather, a career is a process that is lifelong and affected by forces within and outside a person. Some experts in the field even use the term "life/career" as a way to connect life processes to the idea of career.

Working out indicates that career is the result of compromises and tradeoffs between what a person might want and what is possible, between the ideal and real. A career develops as a result of a continuing series of choices that the person makes when considering the costs and risks of particular options in light of the rewards. There is no "perfect" career path for a person, but there may be one that is optimal.

Purposeful means that a career has meaning for the person. A career doesn't just happen by accident or luck; it is planned, contemplated, worked on, and executed. A career develops because of the motivation, aspirations, and goals of the person. It reflects the person's values and beliefs.

Life pattern means that a career is more than a person's employment or job. Career encompasses all the adult life roles (e.g., parent, spouse, homemaker, student) and the ways in which the person blends and arranges those roles.

Work is probably one of the most misunderstood words in the career field. We all have an idea what it means, but among career professionals *work is an activity that produces something of value for oneself or others.*

Work, then, is not limited to activity for which we get paid. It can include unpaid, volunteer activity if it produces something valuable for us or another person, such as coaching youth baseball, leading the church choir, painting landscapes, or mastering a computer program. Thus, leisure activities can be part of one's career, and sometimes a very important part. Work, not employment, is the way in which the concept of career is operationally defined.

To make this point even clearer, Cawsey, Deszca, and Mazerolle (1995, p. 44) cited Handy's (1989) description of five types of work. As a college student, you are already engaged in some of these types of work, especially number 5:

1. *Wage work*, where payment is for time and effort.
2. *Fee work*, where payment is for results.
3. *Home work* is done in the home—child raising or lawn care.
4. *Gift work* is voluntary or charitable work.
5. *Learning work* is studying and learning new skills.

Finally, *undertaken by the person* underscores the idea that a career is unique to the person. In reality, no two people have the same "career" because the career is based on an individual's unique history and situation. Although people may have similar interests or skills and be employed in the same occupation and work for the same organization, their careers are different.

In summary, this definition of the word *career* changes the focus from "finding a career out there that's right for me" to "developing the career that is me." The good news for some people is that the focus of career planning shifts to oneself. For others, the responsibility of developing a career is frightening. The purpose of this book is to help you acquire tools to make good career choices and to take responsibility for them.

Those involved in solving career problems and making career decisions often confuse the terms career, occupation, position, and job. In a nutshell, careers have meaning in terms of people, and they are all unique to each individual. Occupations, positions, and jobs, on the other hand, exist in organizations and industries, separate from what people bring to them. We can use our research skills to find out about them because the information exists "out there."

OCCUPATION. A group of similar positions found in different industries or organizations.

An occupation, which might be a trade or a profession, exists apart from a person. It is found in an industry or an organization. Accountant, for example, is an occupation, and it might exist in the pharmaceutical industry or the Federal Bureau of Investigation (FBI), an organization.

POSITION. A group of tasks performed in an organization; a unit of work with a recurring or continuous set of tasks. A task is a unit of job behavior with a beginning point and an ending point performed in a matter of hours rather than days.

Positions are formed when an organization identifies an area of knowledge or a set of skills—tasks—that will enable the organization to function better if the tasks are completed. For example, the X-Y-Z Company decides it needs someone to improve the information flow among employees, customers, and investors. The company writes a new position description for a "communication specialist" and then seeks to hire a person to do the job.

A position exists whether it is vacant or filled, though when one is "looking for a job," he or she typically applies for a vacant position. A person may work in many different positions over the course of lifelong employment, even if it is in the same organization or occupation. Ordinarily, positions are filled by paid employees, but some organizations have identified unpaid, volunteer positions.

JOB. A paid position requiring some similar traits or attributes held by a person.

A job may consist of one or a group of similar paid positions that are traditionally performed within a 40-hour week. A person may work in numerous different jobs over the course of a lifetime. Jobs may involve self-employment or have special meaning if employment is in a particular organization. Jobs are held by people, and they are task-, outcome-, and organization-centered. To help you compare and contrast the terms *position* and *job*, think of them this way: People lose or gain *jobs*; organizations lose or gain *positions*.

In conclusion, remember that only career is unique to each person as he or she makes life choices over the years. A career may or may not include one's occupational activities, which means that all of us are already in our career. A career isn't really something we prepare for—that's an occupation or a job—but it's something that we live, experience, and are already in the process of becoming. Ultimately, our career is a vital aspect of our lives.

We told you that this book would present some new ideas about the idea of career, and these concepts and their definitions, which will be used throughout the book, will help you understand exactly what we are talking about.

Factors Involved in Career Decisions

Thus far, we have outlined some of the current ways of thinking about careers from individual, organizational, and national perspectives to help you expand your perception of the scope of the career field beyond that of simply an individual making a single career choice. Successful career planning in today's world requires considerable knowledge and skill.

One career theorist, Dr. Anne Roe, devoted a major part of her life to unraveling some of the complexities associated with career decisions and shedding some light on what leads a person to choose a particular occupation. She studied the career behavior of scientists and artists in the 1940s. She theorized that there were 12 different factors that could be grouped into four different categories that explain a person's occupational choice (Roe & Lunneborg, 1990). She arranged these factors into an algebraic formula, shown in Table 1.1, which looks a bit scary but really helps us understand more fully the complexity of career choices. Let's take this formula apart piece by piece. Roe used the lowercase letter to show how each of the 12 general factors, shown in upper case, can be affected by the unique characteristics of a person at a particular point in time, given a person's unique circumstances. Each person's formula would be unique. It is interesting to note that only S (sex) has no modifier before the factor, but it is a general modifier that affects all 11 other factors. Do you think gender is that important in occupational choice?

Table 1.1

Roe's Formula

Occupational Choice = S[(eE + bB + cC) + (fF, mM) + (lL + aA) + (pP × gG × tT × iI)]S = sex

E = the general state of the economy	A = special acquired skills
B = family background, ethnicity	P = physical characteristics
C = chance	G = cognitive or special natural abilities
F = friends, peer group	T = temperament and personality
M = marital situation	I = interests and values
L = general learning and education	

From *Career Choice and Development: Applying Contemporary Theories to Practice*, 2nd Edition by D. Brown, L. Brooks, and Associates. Copyright © 1990 Jossey-Bass Inc., Publishers. Reprinted with permission of John Wiley & Sons, Inc.

Finally, Roe divided the factors (other than sex) into four groups, each within parentheses. In general, the first group includes factors over which a person has little control, whereas the factors in the last three groups include those that are based on both inheritance and experience. We assume that individuals can to some degree choose their experiences or interests. Roe's analysis helps us understand why career development and occupational choice are sometimes so difficult. Solving career problems and making career decisions are complex tasks, but with time, motivation, and effort, we can develop skills and learn how to take control of our career. That is the philosophy of this book.

Theories of Career Choice and Development

Since Parsons began his work in the early 1900s, psychologists, sociologists, economists, and educators have sought to improve our understanding of how people make career choices and solve career problems. The knowledge they have accumulated can be thought of as a discipline or a body of knowledge. The field of career development is multidisciplinary and includes vocational psychology, occupational sociology, labor market economics, and vocational behavior.

The research and theory presented in this book are the foundations of the practical suggestions on how you can increase the likelihood of career satisfaction. You are likely to make better career decisions if you use information based on scholarship and approach the task systematically.

There is another practical reason to learn about career theories. Simply stated, we intuitively use our Personal Career Theory, or PCT (Holland, 1997), in solving career problems and making career decisions. For example, you might say, "I'm an outdoor kind of person, and I like the water and my biology classes. I think I'll be a marine biologist." People who know you well might say, "I think you'd be a great elementary school teacher." In both instances, knowledge of yourself and educational and occupational options were used to create a match and specify an occupation. Some career theorists (Holland is one example) have studied these kinds of matches for 60 years. Learning more about Holland's theory might help you improve your PCT.

> *When your PCT breaks down and no longer is effective in helping you solve career problems and make career decisions, then you might consult a professional career counselor or obtain special assistance to improve your PCT. The purpose of this book, in a real sense, is to help you improve the quality of your PCT and to enable you to become a more effective career decision maker.*

In this book, we draw upon the work of several career theorists whose ideas have taken shape in many of the inventories, computer systems, and materials used in this course as career interventions. We will begin with the work of Frank Parsons and John Holland and conclude with the work of Donald Super and the group at Florida State University.

PARSONS. Frank Parsons is considered a structured theorist. Why? He focused on each occupational or career choice separately and independently, and he wanted to examine all the factors associated with both the individual and the occupational alternatives. Parsons emphasized the need for good information in career decision making, both for the person and his or her options. For Parsons, the final step was for the person to carefully use logical reasoning skills to decide which option was best. A person with poor information about him or herself or occupations and jobs and/or a person with poor reasoning skills would be in danger of making a poor occupational choice. Parsons viewed high-quality self-assessment and occupational and employment information combined with a skilled counselor as essential to helping persons solve career problems.

HOLLAND. Dr. John Holland (1997) developed a "typological" theory about personality types and matching environmental groups. We will examine more closely Holland's RIASEC theory later, because his work since 1950 has led to the creation of the most widely used tools and materials in the career field. Holland's theory continues to produce a great amount of research—more than 2,000 published studies—on how people choose occupations. His interest inventory, the Self-Directed Search, has sold over 30 million copies and been translated into 25 languages since it was introduced in 1970. Holland's approach can also be used to study various social and work environments, including occupations, positions, organizations, schools, and interpersonal relationships.

SUPER. One of the most important "process" theorists was Dr. Donald Super. Super (1990) began to introduce new ways of thinking about career development in the early 1950s. For example, he noted that an occupational choice is based partly on a person's self-concept; that is, a person seeks to implement his or her self-concept through the choice of occupation(s). This idea bound together the concepts of personality and occupation, resulting in the idea of career.

Super introduced the life/career rainbow because he believed that nine life roles was a good way for us to understand the concept of career. Each person occupies one or more of these roles at different times throughout his or her lifetime. In addition, the intensity or strength of each role varies over time for each person. The combination and intensity of life roles are the basis of the person's career. Some roles are defined in terms of biology and inheritance, and some are chosen by the individual (this is similar to what Roe observed). As you can see in Figure 1.1, the nine roles are (a) child (son or daughter), (b) student, (c) leisurite, (d) citizen, (e) worker, (f) annuitant/pensioner, (g) spouse or partner, (h) homemaker, and (i) parent or grandparent. Which roles do you anticipate having in your life/career? How strong or intensely will you be involved in those roles? At what age or ages will those roles be active? Which forces are internal and which are external?

figure 1.1

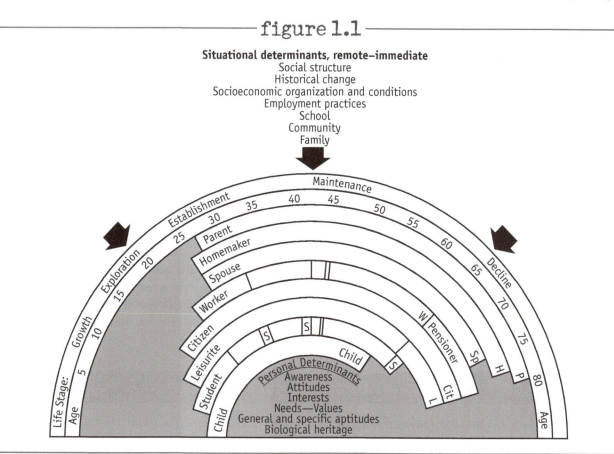

Super's Life/Career Rainbow

Journal of Vocational Behavior by Academic Press. Reproduced with permission of Academic Press in the format Journal via Copyright Clearance Center.

By focusing on career development in terms of a person's self-concept, age, and life roles, Super helped us more clearly understand what is involved in career development and decision making. Clearly, career planning involves more than selecting a college major, an occupation, or a place of employment. It involves a thorough examination of oneself and all of the roles we play in life.

Now that we have examined these scholars' thoughtful contributions to our understandings of career behavior, we can now venture forth in our efforts to further engage the process of career problem solving and decision making and take a look at the cognitive information processing (CIP) approach to understanding career development.

Cognitive Information Processing

In 1991, Drs. Gary Peterson, James Sampson, and Robert Reardon wrote *Career Development and Services: A Cognitive Approach.* This book presented a new way of thinking about career development. This CIP approach was based on eight assumptions. The essence of these assumptions is as follows:

1. Career choices are based on how we think and feel.
2. Making career choices is a problem-solving activity.
3. Our ability as career problem solvers is based on what we know and how we think.
4. Career decisions require a good memory.
5. Career decisions require motivation.
6. Career development continues as part of our lifelong learning and growth.
7. Our career depends largely on what and how we think about it.

8. The quality of our career depends on how well we learn to make career decisions and solve career problems.

What do we mean by cognition? Basically, it is the way we think or how we process information in our heads. Psychologists believe that we maintain several different kinds of knowledge structures or components in our long-term memories that are important in career decision making. First, we deal with facts and concepts about occupations, majors, and so forth. Second, we maintain memories about experiences and past events in our lives. Third, we have sets of rules and guidelines that we use in finding solutions to problems. Fourth, we have more general strategies or rules of thumb that we use in problem solving.

The CIP approach (Peterson, Sampson, Lenz, & Reardon, 2002; Sampson, Reardon, Peterson, & Lenz, 2004) used in this book is ultimately based on ideas about how our brain takes in, codes, stores, and uses information and knowledge in career problem solving and decision making.

Learning more about how to process information is especially important in career decision making because there are so many facts, data, and opinions bombarding us daily on this matter. The science of decision making has shown that more information can actually lead to poorer choices (Begley, 2011). For these reasons, we believe the CIP approach can help people make better use of all the information available for career decisions. At this point we will move on to how CIP works in practice.

What Is Involved in Career Choice

We believe that career problems have some common characteristics.

1. They can be defined in terms of a gap between what exists and what we want. It's the difference between what's happening and what, ideally, we want to happen.
2. Career problems are often complex and involve feelings; they present ambiguous cues or signals. The complexity comes from conflicting desires and motives, pressures from others, and feelings such as worry and embsarrassment.
3. The solution to career problems often involves multiple options, not just a single correct choice. Each option seems to affect others, interdependently, so the best solution is typically a combination of options.
4. There is almost always some uncertainty about the outcome of the choice. No chosen solution to a career problem comes with a guarantee for success and satisfaction.
5. A decision about a major career problem almost always leads to another set of problems that are not fully known beforehand.

We think these five things are common to all career problems. How many of these relate to your present career situation?

An Information-Processing Pyramid

Figure 1.2 shows a pyramid with the components involved in making a career choice. The bottom two parts of the pyramid are called the *knowledge domain*, and they include knowing about myself (*self-knowledge*) and knowing about my options (*occupational knowledge*). Self-knowledge includes knowing about my values, my interests, my skills, and related personal characteristics. Occupational knowledge includes understanding about specific occupations, college majors, and/or jobs and how they can be organized.

The bottom of the pyramid, the knowledge domain, can be likened to the data files stored in the memory of a computer. The bits of information are stored as schemata (plural: schema), or a dynamic piece of information. These schema enable us to work with and process information in career

figure 1.2

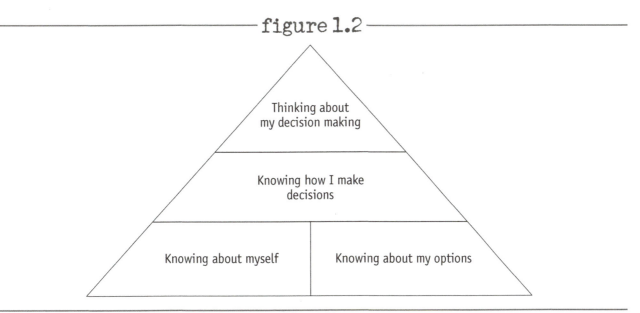

Pyramid of Information-Processing Domains in Career Decision Making

Reprinted from *The Career Development Quarterly, 41*, 1992, p. 70, copyrighted NCDA. Reprinted with permission of the National Career Development Association. Used with permission.

problem solving and decision making. In the occupational knowledge domain, for example, as we learn more about accountants, we develop better, more detailed schema about an accountant's job, skills, interests, and so forth. Likewise, in the self-knowledge domain, when we take an interest inventory, we may grasp a clearer picture of our interest patterns.

The second level of the pyramid, knowing how I make decisions (*decision skills domain*), includes the five-step guide to good decision making (see Figure 1.3). This level can be likened to the computer programs that use facts and data stored in the memory and files of the computer. Career problem solving uses a lot of memory space and requires a lot of information-processing capacity in our brains. To do it well, we have to be focused and concentrate, just like an athlete preparing for a race. This leads us to the top of the pyramid.

Thinking about my decision making (*executive processing domain*) is the top of the pyramid. This part of the pyramid is like the job-control function that tells the computer in what order the

figure 1.3

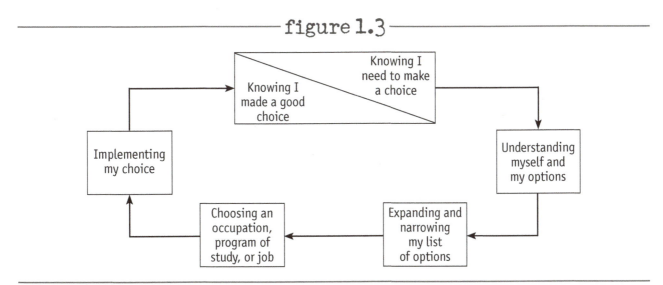

Guide to Good Decision Making

Reprinted from *The Career Development Quarterly, 41*, 1992, p. 70, copyrighted NCDA. Reprinted with permission of the National Career Development Association. Used with permission.

programs in the second level of the pyramid are to be run. For example, you might work on solving the problem of choosing a major before you focus on occupations and organizations to work for, or you might focus on your preferred lifestyle (e.g., frequent travel) and then work on occupational choices. These thoughts govern when and how we decide to work on our goals or the way in which we will solve career problems. And these kinds of thoughts help us figure out when we have reached our goals.

This CIP approach is a simple, effective way to help you learn how to solve career problems and make career decisions. It improves career development because it focuses on how to locate, store, and use information in decision making. What does your Pyramid of Information-Processing Domains look like? Is it strong in the knowledge domains and weak in decision making (e.g., CASVE Cycle)? Does it change as you acquire new information about yourself or the world of work? What is the quality of your thinking (negative or positive) in the executive processing area? The nature of a person's Pyramid can provide information about how effective that person will be in solving career problems and making career decisions. This book should help you improve the quality of the information-processing in your PCT.

Summary

In this chapter, we looked at social forces that led to the beginnings of the career development field in the early 1900s. Examples of why and how career problems are important for individuals and nations were provided. We also reviewed some of the highlights of how modern experts view the career area and how those views differ from traditional, more common views. Finally, we briefly introduced the CIP approach and the Pyramid of Information-Processing Domains, which are explored in more detail later in the book.

References

Begley, S. (2011, March 7). I can't think. *Newsweek*, 28–33.

Bolles, R. (2012). *A practical manual for job hunters and career changers: What color is your parachute?* Berkeley, CA: Ten Speed Press.

Bruyere, C. N., Podgornik, G. L., & Spletzer, J. R. (2011). Employment dynamics over the last decade. *Monthly Labor Review Online, 134*(8), 16–29.

Cawsey, T. F., Deszca, G., & Mazerolle, M. (1995, Fall). The portfolio career as a response to a changing job market. *Journal of Career Planning and Employment*, 41–46.

Clifton, J. (2011). *The coming jobs war.* New York, NY: Gallup Press.

Handy, C. (1989). *The age of unreason.* Boston, MA: Harvard Business School Press.

Holland, J. (1997). *Making vocational choices* (3rd ed.). Odessa, FL: Psychological Assessment Resources.

Parsons, F. (1909). *Choosing a vocation.* Tulsa, OK: National Career Development Association.

Peck, D. (2010, March). How a new jobless era will transform America. *The Atlantic Online.* Retrieved from http://www.theatlantic.com/doc/print/201003/jobless-america-future

Peterson, G. W., Sampson, J. P., Jr., & Reardon, R. C. (1991). *Career development and services: A cognitive approach.* Pacific Grove, CA: Brooks/Cole.

Peterson, G. W., Sampson, J. P., Jr., Lenz, J. G., & Reardon, R. C. (2002). A cognitive information processing approach in career problem solving and decision making. In D. Brown (Ed.), *Career choice and development* (4th ed., pp. 312–369). San Francisco, CA: Jossey-Bass.

Roe, A., & Lunneborg, P. (1990). Personality development and career choice. In D. Brown & L. Brooks (Eds.), *Career choice and development* (2nd ed., pp. 68–101). San Francisco, CA: Jossey-Bass.

Sampson, J. P., Jr., Reardon, R. C., Peterson, G. W., & Lenz, J. G. (2004). *Career counseling and services: A cognitive information processing approach.* Pacific Grove, CA: Wadsworth-Brooks/Cole.

Sears, S. (1982). A definition of career guidance terms: A National Vocational Guidance Association perspective. *Vocational Guidance Quarterly, 31,* 137–143.

Super, D. (1990). A life-span, life-space approach to career development. In D. Brown & L. Brooks (Eds.), *Career choice and development* (2nd ed., pp. 197–261). San Francisco, CA: Jossey-Bass.

Chapter Two

Knowing about Myself

Students come to the career center needing to decide on their major field of study, and their first question is often, "What major will guarantee that I get a job when I graduate?" Others sometimes ask "What are the best-paying jobs available to me after I graduate?" In both cases, the students are looking for information about things "out there" in order to make a career decision.

These students are focusing on the part of the Pyramid of Information-Processing Domains that involves "knowing about my options." As we explained in Chapter 1, this is one part of the knowledge domain where facts and information are stored. This is where some people want to begin the process of solving career problems and making career decisions.

However, we think it is better to start with the part of the knowledge domain that involves "knowing about myself" (see Figure 2.1). Starting with this area puts the initial focus on you, the decision maker. Ultimately, you will be the one who must take the final responsibility for making your career choices. Also, it is easier and less confusing to begin the career-planning process by looking at yourself. This information is already available to you in your life experiences, the episodes that have shaped your life thus far.

---

figure 2.1

What's Involved in Career Choice

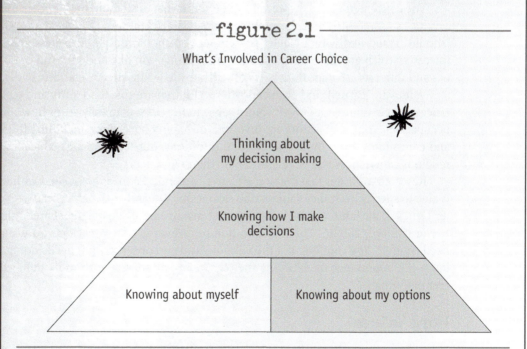

Self-Knowledge—CIP Pyramid

Reprinted from *The Career Development Quarterly, 41,* 1992, p. 70, copyrighted NCDA. Reprinted with permission of the National Career Development Association. Used with permission.

The facts and data about occupations, employers, and fields of study can be overwhelming; the *Dictionary of Occupational Titles* (U.S. Department of Labor, 1991) described over 12,000 different occupations, and new ones are created every day. We believe you know yourself well enough to specify some things you like and don't like, and this should narrow the options "out there" that you need to get more information about. This can help you avoid wasting time and energy learning about occupations that aren't important to you, may not exist tomorrow, and don't match your interests and skills.

> *Self-knowledge will be the cornerstone of your career planning. We will examine some ways that you can improve your self-knowledge for career decision making and provide some methods for you to use in that process. You should use this information to improve the quality of your Personal Career Theory, especially with respect to the Pyramid of Information-Processing Domains and CASVE Cycle.*

In Chapter 1, we reviewed the work of some of the more important career theorists. We noted that Dr. Anne Roe identified 12 different factors that were important in choosing an occupation. Other psychologists have identified even more personal characteristics that they believe are involved in career decisions. Although more detailed lists of self-knowledge factors are sometimes useful in special cases, we believe that three factors—values, interests, and skills—are the most essential parts of self-knowledge in career decisions made by college students. We will examine how each of these three contributes to improved self-knowledge and career planning.

Values

Beginning in the 1950s, Dr. Donald Super, Dr. Martin Katz, and other psychologists began to study how values, or more specifically work values, might be involved in career choices. This research has shown that values are indeed a factor in career decision making, and they are also related to levels of later job satisfaction. A person's well-being and self-esteem are highest when that person lives according to his or her values.

The concept of values, however, can be somewhat difficult to define. One useful way of defining a value is "something that is important or desirable to you." There may even be an element of "should" associated with a value, "something you should do." Values are sometimes confused with interests, which are more likely thought of as "things you like to do for fun or enjoyment." Both values and interests are important parts of self-knowledge in career decisions.

Values are learned, and even very young children are able to identify and rate the relative importance of their values. Our work values seem to develop separately from how much we know about occupations. A host of factors are involved in shaping our values, including the values of our family and community, our ethnic and cultural traditions, our teachers and educational experiences, our religious experiences and beliefs, and our friends and peers.

Research indicates that making effective career decisions is associated with how clearly a person is able to specify his or her values—the clearer our values, the easier the career-planning process. Peter Drucker, the famous social observer and management consultant, shared this observation with a friend (Buford, 2009): "The first question to answer is not 'What do you want to do?' but 'What needs doing?' You can look out the window, and you observe what needs doing." This insight highlights the importance of clarifying the relative importance of your individual values in effective career planning.

Work Values

Super and others (Nevill & Super, 1986) studied the idea of work importance, sometimes called work salience, from the standpoint of values. They discovered that some people don't place very much value on work, which is why they may have difficulty in career decision making. They may place more importance on parenting and family life, spouse or partner relationships, leisure and play, or learning and being a student. We will examine this idea more in Chapter 10 when we explore changing work and family roles.

However, another psychologist, Martin Katz, identified work-related values that might help a person clarify the rewards and satisfactions available in an occupation. In the late 1960s, Katz (1993) conducted an exhaustive study of about 250 occupations to determine how they might be rated on 10 career values. Table 2.1 shows the eight values currently being used and the definitions for each. Katz eventually developed a values-clarification exercise for use in a computer-based career guidance system called System for Interactive Guidance Information (SIGI, pronounced "Siggy"). The current version is called SIGI3 (Valpar International Corp., 2007).

Table 2.1

SIGI Career Values

Contribution to Society
Almost all work contributes to the functioning of society. But you want your work to be devoted mainly to the improvement of the health, education, or welfare of society as a whole.

High Income
You want an occupation in which the median income is high compared with other occupations. The median is the point at which half earn more, half less.

Independence
You want to work without close supervision, not be required to follow daily instructions to the letter.

Leadership
You want to guide others, tell them what to do, get them to work together, be responsible for their performance. You're willing to accept the blame when things go wrong.

Leisure
You want short hours or long vacations. You feel that the satisfactions you get off the job are so important that work must not interfere with them.

Prestige
You want an occupation that will lead people to look up to you, listen to your opinions, or seek your help in community affairs.

Security
You want work that is not sensitive to recession, abrupt changes in technology, government spending, or public taste. You want to avoid seasonal ups and downs in income.

Variety
You want different activities and problems, people, or places—not a fixed routine. You probably get bored if the work doesn't change.

Reprinted by permission of Valpar International Corporation, the copyright owner of SIGI and SIGI PLUS. SIGI is a registered trademark of Valpar International Corporation.

One aspect of Katz's exercise was the idea that one must prioritize values because it may not always possible to have all of one's important values implemented in an occupational choice.

Occupations and jobs have not been created for the purpose of fulfilling all of our important values. Another idea from Katz was that a person's system of values—that is, how compatible or harmonious several top values were with one another—was as important in career decisions as the person's most important value. For example, the values of "high income" and "security" are often not very compatible. Katz believed that values were more important than interests in career decision making, but as we shall see, other psychologists disagree on this point.

Values Clarification

People who have a clear sense of their values often have less difficulty in career planning. Some experts (Raths, Simon, & Harmin, 1966) have suggested that it is the process of clarifying one's values that is most important, not the actual content of the values themselves. They have identified seven steps in the valuing or values clarification process, grouped into three phases. The *first phase* in the valuing process is choosing a value, in which you (a) select a value freely and without pressure from other persons, (b) from among other alternative values, and (c) after thinking about the results from each choice. The *second phase*, prizing your values, involves (d) cherishing or being pleased with your values choices and (e) being willing to state your choice publicly to others when appropriate. The *third phase* in the valuing process, acting on your values, involves (f) doing something behavioral in relation to your choice (such as voting) and (g) acting in a pattern that is consistent and repetitive with your values choices.

Think about one of your important work values and see if you can "clarify" it by going through the seven steps identified above.

Interests

Interest- things one enjoys and have fun..

From the earliest days of Frank Parsons, career development experts have zeroed in on interests as an important part of occupational choice. Before psychological tests and inventories were developed, career counselors would ask persons to list their hobbies, identify people they admired, or describe their likes and dislikes in an autobiography. Even today, these are good ways to identify a person's interests. Identification of a person's interests was seen by early career counselors as a way to identify possible future occupations.

We defined interests as "those things a person does for fun or enjoys." Interest inventories and tests were developed by Dr. Frederick Kuder, Dr. E. K. Strong, and other psychologists in the 1940s that were geared to helping people sort out their likes and dislikes. These psychologists had discovered that people working in various occupations had distinctive patterns of interests. For example, the interests of accountants were different from those of engineers and nurses. Thus, if interests could be quickly and reliably measured, it would simplify the career-planning process.

The development and extensive use of these interest inventories were highly successful. The Strong Interest Inventory (Strong, 1994), the Kuder Career Search with Person Match (Zytowski & Kuder, 1999), and many other such tests are still widely used today. The essence of these interest inventories is that they measure a person's responses to several hundred items about personal likes and dislikes, and then the inventories compare the person's profile with the profiles of others already in occupations to see if there are any matches.

Holland's Typology

In the early 1970s, another psychologist, Dr. John Holland, began to introduce some new ways of thinking about interests and interest measurement (Holland, 1997). Holland suggested that interests were simply another way of describing personality characteristics and that it was really the broader concept of personality that was most important in occupational choice. Personality was seen as a combination of interests, values, needs, skills, beliefs, attitudes, and learning styles. With respect to occupational choice, however, interests were the most important part of personality on which to match people with occupations.

Holland also discovered that interests could be quickly and reliably measured by asking a person to list in order the occupations they would most like to enter. He called this "expressed" interest measurement. Whereas some psychologists used longer inventories with many test items to measure interests—sometimes called "assessed" interest measurement—Holland focused on expressed interest measurement. Holland's approach took some of the mystery out of interest measurement and occupational choice and placed in the hands of ordinary people the tools to search for occupations compatible with their personalities.

How does Holland's idea work? The reason for the success of this new matching approach was based on Holland's development of a hexagon model for examining how interests in one area compared with interests in another area and ultimately for matching people and occupations. In a nut-shell, the theory is based on four ideas.

1. Most people can be categorized as one of six RIASEC types: Realistic, Investigative, Artistic, Social, Enterprising, or Conventional.
2. There are also six kinds of RIASEC environments: Realistic, Investigative, Artistic, Social, Enterprising, or Conventional (see Table 2.2 for more information).
3. People search for environments that will let them exercise their skills and abilities, express their attitudes and values, and take on agreeable problems and roles (see Table 2.3 for more information).
4. A person's behavior is determined by an interaction between his or her personality and characteristics of an environment.

Let's examine these four basic assumptions or ideas behind Holland's theory in more detail. First, the idea that people can be categorized into types is a familiar one in psychology. People or, more precisely, their personalities are sometimes grouped in terms of friendliness, competitiveness, creativity, and other characteristics. Holland's idea of using six different categories for sorting personality is based on this familiar idea. However, the six RIASEC types that Holland identified have been shown, through extensive research since the late 1950s, to be useful, reliable ways to categorize personalities. More importantly, this research demonstrated that interests can be reliably measured in terms of these six different types and that our personality is basically composed of combinations of these six types. A person's interests and personality for the most part become more stable and less likely to change beginning at about age 21. It may be helpful to think of personality as a pie with six slices, some of which may be much larger than others. Each person's pie is a unique combination of these six interests, but usually one of the six types is the largest piece.

Second, what about the idea of six environments like the six types? For Holland, an environment could be an occupation, a job, a leisure activity, an educational program or field of study, a college, or even the culture of an organization. Environments can be thought of as dominated by a given type of personalities, that is, the Realistic environment is dominated by or has the largest percentage of Realistic types. An environment can even be thought of as a social relationship with another person. For example, your "realistic" friend creates a realistic environment for you because of her interests, hobbies, skills, and so forth.

Third, people seek out environments where their personality characteristics will be respected, valued, rewarded, and used. Think of this as the "birds of a feather flock together" saying. For example, Artistic persons will seek out Artistic environments—jobs, leisure, clubs, friends—where their creativity, independence, and idealism will be valued.

Fourth, a person's behavior is the result of the interaction between personalities and environmental characteristics. If a Realistic person ends up in a Social environment, he or she may be unhappy, tense, stressed, and alienated, perform poorly, and soon take steps to get out of that Social environment.

Inspection of the hexagon in Figure 2.2 provides some additional insight into Holland's typology theory. First, you will notice that the types that are adjacent or closest on the hexagon have relatively more in common, for example, E and S. Second, notice that the types farthest apart on the hexagon have the least in common: R and S or C and A. One of Holland's colleagues discovered that the six types relate to one another in ways that resemble this hexagon figure. One of the practical results of this finding is that people and occupations typically include types that are adjacent or alternate on the hexagon.

Holland developed a number of practical devices for helping people identify their type and compatible environments. For example, the Self-Directed Search (SDS) (Holland, 1994) is widely used to help people identify their interests or personality type in relation to career planning. When persons complete the SDS inventory, they obtain a three-letter "summary code," because the results are reported in the three-letter combination that best describes their personality characteristics. For

Table 2.2

RIASEC Personality Typology

Attribute	Personality Type					
	Realistic	Investigative	Artistic	Social	Enterprising	Conventional
Preferences for activities and occupations	Manipulation of machines, tools and things	Exploration, understanding and prediction or control of natural and social phenomena	Literary, musical, or artistic activities	Helping, teaching, treating, counseling, or serving others through personal interaction	Persuading, manipulating, or directing others	Establishing or maintaining orderly routines, application of standards
Values	Material rewards for tangible accomplishments	Development or acquisition of knowledge	Creative expression of ideas, emotions, or sentiments	Fostering the welfare of others, social service	Material accomplishment and social status	Material or financial accomplishment and power in social, business, or political arenas
Sees self as	Practical, conservative, and having manual and mechanical skills—lacking social skills	Analytical, intelligent, skeptical, and having academic talent—lacking interpersonal skills	Open to experience, innovative, intellectual—lacking clerical or office skills	Empathic, patient, and having interpersonal skills—lacking mechanical ability	Having sales and persuasive ability—lacking scientific ability	Having technical skills in business or production—lacking artistic competencies
Others see as	Normal, frank	Asocial, intellectual	Unconventional, disorderly, creative	Nurturing, agreeable, extroverted	Energetic, gregarious	Careful, conforming
Avoids	Interaction with people	Persuasion or sales activities	Routines and conformity to established rules	Mechanical and technical activity	Scientific, intellectual, or abstruse topics	Ambiguous or unstructured undertakings

Table 2.3   RIASEC Environmental Typology

Attribute	Environmental Type					
	Realistic	Investigative	Artistic	Social	Enterprising	Conventional
Requires	Manual and mechanical competencies, interaction with machines, tools, and objects	Analytical, technical, scientific, and verbal competencies	Innovation, or creative ability, emotionally expressive interaction with others	Interpersonal competencies, skill in mentoring, treating, healing, or teaching others	Skills in persuasion and manipulation of others	Clerical skills, skills in meeting precise standards for performance
Demands and rewards the display of	Conforming behavior, practical accomplishment	Skepticism and persistence in problem solving, documentation of new knowledge, understanding or solution of problems	Imagination in literary, artistic, or musical accomplishment	Empathy, humanitarianism, sociability, friendliness	Initiative in the pursuit of financial or material accomplishment; dominance; self-confidence	Organizational ability, conformity, dependability
Values or personal styles allowed expression	Practical, productive and concrete values; robust, risky, adventurous styles	Acquisition of knowledge through scholarship or investigation	Unconventional ideas or manners, aesthetic values	Concern for the welfare of others	Acquisitive or power-oriented styles, responsibility	Conventional outlook and concern for orderliness and routines
Occupations or other environments involve	Concrete, practical activity: use of machines, tools, materials	Analytical or intellectual activity aimed at troubleshooting or creation and use of knowledge	Creative work in music, writing, performance, sculpture, or unstructured intellectual endeavors	Working with others in a helpful or facilitating way	Selling, leading, manipulating others to attain personal or organizational goals	Working with things, numbers, or machines to meet predictable organizational demands or specified standards
Sample occupations	Carpenter, truck operator	Psychologist, microbiologist	Musician, interior designer	Counselor, clergy member	Lawyer, retail store manager	Production editor, bookkeeper

Reproduced by special permission of the publisher, Psychological Assessment Resources, Inc., 16204 North Florida Avenue, Lutz, Florida 33549, from the *Dictionary of Holland Occupational Codes—Revised* by Gary D. Gottfredson, Ph.D. and John L. Holland, Ph.D. Copyright 1992, 1996.

figure 2.2

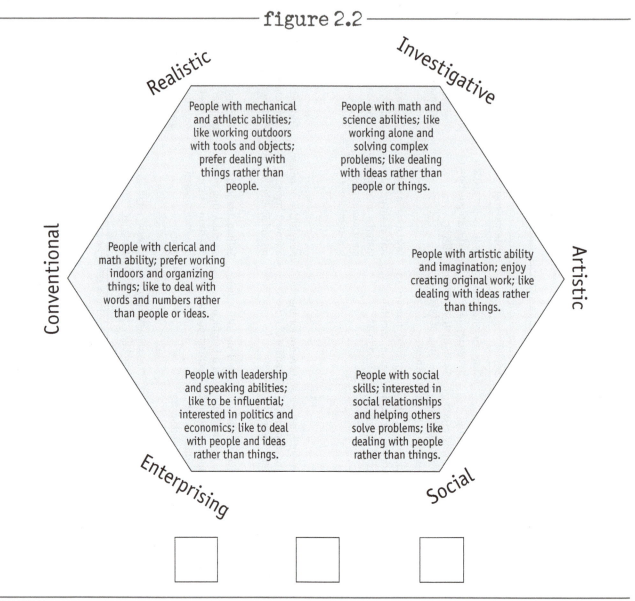

Realistic

Investigative

People with mechanical and athletic abilities; like working outdoors with tools and objects; prefer dealing with things rather than people.

People with math and science abilities; like working alone and solving complex problems; like dealing with ideas rather than people or things.

Conventional

People with clerical and math ability; prefer working indoors and organizing things; like to deal with words and numbers rather than people or ideas.

People with artistic ability and imagination; enjoy creating original work; like dealing with ideas rather than things.

Artistic

People with leadership and speaking abilities; like to be influential; interested in politics and economics; like to deal with people and ideas rather than things.

People with social skills; interested in social relationships and helping others solve problems; like dealing with people rather than things.

Enterprising

Social

RIASEC Hexagon

example, a person might obtain a code of IAS, which would indicate the three letters associated with this interest type. These could be thought of as a pie graph, with the "I" having the largest slice, the "A" the next largest, and so on. Regarding environments, Holland developed the *Occupations Finder—Revised Edition* (Holland, 2011) and the *Dictionary of Holland Occupational Codes* (Gottfredson & Holland, 1996) to identify Holland codes for 1,335 and 7,500 occupations, respectively. Other instruments were created to identify Holland codes for leisure activities and fields of study.

Other Classifications of Interests

Besides Holland's scheme, there are several other assessments and classifications of interests and personal characteristics that are sometimes used in various career services settings. These include the ACT World-of-Work Map (ACT, 2001) and the Myers-Briggs Type Indicator® (MBTI; McCauley, 1990).

ACT WORLD-OF-WORK (WOW) MAP. This system is included in the Career Planning Program developed by ACT (ACT, 2001). You may have used this program when you were taking the ACT as a part of college entrance examinations. The UNIACT Interest Inventory and WOW Map are also included in the DISCOVER computer-based career guidance system, which is similar to the SIGI PLUS program mentioned earlier. The UNIACT Interest Inventory enables a person to develop a profile of interests and personality characteristics related to six types that are almost exactly the same as those developed by John Holland. (The major difference between the UNIACT and the SDS is that the former uses norms to determine scores, whereas the latter uses raw scores only.) In addition to the six types, the profile provides information related to four quadrants divided by data-ideas and people-things (see Figure 2.3).

The WOW arranges 26 career areas (groups of similar jobs) into 6 career clusters. Together these regions cover almost all U.S. jobs. The location of each career area on the WOW Map is arranged according to four job clusters: (a) DATA, facts, numbers, files, accounts, business proce-

figure 2.3

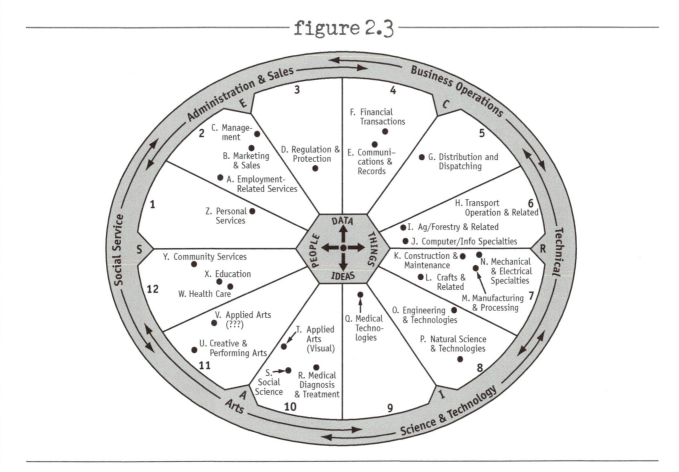

About the Map

- The World-of-Work Map arranges 26 career areas (groups of similar jobs) into 12 regions. Together, the career areas cover all U.S. jobs. Most jobs in a career area are located near the point shown. However, some may be in adjacent Map regions.
- A career area's location is based on its primary work tasks. The four primary work tasks are working with—
  DATA: Facts, numbers, files, accounts, business procedures.
  IDEAS: Insights, theories, new ways of saying or doing something—for example, with words, equations, or music.
  PEOPLE: People you help, serve, inform, care for, or sell things to.
  THINGS: Machines, tools, living things, and materials such as food, wood, or metal.
- Six general types of work ("career clusters") and related Holland types (RIASEC) are shown around the edge of the Map. The overlapping career of cluster arrows indicate overlap in the occupational content of adjacent career clusters.
- Because they are more strongly oriented to People than Things, the following two career areas in the Science & Technology Cluster are located toward the left side of the Map (Region 10): Medical Diagnosis & Treatment and Social Science.

World-of-Work Map, Third Edition

dures; (b) IDEAS, insights, theories, new ways of saying or doing something, possibly with words, equations, or music; (c) PEOPLE, people you can help, serve, inform, care for, or sell things to; and (d) THINGS, machines, tools, living things, and materials such as food, wood, or metal.

Table 2.4 shows how approximately 500 occupations can be grouped into 6 job clusters and 26 career areas. Note that the six clusters are very similar to Holland's six RIASEC types.

Table 2.4

Six Career Clusters and 26 Career Areas

ADMINISTRATION & SALES CAREER CLUSTER

1. Employment-Related Services
Employee Benefits Manager; Employment Interviewer; Human Resources Manager; Labor Relations Specialist; Training/Education Manager

2. Marketing & Sales
Advertising Manager; Buyer; Insurance Agent; Real Estate Agent; Sales/Marketing Manager; Travel Agent

3. Management
Financial Manager; Foreign Service Officer; General Manager/Executive; Hotel/Motel Manager; Property/Real Estate Manager

4. Regulation & Protection
Customs Inspector; Detective (Police); FBI Agent; Food & Drug Inspector; Park Ranger; Police Officer

BUSINESS OPERATIONS CAREER CLUSTER

5. Communications & Records
Abstractor; Court Reporter; Hotel Clerk; Medical Record Technician; Title Examiner/Searcher

6. Financial Transactions
Accountant/Auditor; Bank Teller; Budget/Credit Analyst; Insurance Underwriter; Real Estate Appraiser; Tax Accountant

7. Distribution & Dispatching
Air Traffic Controller; Flight Dispatcher; Mail Carrier; Shipping/Receiving Clerk; Warehouse Supervisor

TECHNICAL CAREER CLUSTER

8. Transport Operation & Related
Aircraft Pilot; Astronaut; Bus Driver; Locomotive Engineer; Ship Captain; Truck Driver

9. Agriculture, Forestry & Related
Aquaculturist; Farm Manager; Forester; Nursery/Greenhouse Manager; Tree Surgeon (Arborist)

10. Computer & Information Specialties
Actuary; Archivist/Curator; Computer Programmer; Computer Systems Analyst; Web Site Developer

11. Construction & Maintenance
Carpenter; Electrician; Firefighter; Plumber; Security System Installer

12. Crafts & Related
Cabinetmaker; Chef/Cook; Jeweler; Tailor/Dressmaker; Winemaker

13. Manufacturing & Processing
Printing Press Operator; Sheet Metal Worker; Tool & Die Maker; Water Plant Operator; Welder

14. Mechanical & Electrical Specialties
Locksmith; Millwright; Technicians in various fields (for example, Automotive, Avionics, Broadcast, Sound)

SCIENCE & TECHNOLOGY CAREER CLUSTER

15. Engineering & Technologies
Architect, Engineers (for example, Civil, Mechanical) & Technicians (for example, Energy, Quality Control) in various fields; Production Planner; Surveyor

16. Natural Science & Technologies
Biologist; Food Technologist; Geologist; Meteorologist; Physicist

17. Medical Technologies
Dietician/Nutritionist; Optician; Pharmacist; Radiographer Technologists in various fields (for example, Medical, Surgical)

18. Medical Diagnosis & Treatment
Anesthesiologist; Dentist; Nurse Practitioner; Physical Therapist; Physician; Veterinarian

19. Social Science
Anthropologist; Criminologist; Political Scientist; Experimental Psychologist; Sociologist

ARTS CAREER CLUSTER

20. Applied Arts (Visual)
Animator; Fashion Designer; Graphic Artist (Software); Photographer; Set Designer

21. Creative & Performing Arts
Actor; Composer (Music); Dancer/Choreographer; Fashion Model; Musician; Writer/Author

22. Applied Arts (Written & Spoken)
Advertising Copywriter; Columnist; Editor; Interpreter; Librarian; Reporter/Journalist

SOCIAL SERVICE CAREER CLUSTER

23. Health Care
Athletic Trainer; Dental Hygienist; Health Services; Administrator; Psychiatric Technician; Recreational Therapist

24. Education
Athletic Coach; College/University Faculty; Educational Administrator; Teachers in various specialties (for example, Art, Foreign Language, Music)

25. Community Services
Counselors in various specialties (for example, Mental Health, Rehabilitation); Director (Social Service); Lawyer; Social Worker

26. Personal Services
Barber; Flight Attendant; Gaming Occupations Worker; Hairstylist/Cosmetologist

MYERS-BRIGGS TYPE INDICATOR[(2)] (MBTI). The MBTI® is one of the most widely used personality inventories (McCaulley, 1990). Like the SDS, it is based on a typological theory of personality. The theory is based on four dimensions of personality, and various instruments produce scores that identify the person as one of 16 types (all possible combinations of the eight letters). As with Holland codes, people sometimes characterize themselves by their code letters—for example, "I'm an ESTJ" or "I'm an INFP." The MBTI® is widely used in solving career problems, especially in organizational settings involving worker supervision and team building.

Interests are probably the most important aspect of self-knowledge related to career decision making and occupational exploration. They are like a beacon that points the direction a person will probably move in his or her career development, so it is important for people to understand and pay attention to their interests in the career decision-making process.

In summary, John Holland's theory and instruments have dominated the career development field for over 50 years and it is the reason we emphasize RIASEC theory in this book. More than 1,600 publications (Ruff, Reardon, & Bertoch, 2008) have explored the theory and have shown the usefulness of the practical devices he has created to help people identify occupations that would be compatible with both their interests and personality.

Skills

Besides values and interests, we believe that skills are a third important part of self-knowledge. The area of skills is one that is of special interest to employers and focuses on the question "What can you do?" Like values and interests, skills are an important part of our personality. They distinguish us in terms of the things we can do well (or poorly), the behaviors we have learned or acquired along the way, and the special talents and abilities that we have.

The Collegiate Employment Research Institute (CERI) at Michigan State University surveys thousands of employers annually, and it reported that students will need to demonstrate the use of higher-order thinking skills, even in their first job (CERI, 2010). New hires will be asked to analyze, synthesize, evaluate, and create information and knowledge to help the organization solve problems and grow. "The [students'] ability to communicate ideas, both justifying their positions and persuading organizational coworkers and clients to adopt their recommendations with a willingness to negotiate modifications, has become essential" (CERI, 2010, p. 4). And in the second and third job the skill demands will be even greater.

In this regard, skills are different from aptitudes, another term often used in career assessment, or talents, sometimes associated with artistic endeavors. Skills involve knowledge and physical behaviors that are developed and learned, whereas aptitudes or talents refer to our inherited capacity or untapped capabilities to learn or develop skills.

Skills Identification

Over the years, numerous psychological tests have been developed to measure skills thought to be related to particular jobs and occupations. The most widely used tests include the Differential Aptitude Test (DAT) and the General Aptitude Test Battery (GATB). Both of these tests were developed for use with people having a high school education or less and are not as useful with college students. These tests measure abilities such as vocabulary, computational skills, hand-eye coordination, clerical speed and accuracy, and mechanical reasoning. (In this text we view the terms *abilities* and *skills* as interchangeable.)

Some employers, professional groups, and industries have developed highly specialized aptitude tests to measure traits that predict the ability to learn specific job skills, for example, sorting, dentistry, welding. However, these tests are used mostly to admit applicants to training programs or to qualify them for particular positions in organizations. In the performing arts, auditions and portfolio work samples are used, rather than paper-and-pencil tests, to assess skills in dance, music performance, and graphic arts.

For most college-level and professional jobs, tests do not typically provide useful results that will tell people what their skills are and whether they will be successful in a professional-level occupation or job. Scholastic aptitude tests such as the SAT, MAT, ACT, LSAT, and MCAT are used to predict the ability to acquire the high-level verbal and quantitative skills necessary to process technical information. We find it more helpful to rely on expressed measurements rather than assessed measurements to identify skills related to self-knowledge for career decisions.

Some of the most common and widely used ideas about skills and career decision making are included in a best-selling book by Richard Bolles, *What Color Is Your Parachute?* Bolles' (2012) basic idea is that people who want to make career decisions need to identify their skill competencies, which have been developed in various life activities such as school, leisure activities, volunteer work, or prior jobs. Once they have completed a thorough inventory of their skills, people can then begin to prioritize their skills in terms of those that are important or satisfying to them, those that might be related to employment, or those that need to be further developed. Bolles believes that many people underestimate and overlook their skills, which limits their ability to solve career problems.

Another method of skills identification can be illustrated using the Florida State University Career Portfolio system (Lumsden, Garis, Reardon, Unger, & Arkin, 2001). This program lists nine basic, general skills that transcend any specific job—they are transferable from one job to another, or one life role to another. These nine skills were identified by a consensus of career center staff, faculty, and employers associated with the university. They are broad skills, not unique to any specific major field of study such as engineering or nursing, which may train a person in a more specialized skill area.

These are also the kinds of skills that often appear on one's resume and are discussed in employment interviews. Managers and leaders use most of these general skills. What are they?

1. Communication
2. Creativity
3. Critical thinking
4. Leadership
5. Personal management
6. Social responsibility
7. Teamwork
8. Technical/scientific
9. Research/project development

A detailed description of these nine basic skills is provided in Table 2.5. A portfolio of accomplishments is a good device for documenting these skills, because they are not readily measured with a paper-pencil test.

Transferable Skills

The notion of transferable skills is important because recruiters see these as important for any field or career one might choose. Some view "interpersonal skills" as the most important to prospective employers (Crane & Seal, 2011). Such skills include communication, problem-solving adaptability, responsibility, positive demeanor, and teamwork. These interpersonal and intrapersonal skills are sometimes identified as "social and emotional competence or intelligence" because they are a set of interrelated behaviors that involve recognition, regulation, and impact of one's emotions and the emotions of others. It is easy to see how organizations would seek persons with such demonstrated skills given the stress, diversity, and change present in the current workplace.

Table 2.5 | General Career Portfolio Skills

COMMUNICATION SKILLS

Communication skills include reading, speaking, writing, editing, listening, presenting, and interpersonal relations. These skills are critically important in the workplace because they involve the transmission of information among people. Think about projects in and out of class that have emphasized communications or that might be available to you in the future. This could include working on the school yearbook, writing up a research project, or authoring an essay for a class; personal courses and skill training; or other experiences that are related to communication skills.

CREATIVITY

Creativity may include skills in many different areas (e.g., artistic, literary, mechanical, and social areas). Think about a time that you came up with an innovative solution to a problem and what made it unique. What experiences could you seek in the future to develop skills in creativity?

CRITICAL THINKING

Critical thinking involves things such as identifying problems in a situation or organization, thinking about the complexity of problems, gathering evidence through research, evaluating options to solve the problem, and deriving a conclusion or solution. In developing options to solve a problem, you may need to think about what are both possible and likely solutions. To compare these options you need some type of measurement criteria or standard, and this may be drawn from various sources. Coming to a position, taking a stand, and making a recommendation to solve a problem are the culmination of critical thinking. Think about situations in classes or working on projects where you have exercised critical thinking in the past. Think about situations where you could develop this skill in the future.

LEADERSHIP

Leadership is the ability to set goals and point out directions for the group to take. You have been a "formal" leader when you have suggested a plan or a way to achieve a group goal. This might have involved making a motion to move a group to take action on an issue. Leadership also involves the ability to delegate responsibility or authority to someone else. It involves the skill of motivating others. An example of this might be asking clarifying questions about the team's goals or presenting a proposal to your group as a way to solve a specific problem. Think about where you might have held or would want to hold a leadership role in a class group project, campus organization (officer, committee chair, etc.), or a community or church group.

LIFE MANAGEMENT

Life management includes such things as managing time, both for long-term projects and activities, as well as day-to-day time management (e.g., finishing class projects and effectively managing work and school demands on a weekly basis). This includes being on time and being prepared to act. Life management can also include the ability to adapt to change. Your personal life-management skills may also include the ability to manage finances (e.g., writing budgets, assessing expenses and income, and keeping accurate records). Think about where you have demonstrated life-management skills in the past, or how you could demonstrate these skills in the future.

RESEARCH/PROJECT DEVELOPMENT

Research and/or project development involves finding and using information for problem solving and decision making. In researching an issue or problem, individuals read and evaluate reports of prior work or collect new data that can be summarized in a written or oral presentation in order to provide new information. In addition to investigating a problem, individuals may develop plans for projects that provide a logical series of activities for eliminating the problem. This includes planning for the direction and coordination of a project to ensure that the goals and objectives are met in a cost-effective way and within budget. Think about research papers assigned in classes by your professors, work projects given by your job supervisors, and service projects for clubs and organizations (e.g., orienting new members, fundraising).

SOCIAL RESPONSIBILITY

Social responsibility involves respecting individual and cultural differences. Finding admirable qualities in others—especially those who appear to be quite different physically, mentally, or in personality—are acts of being a socially responsible person. Social responsibility relates to good citizenship. Individuals with skills in this area actively take part in community-building projects on a regular basis. Think about instances when you were involved in your community (e.g., being a member of a community service group, a church group, a recreation group, as well as providing some community service).

(continued)

Table 2.5 continued

TEAMWORK

Teamwork may include initiating ideas within a team or having team members cooperate and negotiate with each other. Effective teamwork behaviors involve a commitment to join with others to achieve a goal (cooperation). Teamwork involves recognizing your and others' strengths and weaknesses and encouraging team assignments that draw on strengths and minimize weaknesses. Think about situations where you have been (or could be) a team member in a class group project, campus organization (officer, committee chair, etc.), community, or church group and you used (or could use) teamwork skills.

TECHNICAL/SCIENTIFIC

Technical/scientific skills relate to experiences in the social, biological, and physical sciences. The most popular current application of technical/scientific skills involves the applications of computers. Think about a time where you used a software program for a particular project or activity. Technical skills may include system management (e.g., managing data warehouses or web services) and using the Internet for research and related activities. What experiences could you seek that would enhance skills in this area?

Summarizing Values, Interests, and Skills

In summarizing our description of the three areas of self-knowledge important in career decision making—values, interests, and skills—we noted that external, objective measures are often not completely helpful in improving our self-knowledge. Objective measures, such as those provided by psychological tests or expert career counselors, may be less useful than our own self-examination and reflection. We noted that expressed measures, together with assessed measures, could be useful in improving self-knowledge about values, interests, and skills.

In a nutshell, values involve figuring out what is important and what matters to us. That knowledge will sustain our motivation and persistence. Interests involve things we like and enjoy, and they provide direction in career decisions. Most people end up doing what they enjoy in their jobs or leisure. Skills involve the tools, the behaviors that will move us forward to implementing our values and engaging in the things we like. As the career process unfolds, we can try to get closer to having all three of these mutually reinforcing forces present in our lives.

Improving Our Self-Knowledge

In the process of getting to know ourselves better in order to make career decisions, there are several things we can do. First, we can make sure that we keep a positive attitude about ourselves and that we don't let negative thoughts mess up our thinking about our values, interests, or skills. We need to make sure we are thinking "better" about ourselves and as clearly and accurately as we possibly can. Second, we need to know how to improve the quality of the information about ourselves that we use in making career decisions.

Thinking "Better" about Myself

What kinds of things can we do to improve the quality of our self-knowledge? First, we need to be careful about overgeneralizing from past experiences. Perhaps you once had a bad experience solving math problems or dealing with bugs on a camping trip, and as a result you decided to exclude all occupations involving math or the outdoors from your career explorations. Such generalizing can severely limit your ability to successfully explore all of the possible occupations that could bring you satisfaction. We can generalize on the basis of positive experiences, too. Doing really well in one math class might not mean that you should pursue advanced education in a top-flight engineering school.

Second, we need to be careful about relying too much on another person's opinions about what our values, interests, and skills might be in relation to our career choice. This is especially true in the case of people with greater prestige or social power, such as family members, teachers, supervisors, and even career counselors.

Third, we need to avoid making career decisions if we are in some kind of emotional crisis. We sometimes see students who have just failed a chemistry course and then decided to forget about all occupations in the health care field. Other students may have received a letter from their parents informing them that further college costs would not be paid unless the major was in business. When you are in a highly emotional state, it is almost impossible to consider all the relevant information about your values, interests, and skills that is important in making a good career decision.

Finally, it is important to make full and thoughtful use of the tools that are included in state-of-the-art career interventions. Many of us can use some of these materials with little outside assistance, but professional career counselors can provide expert assistance in selecting and interpreting the results of inventories, psychological tests, computer-based career guidance systems, and other devices.

Approaches to Improving Self-Knowledge

It is important to understand that our storehouse of self-knowledge information is based on our experiences, on events that have happened in our lives that we can recall. Although the events themselves are important, it is our recollection of them that is particularly important. Therefore, we should seek out and acquire as many different career/life experiences as we possibly can. Even if the experiences turn out to be things we don't like and are unhappy about, the experiences will improve our self-knowledge. It is also important to process and talk about our experiences, to reflect on the feelings related to the experiences, because they are the building blocks of self-knowledge that clarify our values, interests, and skills. Ultimately, it is our feelings about these things that are valuable in career decision making.

We should also connect and relate these life events and experiences to each other. What are the relationships between your values, interests, and skills? Do they connect in meaningful ways? Are they related? For example, a person who likes being with children (interests) and has experience developed in babysitting and teaching church school (skills) determines that childhood education is a career to pursue because the future of the nation is connected to providing high-quality education to children (value). However, another person with a very good academic record in math (skills) and wanting to make a lot of money (value) may not choose to become an actuary or accountant because of liking the outdoors (interests). It is important to understand not only your skills but also the values and interests related to your skills.

The clearer, sharper, and stronger our self-knowledge regarding our values, interests, and skills, the more likely we will be able to solve career problems and career decisions. How is this done? We can develop stronger images of ourselves by getting varied experiences in many different work settings and by paying attention to our feelings and reactions to these experiences. As the old saying goes, "If you follow your own nose, you'll never get lost." This can mean that even a part-time, volunteer experience may help you sharpen and clarify your values, interests, and skills related to occupations and work. Teaching six-year-olds may help you realize how happy or frustrated you become when working with children. "Watch your feet" to see how you're really thinking and feeling, because we talk with our mouths but "vote" with our feet.

Finally, you must realize that improving self-knowledge related to career decision making is a lifelong process; it is never finished. Every new life event and experience adds to our storehouse of information about values, interests, and skills. Moreover, no life experiences are wasted—important lessons come from experiences that are sometimes initially considered failures. Sometimes, students say that they have gotten into the wrong major or that they took the wrong job. That's usually the short-term evaluation. In the longer term, those experiences can be used to sharpen and clarify one's career journey. For example, one of the most distinguished clinical psychologists at our university once noted that he had majored in chemistry as an undergraduate, and had later come to realize that his knowledge of chemistry had enabled him to more fully appreciate the importance of physiology and brain chemistry in explaining human behavior. Perhaps there is indeed a "seamless web of knowledge" at work in the world that we sometimes fail to appreciate in our career decision making as we try to understand our options and opportunities.

Summary

In this chapter we examined the area of self-knowledge—"knowing about myself"—as a beginning point in career decision making. Three areas—values, interests, and skills—were highlighted as important parts of self-knowledge. The differences in assessed and expressed measurement approaches were outlined, and strategies for developing and improving self-knowledge in the areas of values, interests, and skills were presented. This should help you improve the quality of information in the self-knowledge domain of your Personal Career Theory.

References

ACT. (2001). *Career Planning Survey technical manual.* Iowa City, IA: Author.

Bolles, R. (2012). *A practical manual for job hunters and career changers: What color is your parachute?* Berkeley, CA: Ten Speed Press.

Collegiate Employment Research Institute (2010, February). Under the economic turmoil a skills gap simmers. *CERI Research Brief 1-2010*, pp. 1–18.

Crane, D. D., & Seal, C. R. (2011). Student social and emotional competence in the hiring process. *NACE Journal*, 26–30.

Gottfredson, G., & Holland, J. (1996). *Dictionary of Holland occupation codes* (3rd ed.). Odessa, FL: Psychological Assessment Resources.

Fulford, B. (2009, November/December). An interview about the stages of life—part I. *Career Planning & Adult Development Network Newsletter*, 7–9.

Holland, J. (1997). *Making vocational choices* (3rd ed.). Odessa, FL: Psychological Assessment Resources.

Holland, J. (2011). *Occupations finder—revised edition.* Odessa, FL: Psychological Assessment Resources.

Holland, J. (1994). Self-Directed Search. Odessa, FL: Psychological Assessment Resources.

Katz, M. (1993). *Computer-assisted career decision making: The guide in the machine.* Hillsdale, NJ: Lawrence Erlbaum.

Lumsden, J., Garis, J., Reardon, R., Unger, M., & Arkin, S. (2001). Developing an on-line career portfolio. *Journal of Career Planning & Employment, 62*(1), 33–38.

McCaulley, M. H. (1990). The Myers-Briggs Type Indicator: A measure for individuals and groups. *Measurement & Evaluation in Counseling & Development, 22*, 181–195.

Nevill, D., & Super, D. E. (1986). Salience Inventory. Palo Alto, CA: Consulting Psychologists Press.

Raths, L., Simon, S., & Harmin, M. (1966). *Values and teaching: Working with values in the classroom.* Columbus, OH: Merrill.

Ruff, E. A., Reardon, R. C., & Bertoch, S. C. (2008, June). Holland's RIASEC theory and applications: Exploring a comprehensive bibliography. *Career Convergence.* Retrieved from http://associationdatabase.com/aws/NCDA/pt/sd/news_article/5483/_self/layout_details/false

Strong, E. (1994). Strong Interest Inventory. Palo Alto, CA: Consulting Psychologists Press.

Super, D. E. (1970). Work Values Inventory. Boston, MA: Houghton Mifflin.

Super, D. E., & Nevill, D. (1986). Values Scale. Palo Alto, CA: Consulting Psychologists Press.

U.S. Department of Labor. (1991). *Dictionary of occupational titles* (4th ed., revised 1991). Washington, DC: U.S. Government Printing Office.

Valpar International Corp. (2007). SIGI3. [computer software]. Tucson, AZ: Author.

Zytowski, D. G., & Kuder, F. (1999). Kuder Career Search with Person Match. Adel, IA: National Career Assessment Services, Inc.

Chapter Three

Knowing about My Options

Career problems and career decisions require learning about oneself, but they also involve exploring fields of study, occupations, and leisure activities. Knowledge about self and career options is the information base, the foundation stones, for career decision making.

In our world, the number of options to work, learn, and play is very great and can even be overwhelming at times. However, living and working effectively and responsibly in today's complex global economy means digging into information about options and understanding how options are organized and connected to one another. As we noted in Chapter 2, it is better to begin this process of exploring options by first developing and understanding information about yourself.

This chapter focuses on the second part of the knowledge base of the Pyramid of Information-Processing Domains. This includes what we know about options in fields of study, occupations, and leisure activities. We will examine labor market and occupational information, how it's organized, and how to find and evaluate it; we will learn about education and training options, including sources of financial support; and we will explore leisure and vocational options. Finally, we will review how you can improve your knowledge about occupational, educational, and leisure options.

Option knowledge is the second cornerstone of your career planning. We will examine some ways that people can improve their option knowledge and provide some materials for you to use in that process. This information will help you improve the quality of your Personal Career Theory, especially the Pyramid of Information-Processing Domains and the CASVE Cycle (see Figure 3.1).

Connecting Occupations, Education, and Leisure

Besides What Color is Your Parachute?, Richard Bolles wrote *Three Boxes of Life* (Bolles, 1981), which analyzed the connections between education, work, and retirement.

Bolles suggested that many people believe that education, work, and retirement (or play) occur during three separate periods, or boxes, of life. Earlier generations viewed these three periods as very distinct and divided, and a person sought to prepare for and live effectively in each time period as if it were unrelated to the others. Bolles believed it is more important to view education (learning), work (working), and play (retirement) as three interconnected aspects of life/career. Perhaps you can think about how you blend learning, working, and playing into your life right now; how you did this in the past; and how you will do it 20 years from now. Given Bolles' observations, it is appropriate to view education, work, and leisure as related options to be explored in career problem solving.

Educational, work, and leisure options exist "out there," and much information can be obtained from Web-based resources, publications, or from talking with people who

figure 3.1

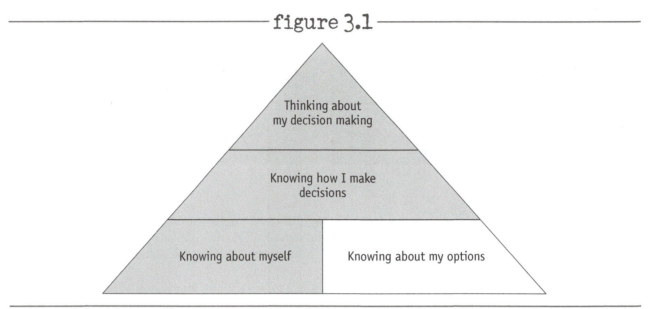

Option Knowledge—CIP Pyramid

Reprinted from *The Career Development Quarterly, 41*, 1992, p. 70, copyrighted NCDA. Reprinted with permission of the National Career Development Association. Used with permission.

are already there. Some information about options is in the form of tables that detail salaries, training requirements, costs, and other characteristics. In this way, our knowledge and information about options is very different from knowledge and information about ourselves, which is stored mostly in memories of our experiences. For example, occupational knowledge is broadly shared in government documents, written reports, biographies, computer files, and other media sources. These are concrete, objective sources of information, and they exist apart from our direct, subjective experience of them. Information about options can be stored on the Web, library shelves, in book chapters, and in a variety of media formats.

Occupations

First we should review the definitions of *work*, *career*, *occupation*, *job*, and *position* that were introduced in Chapter 1. We defined *occupation* as a group of similar jobs found in different industries or organizations. This chapter presents the essential elements of occupational information, changes in knowledge about occupations, common schemes for classifying occupations, and major sources of information about occupations. (It is worth noting that some sources use these five terms interchangeably and, thus, incorrectly.)

Number of Occupations

We noted in Chapter 1 that a publication developed a number of years ago, the *Dictionary of Occupational Titles* (U.S. Department of Labor, 1991), defined over 12,700 different occupational titles, with as many as 17,000 titles cross-referenced. How do we make sense out of all that? Well, the first step is to figure out meaningful ways to combine, group, and categorize them into smaller units. This could be by educational level, by income, by similarities of work activities, or by any way that would help simplify learning about them. Over the past 60 years, many different schemes have been used to group similar occupations, and we will look at some of them.

The fact that over 20 years ago, there were more than 12,000 different occupations that had been classified is only part of the story. Some of these occupations are identifiable but not very significant in most people's day-to-day working lives. Do you know what a snout puller is? A debunker? A hod carrier? (By the way, the first two occupations involve working in a slaughterhouse pulling facial parts from pigs and chickens.) Some experts have estimated that about 95% of the workforce is employed in about 400 occupations. Four hundred is still a lot of occupations but far fewer than 12,000.

For almost 50 years the *Dictionary of Occupational Titles* (U.S. Dept. of Labor, 1991) was the standard basic reference for information about occupations. In later years, it was replaced by the O*NET, http://online.onetcenter.org/, a comprehensive database that provides information about 780 occupations, worker skills, and job-training requirements. Each year hundreds of occupations in O*NET are updated with new research findings. O*NET is now the primary source of U.S. occupational information, and its data are included in many computer-based career-information delivery systems. O*NET is sponsored by the U.S. Department of Labor's Employment and Training Administration (http://www.doleta.gov/).

About Occupations

Most occupational information in the United States is compiled by the Department of Labor. More particularly, the U.S. Bureau of Labor Statistics regularly produces reports on working in America, who does it, when they do it, how much they earn, and so forth. The Occupational Employment Statistics (OES) is the primary data bank of information about occupations. Many federal government departments, such as Commerce, Education, Defense, Labor, Census, Interior, State, Agriculture, and others, contribute data to the OES (we talk more about the OES in Chapter 7).

An example of what we know about occupations can be seen in the topics used in Choices® Planner, a computer-based career information delivery system (CIDS). Florida residents can access the program at this Web site, http://www.bridges.com/cpflorida/. Choices® Planner has 23 different topics for classifying occupations, such as educational level, money and outlook, skills, interests, work values, physical demands of the work, work hours, and working conditions. These topics are further divided into about 172 different factors that are used to describe about 650 different occupations in the program (see Table 3.1). These same topics and factors can be used in this CIDS to search for occupations. That's a lot of information about occupations. CIDS used in other states provides similar, detailed information about occupations.

In 1998, a federal/state initiative called America's Career Resource Network (ACRN) took responsibility for compiling and improving the quality of occupational information available throughout the United States. It provided quality information and resources to help youth and adults make informed career decisions. States and territories have Career Resource Networks (CRNs) designed to make available to all citizens the most current information about occupations, educational programs, financial aid for education and training, and job vacancy listings. It is wise to become familiar with and take advantage of our national and state systems of occupational information. You can freely explore information about occupations in all regions of the country. This type of information is accessible through America's Career InfoNet, www.careerinfonet.org.

Besides the U.S. Department of Labor and America's Career InfoNet, there are many other private providers of occupational information. These include professional associations, career Web sites, private authors and publishers, local governments, educational organizations, industry and commercial organizations, foreign governments, and private foundations. It's useful to note that many Web-based resources often repost information from "official" sources like government agencies (e.g., Department of Labor) and professional associations. As a consumer of career information, you need to use your best critical-thinking skills in evaluating the information. We'll say more about this later in the chapter. Besides these more formal sources of occupational information, we can also learn a great deal by talking to and observing people in occupations. You may even find yourself interacting with people blogging about their work, who are willing to chat online in real time!

Are Occupations Changing?

Occupations do change and information about occupations also changes. Occupational information is very fluid and dynamic, like water that flows past the dock—the water may look the same, but it is

Choices® Planner Topics and Factors

Table 3.1

Topic	Factor
Education level	No high school through professional or graduate degree levels
Physical demands	Sedentary to very heavy (100+ lbs.)
Earnings	Ten categories from $10,000 to $100,000
Aptitudes	Examples: general learning ability, verbal aptitude, manual dexterity, eye-hand coordination, form perception
Work hours & travel	Examples: rotating shift work, weekend work, overtime work, overnight travel, regular work hours & limited travel
Work conditions	Twenty-five categories specified, e.g., avoid indoor work
Career areas & GOE	Examples: artistic, scientific, nature, law enforcement, business detail, humanitarian, physical performing
Workplace skills	Examples: social complex problem solving, resource management
Interests	Realistic, investigative, artistic, social enterprising, conventional
Physical abilities	Twenty-one categories specified, e.g., avoid color discrimination
Future outlook & employment	Increasing, stable, decreasing; all occupations
Apprenticeships	Yes or no
School subjects	Twenty-three categories specified, e.g., art, biology
Fields of work	Twenty-three categories specified, e.g., avoid production occupations
Work hours & travel	Six categories specified, e.g., avoid overnight travel
Basic skills	Nine categories specified, e.g., writing, speaking, critical thinking
Career pathways	Arts & communications; business, information management, & marketing; health & related services; social & human services; engineering & industrial technologies; agriculture & natural resources
Career clusters	Sixteen categories, specified, e.g., construction, financial services
Work values	Achievement; independence; recognition; relationships; support
Postsecondary programs/majors	Categories change annually based on information provided by schools
ASVAB	
Military	
Careers by gender	

always different. This happens because new occupations develop and long-standing occupations disappear. Generally, occupations employing large numbers of people change the least. The vast majority of occupations change very little. Indeed, there are still millions of jobs in manufacturing even though that part of the U.S. economy has declined in the past 30 years.

It is information about positions in industries and work organizations that is frequently changing, not information about occupations. This is especially true of employment-related topics such as the numbers of openings, the outlook, and salaries. Other occupational information doesn't change so rapidly, such as typical work duties, training requirements, and working conditions. Thus, it is best to be somewhat tentative about occupational information because it never represents all of what is really happening at any one time with a particular employer or industry.

Occupational Classifications

It is useful to group and classify occupations according to some common characteristics. We have already talked about the *Dictionary of Occupational Titles* and Holland codes, but in this section we want to focus on the newest classification system, the Standard Occupational Code (SOC; U.S. Dept. of Labor, 2010, www.bls.gov/SOC/).

The SOC, like RIASEC codes, is used in computer-based career-guidance systems such as Choices® Planner. The SOC is designed to cover 840 detailed occupations where work is performed for pay or profit; both military and civilian occupations are included. It uses a four-level system, with each level providing more detail. The 23 divisions are shown in Table 3.2. *If you know the SOC codes for occupations you are interested in learning more about, then you have a "key" that unlocks information for you.*

Table 3.2   SOC Major Groups

1. Management occupations
2. Business and financial operations occupations
3. Computer and mathematical occupations
4. Architecture and engineering occupations
5. Life, physical, and social science occupations
6. Community and social services occupations
7. Legal occupations
8. Education, training, and library occupations
9. Arts, design, entertainment, sports, and media occupations
10. Healthcare practitioners and technical occupations
11. Healthcare support occupations
12. Protective service occupations
13. Food preparation and serving related occupations
14. Building and grounds cleaning and maintenance occupations
15. Personal care and service occupations
16. Sales and related occupations
17. Office and administrative support occupations
18. Farming, fishing, and forestry occupations
19. Construction and extraction occupations
20. Installation, maintenance, and repair occupations
21. Production occupations
22. Transportation and material moving occupations
23. Military specific occupations

Industry Classifications

In learning about options for ways and places to work, most people typically think first about the kind of job they want, the "occupation." But what about the industry or the setting where the work could be performed? According to the *Career Guide to Industries, 2010–2011 Edition* (http://www.bls.gov/oco/cg/indchar.htm) there were 8.8 million private business establishments in the United States in 2008, predominantly small establishments. About 61.6% of all establishments employed fewer than 5 workers, although the medium-sized-to-large establishments employ a greater proportion of all workers. For example, establishments that employed 50 or more workers accounted for only 4.5% of all establishments yet employed 56.2% of all workers. The large establishments—those with more than 500 workers—accounted for only 0.2% of all establishments but employed 16.7% of all workers. *This information is especially relevant for job hunters because it tells us where the jobs actually are.*

Understanding how industries are classified can be especially useful when thinking about career options. The Standard Industrial Classification (SIC) was developed in the 1930s to classify different kinds of businesses and employing organizations, which could then be used to obtain information about occupations and related jobs. For example, if you were interested in physical therapy jobs, you could find the names of potential employers by finding the SIC codes for hospitals, physical therapy centers, and other businesses where you can then get more information about occupations and employment.

However, the SIC system became dated with changes in the economy, and it was replaced by a newer system. The North American Industry Classification System (NAICS; U.S. Bureau of Census, 2007; also available at http://www.census.gov/epcd/www/naics.html) was developed in cooperation with Canada and Mexico and significantly changed the old SIC system. NAICS groups establishments into industries based on the economic activity in which they are primarily engaged. Establishments using similar raw material inputs, similar capital equipment, and similar labor are classified in the same industry. In other words, establishments that do similar things in similar ways are classified together. In developing NAICS, every sector of the economy was restructured and redefined. For example, a new Information sector combines communications, publishing, motion picture and sound recording, and online services, recognizing our information-based economy. Manufacturing is restructured to recognize new high-tech industries. In addition, eating and drinking places are transferred to a new Accommodation and Food Services sector. NAICS classifies all economic activity into 20 industry sectors, whereas the old SIC only used 10 (see Table 3.3).

How could you use this NAICS system in your career planning? Let's say you were interested in finding organizations involved in Professional, Scientific, and Technical Services because you wanted to work in those industries. There are six major categories of these organizations in the NAICS system:

1. Accounting, tax preparation, bookkeeping and payroll services;
2. Architectural, engineering, and related services;
3. Computer systems design and related services;
4. Management, scientific, and technical consulting services;
5. Scientific research and development services; and
6. Advertising and related services.

More specifically, if you were interested in working in the sports industry, you could go to NAICS section 711 Performing Arts, Spectator Sports, and Related Industries, then to section 7112 Spectator Sports, and finally to section 71121 Spectator Sports. There you would find that this industry includes (a) sports teams or clubs primarily participating in live sporting events before a paying audience; (b) establishments primarily engaged in operating racetracks; (c) independent athletes participating in live sporting or racing events before a paying audience; (d) owners of racing participants, such as cars, dogs, and horses, primarily engaged in entering them in racing events or other spectator sports events; and (e) establishments, such as sports trainers, primarily engaged in providing specialized services to support participants in sports events or competitions. The final step would be to find the names and contact information for organizations in this industry section, 71121 Spectator Sports, so you could contact them about jobs.

Locating Occupational Information

As a college student, you are in an ideal situation to locate occupational information. The two best sources are usually the career library or information room in a career center or counseling center, followed by reference librarians based in a school library. Both of these places are likely to have staff with expertise in using the Internet to find high-quality information. In some cases, you can chat live with an information professional to get help locating the information you need.

North American Industry Classification System (NAICS) Categories

Table 3.3

1. Agriculture, Forestry, Fishing, and Hunting
2. Mining
3. Utilities
4. Construction
5. Manufacturing
6. Wholesale Trade
7. Retail Trade
8. Transportation and Warehousing
9. Information
10. Finance and Insurance
11. Real Estate and Rental and Leasing
12. Professional, Scientific, and Technical Services
13. Management of Companies and Enterprises
14. Administrative and Support and Waste Management and Remediation Services
15. Educational Services
16. Health Care and Social Assistance
17. Arts, Entertainment, and Recreation
18. Accommodation and Food Services
19. Other Services (except Public Administration)
20. Public Administration

In this Information Age, where a student's first thought when seeking information is often "I'll just Google it," it's important to know that on your campus there may be collections of information specifically designed to help you with your career exploration and decision making. The best place to start is your career services office. Remember the distinctions we made earlier in Chapter 1 between occupational, employment, and educational information, because each of these three kinds of information may be housed in a different place. In a career services office, there is probably at least one staff member who has primary responsibility for managing career-information resources, and that is the person who can best help you find the information you need. Plus, the resources are organized in one setting so you can move easily between types of information; for example, looking at options related to your major, exploring internship opportunities, and finding out what type of employers hire people with your major. Beyond the career services office, a campus library may have specialized resources such as employer and association directories that can be a valuable source for career planning and job hunting.

If you are not at a college campus, consider visiting a library in your community. This library may have a special collection or a librarian who can assist you with career-related information searches. You may also find other occupational information at a workforce center or state CRN office, or in a public or private career counseling or vocational rehabilitation services office.

There are some particularly good and important publications with occupational information. In the following paragraphs we list several reference sources to look for when you are on the Internet or in the library.

The best U.S. government publication is the *Occupational Outlook Handbook* (OOH; U.S. Dept. of Labor, 2012; also available at http://www.bls.gov/oco/), which is revised every two years and provides the latest information on over 250 occupations accounting for 90% of U.S. jobs. This information includes the nature of work, places of employment, training and other qualifications, advancement, employment outlook, earnings and working conditions, and sources of additional information.

Another reference book, originally produced by the federal government, is the *New Guide for Occupational Exploration, Fourth Edition* (GOE; Farr & Shatkin, 2006). The most recent GOE provides descriptions of over 900 occupations employing about 95% of the U.S. workforce. The occupations in the GOE are categorized in relation to 16 interest areas, such as "Arts, Entertainment, or Media" or "Sales and Marketing," and one can search for fields based on these 16 areas.

Finally, the *Occupational Outlook Quarterly* (OOQ; U.S. Dept. of Labor) is a government publication that describes new trends in occupations and the relationships of education and training to occupational activity. New information published in the OOQ eventually may find its way into the newest edition of the OOH, but it may take some time. It is available online at http://www.bls.gov/opub/ooq/ooqhome.htm.

Since 1995, information about the labor market, including specific job vacancies, occupations, and training opportunities, has become available through hundreds of Web sites. For example, the U.S. Department of Labor has developed online resources about labor market and related career information at http://www.CareerOneStop.org. This Web site provides a one-stop site for job hunters and people seeking to learn more about career exploration, resume writing, military-to-civilian transitions, and more.

Private publishers also produce a great deal of reference information about occupations. *The Encyclopedia of Careers and Vocational Guidance* (13th ed.) published by Ferguson is a five-volume set that covers over 2,500 occupations. Professional associations produce much information describing occupations in their fields, and the *Directory of National Trade and Professional Associations* (Columbia Books), published annually for 39 years, includes more than 8,100 association listings. Association directories, which can include member information and accredited training programs, are often overlooked as a source of inside information about career fields. These types of large reference resources are typically not available for free on the Internet. That's why it's important to not overlook career resource centers and libraries as valuable sources of information. They purchase and make available specialized information resources so a wide range of users can have access to the materials.

There are many specialized publications about career fields and occupations, such as *Black Collegian Magazine* (www.black-collegian.com/), *Working Woman, The Collegiate Career Woman, Equal Opportunity Careers* (www.eop.com), *Careers and the Disabled, Career World, Corporate Job Outlook*, and *Hispanic Business* (www.hispanicbusiness.com/magazine/).

Now when you go on the Internet or to a career or public library and ask for assistance, you will have some ideas about the kinds of books, publications, and Web sites you can use.

Knowledge about Education and Training

Our knowledge about education and training is very extensive, but basically we can think about it in terms of the level and length of the experience. Most CIDS and other career-information systems use level and length of training as a way to describe occupations. Level is defined in terms of General Educational Development, or GED. GED Levels 1 and 2 are elementary or less; Levels 3 and 4 are high school and some specialized training; and Levels 5 and 6 involve college and postgraduate training. As a college student, you'll be most interested in occupations at GED Levels 5 and 6.

The length of training is defined in terms of Specific Vocational Preparation, or SVP. SVP refers to how long you must train to master the skills of a particular job, and every occupation can be rated from 1 to 9. An occupation with an SVP rating of 4 requires 3 to 6 months of training, whereas one with an SVP rating of 8 could require 4 to 10 years of training. An occupation with a lower GED level can have a higher SVP rating and vice versa. Other jobs, like surgeon, could have high ratings on both measures.

We will now examine different ways that educational programs and fields of study are defined; some of the different kinds of training programs available; the differences between certification and licensure; learning as a lifelong process; providers of education and training, including financial support; and sources of educational and training information.

Classifying Educational Programs

Educational and training programs can be classified in some of the same ways as occupations. For example, Holland types and GOE clusters both group fields of study and educational training programs in terms of these two classification schemes.

Holland codes are used to classify over 900 college majors and vocational-technical training programs in the *Educational Opportunities Finder* (Rosen, Holmberg, & Holland, 1994). These fields of study are also listed alphabetically and by degree level (two-year, four-year, postgraduate). GOE clusters are used in the *Guide for Occupational Exploration* (Farr & Shatkin, 2006) to identify and group over 550 school subjects at the secondary and postsecondary level.

College Training Options

Can you name all the majors and degrees at your college or university? What should you know when thinking about educational programs in higher education? Here are some ideas.

First, remember that there is often a difference between a department and a major field of study (usually just called a "major"). A "department" is an administrative unit of the educational institution, and it may include several majors and degree programs. Departments are located in schools or colleges, a higher-level administrative unit. A "program of study" may mean either a department or a major, depending on the organizational structure of the school.

A second thing to remember is that some programs of study are directly tied to occupations through certification and accreditation. Other academic programs, like liberal arts or sciences, are not directly connected to a profession or occupational activities. Understanding the organizational structure of academic programs at your institution is important in educational decision making because it is the way in which options are organized and made available to you. In some universities, the majors most directly linked to occupations are located in "professional schools."

When compared to the occupational classification systems examined earlier in this chapter, it is clear that classifications of majors and occupations differ significantly. Only students pursuing pre-professional, certificated majors can productively think of major and occupational choice as closely related.

Academic program classification systems may vary widely from one college to another. For example, the advertising major might be located in the business college on one campus and the communication school on another. A graduate program in counseling might be located in psychology on one campus and education or social work on another. Information technology might be located in business, computer science, engineering, or library science departments, or in combinations of all of these.

COLLEGE EDUCATION AND EMPLOYMENT. There is a widespread assumption that college training is a way to ensure employment, but that is not always the case. The U.S. Department of Labor reports that in the period 2006–2016, only 20% of the jobs will require a bachelor's degree (Franklin, 2007). We will examine other training options besides college that are more directly employment related.

A second problem with assuming that a college degree guarantees a job is that it minimizes the importance of the person. Employers hire people—not degrees or majors. For example, a degree in computer science will not necessarily translate into job offers. Moreover, even industries and occupations that are stable or declining continue to hire many people, sometimes thousands of workers each year.

However, college degrees do pay off in several ways. First, over the course of your working life you will, on average, earn more total income with a college degree than with only a high school diploma. Second, you're less likely to be unemployed, or you will be unemployed for shorter periods, if you have a college degree. Thus, in these two ways, on average, college pays off with respect to employment. (We discuss this more fully in Chapter 7.)

What about liberal arts majors and career preparation? It is important to know that a liberal arts degree can provide you with a variety of work-related skills that are transferable. Majoring in a pre-professional degree will not automatically make you more job ready than someone with a liberal arts degree. Many business leaders completed liberal arts majors and they philosophically value this learning in new hires, even though front-line managers may be looking for technical skills in hiring new college graduates. Two of the most familiar professions, law and medicine, do not require a specific undergraduate major.

Your best strategy is to major in areas related to your values, interests, and skills, because this will likely produce the highest academic performance (i.e., grades), and, in general, better grades keep future options open to you. In addition to completing your major degree requirements, you can do several other things to improve your employability: obtain experience through an internship, cooperative education, summer or volunteer job; select a minor field of study that balances your major; develop a high-quality resume and/or portfolio; and network with people who already work in your areas of interest.

Noncollege Training Options

There are thousands of training programs outside of the traditional four-year college. Indeed, some have reported that noneducational organizations in the United States—for example, government agencies, business and industry, and labor unions—spend more than $60 billion annually on training. In contrast, all elementary and secondary education accounts for only about $32 billion. Some training options are described below.

VOCATIONAL EDUCATION. "Voc ed" may occur at the secondary, postsecondary, or adult education levels. Vocational education is job oriented; it is designed in response to an assessed employer need for trained workers for particular jobs in a local area. Vocational education programs may last from a few months to several years, and they usually involve completion of a certification rather than a degree. Sometimes the word *technical* is added to this definition, making it vocational-technical education.

In recent years there have been some problems with vocational educational programs provided by private companies as opposed to state or local governments. These private or proprietary educational providers have not always been able to obtain a high job placement rate for students; in other words, the training programs have not been set up in response to assessed employer needs for trained workers. It is a safe bet, however, that there is some kind of training program for virtually any kind of job-related skill.

APPRENTICESHIPS. Training for many skilled and technical trades, such as electrician and steelworker, are provided through apprenticeships. The U.S. Department of Labor's Office of Apprenticeship (http://www.doleta.gov/oa/) works with industry at the national, state, and local levels to promote structured on-the-job training in a variety of industries. Apprenticeships may involve several years of supervised work by a highly skilled senior worker, plus a series of written examinations. Apprenticeship training provides advanced learning experiences in field settings, where trainees can develop real-life problem-solving skills related to job performance. Terms such as *helper* and *journeyman* are used to describe the different levels of apprenticeship.

CONTINUING EDUCATION. Virtually every occupation, whether it is a profession or skilled trade, now incorporates continuing education experiences. Because occupations and the knowledge required to perform competently in them change over time, continuing education is mandatory for people in almost any line of work. This continuing education is sometimes also called professional development, in-service training (as opposed to preservice training, which you obtain while still a "full-time" student), or staff development. Credit for continuing education is typically given in the form of continuing education units (CEUs), which is a standard measure for continuing education. One CEU is equal to 10 hours of time in training. In this way, a CEU is like a semester or quarter-hour of academic credit in a traditional college.

Some examples of continuing education include a half-day workshop at a community college, a two-day training program offered by a visiting consultant at the job site, completing correspondence courses, an employer-sponsored weekend MBA program, or instructional modules available through a Web-based learning tool. Distance learning is sometimes used when talking about continuing education and simply refers to the fact that the learner is in a different location from the instructor. Continuing education is increasingly being provided in innovative, nonclassroom-based instructional programs.

MILITARY TRAINING. The largest provider of noncollege training in the world is the U.S. Department of Defense. This country's armed services offer many training programs in vocational and technical areas because the extensive nature and sophistication of military weapons, transportation, communication, and community-support systems requires a very highly trained workforce. It should be noted that crosswalks have been created that link civilian and military jobs and training programs to one another. These crosswalks are often available through state CIDS. The www.careeronestop.org site mentioned earlier contains a section that helps individuals convert military experience to civilian careers.

CREDIT FOR PRIOR WORK. There are some schools that will provide academic credit for prior work. The system is based on a careful documentation of work-based learning and training, sometimes using a log or portfolio of prior learning. Schools that are members of the Council for Adult and Experiential Learning (CAEL; http://www.cael.org/) have agreed to incorporate a person's on-the-job training and other prior learning into the design of an educational degree program and to give credit for this prior learning. Although postsecondary schools typically do not give credit for prior learning, it is something to be aware of as you acquire training experiences throughout your career.

Accreditation, Ranking, Certification, and Licensure

The relationships between occupations and training are often connected by the processes of accreditation, ranking, certification, and licensure. These terms can be very confusing for people engaged in educational and career planning, so it is helpful to compare and contrast the meanings of these four terms.

Accreditation is a designation given by a professional association or governing group to a training program. It is not a designation given directly to students or trainees. An accredited training program is one that has met standards set up by an association, board of experts, or some other recognized body. In general, you will want to complete your studies in programs that are accredited by the groups that are the most powerful and influential in a field. Completing your training at an accredited program has many advantages for you, including ease in obtaining financial aid and later employment, more prestige and credibility in the profession, and getting certified and licensed.

A word should be said here about **rankings**. Students sometimes want to know the ranking of the school or degree program they are considering, and they often consult the annual report provided by *U.S. News* (http://www.usnews.com/). In addition, employers are also interested in such rankings (Koc, 2009). Although it seems logical to consider this factor in planning your education, there are some problems. First, the ranking is probably based on a "reputational analysis," a fancy way of saying popularity contest. Typically, some group will ask deans, faculty, or another sample of people to rank schools or programs in their field, and the result is the ranked list. Second, the perceptions of quality may be based on history, what the program accomplished many years ago, and not reflect current conditions and information. Third, a "halo effect" can operate. Harvard always seems to get high rankings, mostly because it is Harvard. However, it is uncertain whether all the programs there are of equally high quality. Fourth, rankings of undergraduate programs are especially unreliable because they may be based on the quality of the graduate program. After studying the matter carefully, Koc (2009) concluded that "there are simply not the data available to make a truly defensible ranking of the 'best' colleges in the United States" (p. 20).

Rankings may be useful in your educational planning if they are (a) based on specific outcome criteria that matter to you (e.g., salaries of graduates, percentage of bar exams passed); (b) if they help you identify important characteristics of notable programs so you can use this information to evaluate other, unranked, programs; (c) if they are current; and (d) if they describe why and how the ranking was obtained.

Certification is a designation that a professional association or independent group gives to you after you have completed a specified training program, possibly including supervised field experience and perhaps an examination. It is a public affirmation that you have completed all the requirements as a professional in a field and that you can be designated by a name or title. Certification is typically provided by a national group, but teaching is one occupation where certification is typically provided by a state agency.

Licensure, unlike certification, is provided by a governmental agency, not a professional group (one exception is law). Licensure is often made available by a state, and it means that you can practice or offer services for a fee as a member of a particular profession or trade in that state. Hundreds of occupations require licensure for legal employment, but states may differ in the actual licensure requirements. Some states offer reciprocal arrangements with one another, so you can relocate to a state without repeating the time-consuming, expensive process of becoming licensed.

Licensed occupations have become modern-day guilds (Hoppough, 2008). About 28% of U.S. workers now work in a licensed field, up from 4.5% 50 years ago. For example, there are over 1,100 licensed occupations in California. Typical requirements include hours of classroom study (e.g., 150 hours of college coursework for accountants) and a passing score on a state licensure examination.

What can these distinctions mean for your educational and career decision making? First, it is important to note that educational and training programs don't certify or license you for anything. This is only done by national associations or boards and governmental organizations. Second, completion of an accredited training program may ease your preparation for the certification and licensure process, but it will not guarantee success for you. Third, ranking is relatively unimportant in evaluating educational and training programs. Fourth, you should inquire of educational and training providers about the past performance of graduates in completing certification and licensure requirements.

Education and Training: A Life/Career Process

When we examined Super's (1990) Rainbow in Chapter 1 (see Figure 1.1), we noted that training periods kept recurring throughout the person's career. We have seen how training is lifelong in nature and how education can help you develop transferable skills. Education and training can be early indicators of what will happen later to a person with regards to occupational and leisure activities. For example, a person who enrolls in a welding class to learn more about the process and develop some skills for a hobby may years later start a welding business. The class experience also provided an opportunity to meet other people with similar interests, to learn something about the need for more welders and welding services in the local community, and to refocus broader career goals.

In this sense, it is important to recognize that education and training are already part of one's career; they are not something that will prepare you for some future career. If you are a college student now, you are already in your career.

Sources of Information and Support

Computer-based CIDS and other Internet-based programs have made dramatic changes in the delivery of educational information (e.g., Choices® Planner, DISCOVER®, CIS, GIS, Focus, and SIGI3). You can use these systems to search for educational programs that meet your criteria. Let's say you're interested in searching for bachelor's degree programs in marine biology by state, enrollment size, tuition costs, and the kinds of athletic programs available on the campus. The system will scan many thousands of combinations of options to compile a list of programs in the states you specify. You can also use the computer to get specific information about more than 5,000 programs from up to 4,000 schools that may be included in a typical database of one of these systems.

In addition to computers, most libraries and career or counseling centers have reference books on educational and training options that are updated annually. Standard sources include *The College Handbook* (College Entrance Examination Board); *Barron's Profiles of American Colleges and Guide to Two-Year Colleges* (Barron's Educational Series); *Peterson's College or Graduate School Planners* (Peterson's, A Nelnet Company, http://www.petersons.com/); the *College Blue Book* (Macmillan Publishing); and the 650 *Chronicle Occupational Briefs* (Chronicle).

Financial Assistance

Financial support for education and training is available in many forms. State CIDS and other computer-based career guidance systems provide lists of federal and private sources of financial support for vocational technical and higher-education training. A college financial aid office and a public library can provide reference books.

The school providing the training will likely have specialized rules and sources of financial assistance that may be especially important to you. These local sources may be useful for you to pursue. Employers and unions sometimes provide funds for training as a benefit of employment or membership, sometimes even for spouses and children of employees. Remember that there are some illegal and unethical operators in this field who will take your money and do nothing more than search a CIDS database, which you probably could have done better yourself. Finally, start early in the financial assistance search process. Ten months may be the best lead time in applying for financial and scholarship aid.

Leisure

When Bolles (1981) described the three boxes of life, the last one pertained to retirement, play, and leisure, and it was viewed as the last phase of life/career. In the United States, people have widely differing views about leisure time. Some view it as a positive thing and a desirable part of living. Others see it negatively and regard it as wasteful and useless. How did we arrive at such opposing views? Why is leisure an important part of career planning?

A Historical View of Leisure

Our conflicting views about leisure had their origins many years ago. The ancient Greeks, at the time of Plato and Aristotle, prized leisure as a time for learning, creativity, and sports competition by citizens. They had no word for work, because only slaves and other noncitizens were involved in labor. The fall of the Greek civilization led to a complete change in the concept of leisure. In the later Roman Empire, leisure was seen as depraved, degrading excesses in drunkenness and self-indulgence. Early Christian leaders and, later, Protestant reformers viewed leisure as idleness, and idleness was seen as moral depravity. Even today, some consider leisure the seedbed of substance abuse, antisocial acts, and financial waste. Given this brief sketch of Western cultural traditions, it is no wonder that as a society we are often very confused about the value of leisure.

Despite this low opinion of leisure by some people, others spend a lot of time indulging in it. Jeremy Rifkin (1995), author of *The End of Work*, reported that about 51% of Americans, about 94.2 million adults, gave an average of 4.2 hours per week to various causes or organizations in 1992. He has noted that this third sector of the economy includes more than 1,400,000 nonprofit organizations whose primary purpose is to provide a service or advance a cause. Much of this time is volunteered (unpaid), and it represents a significant allocation of effort on the part of many citizens.

How is leisure viewed in terms of work and career by most career-development experts? We defined work as activity that produces something of value for oneself or others. This definition included unpaid work and/or leisure activities. We further defined career as the time extended working out of a purposeful life pattern through work undertaken by the person. With these definitions, we can include leisure as an important, significant part of our career. A definition of leisure is provided below.

> *Leisure. Relatively self-determined activities and experiences that are available due to discretionary income, time, and social behavior; the activity may be physical, intellectual, volunteer, creative, or some combination of all four.*

Some other important points should be considered. First, leisure is self-determined, just like other aspects of career. You choose the part that leisure plays in your life. Second, the money, time, and social relationships involved in leisure are discretionary; they are not something you "have" to do, but rather that you "choose" to do. And, third, leisure activities may be physical, intellectual, private, social, routine, spiritual, creative, or some combination of all of these.

Viewed this way, leisure is an essential part of our career development and something that we need to better understand and know about in order to effectively solve career problems and make career decisions. *As with other options for occupations and education, it is important for you to begin with knowing yourself before you start to explore leisure options.*

Leisure, in relation to other occupational and educational activities, can be (a) complementary, (b) supplementary, or (c) compensatory (Blocker & Siegal, 1981).

- As **complementary**, leisure extends and magnifies your job activities. If you are a professional musician in a symphony, you could spend your weekends teaching other gifted musicians the fine points of mastering your musical instrument.
- As **supplementary**, leisure could enrich your life in ways that go beyond job satisfaction. It rounds you out. If you are a high school football coach, you could join a class in ceramics as a way to meet different kinds of people and enjoy solitary work.
- As **compensatory**, leisure could make up for deficits and dissatisfactions in your job. If you are an office manager of an accounting firm and want to be more active and work with children, your leisure might involve coaching a youth soccer team.

Leisure Classifications

How many different kinds of leisure activities are there? Overs, Taylor, and Adkins (1977) listed over 725 different leisure activities in a three-level classification. The *Leisure Activities Finder*, another classification of over 760 leisure activities based on two-letter Holland codes, was developed by Holmberg, Rosen, and Holland (1990). They based their groupings on Holland's six environmental models, which have been used to classify occupations, fields of study, and now leisure activities. Each leisure option has a group label, such as collecting, nature, or entertainment, as a way of helping define the nature of the leisure activity.

Sources of Leisure Information

Information about leisure activities is everywhere. There are clubs, organizations, and online chat groups devoted to virtually every kind of leisure activity. These organizations provide demonstrations, training, organized events, memberships, and virtual communities for people interested in the activity. There are Web sites and publications devoted to virtually every leisure activity. Your local newspaper and Yellow Pages are sources of information about community leisure organizations, and a student activities office or Web site at a school or college will have information about school-based organizations and activities. Resorts, community recreation centers, volunteer agencies, and other community organizations can provide information and assistance to people seeking information about leisure options.

Improving Our Options Knowledge

There are a number of things one can do to learn more about options for solving career problems and making career decisions. Improving our knowledge about occupational, educational, and leisure options involves more than simply acquiring additional facts and data. Below we present some ways to do that.

First, develop a conceptual framework or mental map (cognitive psychologists call these "schema") for thinking about options in each of the three areas. For example, Holland's six types provide a hexagonal model for thinking about options in all three areas. This chapter has reviewed other frameworks, but we like Holland types because they can be used to structure and classify self-knowledge as well as knowledge about the three areas of options. Thinking about options as types and combinations of types can free you up to think about options in new ways.

Second, develop ways of thinking about options based on your useful distinctions among them. For example, some information about a field of study, such as the percentage of men in nursing and elementary education, may not be particularly important or useful for you in differentiating among major fields of study. You need to focus on the aspects of your options that are important to you and then examine the facts about those options. In other words, think about your values, interests, and skills as you examine the distinctions among options.

Third, think in complex ways about occupational, educational, and leisure options. You now know that there are many different ways to think about options. For example, options related to occupations, industries, education and training, and leisure are all simultaneously interrelated, changing, and separate. There are local, state, regional, national, and international perspectives on all these areas. This complexity is part of what makes career problem solving and decision making difficult.

Fourth, don't use information about options that is biased, superficial, or inaccurate. For example, some of the information that is available about options is produced for recruitment purposes; it is intended to put a positive spin on the option and make it more attractive.

Using Information about Options

What can you do to improve your information about occupational, educational, and leisure options? First, apply the research skills you have already developed in school to your career decision making. Much of the information about your options is online or in libraries or similar settings, and you have skills for finding and using computer-based indexes, databases, books, periodicals and files, multimedia resources, reference materials, and other sources. Indeed, using your research skills to develop information about your personal, life/career options may be the most important research you ever do.

Second, remember that finding information about options takes time. It is not something that you can rush along or take shortcuts to complete. A good way to look at it is if you spend more than 86,000 hours working in some kind of employed position (calculated at 8 hours per day × 5 days per week × 50 weeks per year × 43 years), and you spend 100 hours in the next year studying and researching information sources related to your options, it would only be about 1/1000 of the time you spend in your occupational option. That's equivalent to about 28 seconds out of an 8-hour day. That doesn't even include the thousands of hours in learning and leisure that you will need to include in your planning. Common sense suggests that it would be important to invest the time now in this personal research in order to get the payoff of increased life/career satisfaction in the years to come.

Third, information about your options is available to you in formats that involve you in (a) reading, (b) listening, (c) observing, (d) writing, (e) visiting, and (f) talking. Think about some ways that these six actions can help you acquire information related to your options. One way you can assess your improvement in acquiring additional information about your options is to check off each time you engage in one of these six behaviors and keep track of exactly what you did. For example, you would list the resources you read, the people and associations you contacted for information about occupations, or the information interviews you conducted. Each of these actions can be used to provide information about your options that is slightly different in nature; for this reason, it is good to use several of these behaviors to get information about each option you are exploring.

Fourth, make it a habit to constantly acquire occupational information from friends, family members of friends, relatives, acquaintances, or even people sitting next to you on airplanes or buses. Church activities and volunteer organizations also provide a means to meet people working in a variety of occupations. Individuals who engage in purposeful information-seeking behavior are in a better position to acquire quality information for their career and life decisions. Without such an approach, the occupations of your family members and teaching may be the only occupations and jobs with which you will be directly familiar.

Fifth, make it a point to learn about and become a critical reader of sources of occupational, educational, and leisure information. They are all around us. Web-based publications, major national newspapers, popular magazines, professional and association newsletters, seminars, blogs, and television regularly contain information about career options. As we noted previously, many of these sources distill and summarize highlights from government reports, university research studies, and public surveys into informational reports that are easier to understand. If you are a college student, pay attention to the resources in your campus career center and on the center's Web site. This center is a collection point for hundreds of items each week that can inform you about your options.

Finally, use the services of a career services professional, librarian, or other information professional to help you locate and evaluate various sources of career information. Many public and educational libraries have a reference or adult services librarian who specializes in career information, including job vacancy listings, company and industry information, and so forth. These professionals can help you clarify what the information means, whether or not you have enough of it, and where you are in the decision-making process.

Summary

This chapter has introduced the topic of life/career options; the areas of occupational, educational, and leisure information. These three areas were examined in terms of organizational classifications, sources of information, and suggestions for improving the quality and quantity of information in each area. The interrelationships of these three areas were also highlighted, and suggestions were made for developing more complex ways of thinking about options in order to improve career problem solving and decision making. The goal was to help you improve the quality of information in the option knowledge domain of your Personal Career Theory.

References

ACT. (2012). DISCOVER® [computer software]. Iowa City, IA: Author.

Bolles, R. (2012). *A practical manual for job hunters and career changers: What color is your parachute?* Berkeley, CA: Ten Speed Press.

Bolles, R. (1981). *The three boxes of life, and how to get out of them.* Berkeley, CA: Ten Speed Press.

Bridges Transitions Co. (2008). Choices® Planner [computer software]. Oroville, WA: Author.

Farr, M., & Shatkin, L. (2006). *New guide for occupational exploration* (4th ed.). Indianapolis, IN: JIST Works.

Franklin, J. C. (2007, November). Employment outlook: 2006–16: An overview of BLS projections to 2016. *Monthly Labor Review,* 3–12.

Gottfredson, G. D., & Holland, J. L. (1996). *Dictionary of Holland occupational codes* (3rd ed.). Odessa, FL: Psychological Assessment Resources.

Holland, J. L. (2011). *Occupations finder—revised edition.* Odessa, FL: Psychological Assessment Resources.

Holmberg, K., Rosen, D, & Holland, J. (1990). *Leisure activities finder.* Odessa, FL: Psychological Assessment Resources, Inc.

Hoppough, S. (2008, February 25). The new unions. *Forbes,* 100–101.

Koc, E. W. (2009, September). NCE research: The frustration and futility of college rankings. *NACE Journal,* 16–28.

Overs, R. P., Taylor, S., & Adkins, C. (1977). *Avocational counseling manual: A complete guide to leisure guidance.* Washington, DC: Hawkins & Associates.

Rifkin, J. (1995). *The end of work.* New York, NY: Putnam's.

Rosen, D., Holmberg, K., & Holland, J. (2011). *Educational opportunities finder.* Odessa, FL: Psychological Assessment Resources, Inc.

Super, D. (1990). A life-span, life-space approach to career development. In D. Brown & L. Brooks, (Eds.), *Career choice and development* (2nd ed.) San Francisco: Jossey-Bass.

U.S. Bureau of Census. (2007). *North American industry classification system: United States 2007.* Washington, DC: National Technical Information Service.

U.S. Department of Labor. (2010). *Standard occupational classification (SOC) system manual 2010.* Washington, DC: U.S. Government Printing Office.

U.S. Bureau of Labor Statistics, U.S. Department of Labor. (2012, March 29). *Career guide to industries, 2010–11 edition.* Retrieved from http://www.bls.gov/oco/cg

U.S. Department of Labor (1991). *Dictionary of occupational titles* (4th ed.). Indianapolis, IN: JIST Works.

U. S. Bureau of Labor Statistics, U.S. Department of Labor. (2012, March 29). *Occupational outlook handbook, 2010–11 edition, bulletin 2800.* Retrieved from http://www.bls.gov/oco

U.S. Department of Labor. (2007). *Occupational outlook quarterly.* Washington, DC: Author.

Chapter Four

Career Decision Making

*Problem*solving and decision making are the essence of our lives—we are constantly involved in sorting through what we want and like out of what's possible. Think about it. You have probably already made a series of decisions today. What should I wear? What do I want to eat? When should I call my friend? Each of these decisions involved checking out information about yourself and your surroundings. For example, deciding what to wear might have involved assessing how you were feeling at the time—cold, sexy, tired—and it might have involved checking the weather forecast, how much outside walking you would be doing, and who you might be meeting during the day. In other words, the decisions you made about what to wear were based on knowing about yourself and your options.

Career problem solving and decision making involve considering information about your values, interests, and skills and about your occupational, educational, and leisure options. In Chapter 1, we likened self-knowledge and occupational knowledge to computer data files stored in our memory that form the basis of career planning. We identified self and occupational knowledge as the base, the knowledge domain, of the Pyramid of Information-Processing Domains. Chapters 2 and 3 examined each of those areas.

The Information Age in which we live means that with an Internet hookup we can obtain large amounts of current information about almost anything. This avalanche of information has led to problems in decision making. For example, Schwartz (2004) reported that the RAND Corporation conducted an assessment of Web sites providing medical information and found that with only a few exceptions, these sites were not doing a good job. "Sometimes important information was omitted, and sometimes the information presented was misleading or inaccurate. Moreover, surveys indicate that these Web sites actually influence the health-related decisions of 70% of the people who consult them" (pp. 55–56). There is no reason to believe the same situation might not be true for career information.

Our response to this problem in decision making is found in Chapter 4, which examines the second level of the pyramid, the decision skills domain (see Figure 4.1). The focus here is on "knowing how I make decisions." The decision skills domain is like a software program that takes selected data from the files and uses it in preset ways to answer questions. The decision skills domain specifies five phases involved in decision making and helps us understand a systematic process for solving career problems.

This chapter provides information that will help you improve your problem-solving and decision-making skills in relation to your career planning. You should use this information to improve the quality of your Personal Career Theory, especially the CASVE Cycle in the Pyramid of Information-Processing Domains. After reading this chapter, you will be able to specify one or more CASVE phases with respect to your decisions about fields of study, occupations, or employment.

———————————— figure 4.1 ————————————

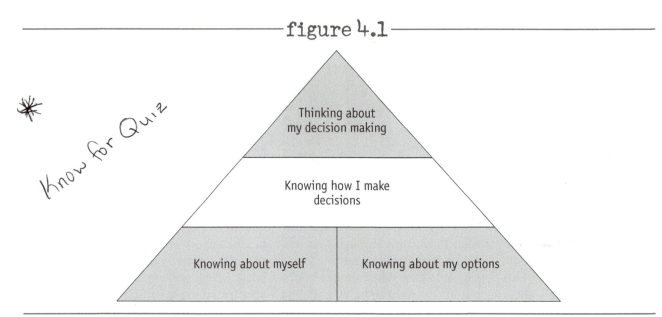

Know for Quiz

Decision-Making Skills—CIP Pyramid

Reprinted from *The Career Development Quarterly, 41*, 1992, p. 70, copyrighted NCDA. Reprinted with permission of the National Career Development Association. Used with permission.

Topics Related to Decision Making

First, we will review several topics related to the career decision-making process. These include (a) why it is important to know to make good decisions; (b) types of career decision making; (c) basic approaches to making personal decisions; (d) barriers to effective decision making; and (e) decision making as a basic skill for general problem solving.

Importance of Good Decision Making

Sometimes we see students who seem to have good self-knowledge and information about their options make very poor decisions. They are constantly trying to "get it right." Other students take inventories to develop information about their interests, values, and skills and spend hours using computer-based career systems and books, and still they are unable to make a decision. In both cases, all the good effort to improve self and occupational knowledge was undermined by poor decision-making skills.

Decision making is very important because one test of our effectiveness in living is the quality of *the way* in which we make personal decisions. Note that the emphasis is on *how* the decision was made. This is especially true of major life decisions, such as what occupation to pursue, with whom to develop a relationship, and so on. These major life decisions, which have long-term implications covering many years, can be especially difficult. Other people know and evaluate us by the way we make important decisions. Sometimes, it is not so much the outcome of the decision that is important to others but the process that was used in making the choice. This is the position we take in this book—it is the process, not the outcome, that we want to focus on. Remember this point.

How do we learn to make personal decisions? Some of it is by trial and error; we learn by practice and from our past experience. Some of it is by observation; we watch others go through the decision-making process and we learn from watching them. However, most of our training for personal decision making is indirect rather than direct. You have probably never had a course on the topic, and yet *much* of your college coursework is designed to help you become a more effective personal decision maker.

The general education courses you take in college, such as those in history, literature, humanities, biology, and psychology, are designed to both inform you about the discipline undergirding the course and to help you learn to apply that knowledge in personal decision making. For example, coursework in biology, history, geography, or economics can help you develop a personal understanding of the issues and importance of the environmental movement and ecology and to make personal decisions in this regard. The CASVE Cycle, which we will explore in more detail in this chapter, is based on the common problem-solving ideas behind those general education courses.

ecision Makers

stinguish who is decided, undecided, or indecisive with respect to career
are decided on our career goals and have a career plan, we may still ex-
tainty and indecision over particular aspects of our situation. Peterson,
991) reviewed theory and research literature in this area and identified
f career decision makers. These three kinds of individual decision mak-
ided, and (c) indecisive.

people who independently integrate knowledge about self and knowl-
bles them to develop a career plan that is satisfying and beneficial to
a whole. They need to confirm a decision or to implement one. A key
viewed all of the relevant facts and data about self and about options in
other words, a person is "decided" because of internal decision-making
he external judgments by others. However, a "false" decided person
ion in order to reduce immediate stress. For example, a student might
college application form to avoid being identified as "undecided" by
officials), even though the student is uncertain about which major to

people who have not made a commitment to an occupational or edu-
led people may be considering options, but for very appropriate rea-
aring a first choice. Other undecided people want occupational cer-
not being able to declare a first choice. This lack of comfort may lead
or to get more information about their occupational and educational
people may have many interests and skills and are unable to make a
al choice due to the numerous options that fit their interests and

people who are often unable to make career decisions and continually
their lives. They often find it difficult to make plans in many areas
on outside events or people in making decisions. In some cases, in-
o explore options because of their anxiety; they put off or procrasti-
responsibility for the decisions to someone else; or they exaggerate
s of various options.

n states are sometimes difficult to identify with respect to specific
help us understand what kind of career assistance may be needed.
eed special assistance in their career decision making.

Decision Making

ere with effective decision making? The following are some of the
are of these problems can help you take the necessary steps to set
sion-making process.

We need to be in good physical, emotional, and mental condition to engage in effective decision making. If we were competing in an athletic event, we would want to be in top form and well prepared so we could succeed and have the best chance of winning the event. Being tired or stressed and unable to focus on the decision-making activity will not ensure a good performance. This may sound obvious, but career counselors find that people who have difficulty in career decision making are often not in good decision-making condition. Their general lack of life-management skills provides little foundation for effective decision making.

FAMILY. Family members and relationships with significant others can interfere with effective decision making. (They can help too, of course, but we're looking at problem areas for now.) For younger people, the problems may be with parents; for older individuals, problems may be with spouses, partners, or children. Scholars who study family systems and career decision making have observed that people who are too interconnected with another family member can have difficulty separating themselves emotionally and psychologically in decision making. For example, when there is a lack of distinction between what a significant other thinks you should major in and what you think you should major in, and you can't keep it all separate, then you can have a problem. A lack of agreement among family members about things like duty, money, responsibility, achievement, and values can present problems in personal decision making. (As an aside, it is important to note that in some cultures, it is considered proper and appropriate for older family members to actively participate in the career decisions of younger members. We will explore these ideas more in Part Two of this book.)

SOCIETY. Social, economic, historical, and cultural forces can interfere with effective career decision making. A national economic recession, gender, ethnic prejudice shared among residents in a community, or age discrimination can complicate one's career options and decisions. In the case of a recession, none of the options may be very good, unless you work for a company that tries to find jobs for workers that have been "dehired."

Altogether, these three factors can make decision making even more difficult than usual, but they are all likely to be a part of many career decisions. Effective career decision makers learn to develop strategies for overcoming personal and social factors that interfere with their decision making.

Decision Making Contrasted with Problem Solving

You have probably noticed that in the first four chapters of this book, the phrases "problem solving" and "decision making" have been used repeatedly. What are the similarities and differences between these terms? Understanding the distinction is important if this book is to be helpful.

Cognitive psychologists view a "problem" as a gap between a current state and a more desired state of affairs. The desire to remove the gap is the source of motivation to engage in the career problem-solving and decision-making process.

Problem solving, then, involves thinking or processing information that will lead to a course of action to remove the gap. This thinking process involves (a) recognizing the gap, (b) analyzing its causes, (c) coming up with different ways to remove the gap, and (d) choosing one of these ways to remove the gap. Thus, problem solving involves a choice among plausible alternative courses of action.

In contrast to problem solving, cognitive psychologists view decision making in a broader way. It includes the four steps of problem solving, but it adds (e) the development of a plan or strategy for implementing the chosen solution and the adoption of a risk-taking attitude and commitment to carry the plan to completion. Decision making, then, adds our feelings and behaviors to the problem-solving process. Decision making includes the implementation of a choice.

For example, when you were selecting a college to attend, you used problem-solving processes to select a course of action (choosing to come to your current college) and to remove a gap between a real and ideal state (being able to tell anybody who asks where I'm going to college). Decision making occurred when you adopted a risk-taking attitude (your application could have been rejected;

your friends could have laughed at you) and you committed energy and resources to attend your first choice (paid a housing deposit, saved money, arranged for transportation). Both problem solving and decision making are involved in career planning, and understanding the distinctions between the two can help you focus your efforts and be more effective.

Decision making is a broader life skill, the one that applies more to life/career development and planning.

The CASVE Cycle

The second level of the Pyramid of Information-Processing Domains pertains to decision making, and the CASVE (pronounced ka SAH' ve) Cycle guides you through the career problem-solving and decision-making process (Sampson, Reardon, Peterson, & Lenz, 2004). Figure 4.2 shows the five phases of the CASVE Cycle: Communication, Analysis, Synthesis, Valuing, and Execution, and the order in which they proceed.

Quiz

figure 4.2

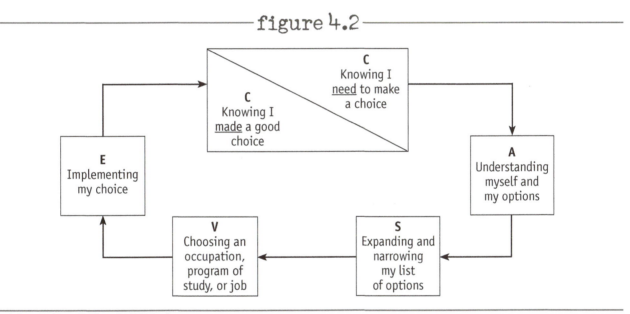

Decision-Making Skills—CASVE Cycle

Reprinted from *The Career Development Quarterly, 41*, 1992, p. 70, copyrighted NCDA. Reprinted with permission of the National Career Development Association. Used with permission.

Communication

The word *communication* is used to describe the first phase of the CASVE decision-making process because this is when we receive information that communicates a gap between the ideal and current situation. This information may be communicated to us by internal or external means. Internal communications might include emotions, such as being anxious about choosing a major or putting off starting a job search, and body signals, such as headaches or stomach problems. External communications might include a note from a dean to declare a major, questions from your family members about your plans after graduation, a layoff notice from your boss, or a newspaper article reporting that your field is becoming obsolete.

This is the "knowing I need to make a choice" phase. It involves becoming fully in touch with a problem cognitively and emotionally. When we become fully aware of these communications indicating that there is a problem or gap that we can no longer ignore, we can then begin to analyze the sources of the problem and explore its causes. The *Guide to Good Decision Making* shown in Appendix F provides some ways for you to think more specifically about your own "communications" in career decisions.

Analysis

The word *analysis* is used to describe this second phase of the CASVE decision-making process, because this is when good problem solvers take a moment to think, observe, research, and more fully understand the gap and their ability to respond effectively. Some of the questions they might ask include the following:

(handwritten note in margin: Good Notes)

- "What do I need to know about myself and my situation to solve this problem?"
- "What exactly do I need to do to solve this problem?"
- "Why am I feeling this way?"
- "What do my significant others think about my choice process?"
- "Where is the pressure coming from to make a choice?"

Good decision makers do not act impulsively to remove the tension or pain experienced in the Communication phase, because they know that impulsive, thoughtless actions may be either inefficient or ineffective, or they make the problem worse.

This is the "understanding myself and my options" phase. During the Analysis phase, a career problem solver often takes steps to improve self-knowledge, especially in the areas of interests, values, and skills, as well as to improve knowledge about options with regards to occupations, fields of study, leisure areas, kinds of work organizations and industries, geographic areas, and so forth. In a nutshell, Analysis involves learning everything possible about all the factors that have led to creating the gap communicated in the first phase. In Chapters 2 and 3, we learned about instruments, activities, and resources that can help us improve our knowledge of ourselves and our options for career problem solving.

The Analysis phase may include more than simply increasing one's knowledge about self and options. For example, "analysis" might involve learning about relationships or connections between self-knowledge and occupational (option) knowledge. We can draw upon the prior work of scholars and other thoughtful people for information about the connections between these two domains. Holland's hexagon and the World-of-Work Map are two examples of how this has been done. For example, we know that particular occupational options are more closely associated with the Realistic type, and similar knowledge exists for the other five Holland types. This might be a good time to review the information in Chapters 2 and 3 to make sure you understand the schemes that have been developed to link self and occupational knowledge.

Finally, Analysis may involve learning more about how you usually make important decisions. What is your attitude about this career problem-solving and decision-making process? How do you think about it? The *Guide to Good Decision Making* provides some examples related to self-talk, self-awareness, and awareness and control of self-talk.

Synthesis

(handwritten note in margin, rotated: Synthesis Elaboration — Expanding list   Synthesis Crystallization — Reduce list)

The term *synthesis* is used to describe the third phase in the CASVE Cycle because it is the time for synthesizing or processing information uncovered in the Analysis phase in order to identify courses of action to remove the problem or gap. The basic question in the Synthesis phase is, "What can I do to solve the problem?"

This is the "expanding and narrowing my list of options" phase. Synthesis actually occurs in two subphases: *expanding* and *narrowing* the possible options for removing the gap. *Synthesis Elaboration* is the subphase when problem solvers expand the list of possible options to solve the problem, to think divergently about every possible solution to the problem. Sometimes groups use the "brainstorming" process to elaborate or expand the list of possible problem solutions. This can be difficult to accomplish, especially if you are tense, threatened, or pressured. One mental image that sometimes helps is to think of yourself fishing in a pond and using a big net to scoop up everything that you might want to keep. Obviously, not everything in the net will satisfy your needs or remove the gap (get fish for dinner), but the process is useful as one part of the problem-solving process. In career problem solving, this is the time to list all the possible occupational, major, or job options that loosely fit at least some of your values, interests, and skills.

Synthesis Crystallization is the second subphase of Synthesis. This is the time when problem solvers reduce the list of alternatives to a smaller number, usually three to five options. Cognitive research suggests that we can most effectively remember and work with this number of options in our minds. That is one reason why phone numbers are broken down into three- or four-digit groups. To narrow down the list of possible options, problem solvers return to the results of the Analysis phase and pick the best three to five options that remove the gap identified in the Communication phase.

At this point, you have probably noticed that the Analysis and Synthesis phases involve repeatedly checking out the quality of the information and of the decision-making processes in terms of whether or not the gap is being removed. Review the *Guide to Good Decision Making* to help you think more concretely about this phase of the CASVE Cycle and to prepare for the next phase.

Valuing

The term *valuing* is used to describe the fourth phase of the CASVE Cycle. This is the "choosing an occupation, job, or field of study" phase.

The first part of Valuing involves evaluating each option in terms of how it affects you and important people in your life. For example, if you select Occupation A, then how will that choice affect your friends, parents, spouse, family, neighborhood, community, gender, or ethnic group? The impact of selecting each option is examined in terms of both costs and benefits to oneself and others.

However, "valuing" also involves judging each option in terms of the problem solver's moral ideals, his or her sense of right and wrong. As you can see, "valuing" in career decision making at this phase involves making moral judgments of right and wrong. Each of us is ultimately faced with making choices about (a) "What is best for me personally?" or (b) "What is best for significant others in my life?" and (c) "What is best for my community at large?" Sometimes, the Valuing process might reveal options that are good for both the individual and society. Some social groups have strong beliefs about what options are most valuable. These social groups might include racial and ethnic groups, recent immigrants to the United States, religious groups, patriotic groups, and so forth.

The second phase of the Valuing process involves ranking or prioritizing the options carried forward from the Synthesis phase. The option, perhaps an occupation or college major, that best removes the gap between the existing and the ideal state of affairs identified in the Communication phase is given the first priority or ranking, the next best option is ranked second, and so forth. Review the *Guide to Good Decision Making* and identify some specific things to consider in the Valuing phase.

At this point, a good problem solver selects a best option and makes an emotional commitment to implement it. The career problem is then solved. One has thus successfully engaged in a career problem-solving activity. However, one must make sure that the other options ranked lower in the Valuing phase would also be suitable backup options in case the first priority did not work out successfully for some reason. In other words, before we can be sure the first option selected is the best final solution, we must implement that option in the real world. This takes us to the next phase in the CASVE Cycle.

Execution

The word *execution* is used in the final phase of the CASVE Cycle because this phase involves converting thoughts into action through the formulation and implementation of an action plan. Execution involves forming means-ends relationships and determining a logical series of steps to reach a goal. With respect to the results obtained in the Valuing phase, it is a matter of reframing the first option as a goal and then focusing on the concrete, active things that lead to accomplishing the goal.

This is the "implementing my choice" phase. For many people the formulation of an action plan in the Execution phase is enjoyable and rewarding because they feel that they are taking positive action to solve the career problem identified in the Communication phase. They are now focused, energized, and getting feedback from outside sources regarding their actions. However, people who are indecisive may experience stress at this phase because they have to give up their tentativeness and uncertainty in order to follow up on their commitment to their first priority. This commitment to a direction or specific goal brings with it the unavoidable risk of failure.

The *Guide to Good Decision Making* shows that three specific activities are associated with Execution: (a) planning, (b), trying out, and (c) applying. Planning involves making a written plan for obtaining education and training, including dates and addresses. Trying out could include getting related experience through cooperative education, volunteering, part-time work, or taking classes to get more information about how to implement an option. Applying could include filling out application forms, registering, paying fees, and taking other concrete steps to implement a planned course of action.

Communication Recycled

The CASVE Cycle is a continuous cycle that repeats itself. Following the Execution phase, one returns to the Communication phase to determine whether the chosen option was a good one—if the gap between the real and the ideal state has been removed. The *Guide to Good Decision Making* graphically shows this process. If the problem-solving and decision-making process in the CASVE Cycle is successful, the negative emotions originally experienced in the Communication phase will be replaced by positive ones.

This is the "knowing I made a good choice" phase. In problem solving and decision making, people may go through the five phases of the CASVE Cycle quickly in some cases or linger in one particular phase. The CASVE model can be useful for solving both individual and organizational problems. It can help you make more careful and informed choices. Thinking through the five phases in a systematic way can provide a useful tool for becoming a more effective person.

Improving Career Decision Making

Each of the five CASVE phases can improve your problem-solving and decision-making skills in distinct ways. It is important to remember that the suggestions for using each phase build upon the material in Chapters 2 and 3 on improving skills related to self-knowledge and occupational knowledge. Each layer of the Pyramid of Information-Processing Domains builds upon the lower levels.

Understanding the Process

Career problem solving and decision making are continuing processes, not events. The successful completion of the process depends on successful work in each of the five phases. The process is only as strong as the weakest phase. Our research suggests that problems in any one phase can shut down or derail the entire problem-solving process.

There are three critical places where this can happen. It can happen in the Communication phase. People become overwhelmed with the problem. They feel bad, and they're anxious, frustrated, or depressed. Most of all, they're confused and don't know how to begin or approach a seemingly overwhelming task. As a result, they never get past these feelings to move into Analysis or Synthesis.

People can also become stuck in the Valuing phase. They find it impossible to make a commitment to one option after narrowing them down. When this happens, they may become frustrated, anxious, depressed, and find themselves back in the Communication phase, perhaps stewing over not yet having found the "perfect" occupation that meets all their needs.

A third area of difficulty is in the Execution phase. People have trouble following through on their first choice because (a) they are not able to break down Execution into smaller action steps, (b) they are uncertain about which task to do first, (c) they are overwhelmed by the ambiguity and uncertainty of the tasks, or (d) they view negative external forces as so powerful that it is pointless to try anything. Therefore, it is important for us to concentrate on completing each phase of the CASVE Cycle to successfully solve career problems and make career decisions.

The CASVE Cycle is one of many problem-solving or decision-making models that have been described in the career literature. Using any of these models may seem a little awkward at first, but with practice, thoughtful review, and some success, using the CASVE Cycle can become almost automatic. At the early phases of learning to use this cycle, it may be important to examine decision-making problems in terms of where the CASVE process is breaking down in your situation. Sometimes, people get stuck at a particular phase, and they may have to take extra measures to get past that sticking point. The goal is to develop a high state of problem-solving efficiency with the CASVE Cycle applied automatically to resolve important life problems.

It is also important to remember that career problems are continuous, meaning that they tend to build upon one another. Successfully using the CASVE Cycle to solve one problem invariably leads to using the CASVE Cycle again to solve the next problem. For example, deciding which college to attend may then lead to problem solving regarding living arrangements, paying the costs, and deciding when to start school.

Improving Decision-Making Skills

Working with a counselor or career advisor, you can complete an assessment activity that can help you learn more about your skill in career decision making. Possible instruments include the Career Thoughts Inventory (CTI), the Career Decision Scale, or the Career Beliefs Inventory. A computer-based career guidance system such as Choices® Planner, Discover, or SIGI3 can also help you practice and improve your career decision-making skills. In addition, career courses, workshops, individual counseling, career planning books, and other career interventions can help you become more skillful in career decision making.

You might also use the *Guide to Good Decision Making* to learn more about the steps you can take in solving a specific career problem and improving your Personal Career Theory (PCT). Have a trusted friend or a career counselor ask you questions about your feelings in the Communication and Valuing phases, the information sources you used in the Analysis and Synthesis Elaboration phases, and the specific actions you plan to take in the Execution phase. Have this other person share his or her views or experiences in each area of the CASVE Cycle as it relates to your situation. Talking out the CASVE phases with another person may help you get new insights into your strengths and weaknesses in decision making.

Read biographies of important people in fields you plan to enter, and analyze the ways they solved important life and career problems with respect to the CASVE Cycle. You can also conduct information interviews with people in career fields of interest to you, and try to understand how they solved work-related problems with respect to the CASVE Cycle. Such activities can accomplish two important things: getting information about career fields of interest and getting practice using the CASVE Cycle.

To improve your skills in the Communication phase, such as identifying the gap between the real and ideal states or achieving a better understanding of your decision-making style, you could do the following:

- trace how you made important decisions in the past, identifying common themes in past decision making;
- recall your feelings at the time and how they affected your decision making;

- develop your skills in progressive relaxation and imaging in order to obtain a clearer picture of the gap;
- talk with people who have recently gone through an important career change process, especially regarding their feelings at the time; and
- identify the role and impact of important people in your life while you were in the Communication phase of decision making.

To improve your skills in the Analysis phase, identify all the causes of the problem (either within or outside of yourself), you could do the following:

- inventory your values, interests, and skills to make sure you know yourself well;
- make sure that the information you have about your options is relatively free from bias or the inappropriate influence of outsiders;
- write an autobiography describing important factors shaping your life;
- look for discrepancies between the informal and the formal information that you have about your options; and
- look for themes and categories that connect your personal characteristics with possible options, such as Holland codes.

Concentrating on the quality of the information that you have in these areas will help you improve your skills in the Analysis phase.

To improve your skills in the Synthesis phase, such as formulating alternative choices and/or eliminating unlikely alternatives, you could:

- find resources and obtain lists of all possible options that meet your minimum requirements;
- develop categories for grouping options together that have common characteristics;
- identify factors for each option that make an important difference in how you evaluate the option;
- practice brainstorming and right-brain activities; and
- identify the factors that limit the usefulness of an option, such as cost or distance, and eliminate those options from your lists.

Remember that Synthesis involves both expanding and narrowing your lists of options in order to come up with the three to five best options.

To improve your skills in the Valuing phase, such as establishing a prioritized, ranked list of three to five options, you could:

- identify the strongest values in your family or cultural background and in the people with whom you have the closest relationships;
- examine how your strongest values match up or conflict with one another;
- write an autobiography and trace the important decisions you have made in the past and how your values were involved in those decisions;
- examine the most important considerations in making prior life decisions;
- examine how your various life roles, such as student, child, worker, citizen, are affected by each option you have identified; and
- talk with others to see if they have similar perceptions of the values for the options you have identified; and identify important values associated with each of your most favored options.

Clarifying your values and being able to act on them consistently in public are important problem-solving skills related to the Valuing phase.

To improve your skills in the Execution phase, such as designing a plan to achieve your first option for solving a problem, you could:

- learn about planning concepts, such as milestones, timelines, flowcharts, and budgets;
- apply each of these concepts to developing a plan for implementing your first choice;
- put your plan into a written, narrative form to explain it and charts and graphs to show it; and
- review your plan with important people in your life and incorporate their useful suggestions in improving your plan.

Successful undertaking of these steps will assist you in improving your skills in the Execution phase. Talk with a career services person if you feel stuck or unsure about how to move forward.

Summary

This chapter examined the second domain of the Pyramid of Information-Processing Domains, the CASVE Cycle. This cycle for guiding a person through the career problem-solving and decision-making process was explained in detail. We explored common problems in effective decision making and examined three decision states of decision makers: decided, undecided, and indecisive. We presented observations and suggestions for improving career problem-solving and decision-making skills in the CASVE Cycle. The goal was to help you improve the quality of information in the decision skills domain of your Personal Career Theory. With respect to choosing a major, specifying an occupation, or choosing a job, after reading this chapter you should be able to answer to the question "Where am I in the CASVE Cycle?"

References

Peterson, G. W., Sampson, J. P., Jr. & Reardon, R. C. (1991). *Career development and services: A cognitive approach*. Pacific Grove, CA: Brooks/Cole.

Sampson, J. P., Jr., Reardon, R. C., Peterson, G. W., & Lenz, J. G. (2004). *Career counseling and services: A cognitive information processing approach*. Pacific Grove, CA: Wadsworth-Brooks/Cole.

Schwartz, B. (2004). *The paradox of choice—Why more is less*. New York, NY: Harper Perennial.

Chapter Five

Thinking about My Career Decisions

Career problems and decisions are among the most complex issues that most of us confront during our lives. We have been introducing a cognitive information processing (CIP) approach, including the Pyramid of Information-Processing Domains and the CASVE Cycle, as devices that can help us sort our way through these issues. *The pyramid and the five-step cycle can be used as guides, like a map or a cookbook, to help us see where we are and where we are going in decision making. They can help us improve our Personal Career Theory.*

This chapter examines the top of the pyramid, the processes involved in "thinking about my decision making." You will remember that as we have worked our way up the pyramid from the knowledge domains, including self-knowledge and occupational knowledge, through the decision skills domain—the CASVE Cycle—we have repeatedly noted how our thinking influences our career decision making.

The top of the pyramid is the executive-processing domain. This area calls the shots. It is here that directions are given on exactly how career decision making will proceed. If you are a *Star Trek* fan, you might think of this as "Starfleet Command." We have used the example of a computer to show how the Pyramid of Information-Processing domains works in our minds. The knowledge domains are like files and data stored on the computer. The CASVE Cycle is like programs that prescribe when, how, and what information will be used. The executive processing domain governs this entire process. For example, it tells the system when to start and stop the CASVE process, how much information is needed from the files, and how well the process is moving along.

Another example of how executive processing works is a football team in a game situation. The knowledge domains include facts, such as the team playbook, the physical characteristics of the players, the weather, and playing field conditions. The CASVE Cycle includes the decisions that the quarterback makes in the huddle. Information has to be processed rapidly in the huddle, so the team relies on its game plan, which specifies what plays will be called in certain conditions. These conditions might include the game score, time left in the game, location of the ball on the field, and the player injury situation.

Executive processing in this example resides with the head coach. The head coach makes the decision to go for two points rather than one late in the game, to go for the win rather than the tie. The head coach decides when to change quarterbacks, depending on if the game is going well or poorly. In effect, executive processing, like a head coach, may direct that some information be ignored, that a time-out be called, or that execution in the CASVE Cycle be carried out in a risky way such as a hidden-ball trick play.

The executive processing function in our brains and our ability to make decisions has been impacted by the Information Age and the Internet. Sharon Begley (2011), the science editor for *Newsweek*, has described how "information fatigue" brought on by the quantity and the rate of information flooding upon us has contributed to poor decision making. "The booming science of decision making has shown that more information can lead to objectively poorer choices, and to choices that people come to regret" (p. 30). We believe that the cognitive-information processing theory featured in this text can help with this problem, for decision making in general and career decisions in particular.

This chapter will explain and analyze the executive processing domain and provide descriptions of new concepts and skills that can improve our decision making ability and avoid "information fatigue." The chapter concludes with strategies for improving our effectiveness in the executive processing area.

The Executive Processing Domain

Having a lot of information or knowledge about yourself and your options and knowing how to use information in a decision-making situation are very important, but they are not sufficient in effective career problem solving. The missing ingredients are referred to as *metacognitive skills,* or the skills that govern how we think about career problem solving and decision making. Remember that "cognition" is the memory and thought process that a person uses to perform a task or attain a goal; it is the thinking process (Peterson, Sampson, & Reardon, 1991). The prefix "meta" simply means "beyond" or "higher," such as "higher-order thinking skills." The pyramid (Figure 5.1) illustrates the position of these higher thinking skills relative to the other two levels. These metacognitive skills help us know when to initiate the CASVE Cycle, when to get more self-knowledge information, and when we are ready to execute a choice. There are three skills that are especially important in the metacognitive area: (a) self-talk, (b) self-awareness, and (c) control and monitoring.

figure 5.1

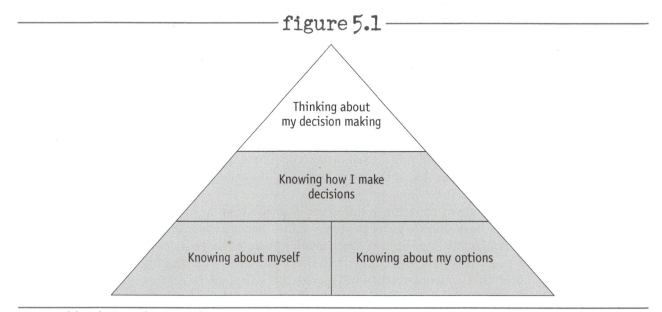

Metacognitions in Executive Processing

Reprinted from *The Career Development Quarterly, 41*, 1992, p. 70, copyrighted NCDA. Reprinted with permission of the National Career Development Association. Used with permission.

Self-Talk

To be an effective career problem solver, you must be able to think of yourself as competent and capable in this area. For example, you can make a positive statement about yourself, such as "I am a good decision maker" or "I can make good decisions for myself." Such positive self-talk does two important things for your decision making: first, it creates a positive expectation, and second, it reinforces positive behavior, such as saying "good work" following a decision-making activity.

Unfortunately, negative self-talk can create problems in career decision making because it interferes with the effective, efficient processing of information. For example, negative self-statements such as "I'll never be able to make a career choice" or "I trust others' judgments more than my own about what is best for me" can disrupt effective problem solving. Sometimes we do a lot of "shoulding" on ourselves: "I should be a good decision maker," "This should be easy for me." Such negative statements tend to shut down the process or create "noise" and "static" in the system that makes it almost impossible to use whatever information is available.

Returning to our football example, coaches who are tentative or doubtful about their teams will not be able to inspire or lead their players. People with more difficult career problems may minimize their metacognitive skills as decision makers, even though they have sufficient information to make decisions. They may find that they are unable to rely on themselves to solve their problems.

A particularly sad example comes to mind. Several years ago a student in a career-planning class was describing his inability to make decisions, concluding that he was a poor decision maker who would never make a successful career decision. The instructor, searching for some positive evidence of career decision-making skill to help change this negative metacognition, noted that the student was well dressed, looked nice, and could obviously make good choices about clothes. She was dismayed when the student responded that he bought the clothes directly off of a store mannequin because he could not trust his judgment in selecting and buying clothes. This is an example of negative self-talk that was quite pervasive in this student's way of thinking and was influencing his ability to make career decisions. Later, we will examine ways to overcome negative self-talk and other dysfunctional metacognitions.

Self-Awareness

Being an effective career problem solver means "having an awareness of one's self as the doer of a task" (Peterson, Sampson, & Reardon, 1991; Sampson, Reardon, Peterson, & Lenz, 2004). An example might be Robert saying, "I'm getting anxious about my ability to make a decision on time." Robert is aware of feelings while working through the CASVE Cycle. He is not just focusing on the specific CASVE phase, but he is aware of his feelings about the overall process of deciding as well.

A simple example comes to mind that may further illustrate this point. Remember your first time on a bicycle? You had to concentrate very hard on the road, the pedals, the seat, your balance, and many other details about bike riding. We might look at these as "lower-order" bike-riding skills. As you developed expertise and confidence in your bike riding, you were able to devote more of your focus on other aspects of bike riding: if you were getting tired or hot, if you were riding on a safe road, if you needed more air in your tires, or how many calories you were burning on your ride. These higher-order thoughts became possible as you mastered lower-order bike-riding skills.

These same principles apply in effective career decision making. Good problem solvers are aware of their feelings as they engage in information-processing tasks. They are able to include an awareness of others' needs and to select options that are good for themselves as well as for society at large. They are able to balance self-interests and the interests of others. Several years ago, a career decision maker stuck in the CASVE process was able to break away by focusing on "what in the world made her angry." By focusing on those feelings, she eventually decided to go into environmental protection work because the loss of wetlands and coastal forests made her angry.

Control and Monitoring

Good problem solving and decision making involves knowing when to move forward and when to stop and get more information. It is the thoughtful balance between compulsivity and impulsivity in decision making. Compulsivity leads to obsessive thinking and endless processing without any action ever being taken. Impulsivity promotes "jackrabbit" decisions, with trial-and-error attempts at problem solving (Peterson, Sampson, & Reardon, 1991). Both approaches generally lead to poor results.

Several years ago, a particularly compulsive student was intent on reading about all 12,700+ occupations in the *Dictionary of Occupational Titles* because she wanted to make sure she knew about all the available options before she made a decision. It took her almost a year to complete the process, with little noticeable positive effect on her ultimate choice. At the other end, an impulsive student recently requested the name of the "best-paying job for college students" because that is what he had decided to enter. Never mind that he had poor math skills and little interest in computers. Good decision makers sense when more information is needed to obtain a better understanding of the gap or the options, and they also intuitively know when they are ready to make a choice and commitment. These are examples of metacognitive skills. (Later in this chapter we discuss *maximizing* and *satisficing* with respect to control and monitoring in career decision making.)

Developing Metacognitive Skills

Improving our metacognitive skills, our ability to think about our thinking, sounds like a difficult task. However, it may be less difficult than it appears. There are specific ways that we can become more aware of ourselves as decision makers and improve our thinking skills in this area.

What Are Metacognitive Skills?

One example of a metacognitive skill is *knowing when to get additional help*. Good career problem solvers know when to seek assistance from outside sources. For example, they know that they need help in learning how their interests and values match up with college majors, occupations, or jobs, and they seek services from a qualified helper. Sometimes, you decide to rely on your intuition or advice from individuals you respect to make a choice after you have exhausted all the rational processes.

A second metacognitive skill is *being aware of effective decision-making strategies*. The important point is to be aware of how a strategy affects the decision-making process. A strategy might involve focusing on the individual steps that need to be taken to avoid becoming overwhelmed.

A third skill involves *being clear about the specific problem that needs to be solved*. Sometimes, relationship problems and career problems are intertwined and difficult to separate. Decision makers need to separate the issues so that the most useful skills and knowledge can be used for the problem at hand. For example, people sometimes try to solve relationship problems by making career decisions, such as "I'll make my father happy by going into business, even though I have no interest in it." It would be better first to separate the decision about which field to enter from the decision about how to improve the relationship with Dad, and then see how the options selected for each decision affect the other.

As you go through the career decision-making process, a fourth important skill is *monitoring how the process is going*. For example, in the CASVE Cycle described in Chapter 4, it is important to pause at the end of each phase and ask, "Am I finished with this step and ready for the next one?" In looking ahead to the end of the cycle, you may also need to determine how you'll know when the problem is solved. You may not always be certain that you've found the ideal solution, but you know that you've expended a reasonable amount of time, energy, and resources in reaching your decision and need to take action. In CASVE terms, we would say: "Have I closed the gap between what I want and where I am?" "Can I commit and act on a choice in the midst of my uncertainty?"

Finally, good problem solvers are not their own worst enemy, rather they give themselves positive self-talk, praise their good efforts, and focus positively on desirable outcomes. Such a *positive attitude* is an important metacognitive skill for tackling many of life's problems.

Improving Metacognitive Skills

Many of our metacognitive skills were formed at an early age, perhaps from ages four through eight. If, as adults, we lack positive, high-quality metacognitive skills, then it can be difficult to learn new ones. It may take assistance from another person, perhaps a professional such as a counselor, minister, or teacher, to help us improve our metacognitive skills. However, it is sometimes possible for individuals to do this through self-directed learning activities once they learn how to identify metacognitive skills that are weak or problematic. Five techniques that can help you improve metacognitive skills are described below.

1. IDENTIFYING NEGATIVE THOUGHTS. Some of us have negative, or self-defeating, thoughts about ourselves or the world of work that make it difficult for us to solve career problems and make career decisions. Some of those thoughts and beliefs are popular, or they have been taught to us by important people in our lives. Nevertheless, these thoughts can present problems in career decision making.

For example, the statement, "I'm afraid I'll pick something and then change my mind" is a thought that can "freeze up" our career decision making. Being afraid is, itself, an emotion that is the opposite of confidence, optimism, and self-assurance, and it is an emotion that negatively affects good decision making. Also, feeling little control over whether I'll change my mind makes it very difficult to make a choice.

We believe there are hundreds of these kinds of negative thoughts that can freeze or short-circuit the decision-making process, and these thoughts must be identified before they can be corrected. Of course, not all negative thoughts always shut down the process, but they can become problems at unexpected times. In some ways, these negative thoughts are like nasty viruses that lurk in our bodies and break out periodically to make us sick. Later, we will see examples of negative thoughts that occur at various points on the Pyramid of Information-Processing Domains and the CASVE Cycle.

The Career Thoughts Inventory (CTI; Sampson, Peterson, Lenz, Reardon, & Saunders, 1996a) helps people learn more about the way they think about career choices. This instrument includes 48 items or statements describing thoughts that some people have when considering educational and career choices. Completing the CTI may help you identify troublesome thoughts related to career problem solving and decision making.

By learning and exploring both positive and negative aspects of ourselves and our options, we can challenge our habitual ways of thinking about career decision making. We'll probably learn that things are not all good or all bad but combinations of good and bad. Career decision making is full of gray areas, and this requires us to think in more complex ways about career problems. In addition, talking out our career problems with a trusted friend or counselor can sometimes help us get our negative thoughts out there in the open, where they can be examined, challenged, and possibly changed.

Sampson, Peterson, Lenz, Reardon, and Saunders (1996b) identified a four-step sequence for changing negative thoughts. The four steps are (a) *identify* the negative thought(s) or statements; (b) *challenge* the appropriateness, usefulness, or truthfulness of the thought-statement; (c) *alter* the negative thought, or reframe it into a more positive thought-statement; and (d) *act* in new ways that are consistent and correspond with the new, altered thought-statement. These four steps might help you remember how to improve your metacognitive skills.

2. TRAIN FOR POSITIVE SELF-TALK. The statement, "I'm not a good decision maker" is an example of negative self-talk that a friend or counselor can challenge and help a person eliminate. You can enlist your friends to help you identify and change such negative statements, and quickly you will learn to monitor your use of these statements. You can train for more positive self-talk by first working to eliminate the negative statements, and then you can learn to start using more positive self-talk. Some people have found that reading self-help books, designed to improve self-esteem and increase self-confidence, enable them to develop more positive self-talk. In addition, professional counseling, positive religious experiences, and positive growth groups can provide opportunities for learning more positive self-talk. Just like a good coach can help you improve your skills in a sport, positive people can help you become more positive about yourself. Indeed, one of the things a good coach does is train you for positive self-talk about you and your sport.

3. REDUCING EITHER/OR THINKING. Another metacognitive skill that helps us become better problem solvers and decision makers involves relative thinking rather than dualistic thinking. Dualistic or all-or-nothing thinking tends to immobilize us. For example, the statement, "All the good jobs require math" might shut us down if we are not interested in math or have few skills in the area. Such a statement could be restated as "Some of the better paying jobs in some organizations are held by people who have skills and interests in math as well as several other areas." As a result of this new thinking about the relationship between jobs and math, we can now examine the matter in terms of degrees rather than all-or-nothing, absolute terms. In the real world of career problem solving and decision making, there are few absolute truths that govern the process. It is almost always a matter of degrees, situations, people, timing, and circumstances, and we function better when our thinking reflects these realities.

4. DEVELOPING SELF-CONTROL. We can learn self-control techniques that help us better manage the factors influencing our behavior. For example, we learn to count to 10 to avoid an outburst when our parent asks why we're not majoring in biology, or we practice deep breathing to relax before starting a job interview, or we use a calming mental image (lying on the beach) when we feel ourselves getting anxious about our career uncertainties. These self-control techniques can help us improve our metacognitive skills and ultimately improve our career decision making.

5. IMPROVED GENERAL PROBLEM SOLVING. The CASVE Cycle provides a general approach to problem solving that can be used in many life situations. When we can quickly and efficiently use such a strategy as the CASVE Cycle to work through career and other life problems, we improve our career decision making. Using the CASVE Cycle without having to think about it can be compared to learning to ride a bike or drive a car—it becomes almost automatic. When that happens, we can more easily move through the decision-making process. The *Guide to Good Career Decision Making* (see Appendix F) can be useful in this regard.

In summary, remember that improving metacognitive skills involves concentrating on the *process* of career decision making, not the event of making a choice. Using another sports metaphor, our focus is not on winning the race (the event), but on improving our strength, using good nutrition and health, being careful about risks, and not missing practice sessions (the process). We have more control over these parts of the process of competing in the race. However, with good career problem-solving and decision-making skills, we do more than run the race well—we can win it, too.

Changing Negative Career Thoughts

Negative, self-defeating thoughts can occur at any place in the Pyramid of Information-Processing Domains (see Figure 1.2) and the CASVE Cycle (see Figure 1.3). Viewing these two figures together as eight areas that include all of the important aspects of effective career decision making, we can examine typical negative thoughts in each of the following areas:

1. Self-knowledge
2. Option knowledge

3. Decision making: Communication
4. Decision making: Analysis
5. Decision making: Synthesis
6. Decision making: Valuing
7. Decision making: Execution
8. Executive processing

Good decision makers use positive metacognitions to effectively solve career problems. Negative thoughts in each of these eight areas can be reframed or restated to make them more positive or helpful metacognitions for good career decision making.

Self-Knowledge

Positive metacognitions related to *self-knowledge* pertain to how we think about our personal characteristics—for example, our interests, values, and skills. Such metacognitions have several characteristics. They are clear, precise, strong, and stable thoughts or statements about the things that we are interested in, indifferent about, and not interested in. The same is true for skills and values. Taken together, these statements clearly describe what is of interest to us, what is important to us, and what we do well.

However, the clarity of these statements should not be confused with rigidity—for example, "I'll never be interested in sales"—because the most useful metacognitions recognize the importance of time and include the idea that we may change our mind about our interests. Another characteristic of positive metacognitions is that they grow out of our personal reflection and experience and are not based on another person's views about us. Finally, positive metacognitions about self-knowledge include information from many experiences instead of a single particularly good or bad experience. For example, getting seasick on a boat one time would not be a reason to eliminate all occupations involving working on or near bodies of water. Positive metacognitions help keep us from overreacting to any single event in life that may exaggerate how we think about our interests, values, and skills.

Here is an example of a negative metacognition about self-knowledge that needs to be changed to a more positive thought: *"No field of study or occupation interests me."*[1]

As you can see, this statement is not a positive metacognition and thus it tends to shut down the process of finding and using self-knowledge information to solve a career problem.

REFRAME With a little work, we can change or reframe this negative metacognition to a more positive thought: "It is possible that I haven't fully determined what my likes and dislikes are. I may need more life experience to really understand my interests. I can get more life experience from full-time or part-time jobs, volunteer work, or leisure activities." This is a more positive thought because it keeps open the possibility of finding new interests in the future, it suggests ways to get new experiences, and it eliminates all-or-none words like "no."

You probably noticed that the more positive metacognition is longer, and this is no accident. Our experience suggests that these more positive metacognitions are, indeed, more complex thoughts and ideas, at least in their initial forms.

Reframing negative career thoughts requires thoughtful concentration and practice. Table 5.1 provides some guidelines and criteria for changing negative thoughts to more positive ones.

[1]Reproduced by special permission of the Publisher, Psychological Assessment Resources, Inc., 16204 N. Fl. Ave., Lutz, FL 33549, from the Career Thoughts Inventory by Sampson, Peterson, Lenz, Reardon, and Saunders, Copyright 1994, 1996 by PAR, Inc. Further reproduction is prohibited without permission from PAR, Inc.

Table 5.1

Guidelines for Creating More Positive Thoughts

Consider the items below in evaluating the quality of the "new" thought. Does the new thought:
- reflect an openness to new things?
- view the person as capable of changing?
- assume responsibility?
- identify the problem (gap)?
- identify multiple options for solving the career problem?
- create an informed and detailed plan for solving the career problem?
- have a realistic estimate of the time required to solve the career problem?
- give a sense of when a person would know the career problem is solved?
- portray optimism about the future?
- acknowledge the need for persistence and commitment?
- acknowledge and cope with feelings?
- acknowledge the ongoing process of decision-making?

Does the new thought:
- avoid words such as "can't," "never," "perfect"?
- avoid words such as "should," "must," "have to?"

Adapted from "Thinking More Helpful Thoughts Activity," by Darrin Carr, Janet Lenz, Gary Peterson, Robert Reardon, & James P. Sampson, Jr., Center for the Study of Technology in Counseling and Career Development, Florida State University.

Option Knowledge

Positive metacognitions related to *option knowledge* pertain to how we think about our options in work, education, and leisure, and also how we group these options in relation to one another. Such metacognitions have several characteristics. For example, they are positive thoughts about reading, viewing, listening, visiting, interviewing, and observing as ways to gain knowledge about options.

Another positive metacognition involves using something like Holland's RIASEC hexagon to group occupations that have things in common and to identify those that are unlike one another. The RIASEC system helps us think about similarities and differences among options at the same time. Finally, positive metacognitions help us appreciate the need to remember information about options and to realize that we can never learn all there is to know about all of our options.

Here is an example of a negative metacognition about occupational knowledge that needs to be changed to a more positive thought: *"Almost all occupational information is slanted toward making the occupation look good."* This statement tends to shut down the process of finding and using occupational information to solve a career problem.

REFRAME With a little work, we can change or reframe this negative metacognition to a more positive thought: "While it is certainly true that some kinds of occupational information are designed to make the occupation 'look good,' it is likely an overstatement to say this about most information. Occupational information may be biased in both directions, good or bad. Helping professionals, like counselors or librarians, can help me determine the quality of various sources of information. It is important to evaluate the source and purpose of each piece of information and determine its usefulness in my career decision making." This statement is a more positive thought about the source, purpose, and quality of occupational information, and it prevents making a negative assumption about information that is needed to solve career problems and make career decisions.

Decision Making: Communication Phase

Positive metacognitions related to the Communication phase in the CASVE Cycle pertain to expectations for successful resolution of a career problem and recognizing that career problems are simply a part of living in our society. For example, positive thoughts in the Communication phase enable us to fully appreciate all of the feelings that are associated with the career problem, such as hopefulness, anticipation, anxiety, anger, frustration, uncertainty, and resentment. Rather than being overwhelmed by these emotions, we accept them, recognize their origins, and resolve to move beyond them.

Here is an example of a negative metacognition about communication that needs to be changed to a more positive thought: *"I get so depressed about choosing a field of study or occupation that I can't get started."* As with the other negative metacognitions, this one tends to shut down the problem-solving and decision-making process.

REFRAME With some work, we can change or reframe this negative metacognition to a more positive thought: "It is important for me to admit that I am feeling depressed about making a career choice, but doing nothing about the problem is not a good idea in the long run. I may need to get help for my feelings of depression or take small concrete steps toward getting the information I need to begin the decision-making process. Such steps might include talking with people in different occupations, reading about occupations, or seeking career assistance to help me develop a plan for taking the next step." This is a more positive thought because it acknowledges the negative feelings associated with the career problem and goes beyond those feelings toward concrete steps that can move the decision-making process forward. This statement helps the person avoid getting stuck or becoming overwhelmed by feelings that limit the processing of information for problem solving.

Decision Making: Analysis Phase

Positive metacognitions related to the Analysis phase in the CASVE Cycle pertain to having the personal motivation and energy to engage the problem-solving task and the expectation of finding a good person-to-environment fit. For example, positive thoughts would be found in statements that express a desire to explore both self and occupational information to find suitable options for oneself. In other words, the person can say with confidence, "I can figure out this relationship between who I am and what fits for me." The opposite of this is "analysis paralysis," or the belief that "I'll never get it figured out and will never solve this career problem." Successfully figuring out all aspects of the career problem means that one is then ready to move on to the Synthesis phase and get lists of options that will solve the problem.

Here is an example of a negative metacognition about Analysis that needs to be changed to a more positive thought: *"I'll never understand myself well enough to make a good career choice."* Here the person has concluded that the lack of self-knowledge makes it impossible to find suitable options and choose one, and this thought can shut down the whole process of finding something.

REFRAME As with the earlier statements, we can change or reframe this negative metacognition to a more positive thought: "It is important for me to be aware of my values, interests, and skills as I make career decisions. Thinking that I must have total understanding of myself before I can make a good career choice may make me feel discouraged and less likely to think carefully about my options. However, going through this career choice process will actually help me better understand myself. There are resources, including printed materials and professionals, that can assist me in gathering enough information about myself to at least take the next step in the career decision-making process." This new, more positive metacognition enables the person to move ahead in the CASVE Cycle and to continue to work on solutions to the career problems.

Decision Making: Synthesis Phase

Positive metacognitions related to the Synthesis phase in the CASVE Cycle pertain to freeing the mind to generate options that draw upon the work done in the preceding four phases to solve the career problem. Information obtained from both the self and occupational knowledge domains, as well as the realization that a career problem exists (Communication) and that it can be examined (Analysis) in terms of person and environment information, leads us to Synthesis.

You will recall that there are two phases in Synthesis, Elaboration and Crystallization, so there are two kinds of positive metacognitions that can help us here. First, positive thoughts help us make sure that no good options are missed, that all possible career solutions are on the table for review. There are no constraints or limits on our listing of possible solutions. Second, positive thoughts also help us let go of the least likely options, to separate and critically analyze each option identified in terms of which are the best possible solutions to the problem.

Here is an example of a negative metacognition about Synthesis that needs to be changed to a more positive thought: *"I can't think of any fields of study or occupations that would suit me."* This negative thought severely impedes Synthesis Elaboration because it shuts down the process of freely generating lists of possible options.

REFRAME Here's how we can change and reframe this negative metacognition to a more positive thought: "Right now I feel discouraged and that may cause me to cut myself off from developing and exploring suitable possibilities. If I think, instead, that it is possible to identify appropriate options, I may free myself up to explore and discover suitable fields of study or occupations. There are tools and resources that can help me do this." You'll notice that this positive reframing statement incorporates the negative feelings embedded in the negative statement and then moves forward to more positive thoughts about how to proceed in solving the career problem.

Decision Making: Valuing Phase

Positive metacognitions related to the Valuing phase in the CASVE Cycle pertain to the ability to prioritize or rank a list of options based on what is best for you, your family and significant others, and society. Stated another way, valuing metacognitions has to do with making a tentative first choice.

Several things may interfere with having these kinds of positive metacognitions, including an inability to think about a first choice from different perspectives: self, others, society. In addition, problems in thinking about a compromise between what is best for both oneself and others can interfere with the metacognitive processes. Unwillingness to take responsibility for a choice, needing to be certain, and desiring to remain uncertain can also interfere with positive valuing metacognitions.

Here is an example of a negative metacognition about Valuing that needs to be changed to a more positive thought: *"The views of important people in my life interfere with choosing a field of study or occupation."* This negative thought makes it difficult to make a choice, because the views of other people have overwhelmed the sense of what choice is best for oneself or society.

REFRAME Here is an example of reframing this negative metacognition to a more positive thought: "The differing views of important people in my life can easily complicate my choice of a field of study or an occupation. Some of the information I get from important people may be useful, while their other ideas may make me more confused or uncertain. However, no matter what suggestions I get from others, I am ultimately the person who is responsible for and capable of making my career choice."

In reframing the negative Valuing metacognition, we have not necessarily chosen to disregard the ideas shared by others about what the person should do, but we have underscored the importance of the deciding person's right and responsibility to prioritize options and make the choice. Such positive metacognitions enable the deciding person to successfully continue in the CASVE Cycle and solve the career problem and make a career decision. We move now to the last part of the CASVE Cycle.

Decision Making: Execution Phase

Positive metacognitions related to the Execution phase in the CASVE Cycle pertain to the ability to think in a logical series of steps in order to make and implement a choice.

These execution metacognitions enable us to think in terms of means-end relationships—for example, "If I improve my grades, I can get into the accounting major." These positive thoughts also help us minimize the idea that luck is the explanation when good things happen in career life, strengthen the attitude that patience and persistence pay off ("I'm willing to ride the bench for two years to get my shot at the starting position on the team"), and recognize the importance of reality testing a tentative choice ("I want to get an internship to test my interest in public relations"). Such beliefs and attitudes foster the development of positive metacognitions in the Execution phase of the CASVE Cycle.

Here is an example of a negative metacognition about Execution that needs to be reframed to a more positive thought: *"I know what I want to do, but I can't develop a plan for getting there."* This negative thought blocks the action phase of the CASVE Cycle; it keeps the person from following through on the choice that has been made. Our experience is that negative metacognitions in Execution are a major barrier to effective career decision making. Often, it is not making the choice that is the biggest problem for many people but the follow-through or execution of the choice.

REFRAME   Here is an example of reframing this negative metacognition to a more positive thought: "In knowing what I want to do, I have already made good progress toward completing my career plans. The fact that I am unclear about my next step shows that I need to find information on career planning or that I need to find a competent person to help me develop a plan, so I can reach my goals." In making this negative metacognition a more positive thought, we have demonstrated how additional information can help in the planning process and how outside, expert assistance may be needed from a counselor, advisor, teacher, or some other knowledgeable person. Positive metacognitions in Execution can help us make sure we get assistance and needed information to boost us along in the CASVE Cycle. In this way, we can assure successful career problem solving and decision making.

Executive Processing

The final aspect of the Pyramid of Information-Processing Domains and the CASVE Cycle is *executive processing*. Positive metacognitions related to the executive processing domain pertain to the ability to control, regulate, monitor, and evaluate all the preceding areas of information processing. It is a key focus for combating the "information fatigue" described by Begley (2011) at the beginning of this chapter.

These metacognitions are probably the most powerful and important in effective career decision making. They have to do with "thinking about thinking," or being aware of one's ability to solve career problems and make career decisions. Positive executive processing metacognitions, as you might expect, have characteristics in common with the metacognitions in the other seven areas.

Maximizers and Satisficers

According to psychologist Paul Schwartz (2004), the growth of options and opportunities for choice has affected our ability to make decisions. He believes that *"the first choice you must make is between the goal of choosing the absolute best and the goal of choosing something that is good enough"* [italics added] (p. 77). People who select the first goal are described as *maximizers* because they need to be assured that every decision is the best that could be made. This creates an impossible situation, as the number of options in this Internet age provides previously unimagined numbers of options. The alternative to maximizing is to be a *satisficer*, to settle for something that is good enough and not worry about the possibility of something better. In a nutshell, the satisficer is content with selecting an *excellent* option rather than the *absolute best* option.

A study of college students in a career course revealed that maximizers often seek out the absolute best options even when this standard cannot be realistically obtained (Paivandy, Bullock, Reardon, & Kelly, 2008). Then, because they are unable to meet their established goal of selecting the absolute best choice, maximizers are more likely to experience negative career thoughts relating to their decision-making ability and commitment to a career path. As a result, maximizers experience more commitment anxiety when their goal cannot be met.

So how does one combat the impact of maximizing and negative career thoughts in the executive processing area? Here is an example of a negative metacognition in executive processing that needs to be reframed to a more positive thought: *"I get so anxious when I have to make decisions that I can hardly think."* This negative thought shuts down cognitive information processing for the person. One can't think about how to solve a career problem—and perhaps other life problems as well.

REFRAME   Here is an example of a more positive thought to replace the negative one: "Many people feel anxious when making important decisions. Anxiety does make it harder to think clearly. However, avoiding decision making or depending on others to make decisions for me is not a good idea. With help from a competent person, I can get the information I need and learn how to make a good career decision." As noted before, this reframing statement pays attention to the negative emotions but points out that unless the cycle of poor decision making is broken, things only get worse. Also, it reminds the person that outside help might improve the situation and reinforces the idea that the person can successfully solve the problem in the long run.

Good thinking in this area avoids *perfectionism* ("I must find the perfect job"), *"top-dogging"* ("I should or must do this better than others"), and *external forces* ("I must go into computers because that is where the best jobs will be"). These metacognitions can contribute to depression, anxiety, lack of self-confidence, lack of persistence, lack of a plan, or lack of self-control, and these all interfere with effective information processing.

Changing negative metacognitions may require persistence, motivation, and outside assistance. The *CTI Workbook*, which shows more examples of reframing statements (Sampson, Peterson, Lenz, Reardon, & Saunders, 1996b), was designed to help people change negative thoughts and develop a positive plan for solving career problems and making career decisions. Metacognitions that are deep seated, pervasive, and long standing may be more likely to require outside help. Having a bad attitude about career decisions may carry over to other areas of life and personality. Counselors and other helping persons are specially trained to assist in overcoming troubling metacognitions, and the fastest, easiest course may be to consult with such a professional.

Summary

This chapter examined the executive processing domain of the Pyramid of Information-Processing Domains. It described three types of metacognitive skills—self-talk, self-awareness, and control and monitoring—and suggested ways to develop and improve metacognitive skills. We discussed positive and negative metacognitions or thoughts in each of the eight areas of the Pyramid of Information-Processing Domains and the CASVE Cycle.

Effective career problem solving and decision making involve the effective use of information in four domains: self-knowledge, occupational knowledge, decision making (composed of the CASVE Cycle), and executive processing. Negative metacognitions in any of these areas short-circuit the problem-solving process. Ideas were offered on how to increase positive, helpful metacognitions in career decision making—away from maximizing and toward satisficing. The goal was to help you improve the quality of your metacognitions in the executive processing domain of your Personal Career Theory.

References

Begley, S. (2011, March 7). I can't think: The Twitterization of our culture has revolutionized our lives, but with an unintended consequence—our overloaded brains freeze when we have to make decisions. *Newsweek*, 28–33.

Brown, A. L. (1978). Knowing when, where, and how to remember: A problem of metacognition. In R. Glaser (Ed.), *Advances in instructional psychology: Vol. 1* (pp. 77–165). Hillsdale, NJ: Lawrence Erlbaum.

Peterson, G. W., Sampson, J. P., Jr., & Reardon, R. C. (1991). *Career development and services: A cognitive approach*. Pacific Grove, CA: Brooks/Cole.

Paivandy, S., Bullock, E. E., Reardon, R. C., & Kelly, F. D. (2008). The effects of decision-making style and cognitive thought patterns on negative career thoughts. *Journal of Career Assessment, 16,* 474–488.

Sampson, J. P., Jr., Peterson, G. W., Lenz, J. G., Reardon, R. C., & Saunders, D. E. (1996a). The Career Thoughts Inventory (CTI). Odessa, FL: Psychological Assessment Resources, Inc.

Sampson, J. P., Jr., Peterson, G. W., Lenz, J. G., Reardon, R. C., & Saunders, D. E. (1996b). *Improving your career thoughts: A workbook for the Career Thoughts Inventory.* Odessa, FL: Psychological Assessment Resources.

Sampson, J. P., Jr., Reardon, R. C., Peterson, G. W., & Lenz, J. G. (2004). *Career counseling and services: A cognitive information processing approach*. Pacific Grove, CA: Wadsworth-Brooks/Cole.

Schwartz, B. (2004). *The paradox of choice—Why more is less*. New York, NY: Harper Perennial.

Chapter Six

Careering in a Changing World

In Chapters 1 to 5, we focused on the idea of "career" and how the Pyramid of Information-Processing Domains and the CASVE Cycle could help us understand and improve our thinking about career problem solving and decision making, our Personal Career Theory (PCT). The goal was to learn how to become better career problem solvers and decision makers and to improve the ways we think about and use career information. We have been examining the person and how the person *thinks* about career.

In Part Two, we examine some of the forces—outside the person—that affect our careers: (a) technology and global economic markets, (b) organizational culture, (c) alternative ways of working, and (d) the relationships between men and women at home and at work.

Jeffrey Sachs (2011), a distinguished economist at Columbia University, noted that the United States and the world have been "buffeted by three global changes: the technological revolution of computers, the Internet, and mobile telephone ushered in by the digital electronic age; the history-changing rise of Asia within the world economy; and the newly emerging global ecological crises. These three changes are the cause of massive and ongoing shifts of incomes, jobs, and investments all over the world, including the United States" (p. 85).

Chapters 6 to 10 will help us refine our thinking about the part of the pyramid that deals with understanding our options: the occupational knowledge domain. We will examine large, powerful forces in terms of how they may limit or increase our options. Stated another way, these macrolevel forces—meaning large, high-level forces—affect all areas of our PCT, the Pyramid of Information-Processing Domains, and the CASVE Cycle.

Our individual perception and interpretation of these macrolevel forces is related to our metacognitions, which, we have already learned, influence how we solve career problems and make career decisions.

The Role of General Education Courses

The liberal studies courses taken in college should influence your thinking about careers. White (2005), writing in the *Wall Street Journal*, noted that future chief executives may require a broader liberal-arts education and wider international experience. Paraphrasing comments by a former corporate recruiter, White suggested that, for future CEOs, it's about maturity and leadership rather than how many accounting courses they took. Furthermore, international experience is a "big deal."

As a college student, you have taken (or will take) courses in general education or liberal studies. What role do these courses play in career planning? Are they simply courses you need to get out of the way before you get into your major? General education courses, apart from those in your major, are intended to broaden your appreciation of what is happening in the world that affects the way we work and live.

Such knowledge directly affects the way we learn to think about our careers. For example, courses in the social sciences provide opportunities to learn about ethnic groups, communities, organizations, and human behavior. Courses in the humanities help us learn about cultures, languages, and the communication of ideas and values, and courses in the sciences help us learn about technology and problem solving. "Clearly students need to have emphasized the intrinsic value of studying history and culture, mathematics and science—*learning broadly about those things that make us what we are and the world about us what it is*" [italics added] (Johnston, Reardon, Kramer, Lenz, Maduros, & Sampson, 1991, p. 192).

The Collegiate Employment Research Institute (CERI) at Michigan State University surveys thousands of employers annually, and it reported that organizations are looking for students who demonstrate global understanding, even when it does not appear in a position description. Global knowledge will be essential in organizations doing business and providing services in a worldwide economy. Moreover, employers view candidates' ability to build and sustain professional, working relationships as essential, the highest-rated ability for new hires (CERI, 2010). We believe the skills in this area draw upon general knowledge obtained in liberal arts courses.

In terms of the Pyramid of Information-Processing Domains, general education courses provide knowledge about work options, such as labor market trends, social changes, and work styles. In terms of the CASVE Cycle, these courses help you learn about and clarify the societal gaps to which you might want to dedicate your career or prioritize the values on which you will base your career decisions. Such courses might help you understand an issue that motivates you to commit to a particular career objective (e.g., global warming, homeless children, family entertainment).

General education/liberal studies courses can enable students to develop more complex and accurate ways of thinking about careers in many ways, including the following:

- A course in *world history* can increase understanding of the decline of nationalism, the rise of tribalism, and the increase in global economic power in relation to geography, culture, technology, and population; such historical interpretations can be helpful in developing schema regarding strategic career planning.
- A course in *sociology* or *economics* can increase understanding of the ways that organizations develop and function, particularly work-related organizations; such knowledge can be helpful in developing career schema regarding work attitudes and organizational culture, because most work is done in organizational settings.
- A course in the *sciences* or *humanities* can increase understanding of the ways that technology has affected work organizations and jobs, which has resulted in new ways of working; such knowledge can be helpful in developing schema regarding work and leisure, unemployment, occupational change, part-time work, and job hunting.
- A course in *communication, sociology,* or *psychology* could increase understanding of gender and interpersonal relationships in relation to work and family life; such knowledge can be helpful in developing and negotiating successful work and family relationships, which are now more complex in the modern world.

Needed: New Career Metacognitions

Jerry Hage (1995), an industrial and organizational psychologist, has studied issues associated with modern work for many years. He made the case that we must develop more complex ways of thinking about life in the modern world:

People must learn to live in complex role-sets, each with a large number of role-relationships in which negotiations about role expectations or behavior become one of the major capacities for successful role performance. Furthermore, to adjust to the constant changes in society that provide the context for both the family and the workplace, people in post-industrial society need to have complex and creative minds, be adaptive and flexible, and know how to understand symbolic communications (p. 487).

If Hage is correct, we have no choice but to think in more complex ways about our careers. In our view, the cognitive information-processing approach provides ways to help us do this.

As you read Part Two, you should be constantly thinking about your metacognitions (your thoughts, beliefs, and attitudes) regarding your PCT, how you think about yourself and your career, and whether the information in these five chapters requires you to reframe or modify your thinking. Remember, metacognitions refer to the process of thinking about thinking. Here are some thought-provoking questions to ask yourself:

- *How can I fully use this information about the sociology of work, economic changes, diversity in the workplace, and alternative work styles to sharpen my PCT career metacognitions, and become a more effective career decision maker?*
- *How does this information relate to my gender? My cultural or ethnic group? My religious preferences? My spirituality? My identification with my community?*
- *How will this information affect my "careering" as I finish school, look for a good job, make plans for a significant personal relationship or family, and undertake job changes (voluntary or forced)?*
- *How can I develop a strategic plan for my career in light of the powerful, rapidly changing socioeconomic forces affecting people today?*

Two metaphors are useful as we begin Chapter 6. First, think of your career as a ship sailing on the sea. These macrolevel forces are like the tides, the wind, the ocean currents, and the temperature—they are the forces that may require you to make adjustments to your ship as you go "careering" over the horizon. They will directly cause you to make changes in the way you sail your "career ship."

Second, in Chapter 1 we examined Roe's formula (see Table 1.1) explaining "occupational choice." Roe observed that the general state of the economy (E); family background (B); chance factors (C), such as technological inventions and new laws; and one's friends, peers (F) and marital situation (M) all combine to shape a person's career options. These are the conditions affecting career behavior that we will explore in Part Two.

The Vision: "To Have a Successful Career"

Almost every college student working through a career problem or decision is really pursuing the vision of "having a successful career." *Webster's* defines *vision* as "a thought, concept, or object formed by the imagination" (Mish, 1997). In a real sense, we are each charged with imagining our career; we have the potential to develop an idea, a dream, of what we want and where we will end up.

As we learned in Chapter 1, a career is *not* something that a person has or possesses. As the cover of our text suggests, it is better to think of career as a course, a journey, or a path, rather than a destination. If we substitute the word *life* for the word *career*, we come closer to the meaning of *career*. Therefore, a career is something we pursue, not something we possess. This is an important reframing of the career metacognition and changes the common understanding of a "successful career." Make sure you fully grasp this thought.

The word *successful* is vague because to be a *success* in something is truly an individual matter. The runner Mary Decker Slaney set 36 national records and 17 official and unofficial world records at various distances, but after four tries she never won an Olympic medal. However, we can still say she had a *successful* running career. Our vision of having a successful career may be a frustrating journey if we are not clear and specific about what success means to us.

Elizabeth McKenna (1997), in *When Work Doesn't Work Anymore*, suggested that men and women (especially women) "have to figure out who they are and what their own definitions of success are (apart from business achievements) in order to negotiate the emotional contract they have made with their careers. And no matter what the decision, there are trade-offs" (p. 38). McKenna made the case that future generations will "have a different definition of success than we have" (p. 21) and a very different way of working.

Reframing Career Metacognitions

Figure 6.1 provides a graphic image to illustrate the point we want to make, and we are indebted to the psychologist Kurt Lewin (1951) for presenting this idea. He noted that it is important to distinguish between the "world out there" and what we actually see (or perceive). The larger circle shows the broader environment (the "real world") in which our careers unfold. This real world or force field includes technology and the global economy (Chapter 7), organizational culture (Chapter 8), alternative ways of working (Chapter 9), and family-career adjustments (Chapter 10). You might think of this as a stage with all kinds of varied sets and props where actors do their work.

The smaller shaded circle indicates that we each view the broader environment in our own unique ways using our metacognitions. We can learn to view this "real world," this force field, in new

figure 6.1

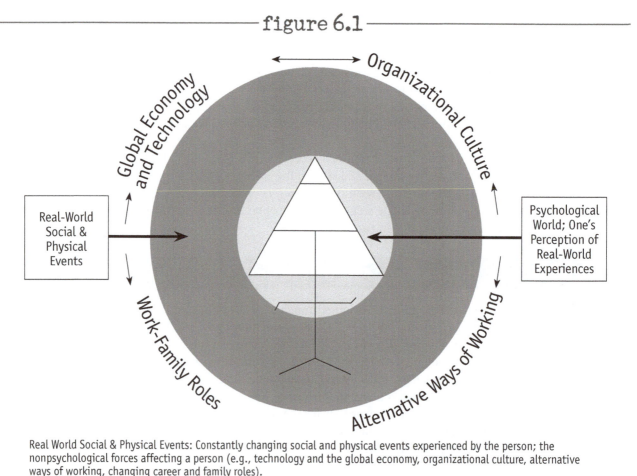

Real World Social & Physical Events: Constantly changing social and physical events experienced by the person; the nonpsychological forces affecting a person (e.g., technology and the global economy, organizational culture, alternative ways of working, changing career and family roles).

Psychological World: The person's psychological world, or "life space"; the person's *perception* of the social and physical events as either positive (supporting) or negative (restraining) forces having an impact on the person's goal achievement.

Career Metacognitions in a Force Field

and different ways, depending on our goals, aspirations, interests, values, and skills. You are the principal actor in your career. The chapters in Part Two are intended to help us to learn more about "the real world" and to improve the quality of our "psychological world" in relation to career problem solving and decision making.

Technology and the Global Economy

Changes are taking place that will continue to affect the way we "career" in the future. Here are some examples of events that have affected even the way we work, including career counselors.

Technology has changed the way many organizations conduct business. For example, in the banking industry, computers are set to automatically move money to and from accounts when certain preset conditions exist. This occurs throughout the world, 24 hours a day. While you sleep, your money is moving around various world exchanges, searching for the highest interest-bearing accounts. The Internet makes it possible for individuals and organizations to have instant contact with one another, at little cost. Financial experts were shocked several years ago when one bank employee, working alone at a computer, was responsible for financial transactions that caused the collapse of one of the largest banks in the United Kingdom.

Trade agreements between nations can dramatically change the way products and services are sold. For example, the North American Free Trade Agreement (NAFTA) between Canada, Mexico, and the United States eliminated many barriers to economic exchanges. In effect, this means that there are no economic borders between these countries, although there are still political ones. As a result of NAFTA, some U.S. companies sell their products or services, such as computer parts or software training, to businesses and organizations in new places that were inaccessible before. Products are manufactured in one country and packaged in another.

Even the authors of this text, who are college faculty and staff in a southeastern university, have been affected by international economic developments. One consulted with people in Turkey about how to improve job training and employment of Turkish citizens. This text has been translated into Chinese and is being used in the People's Republic. In the past 10 years, visitors from more than 40 foreign nations have come to observe how our career center designs and delivers services. It turns out that even the field of career counseling knows no borders in a global economy.

Organizational Culture

Work organizations, including businesses, government agencies, schools, and community centers, are changing the way they function. Increasingly, they are organized differently, they communicate internally and externally in new ways, they treat employees differently, and they think about their customers and products in new ways. These organizational changes are having a dramatic impact on the ways in which we "career," and we will examine them in more detail in Chapter 8.

One example is when organizations significantly cut personnel and then purchase the same services from an outside organization. This is typically called *outsourcing*. For example, Company A, a medical supply service, decides to eliminate its human resources (HR) department (for example, to maintain employee leave records, advertise positions, screen resumes, keep payroll records) and contract with Company B, a firm that specializes in HR services, to do this work for Company A. Company A has reduced the number of employees, which saves Company A some money, but the work still gets done by Company B.

Alternative Ways of Working

Many people have grown up with the idea of working a 40-hour week in a professional job—that just seemed to be the natural order of things. Of course people in certain jobs (e.g., physicians, nurses, plumbers, police officers) work odd schedules, but most of us assumed we would have "regular" weekday jobs. Perhaps nothing else in the career world has changed as much as the way we work. Work patterns include options such as flextime, part-time, job sharing, temporary, and home-based work/telecommuting patterns. We will examine these issues and others in detail in Chapter 9 and focus on how they affect our career planning.

One example of this is *job sharing*. This occurs when one job is shared between two people. Each person typically works 20 hours per week at separate times, although they probably share two or three hours of time on the job each week for joint meetings with supervisors and other staff members. This arrangement is ideal for someone with child care or elder care responsibilities, for whom a 40-hour job might be difficult or impossible. A person completing an educational degree might find it impossible to work full time and attend classes full time. A person might have leisure or entrepreneurial interests that make it difficult to work full time and still pursue these outside interests. A job share typically carries one-half the insurance and other benefits available with the position. This arrangement provides extra support that might not be otherwise available to the part-time worker.

As you contemplate your career journey, be mindful that alternative work arrangements might give you options regarding when and how you work as well as how you engage in other important life activities.

Career and Family Roles

Sociologists have noted that the patterns of work for men and women common today in the United States are only about 100 years old. Before the industrial revolution, both men and women worked on the farm or in the shop and shared childcare and housekeeping duties. With the rise of manufacturing and industry in the late 1800s, men increasingly left the farm to pursue higher-paying jobs in city factories. Women were left at home to care for children and manage the domestic responsibilities. In the past 50 years, beginning during World War II in the 1940s, women have increasingly taken jobs outside the home. The dual-career family, or in some cases the dual-earner family, where both individuals in a relationship are working outside the home, has had a huge impact on the way most of us work today and will work in the future. We will explore these topics in more detail in Chapter 10.

Relocation is an example of a critical issue that may add complexity in career planning for a dual-career couple. When both partners are engaged in career, and relocation opportunities affect one career, the trailing spouse or partner can face considerable difficulties. The same kinds of opportunities may not be present in the new location. Successful relocation in dual-career situations requires considerable skill in negotiation and compromise. In cognitive terms, it means that both people are able to perceive a "win" no matter which option is selected.

The Four Macrolevel Factors

In Part Two, we will look at the "market economy" and how things are changing in this regard. A market is created when one person's wants or needs create a demand for a product or service that another person can satisfy. The market involves the exchange of goods and services between people, typically involving money. *In a market economy, jobs are created because one person is willing to spend money for goods or services. Jobs follow from what someone wants, needs, or is willing to pay for.*

In the present day, market economies—also known as capitalism—are springing up throughout the world. Moreover, there are markets for everything: baseball cards, money, hamburgers, steel, and knowledge. Someone once joked that we could become a nation of hamburger sellers because that's how many of us like to spend our money. Historically, markets have been the largest source of career opportunities for individuals across the globe.

In our analysis, we have emphasized the distinct nature of the four macrolevel changes affecting work today: (a) global economic markets, (b) organizational culture, (c) alternative ways of working, and (d) the relationships between men and women at home and at work. In reality, however, these four influences are impossible to separate, and they have all been affected by technology. Altogether, they function as a complex system where each factor affects the others and vice versa. The phrase "everything affects everything" applies here. Focusing on the independent nature of these four factors in Part Two will make it easier to analyze and understand them.

You might notice that the progression of these four factors is from the most broad and distant to the most specific and immediate. We will begin by looking at global economic events and trends and then examining how these factors are affecting work organizations and the way individuals work now and in the future. We will conclude with the impact of these changes on the lives of men and women in contemporary America.

Finally, the perspective we will take in Part Two is one of change, how things about career and work are changing in the modern world. This reflects some age bias (the authors are all old enough to have experienced many of these changes in their work lives), but many college students born after 1994 may not see these macrolevel factors as changes because they haven't experienced anything else. The present-day world with its technological advances, global economy, instant communication, and changing social roles is all they know.

Strategic Career Thinking

The term *strategic thinking* may not be a familiar one, so we should define it. Years ago, business organizations began to use the concepts of strategic thinking and strategic planning to ensure that their organization was headed in the right direction (Cope, 1987; Omahe, 1982). When "thinking strategically," an organization asks itself the following questions:

- Where does our organization want to go?
- Are we in the right business relative to other businesses we could be in?

Cope (1987) defined strategic thinking for an organization as "the process of developing a vision of where the institution wants to go, and then developing managing strategies (plans) on how to get there" (quoted in Hoadly & Zimmer, 1982, p. 16). Note that strategic thinking begins with the process of developing a vision. *Put another way, strategic thinking is doing the right things (effectiveness), whereas operational planning is doing things right (efficiency).*

Sometimes organizations get so caught up in being efficient and doing things right that they lose sight of doing the right things, of being effective. In other words, effectiveness is doing the right things and thinking strategically, and efficiency is doing things right and operational planning. *Organizations can fail for being either ineffective or inefficient.*

The process of strategic thinking applied to organizations can also be applied to individuals. By thinking strategically about your career, you can (a) formulate a vision of what being "successful" means for you, (b) get yourself organized and prepared to do the "right things," and (c) implement a plan to do "things right." *Strategic career thinking means setting your course and charting your way through important social issues, such as the global economy, changing organizational cultures, alternative ways of working, and changing roles of men and women.*

Thinking and planning your career in a strategic way means that you can set your career direction in light of the internal forces, such as your interests, values, and skills, in relation to the external forces existing in society.

Your task is to develop a vision of your career, based partly on your intuitive, subjective judgment about where the four social forces we examined are taking us as individuals and a society.

As you read the next four chapters, interpret the facts presented in light of your own experience and the other things that you know or have learned about the future. Critically analyze the information in light of your strategic career plan. How does it change how you think about your life/career in the future? Be proactive and forward-thinking in light of the facts that are presented in these chapters about work organizations and work roles, especially with reference to your Personal Career Theory.

A Case Application: From College to Becoming a Manager

Many college graduates find themselves in positions leading an organization and managing projects, programs, or people. Indeed, you may find yourself on this career path in the future. Given this fact, let's examine how the social conditions we have briefly described in this chapter might affect a college student's career thinking.

With respect to the *global economy*, a college student might do the following:

- Consider getting educational and work experiences in multicultural settings
- Take courses in world history, sociology, economics, and languages to learn more about worldwide changes and issues
- Travel to different countries and learn about cultural traditions
- Develop friendships with people from other countries
- Learn about how management is done in other countries
- Look for work opportunities in multinational organizations
- Use the Internet to communicate directly with people around the world

These activities will help you develop a better vision of the existence of worldwide problems and opportunities for working as a manager in your field of interest.

With respect to *organizational culture*, a college student might do the following:

- Interview managers to learn about their actual work histories and experiences in different kinds of organizations
- Reflect on personal work experiences in various organizations with respect to the culture of the organization
- Research the advantages and disadvantages of being a manager in different kinds of organizations and agencies
- Study the occupations and organizations that employ managers, and learn about the laws, inventions, and policies that are affecting those areas
- Learn about the characteristics of family-friendly organizations and other employee-centered practices

These things will help you develop a better understanding of how the culture of an organization affects the way people work together and the overall climate of the place.

With respect to *alternative ways of working*, a college student might do the following:

- Develop a vision of how the roles of parent, spouse/partner, worker, student, child, leisurite, and citizen will be incorporated into one's life over the next 10 or more years
- Examine how significant people in one's life will be involved in shaping a career
- Understand the importance of leisure activities in one's life and how these activities may be selected in relation to work activities and organizational policies
- Learn about alternative work-style patterns and employer benefit options, and set priorities on when and how these would be incorporated into one's career plan

These things might help you develop a vision of a time-extended plan for balancing work and other life roles in one's career.

With respect to *changing roles of men and women*, a college student might do the following:

- Develop a shared career vision of life roles with a partner or significant other
- Learn about successful patterns of balancing work and family life given different kinds of career options and organizational characteristics
- Learn about effective child care options
- Learn about alternative work styles within different kinds of industries

- Study the kinds of stressors—for example, eldercare, relocation, childcare—that affect relationships in dual-career situations
- Study the trends and issues in work and family life for single parents

These things might help you develop a vision of how work and family life might be balanced in a career.

Summary

In this chapter, we introduced four external, social forces that affect the ways individual careers are developing now and in the future. We began with a review of general education/liberal studies courses in relation to strategic career planning and suggested the need for new career metacognitions in this information age.

"Having a successful career" is the vision that many people bring to the career-planning process. The vision of a successful career can be framed within four social conditions: (a) technology and the changing global economy, (b) changing organizational cultures, (c) alternative ways of working, and (d) changing roles of men and women.

The idea of strategic career thinking is one way to project your career vision into the future, accounting for the changing social conditions that will affect future career behavior. The process of career visioning and strategic thinking was illustrated by examining the thinking processes of a college student becoming a manager. The next four chapters will help you improve the part of your Personal Career Theory having to do with occupational knowledge. This, in turn, will enable you to develop new metacognitions for solving career problems and making career decisions.

References

Collegiate Employment Research Institute (2010, February). Under the economic turmoil a skills gap simmers. *CERI Research Brief 1-2010*, 1–18.

Cope, R. G. (1987). *Opportunity for strength: Strategic planning clarified with case examples* (ASHE-ERIC Higher Education Report No. 8). Washington, DC: George Washington University, Clearinghouse on Higher Education.

Hage, J. (1995). Post-industrial lives: New demands, new prescriptions. In A. Howard (Ed.), *The changing nature of work* (pp. 485–512). San Francisco, CA: Jossey-Bass.

Hoadly, J. A., & Zimmer, B. E. (1982). A corporate planning approach to institutional management: A preliminary report on the RMIT experience. *Journal of Tertiary Education Administration, 4*, 15–26.

Johnston, J., Reardon, R., Kramer, G., Lenz, J., Maduros, A., & Sampson, J. (1991). The demand side of general education: Attending to student attitudes and understandings. *Journal of General Education, 40*, 180–200.

Lewin, K. (1951) *Field theory in social science.* New York, NY: Harper & Row.

McKenna, E. P. (1997). *When work doesn't work anymore: Women, work, and identity.* New York, NY: Delacorte Press.

Mish, F. C. (Ed.). (1997). *Merriam-Webster's collegiate dictionary* (10th ed.). Springfield, MA: Merriam-Webster.

Omahe, K. (1982). *The mind of the strategist: The art of Japanese business.* New York, NY: McGraw-Hill.

Sachs, J. D. (2011). *The price of civilization: Reawakening American virtue and prosperity.* New York, NY: Random House.

White, E. (2005, April 12). Future CEOs may need to have broad liberal-arts foundation. *The Wall Street Journal*, B4.

Chapter Seven

Working in the New Global Economy

The world is getting smaller. Communication across continents is easier, global travel is experienced by ever-increasing numbers of people, and an increasing number of businesses have become multinational companies. We live and work in a "global village." Some have gone so far as to describe the world as "flat" (Friedman, 2005). This is the stage on which our careers will unfold.

This chapter examines how factors and trends in the global economy will likely shape the ways we work, play, and learn during the next 10 years. Changes in work activity and production are occurring throughout the world, and we will look at projected economic changes. We explore the scope and shape of the U.S. labor force as it has been affected by international changes in the world of work, especially the services industry. Finally, we will analyze these macrolevel changes in light of cognitive information processing theory, the Pyramid of Information-Processing Domains, and the CASVE Cycle to see how we might improve our metacognitions for career problem solving and decision making.

As you read about these changes in global and U.S. economies, keep in mind your Personal Career Theory and how your strategic career thinking can be improved.

International Changes in Work Activity and Production

Peter Drucker, Robert Reich, Thomas Friedman, and Jeremy Rifkin have all written books on the world economy. Their works can help us understand the place of individual lives and careers in this context.

Drucker's Post-Capitalist Society

Peter Drucker was a management consultant who wrote 35 books about trends in the working world. His views are widely read and often controversial, and his book *Post-Capitalist Society*, is no exception. Drucker (1993) predicted that the world would experience a period of enormous transformation. Earlier transformations are the Reformation, the Renaissance, and the American Revolution.

> *This time it is not, however, confined to Western society and Western history. Indeed, it is one of the fundamental changes that there is no longer a "Western" history or, in fact a "Western" civilization. There is only world history and world civilization—but both are "Westernized." It is moot whether this present transformation began with the emergence of the first non-Western country, Japan, as a great economic power . . . or with the computer—that is, with information becoming central. (p. 3)*

Drucker suggested that by 2010 or 2020 the world would be nonsocialist and postcapitalist. Its primary resource would be knowledge (i.e., useful information); nation-states would be replaced by megastates; and it would be a society of organizations, each devoted to a specific task. One of the leading groups in this new world society would be the "knowledge workers," who know how to allocate knowledge and information to productive use.

> The knowledge society [where knowledge workers will be employed] must have at its core the concept of the educated person. It will have to be a universal concept, precisely because the knowledge society is a society of knowledges and because it is global—in its money, its economics, its careers, its technology, its central issues, and above all, in its information. (p. 212)
>
> Tomorrow's educated person will have to be prepared for life in a global world. He or she must become a "citizen of the world"—in vision, horizon, and information. But he or she will also have to draw nourishment from their local roots, and, in turn, enrich and nourish their own local culture.
>
> Post-capitalist society is both a knowledge society and a society of organizations, each dependent on the other and yet each very different in its concepts, views, and values. Most, if not all, educated people will practice their knowledge as members of an organization. The educated person will therefore have to be prepared to live and work simultaneously in two cultures—that of the "intellectual," who focuses on work and ideas, and that of the "manager," who focuses on people and work. (pp. 214–215)

In reflecting on Drucker's last point, we are reminded of Holland's Investigative and Enterprising types from Chapter 3 and the fact that they are located in opposite points on the RIASEC hexagon. Success will come easier to those who develop I (investigative) and E (enterprising) skills.

In summary, Drucker believed that future careers would occur in a global context where people having management and information-processing skills would work in an information society. Moreover, these knowledge workers will find themselves working as members of organizations and teams, each seeking to accomplish its own limited objectives. This vision is complex and requires thoughtful reflection. We will see Drucker's ideas reinforced by other writers in this chapter.

Reich's Global Enterprise Webs

Robert Reich, a former U.S. Secretary of Labor, is a political economist and a faculty member at the University of California at Berkeley. He has written several books about economic life in contemporary America and what government and business should do to make it better. His ideas also have implications for college students and their career planning.

In 1992, Reich wrote an important book, *The Work of Nations: Preparing Ourselves for 21st-Century Capitalism*. His basic idea was this:

> As almost every factor of production—money, technology, factories, and equipment—moves effortlessly across borders, the very idea of an American economy is becoming meaningless, as are the notions of an American corporation, American capital, American products, and American technology. A similar transformation is affecting every other nation, some faster and more profoundly than others. (p. 8)

However, Reich also noted that there is one aspect of our American economy that remains American, and that is its workforce (this includes all of us). We are relatively immobile; it is not easy for masses of us to cross national borders. Although money, technology, factories, and equipment can be quickly moved to other countries, people are another matter. If the American economy is to succeed, it is the American people who must develop their work knowledge, skills, and attitudes relative to those of citizens in other countries. This is an important point. No matter how much attention is devoted to the global economy, we, as American workers, are the important ultimate stakeholders in this matter.

Reich described the new business organizations as "*global enterprise webs*." To understand this, we have to go back in history. Early in the 20th century, business organizations looked much like a big pyramid—with lots of salaried workers at the bottom, managers in the middle, and top executives in a small area at the top. The power and control of the organization was vested in a few people at the top, while vast amounts of material, buildings, people, and other resources were lodged at the bottom. Business organizations were organized like the army—lots of infantry, guns, and tanks at the bottom and a few generals at the top running the show.

The high point of these organizations occurred in the 1950s. Reich reported that about 500 of the largest American corporations produced half of the nation's industrial output, created about 40% of the nation's corporate profits, and employed more than one out of every eight nonfarm workers. The biggest companies were very large. General Motors, for example, produced goods and services equivalent in value to those produced by Italy. These big companies were the basic American economy in that day. These kinds of business organizations were effective in their time, producing high volumes of materials, goods, and services, but they are now becoming outmoded.

In the modern world, these big, rigid organizations have been increasingly replaced by small groups of information workers who create high value for business organizations by quickly *identifying* and *solving problems*. These workers are joined by a strategic broker in a headquarters who helps them identify work projects and communicate effectively among themselves. For these workers to be effective, they have to be able to communicate directly and quickly with each other, often horizontally rather than vertically. A big bureaucracy with a large number of middle managers just slows things down. These information workers are involved in projects like developing software, designing a new marketing strategy, designing a new employee training program, finding a biological discovery, or developing a new financing scheme.

Reich described these enterprise webs as high-value business enterprises, and they are complex, flexible work organizations, which also may be very temporary. These new enterprise webs are best understood in terms of a spider's web, where each connecting point is a place where information is exchanged by the workers. This is a very different kind of business model compared to the earlier pyramid organization.

In the new enterprise web, speed—or time—is very important; in other words, who will correctly identify and solve the problem first? The knowledge needed to do this work can be obtained from anywhere in the world through computer networks and international travel. These enterprise webs are often global.

Reich described enterprise webs as having many different kinds of shapes that constantly change and evolve. Here are some of the most common ones he identified.

As you read the descriptions of these organizations, think about the implications of this information for your job campaign and the kinds of questions you might ask in an interview.

---

1. **Independent profit centers.** This web eliminates middle management and pushes authority for product development and sales down to engineers and marketers (problem identifiers and solvers). For example, Reich noted that in the 1990s, Johnson & Johnson comprised 166 separate, autonomous companies. As another example, you may have noticed that your textbooks are often published by small publishing companies operating under a larger publisher. Each little company has the responsibility to find and publish books on its own.
2. **Spin-off partnerships.** In this web, strategic brokers at headquarters look for good ideas that bubble up from groups of problem solvers, which are then spun off as new business organizations. Reich cited Hitachi as an example: Hitachi consisted of more than 60 companies, only 27 of which were publicly traded on the stock market. This means that almost half of the companies were small and perhaps temporary.
3. **Spin-in partnerships.** In this web, good ideas bubble up outside the organization from independent problem solvers. Reich noted that this kind of web is common in the software industry, where hundreds of small companies are regularly bought up by big ones such as Microsoft and IBM. The owners of the smaller companies get rich and the big companies get a steady flow of new products and ideas.

4. **Licensing.** In this web, the strategic brokers at headquarters contract with independent businesses to use a brand name to sell special services or products. A good example of this is the franchise arrangement, where ownership and control is left in the hands of the licensee. Much economic activity in America today is based on this kind of web; Starbucks is one example.

5. **Pure brokering.** This is the most decentralized kind of web, and it occurs when strategic brokers contract with independent businesses for problem solving as well as production. Let's say a computer company contracts with one company to make its computer, with another to deliver it, and another to advertise it. This new company sells millions of dollars' worth of computers within weeks of its startup and has fewer than 40 engineers, technicians, and accountants on its staff. This kind of outsourcing has now become common. Reich noted, for example, that in the 1990s, General Motors bought half of its engineering and design services from 800 different companies.

Reich reminded us that these web-like business organizations and relationships play a role in shaping the new global economy. They can be complex structures, with various profit centers, licensees, suppliers, dealers, and spin-offs. Reich noted that even IBM, which in an earlier time had been a very exclusive kind of American company, has joined with dozens of other companies and more than 80 foreign-owned firms to share problem solving, problem identifying, and strategic brokering. It provides services in over 170 countries and has 319,000 employees. Think about it: Is IBM still an American company? Many other companies have also created hundreds of alliances with other organizations to create enterprise webs that produce marketplace value.

Products created by global webs are typically the combined work of many different nations. Friedman (2005) provided a good example with Rolls-Royce. Most people know this as a British company and the manufacturer of a shiny, hand-made car with a uniformed driver. However, Rolls-Royce hasn't made cars since 1972 and the brand was licensed to BMW in 1998. Today it is a technology company that builds power systems for airplanes, ships, and other industries. Rolls-Royce has customers in 120 countries and employs about 35,000 people. Forty percent of its employees are outside the United Kingdom and they represent about 50 nationalities in 50 countries speaking 50 languages. It outsources and offshores about 75% of its work to a global supply chain. Friedman noted that a new manager in this company could be working with a team that is one third in India, one third in China, and one sixth each in Palo Alto and Boston. Such a job would require special skills.

In summary, global webs, whether headquartered in the United States, Western Europe, or Asia, have many characteristics in common. For example, they have no clear connection to any particular nation. Indeed, many have much larger economies than most nations in the world. In addition, such webs involve "an international partnership of skilled people whose insights are combined with one another and who contract with unskilled workers from around the world for whatever must be standardized and produced in high volume" (Reich, 1992, p. 132). Multinational corporations, then, are global and their profits are shared with problem solvers, identifiers, and brokers around the world.

Friedman's Flat World

Thomas Friedman (2005) has written several books about how work has changed because of technological innovations and the global economy. He identifies three historical periods of globalization. The first began in 1492 with Columbus's trip to the New World and lasted until 1800 with ships traveling the world's continents seeking trade. The second era lasted from 1800 to 2000 and was marked by multinational companies using new forms of transportation (e.g., steam and rail) and new forms of communication (e.g., satellites, PCs, telephones). But Friedman views this third period as very different because it is marked by the capacity of individuals to use new software to collaborate and compete globally. Unlike the two earlier eras, this one is not driven by European and American individuals or companies but includes people in China, India, South Korea, Turkey, Japan,

South America, and other parts of the world. Friedman believes that this most recent phase of globalization has truly shrunk and flattened the world—individuals who have the skill and knowledge can now directly participate in the global economy.

The global, web-enabled playing field permits all kinds of new collaborative efforts in education and work and does it in real time with no regard for distance. This, in turn, has led to new forms of business leadership and organizational behavior—new ways of working. Friedman suggests that 3 billion people outside of Western Europe and North America are now able to compete and collaborate in the new global economy. He argues that the discovery and innovation brought about by these changes are unprecedented in world history. For example, he notes that there are more cell phones in use in China than there are people in the United States and that South Koreans far exceed Americans in use of the Internet.

What does all this mean for U.S. college students and their career planning? There are numerous implications (e.g., international experience, ethnic cultural understanding, information technology skills, constant training), but the bottom line is to develop job skills that cannot be outsourced. Anna Kamenetz (2012) writing about the "four-year career" in *Fast Company* magazine, gave the example of a recent college graduate who completed dual degrees in history and international relations. In the span of 6 years, he applied a skill set that involved entrepreneurship, writing, programming, and an apprenticeship in an interactive media-arts lab in South America. We explore this idea of being flexible and having multiple skills later in this chapter.

Rifkin's End of Work

Another important writer in this area is Jeremy Rifkin, an American economist who has produced more than a dozen books on the macrolevel forces affecting the world economy. His most important book, written in 1995, is *The End of Work: The Decline of the Global Labor Force and the Dawn of the Post-Market Era*. Rifkin's basic idea was that the global economy is undergoing fundamental changes that will lead to a steady decline in traditional, 40-hour-per-week "jobs." This will happen as computers, robots, telecommunications, and other technologies replace humans in every area of work. Virtual companies and factories will replace workers in Rifkin's view, and this means that every nation will have to rethink the idea of work. These are powerful ideas, and they obviously have strong implications for individual career planning.

According to Rifkin, the coming of the "Third Industrial Revolution" has been brought about by the rapid advancement of technology throughout the world. The increased use of the microchip is the source of this change. (By the way, the first Industrial Revolution involved the introduction of the steam engine, and the second involved the use of oil.) Rifkin cited many reports to show that in every area of the economy—agriculture, manufacturing, services—and in every nation, machines are increasingly doing the work of people. News reports carry information about these phenomena every day as companies reduce their workforces, restructure their operations, and re-engineer the workplace.

Rifkin offered a few ideas about solutions to the problems he identified. First, he suggested that we must move to shorten the work week, perhaps to 30 hours. This was almost accomplished in the United States in the late 1930s, and it is already being implemented in some European countries. The immediate benefit is the creation of jobs for more workers. Second, Rifkin predicted the development of a more powerful Third Sector, which will contribute to what he calls the "social economy." This Third Sector, also known as the independent, nonprofit, or volunteer sector, will balance the Public Sector (government) and the Market Sector (business).

The Third Sector, or social economy, includes volunteer and community organizations that feed the poor, protect the environment, teach reading, run youth basketball programs, care for the elderly, operate museums, promote women's civil rights, and build churches. The Bureau of Labor Statistics reported that about 64.3 million people volunteered in 2011, primarily in religious organizations, educational and youth service organizations, or social and community service organizations (http://www.bls.gov/news.release/pdf/volun.pdf). To manage these volunteers, Rifkin reported that "more people are employed in third-sector organizations than work in the construction, electronics, transportation, or textile and apparel industries" (p. 241), and the third sector is growing twice as fast as the government and private sectors.

A variation on this idea was offered by Alperovitz (2011), who described the "new-economy movement" as involving organizations that are increasingly green and socially responsible. These "social enterprises" use profits for environmental, social, or community-serving goals; such organizations do not include the 1.6 million nonprofit corporations that sometimes cross into economic activity (e.g., Goodwill). "The American Sustainable Business Council, a growing alliance of 150,000 business professionals and 30 business organizations, has emerged as a leading venue for such activities. Most members are 'triple bottom line' companies and social enterprises committed to the environment and social outcomes as well as profits" (Alperovitz, 2011, p. 21).

Finally, one of the new types of organizations in this Third Sector pertains to social entrepreneurship. This new and rapidly developing field has varied facets, and there is a lack of consensus about exactly how it should be understood. However, an article by Mair and Martí (2005) in the *Journal of World Business* described it "as a process involving the innovative use and combination of resources to pursue opportunities to catalyze social change and/or address social needs" (p. 37). In other words, a social problem is recognized (e.g., bad drinking water in a poor community), and a person or group uses entrepreneurial principles to create and manage a process to fix this problem. A traditional business entrepreneur probably measures performance in terms of profit, but a social entrepreneur focuses on creating social or environmental good works as well.

The Grameen Bank in Bangladesh is an example of a social entrepreneurship organization. It is a community development bank that makes small loans (microcredit) without the need for collateral to poor people. The system is based on the idea that the poor have untapped skills that can be turned into profit-making enterprises (e.g., handcrafts, vegetable growing). Almost all of the loans are made to women. The borrowers conduct their work under strict supervision, which provides for eventual repayment and establishment of good credit. The Grameen Bank was founded in 1976 when Professor Muhammad Yunus, a Fulbright scholar at Vanderbilt University and Professor at University of Chittagong, researched the possibility of designing a credit delivery system to provide banking services for the rural poor. The organization and its founder were jointly awarded the Nobel Peace Prize in 2006. Much of the work in this field is being carried out in global settings, and it will be interesting to see what these types of organizations add to the global economy in the future.

Offshoring and Outsourcing

A discussion of global changes in work and production affecting U.S. jobs would not be complete without mention of the offshoring and outsourcing phenomenon. Friedman offered a distinction between these two terms. He described *offshoring* as the movement of an entire factory to another location where exactly the same goods are produced but the costs are lower. *Outsourcing* means taking some specific organizational function (e.g., research, call center, accounting, human resources) and having some other organization do the work and return the output.

The global economy has been pushed by large multinational companies with operations worldwide. The largest such U.S. companies are General Electric (GE), Exxon-Mobil, Chevron, Ford, ConocoPhillips, Procter & Gamble, Wal-Mart, IBM, and Pfizer (Sachs, 2011). These companies often have more than half of their global workers outside the U.S. Sach notes, for example, that GE had 133,000 workers in the U.S. and 154,000 in over 60 other countries in 2010.

The Changing American Labor Force

Given these changes in the global economy, how are American jobs being affected? In this section, we will learn which occupations are growing and which are declining. We will examine these general labor market trends with reference to the implications for individual career planning. We'll also focus on the earnings gap. The goal is to help you develop "mental maps" of how the labor market works (Wegmann, Chapman, & Johnston, 1989). This, in turn, should help you improve your strategic career thinking.

U.S. Labor Market Trends through 2020

Given this brief review of economic global trends and changes in the nature of work, what is happening in the United States regarding job changes? What are the trends in the growth and decline of occupations? Where are the jobs? What industries are growing? What is the labor market for college graduates?

To begin to answer these questions, we note that large-scale labor market trends are heavily influenced by demography or population characteristics. The aging of the baby-boomer generation is a significant example of these characteristics at work (Toossi, 2012).

HOW NEW OCCUPATIONS DEVELOP. The U.S. Bureau of Labor Statistics (BLS) conducts extensive research to determine if a new occupation should be added to its list of 749 detailed occupations. A new occupation is one that includes duties not previously identified (e.g., biomedical photography), one that has been recognized in small numbers and continues to grow (i.e., now has its own professional association or trade group), or one that is evolving and whose tasks have changed significantly (e.g., database administrator, now database security engineer). These new occupations arise from technological advances, new laws or regulations, or changing demographics. Jones (2008) noted that emerging occupations are increasingly multidisciplinary, specialized, and international, which is the basic theme of this chapter.

WHO WORKS? We reviewed an article in the *Monthly Labor Review* (Toossi, 2012), "Charting the Projections: 2010–2012," for information about the U.S. labor force. Toossi (2012) indicated that 164.4 million people will be working or looking for work in 2020. (To add some perspective, in 2020 the U.S. population of people aged 20–64 years is projected to be 195.9 million.)

The labor force (those 16 and older who are working or looking for work and who are neither in the military nor in prison) in 2000 included about 67% of the U.S. population, and this is projected to decrease to 62.5% in 2020. The labor force will continue to age, with the 55-years-and-older group growing from 19.5% in 2010 to 25.2% in 2020. (*Your parents and grandparents may still be working.*) Toossi (2012) reported that an average of 57% of women and 68% of men are projected to be employed in 2020.

TWO VIEWS OF EMPLOYMENT GROWTH. Figure 7.1 illustrates the two ways in which job growth can be viewed, numeric change and percent change. Numeric change is the actual *number of jobs* gained or lost over a decade. Percent change is the *rate of job growth* or decline during the decade.

The upper chart shows the projected increase in employment for accountants and auditors compared with that for environmental engineers. In numeric terms, more than 11 times as many new jobs were projected for accountants and auditors as for environmental engineers between 2002 and 2012. The percent change tells a different story. As the lower chart shows, the rate of employment of environmental engineers was expected to grow about twice as fast as that of accountants and auditors.

In general, occupations expected to grow at a fast rate do not produce large numbers of jobs. This has implications for those who want to use labor market forecast information in their career planning. Should they pay more attention to occupations that grow rapidly or those with the most jobs? *What do you think about this?*

EMPLOYMENT TRENDS. Before continuing, we should reflect on the accuracy of these labor market forecasts by BLS. In general, the economists who study labor markets and issue projections are accurate in their forecasts, possibly underestimating the trends slightly. On the whole, BLS employ-

figure 7.1

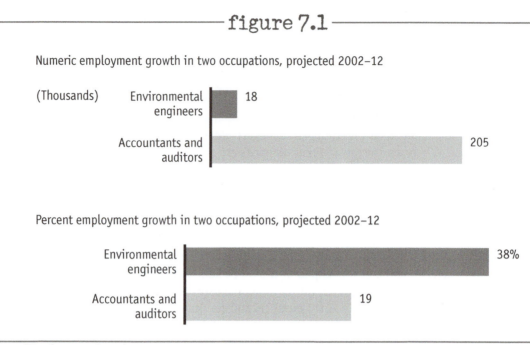

Numeric employment growth in two occupations, projected 2002–12

(Thousands)

Environmental engineers — 18

Accountants and auditors — 205

Percent employment growth in two occupations, projected 2002–12

Environmental engineers — 38%

Accountants and auditors — 19

Two Views of Employment Growth
Source: U.S. Dept. of Labor

ment projections are quite accurate. However, Toossi (2012) noted that these projections to 2020 could change if more young people enter the labor market, older workers decide to keep working, women increase their work outside the home, and immigration rates change.

Moreover, the projections themselves can affect the forecast outcomes. For example, if a shortage of engineers is forecast, which leads to increased enrollment in engineering programs, then the projected shortage will decrease. In addition, economic recessions affect occupations in different ways—for example, career counselors have more work to do, whereas other workers have less to do. The following factors can also affect economic forecasts:

- Natural disasters (e.g., earthquakes, hurricanes)
- World political events (e.g., war, trade agreements, terrorism)
- Changes in government spending (e.g., homeland security)
- New welfare or student financial aid programs
- Technological inventions and breakthroughs (e.g., cloudless computing)
- New laws (e.g., balancing the federal budget)

In general, it is wise to keep these things in mind as you read about labor market forecasts in this chapter.

Tables 7.1, 7.2, and 7.3 provide the following labor market projections:

- The 20 occupations that will employ the most people through the year 2020;
- The 20 occupations that will grow the most rapidly through 2020; and
- The 20 fastest growing occupations requiring a bachelor's degree through 2012.

These data are based on an analysis of Occupational Employment Statistics (see Chapter 3 for a review of OES). We'll also examine Holland codes (see Chapter 2) for these occupations.

OCCUPATIONS THAT EMPLOY THE MOST PEOPLE. Table 7.1 shows the 20 occupations expected to have the most job openings each year through 2020 (Lockard & Wolf, 2012). We might call these "big growth" occupations. Four of these occupations—registered nurses, retail salespeople, home health aides, and personal care aides—will add more than half a million jobs each through 2020. As a college student, the first fact that will probably get your attention is that only two occupations listed require a college degree: postsecondary teachers and elementary school teachers. The registered nurse occupation typically requires an associate degree, and the other 17 occupations require a high school degree or less, or short-term to moderate on-the-job training. Jobs requiring a high school diploma or less will represent more than half of all jobs. However, you should keep in mind that the management and supervision of all these workers probably does require advanced training, and occupations requiring postsecondary training will grow faster.

Table 7.1

Twenty Big Growth Occupations, 2010–2020

Standard Occupational Code (SOC) Number and Occupational Title	2020 Employment (thousands)	Percent Change +	Holland Codes
29-1111 Registered nurses	3,450	26	SIE
41-2031 Retail salespersons	4,968	17	ESR
43-4051 Customer service representatives	2,526	16	ESC
35-3021 Combined food preparation & serving workers, incl. fast food	3,080	15	REC
43-9061 Office clerks, general	3,440	17	CRS
39-9021 Personal care aides	1,468	71	SRE
31-1011 Home health aides	1,724	69	SRC
25-1000 Postsecondary teachers	2,062	17	IRS
37-2011 Janitors and cleaners, except maids and housekeeping cleaners	2,557	11	RES
31-1012 Nursing aides, orderlies, & attendants	1,807	20	SER
43-3031 Bookkeeping, accounting, & auditing clerks	2,157	14	CSR
53-7062 Laborers & material movers	2,087	15	REC
39-9011 Child care workers	1,544	20	ESA
41-2011 Cashiers	3,613	7	CES
41-4012 Sales representatives	1,653	16	ESR
47-2061 Construction laborers	1,211	21	RES
37-3011 Landscaping & grounds-keeping workers	1,392	21	RIS
25-2021 Elementary school teachers, except special education	1,725	17	SAE
43-4171 Receptionists & information clerks	1,297	24	CSE
53-3032 Truck drivers, heavy & tractor-trailer	1,935	21	RCS

Source: *Monthly Labor Review*, January 2012, p. 101.
Notes:
These 20 occupations account for almost 36% of projected new jobs 2010–2020.
Holland Code order: S = 34, R = 30, E = 28, C = 18, I = 7, A = 3, or **SRECIA**; code order in 2016 was SERCIA

Lockard and Wolf (2012) noted that only four of the occupations gaining the most new jobs through 2020 pay $46,000 or higher (registered nurses, postsecondary faculty, sales representatives, and elementary teachers), and 11 pay $30,000 or lower. This is consistent with the idea that many of these occupations do not require education beyond the high school level. They also note that four of these occupations involve the demand for health services.

Finally, occupations with the most openings ("big growth") are not new, different, or unique but familiar and common. Only four new occupations appear in Table 7.1 for 2020 from the list projected for 2016 four years ago. This fact can be reassuring for people involved in career planning. The more things change, the more they stay the same.

Table 7.1 also shows the Holland summary code order of **SRECIA** for these 20 occupations. It is not surprising to see that the Realistic area has become more prominent in the latest projections, given the expected rebound in the construction industry. However, only four occupations were new for this list from the 2016 projections, indicating limited change in big growth occupations. To determine Holland codes for these projections, we consulted the *Dictionary of Holland Occupation Codes* (Gottfredson & Holland, 1996) and the *Occupations Finder—Revised Edition* (Holland & PAR staff, 2010). (You may want to review information about Holland's theory in Chapter 2). We then calculated this summary code by giving each RIASEC letter 3 points for first position, 2 points for second position, and 1 for third.

OCCUPATIONS THAT GROW MOST RAPIDLY. Table 7.2 shows the 20 fastest-growing occupations in the United States (Lockard & Wolf, 2010; Sommers, 2011–12). This list is based on the percentage growth of the occupations. We just saw data pertaining to "big growth" occupations, but the focus here is on "fast growth." Six of the 20 fastest-growing occupations are associated with construction, but this level remains below the 2006 level because of the impact of the 2007–2009 recession. The two fastest growing occupations, personal care aides and home health aides, are affected by demographic changes and the increased need for eldercare (we will address this more in Chapter 10).

As a point of comparison, Lockard and Wolf (2012) examined the projected annual salaries of occupations in the big and fast growth lists through 2020. Unlike the big growth occupations described previously, where 11 out of 20 paid $30,000 or less, 7 of the 20 fast growth occupations pay below $30,000 annually.

Table 7.2 Twenty Fast Growth Occupations, 2010–2020

Standard Occupational Code (SOC) Number and Occupational Title	2020 Employment (thousands)	Percent Change +	Holland Codes
17-2031 Biomedical engineers	25	62	IRE
39-9021 Personal care aides	1,468	71	SCE
31-1011 Home health aides	1,724	69	SER
47-3011 Helpers—brickmasons, tilesetters, etc.	47	60	REI
29-2056 Veterinary technologists/technicians	122	52	SIE
47-3012 Helpers—carpenters	72	56	RCE
47-2121 Reinforcing iron & rebar workers	28	49	RES
47-3015 Helpers—pipelayers, plumbers, etc.	84	45	RES
13-1121 Meeting, event planners	103	44	ESC
29-2032 Diagnostic medical sonographers	77	44	ISA
31-2011 Occupational therapy assistants	41	43	SCE
31-2022 Physical therapist aides	67	43	ESC
47-2121 Glaziers	60	42	RSE
27-3091 Interpreters & translators	83	42	ESA
31-2021 Physical therapist assistants	98	46	SCR
43-6013 Medical secretaries	714	41	CES
13-1161 Market research analysts & specialists	399	41	ISC
21-1013 Marriage & family therapists	51	41	SAI
47-2021 Brickmasons & block masons	125	41	RSE
29-1123 Physical therapists	276	39	SIE

Source: *Monthly Labor Review*, January 2012, p.100.
Notes:
Six of the fast growth occupations relate to construction, but this rate is below the 2006 level.
RIASEC Code order: S = 38, E = 27, R = 22, I = 15, C = 14, A = 4, or **SERICA**; E has moved from 5th to 2nd in code order since 2002

In examining these BLS reports, notice that only two occupations, home health aides and personal care aides, appear on the lists for both big growth and fast growth occupations. This is noteworthy and underscores the earlier observation about the importance of demography in labor market forecasts, more specifically the increased health care needs of the aging baby-boomer generation.

Table 7.2 also lists Holland codes for the 20 fastest-growing occupations. The summary code is **SERICA**. The predominance of the Holland S and E codes shows that the occupations growing at the most rapid rate in the future will employ people with social and enterprising skills and interests—those with "people" skills.

Dixie Sommers (2011–2012), the Assistant Commissioner of the Office of Occupational Statistics and Employment Projections with the Bureau of Labor Statistics, identified the 20 occupations typically requiring a bachelor's degree that are projected to have the most job openings. Her findings appear in Table 7.3. Many of these jobs also require work experience in a related field or on-the-job-training (e.g., 5+ years for financial managers). Many of these projected openings reflect the large

Table 7.3 Twenty Fastest-Growing Jobs Requiring a Bachelor's Degree, 2010–2020

Occupation	Jobs (in thousands)	Median Annual Wages (May 2010)
Elementary school teachers	249	51,660
Accountants and auditors	191	61,690
Management analysts	157	78,160
Software developers, applications	144	87,790
Software developers, systems software	127	94,180
Computer systems analysts	120	77,740
Market research analysts, specialists	117	60,570
Middle school teachers	108	51,960
Network & computer systems administrators	97	69,160
Secondary school teachers	72	53,230
Medical & health services managers	68	84,270
Cost estimators	68	57,860
Personal financial advisors	66	64,750
Information security analysts	66	64,750
Sales representatives	66	73,710
Recreation workers	64	22,260
Training & development specialists	62	54,160
Public relations specialists	58	52,090
Child, family, school social workers	58	40,210
Computer & information systems managers	56	115,780

Source: *Occupational Outlook Quarterly*, Winter 2011–2012, p. 17.

size of teaching occupations, the need to replace teachers expected to retire, and rising student enrollments.

GEOGRAPHY AND OCCUPATIONS. Some occupations are more likely to be concentrated in specific areas because of population density, location of natural resources, or work distinct to an area (Watson, 2010). For example, 89% of political scientists worked in just a few areas in 2009, with two thirds in the Washington, D.C. area. Occupations widely dispersed are often in the services field (e.g., office clerks, retail salespeople, teachers). Not surprisingly, the areas of highest employment, such as metropolitan areas of over one million, also have the largest number of different occupations and 42% of employment. Publications like *Kiplinger* (www.kiplinger.com) that regularly publish articles on good places to live often focus on employment. A recent article (Dewey, 2011) highlighted "great cities for young adults," and the criteria for these cities included employment opportunities with high starting salaries for college graduates.

GROWTH IN INDUSTRIES. Thus far, we have examined growth in occupations through 2020, but what about industries? In individual career planning, it may be more useful to focus on the industry rather than the occupation in planning for your future employment. Workers in many kinds of occupations may be found in an industry. For example, the hospital industry includes electricians, public relations specialists, and janitors, as well as physicians and nurses. Industries vary widely in size and scope. Later in this chapter we'll examine the services industry in more depth, and in Chapter 9 we'll discuss employment opportunities in the staffing services industry.

There are two basic categories of industries in the U.S. economy, goods producing (which includes construction, manufacturing, and mining) and service producing. Sommers (2011–2012) identified the 20 industries expected to produce the biggest employment growth in 2010–2020, and construction is the only industry listed in this table that is goods producing—the other 19 are service producing. Sommers reported that industry employment growth through 2020 is concentrated in the services sector, which includes professional and business services (see Table 7.4). In terms of employment, five of these service industries are related to health care, including offices of health

Table 7.4

Twenty Industries with the Biggest Employment Growth, 2010–2020

Industry	Projected Growth (Thousands of Jobs)
Construction	1,893
Retail trade	1,767
Offices of health practitioners	1,391
Hospitals	878
Home health care services	872
Food services & drinking places	859
Individual & family services	851
Nursing & residential care facilities	822
Wholesale trade	743
Local educational services	740
Computer systems design & related services	671
Employment services	631
Management, scientific, & technical consulting services	575
Junior colleges, colleges, universities, & professional schools	477
Outpatient, laboratory, & other ambulatory care services	394
Architectural, engineering, & related services	358
Services to buildings, dwellings	302
Truck transportation	300
State educational services	284
Child daycare services	249

Source: *Occupational Outlook Quarterly*, Winter 2011–2012, p. 38.

practitioners, hospitals, home health care services, nursing and residential care facilities, and ambulatory care services (e.g., outpatient, laboratory).

Henderson (2012) suggested that 71% of the U.S. economy in 2020 will be service producing, and 23% will be goods producing (the other 6% will be in agriculture, household self-employment, and other areas). He further noted that the construction industry will rebound through 2020 more than some other goods-producing sectors of the economy but will not yet be up to prerecession levels. However, professional and business services are projected to provide the second largest number of jobs during the period 2010–2020. Firms in this industry help organizations respond to globalization, technology changes, and other challenges. This work is led by providers of management, scientific, and technical consulting services.

HOLLAND CODES AND JOBS. In Chapter 3, we pointed out that Holland's RIASEC theory provided a way to classify occupations. Figure 7.2 shows what has been happening in the economy over five decades from 1960 to 2000 (Reardon, Bullock, & Meyer, 2007). Inspection of this figure shows that Realistic jobs have held constant in employing the most people, but the percentage has been declining over the years. Think about the reasons for this in terms of the decrease in manufacturing jobs in the United States. Note that very few people work in the Artistic area and this has remained constant, which is also true of the Investigative area. Note also that the Enterprising area has been increasing slightly.

Following up on this theme, Figure 7.3 shows how annual income varied in 1990 across the six RIASEC kinds of work. (We believe this may still be representative of how income is distributed across the RIASEC areas today.) Remember that the Investigative area of work requires more education and training than the other five areas, so this figure provides some data supporting the idea that education pays.

THE COLLEGE LABOR MARKET. The employment of college graduates is affected by the general economy, so it is no surprise that the level has dropped from 86% in 1994 to 80.2% in 2009, the height of the recession (Koc, 2010). But other factors have contributed to this decline. The labor

figure 7.2

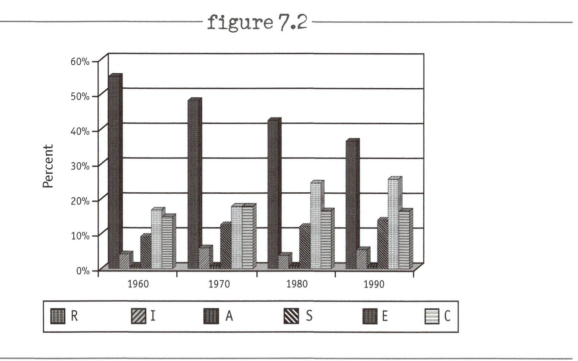

Employment by Six Kinds of Work, 1960–1990

force participation rate for female college graduates has declined since 1998, whereas the rate for males has been stable. At the same time, the number of female bachelor's degree holders has increased by more than 51%.

The Collegiate Employment Research Institute at Michigan State University (2010–2011) had a cautiously optimistic labor market report for college graduates in 2011. They concluded that the reduced uncertainty among employers in 2010–2011 reflected an intention to hire at the 2007–2008 prerecession levels. They found that the college labor market would continue to expand opportunities for graduates in 2011 but at a more moderate rate than in 2010 (Recruiting Trends 2010–2011).

figure 7.3

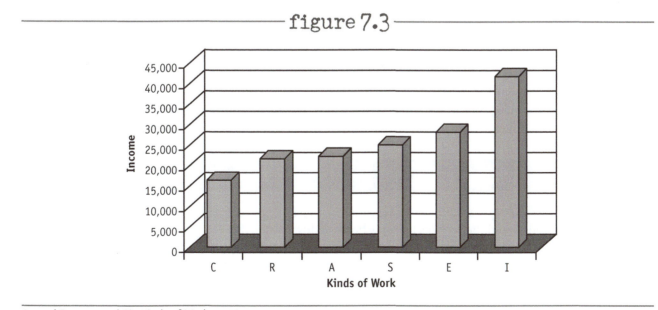

Annual Income and Six Kinds of Work, 1990

New college graduates are also being squeezed by older workers with bachelor's degrees who are working longer because they can and want to remain in the workforce. Surprisingly, the unemployment rate for bachelor's degree holders age 65 and older in November 2009 was 5%, while it was 7.5% for those aged 20–24.

Koc (2010) reported that the unemployment rate for female college graduates was 6.2% and 9.3% for males in November 2009. It seems that female graduates are beginning to dominate this entry-level workforce once dominated by men. (This raises a variety of issues regarding home and work, which we will explore more in Chapter 10). Koc (2011) later noted that the higher employment rate for college women may be the result of being more open to part-time and temporary work than men. (We will discuss this more in Chapter 9.)

UNEMPLOYMENT, EARNINGS, AND EDUCATION. Table 7.5 provides data regarding the relationship of educational completion with respect to employment security and income. The unemployment rate is clearly related to educational attainment—those with more education are less frequently unemployed. The information on weekly earnings is also related to education—more education is connected to more income. It is important to remember that median weekly earnings means that 50% of those with a bachelor's degree earn more than $1,025 weekly and 50% earn less.

Table 7.5 Unemployment Rates and Earnings Related to Educational Attainment

Unemployment Rate 2009	Educational Attainment	Median Weekly Earnings 2009
2.5%	Doctoral degree	$1,532
2.3	Professional degree	1,529
3.9	Master's degree	1,257
5.2	Bachelor's degree	1,025
6.8	Associate degree	761
8.6	Some college, no degree	699
9.7	High school graduate	626
14.6	Less than a high school diploma	454
Average rate, all workers 7.9%		Median earnings, all workers $ 774

Source: *Occupational Outlook Quarterly,* Summer 2010

Finally, we should note that the phenomenon of educational upgrading is occurring in many occupations because of the large numbers of college graduates available for jobs. Stated another way, there is an increasing level of educational attainment required in many occupations. This change has been especially noticeable in the health and protective service occupations and in occupations that usually are considered desirable and well paid, such as airline pilot and flight attendant. Employers increasingly prefer college graduates because jobs are becoming more complex in the global economy, and college graduates are more motivated and have better problem-solving skills, learn tasks more quickly, and have better communication skills (Dohm & Wyatt, 2002).

The Services Industry

What exactly do we mean by services? Is it just health care and social work? It is important to fully understand the services industry because this is where the U.S. economy is growing and where many individuals will find employment. It is expected that employment in the services industry will increase from 76% of total jobs to 79% in 2016 (Figueroa & Woods, 2007).

Henkoff (1994) noted that the services industry has an image problem. Sometimes, it is viewed as less important and worthwhile than manufacturing. You can touch the results of manufacturing, but you only experience the results of services (e.g., an airplane ride or telephone call). Services brings to mind what George Ritzer (1995) called "McJobs," including low-paid burger flippers and floor sweepers who work in highly controlled and tightly scripted jobs. However, the services industry also includes highly paid brain surgeons, defense lawyers, actors, and accountants.

Anthony Carnevale and Stephen Rose (1998) offered another way of thinking about the services industry, which they call the "Office Economy." College students who fear being stuck in an office all day may be alarmed by their views. They reported that office work employed 41% of all workers, often paid the highest salaries, was growing quickly, employed over half of college graduates, and captured 50% of all earnings. Office work includes accountants, managers, sales representatives, and brokers, which account for 44% of office jobs.

Carnevale and Rose suggested that the office has become the new model for the American economy. The office accounts for almost 60% of jobs for people with college degrees, 50% of all earnings, and most of the job growth in the last two decades. They noted that the office economy has been especially beneficial for women and African Americans.

The report by Carnevale and Rose was so significant that the Australian National Training Authority set about to replicate it. They found that office work had become the dominant sector of the Australian economy in comparison to factory, hospital/classroom, farm, or retail sales work, employing 41% of workers, paying some of the highest salaries, employing more educated workers, showing substantial growth, and capturing 50% of all earnings (Doyle, Kurth, & Kerr, 2000). In addition, they found that 56% of office jobs were held by managers and professionals, finance and insurance managers, real estate brokers and agents, and business professionals.

We present three examples of successful companies in the services industry, and will profile them briefly.

TOMS Shoes

This company, a social entrepreneurship, gives away a pair of shoes for every pair it sells (Schectman, 2012). The company founder, Blake Mycoskie, noticed that children in rural Argentina did not have proper fitting shoes. Volunteers initially donated shoes but kids did not always get the correct size. As a result, Mycoskie created a constant revenue stream making sure that each donated pair was backed with a purchase. "Because we incorporated giving [into our mission], customers helped spread the word, [that]got media attention, and retailers even helped market us" (p. 50). See more about TOMS one-for-one commitment at: www.toms.com/one-for-one.

Johnson Controls

Johnson Controls describes itself as a global diversified company in the building and automotive industries (www.johnsoncontrols.com). This company might have built the thermostat or energy system used in your house or apartment. However, the company has moved into managing other companies' buildings. The engineers who designed the heating/cooling systems for buildings have now moved away from their desks and out into the buildings to ensure that occupants of the buildings— their customers—are always comfortable. Johnson Controls, however, expanded beyond heating and cooling and moved into lighting, security, and cleaning operations of office buildings, as well as providing comfort for the "automotive experience." Henkoff described the work of an engineer, Tina, who heads a four-member team that spends half its time in the field helping schools become more energy efficient. The company realized that this market is worth billions of dollars in the United States alone (review Table 7.1 to examine the growth in jobs for janitors/cleaners). Service means doing something that customers cannot or do not want to do for themselves. This explains the basis for the success of such organizations (Henkoff, 1994).

Panera Bread

We're all familiar with what Panera Bread does, and many of us have eaten there. What we probably don't know is that Panera is a $2.6 billion restaurant chain (Rockwood, 2009) that opens a new bakery every five days and in 2012 had over 1,500 locations in 40 states (http://www.panerabread.com/). Besides selling fresh bread with the best ingredients at full price, the company provides an unpretentious atmosphere and no time limit for the customer's visit—indeed, customers are encouraged to linger. As a result, the bakeries have become a community gathering spot. The CEO noted that ". . . we're renting space to people and the food is the price of admission" (Rockwood, 2009, p. 70).

There are many examples of organizations in the services industry; we hope these three illustrate the scope of the work included in this area. New ways of thinking about the services industry, including the idea of sales, can introduce new schema for individual career planning.

State Labor Market Information

In strategic career planning, geographic location can sometimes make an important difference in analyzing labor market information. Economic conditions can vary greatly across states in terms of the factors we have discussed in this chapter (e.g., big growth occupations, fast growth occupations, big growth industries).

It is beyond our purposes here to speculate about the similarities and differences between state and U.S. economic data with respect to labor market forecasts or Holland's typology and the amount of education and training associated with high-employment jobs. However, these data do point out the value of thinking critically about the kinds of jobs available in various geographic regions of the United States, and how you might use something like the RIASEC typology to guide your strategic career thinking.

We should note that labor market reports are often produced for geographic regions, counties, and cities. These may be obtained from a local employment service office or a state department of labor. In Florida, for example, the Agency for Workforce Innovation provides this kind of information (http://www.floridajobs.org/). Many other states have similar services, and you can search for directory information at America's Career InfoNet (http://www.careeronestop.org/).

A CIP Perspective

In this chapter we have examined information related to the emerging global economy, as well as some of the trends in the U.S. labor market. Along the way, we have pointed to facts that might be considered by those engaged in personal, strategic career planning. Now we want to review what we have learned by examining it in light of the Pyramid of Information-Processing Domains and the CASVE Cycle. *Our goal is to improve the quality of your PCT for solving career problems and making career decisions.*

Self-Knowledge

What interests, skills, and values are most relevant in this emerging global economy? A review of information in this chapter suggests several things to us, but readers can think of others in light of their unique career history and goals (their PCT). In general, Holland's Social, Enterprising, Investigative, and Artistic types appear to be in a good place with respect to the changing labor market. It is especially apparent that Social and Enterprising interpersonal skills, essential in teamwork and leadership activities, will be highly valued by organizations.

The global economy will likely seek people with skills in languages and history, and experience in ethnic diversity and multicultural traditions. Technology-related skills, including computers, telecommunications, systems analysis, biology, business, and economics, would also appear to be essential in the global economy.

Rifkin's discussion of the developing social economy suggests that personal values, which include community welfare and social service, will be important. Indeed, there will be jobs for college graduates in this Third Sector.

In general, it is important to constantly explore new interests and develop new skills or to find meaning in a variety of work options. Adaptability, flexibility, compromise, and personal growth are traits that will most likely be rewarded in the new global economy.

Option Knowledge

Understanding the nature of the new kinds of work organizations in the global economy will be essential. We'll examine this topic more closely in the next two chapters.

Among other things, Drucker told us about knowledge workers, Reich told us about global enterprise webs, Friedman told us how individuals with technology skills can participate directly in a global economy, and Rifkin told us about the third sector. These ideas and others make us mindful of the constant need to learn more about the contemporary world, which is changing so rapidly.

Although global economic statistics may show job stability, local economies might show change. For example, larger, dynamic cities, such as Atlanta, Boston, Denver, Orlando, Houston, and San Francisco Bay may provide rich possibilities for individual career development. *Fast Company* magazine annually profiles what they call "fast cities," which are characterized by "bold ideas" that often enrich the local economies and in turn lead to new and exciting job possibilities (http://www.fastcompany.com/magazine/155/fast-cities-2011.html).

Decision Making

Our individual career-planning skills will be increasingly important in the global economy. One reason is the increasing rate of speed in which work projects will be completed and jobs will develop and change. Indeed, people will be actively involved in one stage or another of the CASVE Cycle throughout their lives. Career decision making will be continuous as new training, work, and lifestyle options rapidly emerge. In this chapter, we have learned that periods of unemployment may be increasingly common for many people. For example, we can look at the Execution stage of the CASVE Cycle and be aware that we constantly need to keep our resumes up to date and be ever ready to move into a job-hunting process.

Executive Processing

Many of the ideas presented in this chapter have suggested that careers will be more complex constructions in the future. This means that our individual PCTs will need to become more complex as well.

Careers will no longer be tied to a single company or organization, and individuals will take much more personal responsibility for independently managing their careers. This will require us to think strategically about our career life, to be flexible, to have a sense of timing, and to constantly scan the environment for new information. As we will learn in Chapter 10, careers will also require complex thinking to balance family relationships, organizational roles, leisure pursuits, and personal goals.

In short, *career development in the future will require us to think globally and work locally*. We will need to be ever mindful of the global economy and the changes that will affect the way we work in the future and the strategic direction of our careers. However, we must work locally in the job situation at hand, mindful of the services we provide our clients and customers, the need to constantly improve our job skills, and to actively work in some phase of the CASVE Cycle to solve career problems and make career decisions.

Summary

In this chapter, we introduced some of the important career themes to emerge from the developing global economy. We also examined some of the facts associated with understanding the labor market and trends in the U.S. economy, including states and local communities. Finally, we reviewed this new information in light of the cognitive information-processing paradigm that undergirds this book. This information should help you improve the part of your PCT having to do with options knowledge. This, in turn, will enable you to develop new metacognitions for solving career problems and making career decisions.

References

Alperovitz, G. (2011, June 13). The new-economy movement. *Nation*, 20–23.

Carnevale, A. P., & Rose, S. J. (1998). *Education for what? The new office economy*. Princeton, NJ: ETS.

Collegiate Employment Research Institute (2010–2011). *Recruiting trends 2010–2011*. East Lansing, MI: Michigan State University (also available at http://www.ceri.msu.edu/ceri-publications/).

Dewey, C. (2011 September). *Great cities for young adults*. Retrieved from http://www.kiplinger.com/slideshow/more-great-cities-for-young-adults/1.html

Dohm, A., & Wyatt, I. (2002). College at work: Outlook and earnings for college graduates, 2000–10. *Occupational Outlook Quarterly, 46*(3), 3–15.

Doyle, L., Kurth, B., & Kerr, E. (2000). *Knowledge work: The rise of the office economy (full report)*. Brisbane: Australian National Training Authority.

Drucker, P. F. (1993). *Post-capitalist society*. New York, NY: HarperCollins Publishers.

Figueroa, E. B., & Woods, R. A. (2007, November). Industry output and employment projections to 2016. *Monthly Labor Review*, 53–85.

Fisher, A. (2005, March 21). Hot careers for the next 10 years. *Fortune*, 131.

Friedman, T. L. (2005). *The world is flat*. New York, NY: Farrar, Straus, & Giroux.

Gottfredson, G., & Holland, J. (1996). *Dictionary of Holland occupation codes* (3rd ed.). Odessa, FL: Psychological Assessment Resources.

Henderson, R. (2012, January). Industry employment and output projections to 2020. *Monthly Labor Review, 135*(1), 65–83.

Henkoff, R. (1994, June 27). Service is everybody's business. *Fortune*, 48–60.

Holland, J. L., & PAR Staff (2010). *The occupations finder—revised edition*. Odessa, FL: Psychological Assessment Resources.

Jones, S. (2008, May). Making magic: New and emerging occupations. *NACE Journal*, 37–44.

Kamenetz, A. (2012, February). The four-year career. *Fast Company*, 72–77, 97–98.

Koc, E. W. (2010, April). The evolution of the college labor market. *NACE Journal*, 16–20.

Koc, E. W. (2011, April). Gender and college recruiting. *NACE Journal*, 18–24.

Lockard, C. B., & Wolf, M. (2012, January). Occupational employment projections to 2020. *Monthly Labor Review*, 88–108.

Mair, J., & Martí, I. (2005). Social entrepreneurship research: A source of explanation, prediction, and delight. *Journal of World Business, 41,* 36–44.

Reardon, R. C., Bullock, E. E., & Meyer, K. E. (2007). A Holland perspective on the U.S. workforce from 1960–2000. *Career Development Quarterly, 55,* 262–274.

Reich, R. (1992). *The work of nations*. New York, NY: Vintage Books.

Rifkin, J. (1995). *The end of work*. New York, NY: Putnam's Sons.

Ritzer, G. (1995). McJobs. In R. Feller & G. Walz (Eds.), *Career transitions in turbulent times* (pp. 211–217). Greensboro, NC: ERIC/CASS Publications.

Rockwood, K. (2009, October). Rising dough: How Panera is thriving by selling real food—and a gathering space—in suburbia. *Fast Company*, 69–71.

Sachs, J. D. (2011). *The price of civilization: Reawakening American virtue and prosperity*. New York, NY: Random House.

Schectman, J. (2010, October 1). Good business. *Newsweek*, 50.

Sommers, D. (2011–2012, Winter). Charting the projections 2010–2020: Getting started. *Occupational Outlook Quarterly*, 2–48.

Sommers, D., & Franklin, J. C. (2012, January). Oveview of projections to 2020. *Monthly Labor Review*, 3–20.

Toossi, M. (2012, January). Labor force projections to 2020: A more slowly growing workforce. *Monthly Labor Review*, 43–64.

Watson, A. (2010, Fall). Mapping out a career: An analysis of geographic concentration of occupations. *Occupational Outlook Quarterly*, 12–22.

Wegmann, R., Chapman, R., & Johnson, M. (1989). *Work in the new economy*. Alexandria, VA: American Counseling Association.

Chapter Eight

Organizational Culture and Effective Work

In Chapter 7, we learned how socioeconomic trends, including the emerging global economy and the growth of technology, are affecting organizations. In this chapter, we will focus on organizations because they are the settings where most of us will spend our time working. The organizational context is sometimes overlooked in career planning, but we believe that a better understanding of organizations is essential for career growth. As in Chapter 7, we will focus on what several authors have to say about this topic. Along the way, we will examine related subjects including:

- The changed social contract
- Characteristics of organizations
- Organizational culture
- Kinds of organizations
- Past and present organizational structures
- Leadership in organizational development
- The relationship between career development and organizational development

We will conclude with a cognitive information processing (CIP) perspective on the nature of organizations and the implications for career planning.

As you read about organizational culture and effective work, try to think about how your Personal Career Theory (PCT) and strategic career thinking can be improved by this information. How will it affect occupations you are interested in, and how will it affect the ways you think about working? How will it affect the type of questions you might ask in a job interview? What new, more complex career metacognitions will this information enable you to develop? What will be the organizational context of your work?

The Changed Social Contract

The big story related to the changing culture of organizations pertains to the changed "social contract" between individuals and work organizations. Under terms of the old social contract, it was understood that if workers were loyal to the organization and dedicated their working lives to producing its products and services, the organization would maintain them as employees and pay them benefits in retirement. *Loyalty would be repaid with economic security.* It was a contract for life.

However, the nature of this social contract has changed, and many organizations now view workers like other parts of the production process (e.g., machines, buildings, money). Productive work is a commodity that the organization purchases in the marketplace, just like it buys electricity, water, and raw materials for production. Loyalty and long-term commitments are no longer part of the social contract between workers and the organization.

As William Morin, president of one of the nation's largest human resources consulting firms said years ago, "We've broken the whole mommy and daddy syndrome. Nobody else is responsible for your happiness. You have to see yourself as a business. *That* is your job" (Henkoff, 1993, p. 46). For many, this was a dramatic new way of thinking about careers and working, something we are emphasizing throughout this book.

Indeed, some have suggested that the only thing workers might reasonably expect from an organization is ongoing training to enable them to become more productive and competitive in the marketplace (Gutteridge, Leibowitz, & Shore, 1993). The new social contract is based on the employee's opportunities for training and development, and one's loyalty may be more to the profession than to the organization.

What about job security? The idea has changed from job security to *employability security*, meaning that the worker develops skills and competencies that someone is willing to pay for in the marketplace. As Feller and Whichard (2005) noted: "Skills and competencies tied to adding value to an organization's core mission increasingly determine the quality of jobs workers can expect to attain" (p. 41). Although it is still developing today, workers under the new social contract have strong commitments to their work skills and to their coworkers (or teammates). This appears to be the nature of the new social contract. We will return to these ideas throughout Chapters 9, 10, 11, and 15 when we examine the job campaign.

Characteristics of Organizations

Peter Drucker, Edgar Schein, Susan Mohrman, and Susan Cohen wrote on the issue of organizations in relation to career planning. Some of their ideas are presented below.

Drucker's View

Peter Drucker (1993), who consulted with many organizations over the years to help them improve their effectiveness, noted that "organizations" have not been studied by social scientists until relatively recently. He pointed out that an organization is *not* a "community," "society," "class," "family," "clan," or "tribe." Organizations are not outgrowths of geographic location, wealth or status, marriage, or royalty. However, armies, churches, hospitals, universities, and labor unions are organizations, because "organizations are special-purpose institutions. Organizations are effective because they concentrate on *one task*" (p. 53).

Drucker further noted that organizations function best when they have a clear purpose and specialists working in the organization know exactly how to align themselves with this larger purpose. "Only a clear, focused, and common mission can hold the organization together and enable it to produce results" (p. 53). He suggested that an excellent example of a modern organization is the symphony orchestra, where 250 specialists forego their specialization and play together from one piece of music. Because most of us work in organizations, it is important that we understand the essential task(s) of the organization, its mission.

Sandroff (1993), writing in *Working Woman* magazine, shared this example from American Express. Like other modern organizations with too many good business ideas and goals, American Express decided to set fewer goals in order to encourage a clear sense of purpose. In effect, there were different cultures operating and even competing within the organization. As a result of this lack of shared focus, employees were asked to clear their desks of all work that did not directly pertain to the company goal of "improving cardholder satisfaction." Workers evaluated every assignment in terms of improving cardholder satisfaction, and some common work tasks done in the past were deemed irrelevant. This is an example of an organization arriving at agreement about its culture and its workers arriving at a clear understanding of the organization's purpose.

One of your tasks in seeking employment is to develop an accurate, clear understanding of the purpose of the organization where you seek to work. Erin White (2005) noted that culture clash was one of the primary reasons that new hires failed on the job.

What is the relationship of individuals to organizations? In one way, the contribution of any one person can be swallowed up, because organizations exist to produce goods and services for the outside world. In another way, however, each person's contribution is important and valued. This is because organizations are social systems, and each part (person) is both independent and interdependent at the same time. People become involved with organizations because of decisions by both the individual and the organization. Organizations look for competent, dedicated members, and in this sense they compete among themselves for new members.

Organizations are also always *managed*, which is how decisions are made. As with the symphony, there is a conductor who controls things, an arranger who writes the music, and a manager who makes sure members are paid and can travel. However, Drucker (1993) noted that modern organizations have a new factor to consider. They must be able to function in rapidly changing conditions, to constantly invent new ways to accomplish their tasks, to constantly improve. As we shall learn, these facts of modern organizational life are also played out in the careers of those who work in them.

Organizational Culture

Edgar Schein (1985), a professor of management at the Massachusetts Institute of Technology, is one of the foremost experts on organizations in the United States. He has studied organizational culture for over 40 years.

Schein's definition of "organizational culture" is complex. Let's break it down into some manageable parts:

1. Schein views culture as a characteristic of a stable social group that has a history, and where members have shared important experiences in solving group problems.
2. These common experiences have led the group members to have a shared view of the world and their place in it.
3. This shared view has worked successfully long enough for it to be taken for granted by the group and has now dropped out of members' awareness. They take this shared view for granted as members of the group.
4. "Culture" may be viewed as a learned product of group experience, and it is found in a group or organization with a significant history.

As a new member, or employee, in an organization, it is important for you to learn the culture of the organization. Indeed, the members of the organization will watch you closely to see if you are able to understand and adopt their organizational culture. Why? Because most members have a history of experience in solving the organization's problems, and it is important to them that you learn from those prior experiences, to adopt their shared view. It is important to add this factor to your developing PCT.

In many organizations, there is more than one culture, and each department or work team may have its own subculture. It is essential that you learn about the various cultural traditions in a new organization, especially those held by top managers and your supervisor, if you want to be accepted and succeed as a member.

Organizational culture is practically observable in many ways. Schein offers six examples that you can use when you visit an organization or after you get hired and report for work (see Table 8.1).

Indicators of Organizational Culture

Table 8.1

Indicator	Observable Behaviors
1. Regular behaviors	• Common ways that members greet one another, courtesies extended to senior members of the organization, where people sit at meetings or have lunch. • How members dress. • Artifacts the organization uses to represent or symbolize itself (e.g., furniture, colors, art, nature of publications, images on the home page).
2. Norms	• How hard do members work in the organization, are they willing to work evenings or weekends, is working more than 40 hours per week the norm? • Behaviors related to the use of time and working hard are key indicators of organizational culture.
3. Dominant values	• Our products are of highest quality, customer service is the priority, employee family life is important, employees should have leisure interests. • Organizational culture usually reflects the values of the founder, or the way things "ought" to be. • Organizational culture is directly tied to leadership of the organization.
4. Philosophy	• The overall guiding views toward employees, the local community, serving others, making money, or working hard. • Statements related to the nature of the relationship between the individual worker and the group in the organization.
5. Rules	• Learning the ropes as a new employee, understanding and accepting supervisor's feedback, managing time, and getting along with coworkers. • How new employees are oriented.
6. Feeling or climate	• Physical layout of the facilities, the manner in which employees treat customers and coworkers, the level of trust. • Is the climate marked by tension, happiness, competitiveness, or some combination of these things?

As you review these six indicators of organizational culture, think about organizations where you have worked or volunteered. How would you evaluate an organization's culture using these six topics? We will look at specific ways to assess an organization's culture in Chapter 15 when we analyze the first day on the new job.

Increasing Diversity in Organizations

Organizational culture in the workplace is also being affected by several demographic changes now taking place in the United States. Some of these changes are related to history, some to public policy, and others to sociology. The workplace is increasingly composed of more diverse groups, and these changes have an impact on organizational culture (Howard, 1995).

1. **More older workers.** The labor force is growing most rapidly in the 55-and-older age group. This is happening as baby boomers (born between 1946 and 1964) continue to age, live longer, and seek income to offset health costs and other expenses. As we noted in Chapter 7, the labor force will continue to age, with the 55-years-and-older group growing from 19.5% in 2010 to 25.2% in 2020 (Toossi, 2012).
2. **More immigrants and varied ethnic/racial groups.** Foreign-born workers have come to play an increasing role in America's workforce. The greatest influx of immigrants has come from Latin American and Asia. This is a very different group of workers than those who entered this country from Europe in the early 1900s. Many of these immigrants take positions in the natural and applied sciences, whereas others take low-level jobs in the services industry. The skills and training of immigrants vary widely by country of origin and whether their immigration is legal or illegal.
3. **More people with disabilities.** The passage of the Americans with Disabilities Act (ADA) in 1990 was an effort to increase the entry of people with disabilities into the workforce. The

ADA prohibits discrimination in all employment practices, including job application procedures, hiring, firing, advancement, compensation, training, and other terms, conditions, and privileges of employment. It applies to recruitment, advertising, tenure, layoff, leave, benefits, and all other employment-related activities. Conditions that might impair a person's functioning in a work environment include mental retardation, cancer, multiple sclerosis, cerebral palsy, blindness, orthopedic impairments, arthritis, and many others. The ADA requires organizations to provide "reasonable accommodations" to remove a barrier to functioning in an environment or to adapt the environment so that the person can function on a level playing field. In spite of the ADA, the Kessler Foundation reported a 2011 survey that only 20% of people with a disability are employed compared to 60% of those without disabilities (http://nod.org/assets/downloads/01-2011_Exec_Summary.pdf).

4. **More women.** The participation of women in the labor force has nearly doubled over the last 54 years. The positive change over the last half century in the female labor force participation rate has greatly affected the social and economic condition of women, their families, and our nation's economy (Employment Policy Foundation, 2005). In Chapter 7 we learned that the trend has slowed; however, there are many interesting factors involving career planning associated with women entering work outside the home, and we will review them more fully in Chapter 10.

Ethnic Culture and Organizational Culture

In Chapter 7, we focused on the increasing global economy and the development of multinational corporations. As an aside, it is worth noting that half of the world's largest economies are either nation-states or multinational corporations (Centron & Davies, 2008). As business organizations have become involved in global enterprise webs (Reich, 1992), they have sought to accommodate themselves to the diversity of ethnic and national cultures represented by the new employees. Managers and workers increasingly find themselves coping with this diversity.

Geert Hofstede (1984), a professor at the University of Maastricht in the Netherlands, conducted a study of people working in sales in a major multinational American corporation operating in 39 countries. He studied the work-related values of these employees, and he found that work attitudes and values could be attributed to cultural differences among the 39 countries. He found four major categories for classifying cultures: (a) power distance, (b) uncertainty avoidance, (c) individualism, and (d) masculinity.

1. **Power distance.** This category refers to the relationship between the boss and subordinates, and the social power difference between the two. Hofstede found that in some countries (e.g., the Philippines, Mexico, Venezuela, India) there were strong, clear status differences between bosses and employees, whereas in others (i.e., New Zealand, Denmark, Israel, Austria) there were not. In the United States, social power distance was minimized.

2. **Uncertainty avoidance.** This category refers to the ways different cultures handle stress and anxiety. Hofstede found that the workers in various countries differed significantly in this area. Those avoiding uncertainty had lower job stress, less resistance to change, greater readiness to live day-by-day, and stronger ambition for advancement. Those who were prone to uncertainty had greater fear of failure, less risk-taking, higher job stress and anxiety, and more worry about the future. A person working with someone from a different country might find differences in approaches to work activities in the area of uncertainty avoidance.

3. **Individualism.** This category refers to the ways different national cultures emphasize the individual or group (collectivism). Countries having the highest scores for individualism were the United States, Great Britain, Australia, and Canada, and countries having the highest scores on collectivism were Peru, Colombia, and Venezuela. Countries high on individualism placed importance on employees' personal lifestyle, emotional independence from the company, freedom and challenge of jobs, and working for a small company. Countries

high on collectivism were emotionally dependent on companies, frowned on individual initiative, considered group decisions better than individual ones, and had managers who sought conformity and orderliness.

4. **Masculinity.** This category pertains to cultures that maintain differences between men and women in the workplace. Those in countries scoring high in the masculinity category tended to believe in independent decision making, aspired for recognition, and had stronger achievement motivation. Those scoring lower in masculinity were more likely to believe in group decision making; additionally, they valued security, had lower job stress, and preferred shorter work hours.

How can these ideas affect your individual career planning? These differences between national cultures may affect employee attitudes, interpersonal relationships, and reactions to supervision. An organization founded in the United States may experience "culture shock" as it expands into South America, the Middle East, or Southeast Asia. However, we caution you to use these ideas about national culture as general guidelines, because unique organizational and individual differences exist in all cultures.

Typical Organizational Problems Involving Culture

Our understanding of some common organizational problems (Schein, 1985) can be improved if we pay attention to organizational culture. When you are working in an organization, paying attention to these four areas of organizational behavior can enable you to be an effective worker in light of cultural understanding.

1. **New technologies.** In Chapter 7, we focused on the increasing importance of technology in the global economy. However, an organization's culture may slow the introduction and effective use of technology. For example, computers could bring new information about products, production, and staff to all members of an organization—information that was once only seen by top managers or bosses. The people in power in the organization may resist these technological changes because of their loss of control and status. Almost all organizations that are introducing new technologies into the workplace are also having to deal with issues of organizational culture. This includes schools, hospitals, sports teams, government, and business organizations. The successful introduction of new technologies in an organization is related to its culture.

2. **Intergroup conflicts.** When joining an organization, one quickly becomes aware that subgroups in an organization can have a culture of their own. These groups might be based on physical location, common occupation or job, similar ethnic background, or rank. "Once a group acquires a history it also acquires a culture" (Schein, 1995, p. 39). When sales and engineering or research and marketing have disagreements, these problems may be viewed as intercultural conflicts. In multinational organizations, these problems can become even more complex. A good example involves payoffs between customers and suppliers; in some ethnic cultures these are viewed as normal, and in others they are viewed as kickbacks and bribery. As a new employee in an organization, it is important for you to identify different cultural groups and their values.

3. **Communication breakdowns.** Ineffective communication in an organization can occur in group discussions in meetings, in e-mail exchanges, and direct face-to-face contact. Some might view communication problems as semantics or defensiveness, but social psychologists view these problems as cultural differences—real differences in how people view their history and their group. It goes without saying that people from different cultural traditions will have some difficulties in communication and in fully understanding what another person means in his or her communication. As we find ourselves in organizations working with people from other cultures, including people in different occupations, we may encounter communication problems related to culture.

4. **Training problems.** Every organization spends considerable energy in making sure members "fit" properly. This may be done through training programs, informal socializing, or special orientations. If these efforts are not successful in helping new members learn the culture of the host organization, employees may feel lost and uncomfortable, and the organization may suffer in productivity. Learning an organization's culture is an ongoing process for new members. Organizational culture helps determine who is "in" and who is "out." It helps the group determine who is a member.

In summary, Schein and others have provided us a rich understanding of organizational culture and how it provides the background from which our career portrait will emerge. Many issues associated with work, including staff relationships, training, and negotiating job offers, have their roots in organizational culture.

Kinds of Organizations

People might find themselves working in many different kinds of organizations. We will examine some of the most common.

Profit-Making Organizations

In Chapter 7, Rifkin (1995) noted that about 80% of economic activity is in the market sector of the economy. These organizations include Fortune 500 companies, as well as small family-owned businesses and self-employment (being an entrepreneur). This is the largest sector of the economy and has the most jobs. The most common term for such organizations is *private enterprise* or *business,* but it is important to note that this might include schools and even some charities, religious organizations, and social service organizations. For example, Embry-Riddle Aeronautical University is a private college that makes a profit for its owners. The Chamber of Commerce in a town or state is a good place to get lists of profit-making organizations.

Nonprofit Organizations

Most churches, charities, and social service organizations are included in what Rifkin (1995) called the "service sector" of the economy. Such organizations include the Red Cross, the Humane Society, the Sierra Club, the Environmental Defense Fund, and even the Educational Testing Service, which administers the SAT and GRE. However, this is only part of the story about this group of organizations. The nonprofit sector also includes the National Football League, the Motion Picture Academy of Arts and Sciences (it puts on the Academy Awards), and the National Basketball Association.

Nonprofits employ more than 10 million people. They include nearly every kind of occupation (e.g., managers of volunteers, fundraisers, event planners, grant writers, foundation officers, communications directors, credit counselors, social workers, community organizers, executive directors, and many others). Large nonprofits rival large corporations in facilities and resources, but small ones may have limited budgets requiring creativity in management. One example of such an organization is The Brother's Brother Foundation, which shipped over $262 million in medical books, supplies, and shoes around the world at a cost of less than $1 million in 2006. It employs a staff of 10 (Barrett, 2007). The intangible benefits, such as starting a new program, seeing people helped or a problem solved, or seeing a volunteer have a good experience can be rewarding. Volunteering is probably the best way to see what this kind of work is like.

Entrepreneurial Nonprofits

An emerging form of organization is a combination of two listed above. Shuman and Fuller (2005) described it as a form of nonprofit that uses its profits to advance its ideas. For example, the YMCA operates health clubs to support its youth outreach programs. The American Red Cross draws blood and sells it to hospitals and health centers. Goodwill Industries, which describes itself as a social enterprise, raises more than a billion dollars through the collection, refurbishment, and sale of second-hand clothing and household items and another half billion from fees for contracts and services. And many of us have done business with the Girl Scouts, which generates millions from the sale of cookies. Other nonprofits operate all kinds of business enterprises to generate income to further their organizational goals.

Governmental Organizations

Rifkin referred to government as the "public sector" of the economy and indicated that about 14% of economic activity is in this area. Sometimes when we think of government jobs, we think first about federal employment, but there are also 90,000 state and local governments. Indeed, counties, cities, and municipalities have grown significantly. The largest categories of state and local government services involve education, followed by police and fire protection. There are hundreds of agencies, offices, bureaus, departments, and sections in the executive, legislative, and judicial branches at each of the federal, state, and government level, and each of these has its own organizational culture.

Quasi-Governmental Organizations

Quasi means "semi" or "sort of," and this is an apt description for some organizations that receive government funding but are not, strictly speaking, governmental entities. These organizations have boards that are elected by the organization members, and the boards are accountable to the members. However, much of their funding typically comes from governmental organizations (tax revenues). Water management districts in Florida or rural electric cooperatives in Texas are examples of quasi-governmental organizations.

Public schools are in a special category of organization in this regard. Public schools receive most of their funding from local and state taxes, but local school boards and/or local superintendents make many decisions about employment and programs. Public colleges and universities operate in a similar fashion.

Associations

In state capitals and other geographic locations with a high concentration of government agencies, one will typically find the headquarters for hundreds of trade and professional associations. Such groups are a combination of nonprofits and quasi-governmental organizations. They represent their members before the legislature and other governmental boards, and they try to influence laws and public policy in directions that will benefit their members.

For example, Florida has 1,100 associations, not including charitable not-for-profit organizations, with 10,800 jobs. About 500 have headquarters in Tallahassee, the state capitol, where up to 5,400 jobs exist (Hodges, 2009). Managing meetings and conferences, along with setting standards for the profession or industry, is a big part of association work—lobbying is a small part of what they do.

The Yellow Pages include a listing of associations, and you might be surprised to see the names of the organizations appearing there. Our experience is that college students are not familiar with associations as sources of employment. You can also locate information about associations in directories such as the annual *NTPA Directory, 2012* (National Trade and Professional Associations of the United States; Colombia Books, 2012), which provides detailed contact and background information on over 7,800 trade associations, professional societies, technical organizations, and labor unions in the United States, as well as the 20,000 executives who run them. Virtually every product or service available in the economy is supported by an association. Additional information about associations is available from the Center for Association Leadership (http://www.asaecenter.org/).

figure 8.2

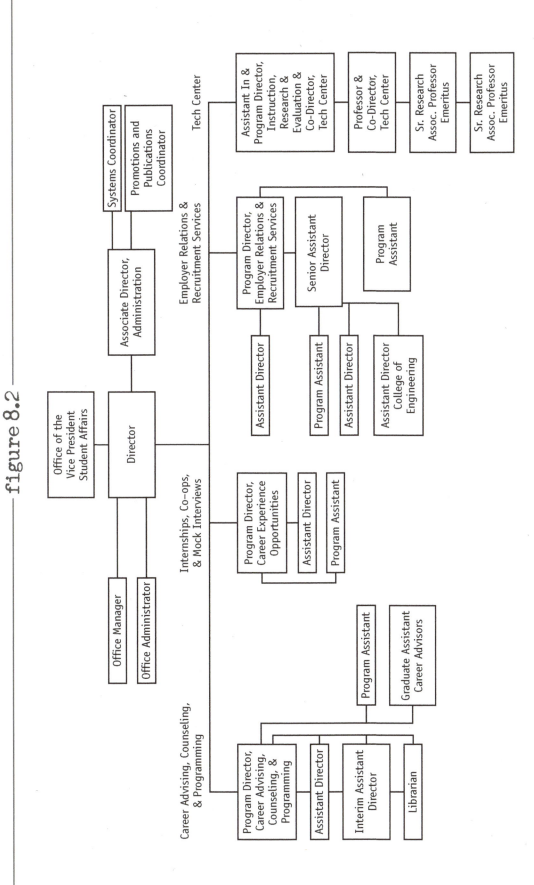

Organizational Chart

Source: Career Center, Florida State University

figure 8.3

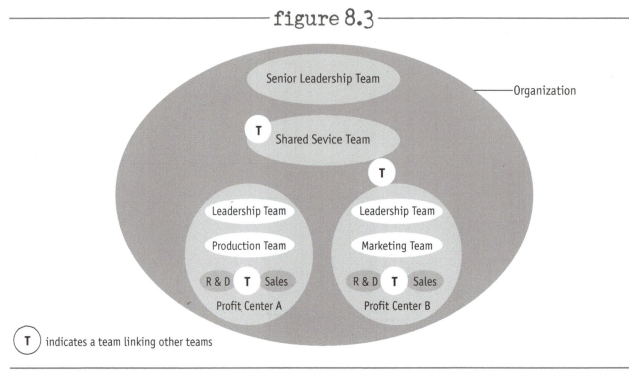

T indicates a team linking other teams

A Team-Based Organization
Source: Career Center, Florida State University

yourself, as you make decisions about organizations in which to work. This is what William Morin meant when he said, "You have to see yourself as a business. *That* is your job."

Workers in these new flat organizations need interpersonal skills (Enterprising and Social types in Holland's terms) that can help them manage conflicts and participate effectively in a team. The irony is that these workers need to make strong commitments, albeit temporary ones, to the work of the organization (including spending extra time completing tasks) and to coworkers, even though the old social contract no longer exists. This is difficult to accomplish and requires new ways of thinking about the relationship of employees to an organization. It represents an unfinished model for what careers will be like in the future.

Leadership in Organizational Development

The founder or founders of a successful organization are the first source of its culture. Organizations are created when founders recognize that a group working together can accomplish more than individuals working alone. An organization's beliefs about its core mission, history, reasons for existence, preferred methods for getting things done, and ideals about how members should treat one another are typically established by the founder(s). The organization's history, as told through personal stories, gossip, documents, and old media reports, are ways in which leaders continue to shape and mold the culture of the organization. Listening to such stories and reading such reports are ways to learn about an organization's culture. We will say more about this in Chapter 15.

Schein (1985) analyzed the close link between organizational culture and leadership. Indeed, he describes organizational leadership as *culture management*. The leader's vision of what the organization should be and do is designed to inspire and guide other members. Sports teams provide a good example of the relationship between organizational culture and leadership. Sports teams have a clear, single purpose—to win games. Winning traditions, hard work, expertise, risk taking, and self-sacrifice are elements of the culture of a successful professional athletic team. However, leadership is also essential. This includes the work of the owner, general manager, head coach, the assistant coaches, the senior members of the team, and the captains who transmit the culture of the team to new members.

Modern organizations are increasingly relying on individual members to provide leadership in work teams, task forces, committees, and other groups. Because organizational leadership is so closely connected to culture, it is important for us to understand these relationships as we assume roles as employees in work organizations. Our personal career development will increasingly be affected by the extent to which we can become effective leaders and managers of the culture in our work settings.

Career Development and Workforce Development

The relationship between the career development of individual employees and the overall development of an organization is a vital one. Indeed, these two factors are often closely linked. An organization can renew itself, change, and grow in new directions through the management and direction of its workers' careers. This is sometimes called *workforce planning,* and it is different from individual career planning, the primary focus of this book. Workforce planning is something that the organization does for itself to make sure it grows properly, whereas career management is something that individuals in an organization do with respect to their interests, values, skills, and goals (Herr, Cramer, & Niles, 2003).

In the past, career development was part of the old social contract between the organization and its employees, but we have learned that this contract model has been broken in many ways. Today, individuals may use career development in the form of organizational programs such as human resources, training and development, supervision, and the organization's career resource center. They can also voluntarily seek lateral moves in the organization to further develop their skills. Of course, the strength of the relationship between career development and organizational development depends on the culture of the organization. Organizations with a culture of *people development* are more likely to have organizational career development programs.

How do organizations get involved in career development? The implementation of a career development program in an organization may take many forms, and there is no one best way for it to occur. Here are some of the most common program activities found in organizations (Greenhaus, Callanan, & Godshalk, 2009; Inkson & Arthur, 2002):

- *Individual career counseling.* This may be provided by professional staff, personnel workers, outside consultants, supervisors, or peers.
- *Group career counseling.* This may take the form of career workshops or special topics seminars on self-assessment, resume writing and interviewing, preretirement, or new employee orientation.
- *Assessment.* This can include job performance appraisals and reviews, self-assessment activities, psychological testing, and assessment center work.
- *Career information.* This could include a career resource center; researching career paths and career ladders in the organization; job posting or bulletin boards, phone message systems, or Web pages; messages about scholarship programs and training/development activities.
- *Training and development.* This can include job enrichment, job rotation, career sabbaticals, tuition reimbursement, in-house training, or external degree programs.
- *Organizational career planning.* This can include the development of labor force projections for the organization and the development of employee skill banks, such as how many employees have data-information management, graphic design, or programming skills.
- *Special programs.* These can include targeted presentations for special groups of employees, minorities, women, people with disabilities, preretirees, plateaued workers, outplaced (fired) workers, young managers, high-performing workers, management trainees, dual-career couples, science/technology workers, and support staff.

In reviewing these career development program activities, you might be surprised to see how many of them are also available in a college career services program. These are things you can learn how to do and participate in while still in college. The existence of a comprehensive, effective career development program might be one of the factors to consider in accepting a job offer from an organization. In researching potential employers, find out what organizations are doing in this area for their workers. If nothing else, it can help you see how your individual career development is linked to the future growth of an organization that might employ you.

A CIP Perspective

Let's review what we have learned about work organizations in light of the CIP Pyramid of Information-Processing Domains and the CASVE Cycle. Use this knowledge to improve the quality of your PCT for solving career problems and making career decisions.

Self-Knowledge

How does information about organizations relate to information about the interests, values, and skills that make up self-knowledge? One thing seems clear—those working in the new kinds of organizations constantly have to cultivate their interests, talents, and skills to enhance person-environment (P-E) matches. These P-E matches, such as those in Holland's RIASEC typology, are no longer stable because organizations are changing. This means that people have to consider making adjustments and compromises in adapting their interests, skills, and values to organizational needs. Moreover, those who value security have been negatively affected by the loss of the old social contract between employers and workers. Individual job security is no longer part of the contract.

We also learned that Holland's Social and Enterprising types, especially the interpersonal, team-building, leadership, and conflict-resolution skills associated with those types, are increasingly valued by organizations. Individuals would do well to enhance their skills in these areas to assure career growth opportunities. In analyzing an organization's culture, individuals first have to assess themselves in terms of preferred supervision and leadership style and the agreement between organizational and personal philosophy and values, among other things. It is out of this improved self-knowledge that one can then more accurately analyze the culture of an organization in making career decisions.

Option Knowledge

Organizational culture is the context in which many of our careers unfold, and our career growth will be related to our ability to understand and effectively act on this knowledge. We know that organizations are increasingly becoming more diverse in terms of worker characteristics, and we will likely find ourselves working in teams with people very much unlike ourselves. Individuals with varied experiences and skills in ethnic and cultural diversity will be sought by organizations.

Increased knowledge about organizations helps us understand the differences between business, government, nonprofit, and other kinds of organizations. All of this information helps us move to more complex schema, beyond just occupations and positions, when thinking about our career options. This kind of thinking helps us improve our PCT.

Finally, we believe it is important to remind ourselves that Holland's environmental typology using the six RIASEC categories can help us understand organizational culture. Indeed, Holland first used RIASEC types to study college and university cultures, and found that a lack of a close match between the student and the environment affected retention. RIASEC theory provides a way to describe organizational cultures or environments as well as personal interests.

Decision Making

Knowledge of organizational culture can have a very important impact on the kinds of educational and career decisions we make. Employment decisions are certainly affected by one's perception of the organizational culture. People have to pay attention to their feelings and instincts as they visit organizations on second and third interviews, and they have to sharpen their skills in reading the signs of organizational culture described in this chapter.

Decisions about career growth are increasingly tied to decisions about the work we want to do in the organization—how we want to retrain ourselves, new skills we want to develop, new roles we want to play in the organization, the option of home-based work. Moreover, these decisions may be related to the matter of remaining with the organization itself or choosing to become an independent contractor who is self-employed.

Executive Processing

Given all these changes in the global economy and organizations, is the idea of "career" now dead? Douglas Hall (1996) a professor of organizational behavior at Boston University who has spent a lifetime studying careers and organizations, believes "career" is still alive.

> The career as we once knew it—as a series of upward moves, with steadily increasing income, power, status, and security—has died. Nevertheless, people will always have work lives that unfold over time, offering challenge, growth, and learning. So if we think of the career as a series of lifelong work-related experiences and personal learnings . . . , it will never die [roman added]. (p. 1)

Hall et al. believe that in the new career, the "notions of caregiving, mentoring, caring and respect, connection, and co-learning (that is, learning through relationship with others), especially co-learning with others with whom one regards as different, provide the clues to growth and success" (p. 4). In this idea of career, personal development becomes a person's most powerful career development tool (p. 265). In CIP terms, this new career schema is based on personal learning and growth. These ideas should be incorporated into your PCT.

In this chapter, we reported Henkoff's (1993) admonition that you have to see yourself as a business in this new organizational culture. In effect, you have to think of yourself as an entrepreneur, even if you work in an organization for someone else. This is a new career metacognition for many, and it will probably add some complexity to your PCT.

We introduced the idea of "employability security," the idea that your career effectiveness is tied to your ability to use a wide variety of skills and to produce value in numerous ways. As long as you keep increasing your skills and knowledge, as well as your ability to use both effectively, you can make yourself employable and can engage in career growth.

Summary

In this chapter, we introduced some of the important ideas associated with organizational behavior, including organizational culture and structure. We believe that organizations provide the context in which much of individual career growth occurs. However, the rapidly changing nature of organizations makes it difficult to adjust career planning accordingly. The implications of emerging trends in organizational life for building your PCT were highlighted throughout this chapter. Finally, we reviewed this new information in light of the cognitive information processing paradigm that undergirds this book.

References

Barrett, W. P. (2007, December 10). Your charity dollars at work. *Forbes*, 180–181.

Deming, W. E. (1986). *Out of crisis*. Cambridge, MA: MIT Press.

Drucker, P. (1993). *Post-capitalist society*. New York, NY: HarperCollins.

Employment Policy Foundation. (2005). *Handbook on 21st century working women*. Washington, DC: Author.

Feller, R., & Whichard, J. (2005). *Knowledge nomads and the nervously employed: Workplace change and courageous choices*. Austin, TX: PRO-ED.

Gottfredson, G., & Holland, J. (1996). *Dictionary of Holland occupation codes* (3rd ed.). Odessa, FL: Psychological Assessment Resources.

Greenhaus, J. H., Callanan, G. A., & Godshalk, V. M. (2009). *Career management* (4th ed.). Thousand Oaks, CA: SAGE.

Gutteridge, T., Leibowitz, Z., & Shore, J. (1993). *Organizational career development*. San Francisco, CA: Jossey-Bass.

Hall, D. T., & Associates. (1996). *The career is dead . . . long live the career*. San Francisco, CA: Jossey-Bass.

Henkoff, R. (1993, July). Winning the new career game. *Fortune*, 46.

Herr, E. L., Cramer, S. H., & Niles, S. G. (2003). *Career guidance and counseling through the lifespan: Systematic approaches* (6th ed.). Boston, MA: Allyn & Bacon.

Hodges, D. (2009, July 5). Association leaders mark 50 years. *Tallahassee Democrat*, 8A.

Hofstede, G. (1984). *Culture's consequences: International differences in work-related values*. Beverly Hills, CA: SAGE.

Holland, J. L. (1997). *Making vocational choices: A theory of vocational personalities and work environments*. Odessa, FL: Psychological Assessment Resources.

Howard, A. (Ed.) (1995). *The changing nature of work*. San Francisco, CA: Jossey-Bass.

Inkson, K., & Arthur, M. B. (2002). Career development: Extending the "organizational careers" framework. In S. G. Niles (Ed.), *Adult career development: Concepts, issues, and practices* (3rd ed., pp. 285–304). Tulsa, OK: National Career Development Association.

Mohrman, S. A., & Cohen, S. G. (1995). When people get out of the box: New relationships, new systems (pp. 365–410). In A. Howard (Ed.), *The changing nature of work*. San Francisco, CA: Jossey-Bass.

Reich, R. (1992). *The work of nations*. New York, NY: Vintage Books.

Rifkin, J. (1995). *The end of work*. New York, NY: Putnam's Sons.

Sandroff, R. (July, 1993). The psychology of change. *Working Woman*, 52–56.

Schein, E. (1985). *Organizational culture and leadership*. San Francisco, CA: Jossey-Bass.

Sheridan, V. S., Qureshi, M. W., Slife C., & Epstein, D. (Eds.). (2012). *National trade and professional association directory*. New York, NY: Columbia Books.

Shuman, M. H., & Fuller, M. (2005, Jan. 24). Profits for justice. *Nation*, 13–22.

Toossi, M. (2012, January). Labor force projections to 2020: A more slowly growing workforce. *Monthly Labor Review*, 43–64.

Wenger, E. C., & Snyder, W. M. (2000, January). Communities of practice: The organizational frontier. *Harvard Business Review, 78*, 139–146.

White, E. (2005, March 29). Savviest job hunters research the cultures of potential employers. *Wall Street Journal*, B1.

Chapter Nine

Alternative Ways to Work

The emerging global economy, the increased use of technology, and changes in organizational culture and structure are having profound impacts on the way we work in the United States. If you consider regular, permanent jobs the crystal vase that has been knocked off the table by the cat, the new ways to work are the little pieces of the broken vase.

Our individual places of employment are increasingly linked by communication networks to other work sites around the world. People in business may be pursuing markets for products and services in several different nations. Moreover, the teams in which we work today have changed job descriptions in many ways. The focus in this chapter is on how the forces reviewed in Chapters 7 and 8 have altered the ways we work. A good understanding of this issue will help you develop new, more complex schema related to career planning and employment and help you improve the quality of your Personal Career Theory (PCT).

Here are the topics we will cover in this chapter:

- The nature of *job creation*. Why are the forms of employment changing?
- *Alternative ways to work* and the growing *contingent workforce*, including the various kinds of employment options associated with it
- The *social forces* that are influencing regular and contingent jobs and how all of this is affecting *retirement*
- *Problems* associated with these new ways of working
- We will conclude with a cognitive information processing (CIP) perspective and a summary.

As you read about these alternative ways to work, try to think about how your PCT and strategic career thinking can be improved by this information. How will this information affect occupations you are interested in, and how will it affect the ways you might think about working. In what kind of job will you work? How will this new way of working differ from what you have thought about in the past?

Job Creation

Where do jobs come from? Before looking at the alternative ways in which we work, it is probably useful to take a few minutes to think about why and how jobs are created. What events or factors lead employers to create jobs? (You might want to review the definitions of *job* and *position* in Chapter 1.)

Sar Levitan and Clifford Johnson (1982), the economists who wrote *Second Thoughts on Work*, explained that jobs are created by the public's desire for goods or services. In effect, jobs are the outcomes of our consumer wants rather than our needs. When we want more clothes, cars, college degrees, elder care, or child care, people who provide these things take the necessary steps to produce more of them. Producing more can be accomplished in two basic ways. The providers can either have the present workers do more, by working more hours or days each week, or the providers can hire more workers by creating new jobs. Of course, when these wants decrease, jobs are lost as providers cut back on production.

Net job increases in the economy are created by small start-up companies and entrepreneurs (Samuelson, 2010). There are 500,000 new start-ups every year, though half of them fail within five years. Many of these businesses provide highly specialized goods and services (e.g., restaurants, auto-repair shops) and are a major source of *new* jobs.

In an effort to control labor costs, organizations have resorted to many new schemes to meet the public's increased wants and to increase the production of goods and services. Among other things, organizations are using contingent workers, who may be likened to rented furniture or a leased automobile. In effect, they are disposable, and employers have no obligation beyond paying the salary. This is a new way of working in America because in the past we believed that when profits and demand were up, the "good jobs" would return. Now we are moving to "just-in-time" employment as well as "just-in-time" manufacturing.

There are many alternatives to permanent, full-time positions. As you read about these different ways of working, think about your occupational and employment goals and how they might be affected by this information.

Alternative Ways to Work

At the outset, it should be noted that Americans work very hard. They have the fewest guaranteed vacation days of any industrialized country, work more weeks per year than any country besides Japan, work more hours annually than any other Western nation, and are the most productive in the world (Begala, 2011). The average American works 1,804 hours per year, or 45.1 weeks at 40 hours per week. College students should be aware of these facts regarding the U.S. workforce as they prepare to join it.

Permanent Full-Time Positions

The most common way of working is 40 hours per week in a regular, permanent job. However, given all that is happening in the economy, it seems a little awkward to talk about "permanent" jobs. For example, Farber (2006) reported a decrease in long-term employment relationships and an increase in "churning," the proportion of workers in jobs with less than one year of tenure. Compared to their parents, new hires are not likely to have a "lifetime" job with a single employer. Sounding a similar note, Kallenberg (2009) described work as a core activity in society that links people to one another and their place in the community, but at the same time he noted that the world is in a transition situation with the rise of "precarious work," defined as "employment that is uncertain, unpredictable, and risky from the point of view of the worker" (p. 2).

Historically, however, the general view was that permanent positions were filled for life, unless the employee really messed up or chose to leave the organization. Although jobs are no longer as permanent as they were before, these kinds of positions for core workers still make up the backbone of most organizations. In Chapter 8, we saw the new diamond-shaped work organizations and saw that core employees make up between 50 and 80% of the workers in these emerging organizations.

Employees in permanent positions work directly for the organization. Permanent employees typically have full benefits, such as health insurance, child care services, and retirement programs.

These employees may also have certain protections with respect to layoffs: they are last to be fired, and their salaries are drawn from more secure funds within the organization. In organizational charts, these positions are in boxes, and there are lines showing relationships to other positions in the organization.

Permanent employees are not typically thought of as part of the contingent workforce, which we will examine later in this chapter. In recent years, organizations have begun to experiment with programs to provide more flexible arrangements for work by people in permanent positions.

Part-Time

Part-time work is defined as 1 to 34 hours per week; it involved 25 million workers in 2006 (Torpey, 2007). This is the most widely used alternative way to work, and it is increasing relative to other kinds of part-time workers. Part-time work is an easy tool for employers to use in making workforce adjustments to accommodate shifting customer demands, and it is desirable to workers who have personal responsibilities away from the job site. A part-time job has the advantage of a regular paycheck, but it may not include benefits such as health insurance.

When you study an organization as your possible employer, it might be helpful to know how many workers are part-time, particularly in an area where you would be working. Also, because it is so widespread, it might be a way to begin working for an organization you're interested in; some organizations use part-time work to screen for full-time workers.

Flextime, Compressed Workweeks, or Comp Time

Flexible scheduling, or flextime, is also widely practiced in organizations. One of the most common practices involves permitting employees to set their work schedules.

There are many ways to "flex," including the following:

1. Working 4 days a week at 10 hours per day (sometimes called a "compressed week")
2. Working from 6:30 a.m. to 3:30 p.m.
3. Taking a half-hour for lunch
4. Working longer hours on some days and a half day on others
5. Working Saturdays and Sundays

Organizations offer such flextime arrangements to help employees meet family obligations and schedule medical care, among other reasons. However, an organization might have a policy that requires all employees to be available from 9 a.m. to 3 p.m. weekdays, for example, or on all Mondays. Local communities like flextime because it reduces traffic at peak hours and places fewer strains on the community infrastructure. An organization's approach to flextime might also reveal something about its culture regarding alternative ways to work.

Another approach to flextime involves the compressed workweek, or working more hours on some days in order to have some days off. For example, a person might work 1 extra hour for 9 days in a 10-day work period, and then take every other Friday off. Related to this is compensatory time off, or "comp time," which means that the hours worked beyond what is required can be accumulated and used later for a vacation.

Overtime

Before discussing overtime work, it might be useful to distinguish between hourly and salaried employees in an organization. Hourly workers typically include blue-collar workers and clerical staff whose work arrangements may be covered by labor union work rules. Their basic way of working is controlled by a time sheet or clock. (In some organizations, certain managers and professional staff may also be hourly workers.) Hourly workers are sometimes called nonexempt or included, meaning that they must conform to federal wage and hour laws, or they are included in a collective bargaining agreement with a union. These workers are protected from abuse by employers, and any work beyond the maximum of 40 hours per week must meet certain requirements, including higher pay.

On the other hand, exempt employees, including most senior managers and professional staff, are not limited to 40 hours of work per week. Indeed, in some organizations such workers may spend up to 60 hours working at their job, at home and/or at the work site.

As we noted earlier, organizations have an option to meet the increased demands for goods and services by having employees work more hours or days—to work overtime. Hetrick (2000) noted that, not surprisingly, when the U.S. economy experiences growth, particularly coming out of a recession, there is a parallel rise in overtime. Many people who work in hourly jobs are regularly faced with a dilemma when employers want them to work more hours each week, because these extra hours cut into time available for spouse/partner relationships, family activities, or leisure pursuits. Refusing overtime work, however, can be interpreted by employers as poor commitment to the organization or lack of interest in the job.

Dr. Arlie Hochschild (1997), who studied a large U.S. company, found that although most workers *said* they wanted more time away from their jobs, they most often *chose* to spend more time on the job, working overtime. (This might have been an instance of workers *saying* what they *wanted* and *choosing* what they *needed*.) A similar thing happens with exempt employees, the senior executives and managers. We will return to some of the reasons for this apparent contradiction in Chapter 10.

When you research an organization, learning about the numbers of employees working overtime and how many hours managers and professional staff work each week can provide insights about the organization's culture.

Shift Work

The shift to lean production and just-in-time production has caused some organizations to move to 24-hour work schedules. The "graveyard shift" was typically limited to blue-collar workers and hospital staff, but this has changed. Nowadays, college graduates will likely do some shift work in their careers. For example, banks and other business organizations may need to operate on a 24-hour basis because what happens in Tokyo financial markets at 2 a.m. Eastern time in the U.S. may require immediate action in New York. Shift work includes night, evening, and weekend work.

Presser and Ward (2011) found that high percentages of Americans work nonstandard schedules over the course of their work life. For example, almost 90% of workers aged 14–18 in 1979 had at least one such experience by age 39. One in five employed Americans work mostly in the evening, at night, or on a rotating shift. Moreover, one third of all dual-earner families with children include at least one spouse working one of these shifts. There are many issues associated with working at nonstandard times, including the health and safety of shift workers and their families.

Moonlighting or Multiple Jobholding

The Bureau of Labor Statistics (Hipple, 2010) reported that in 2009, 5.2% of all U.S. workers (7.3 million people) had multiple jobs. The rate of moonlighting is higher for women than for men, and the incidence increases as workers achieve higher levels of education (7% for those with graduate degrees moonlight). This form of contingent work has remained relatively stable since the mid-1990s. Moonlighting can take several forms, including (a) holding two part-time jobs, (b) working a part-time job in addition to a full-time job, or (c) working more than one full-time job.

Moonlighting can be a person's best option for making more money, learning a new job, or taking care of family members. However, it can also be an indication of financial stress, a poor-quality job market, and high costs of work.

Job Sharing

Job sharing is an alternative to full-time, regular work, although the Bureau of Labor Statistics does not keep track of this kind of part-time work. It occurs when a single job is shared by two people. Given a regular full-time position of 40 hours per week, each person in the job share typically works 20 hours per week at separate times, although they probably share two or three hours of time on the job each week for joint meetings with supervisors and other staff members. Like other part-time work, there can be several advantages to job sharing. For instance, it can enable a worker to:

- handle childcare or eldercare responsibilities that would be impossible when working 40 hours per week;
- complete a degree more quickly by taking additional classes during regular work hours;
- pursue leisure or entrepreneurial interests that are difficult to handle while working full-time;
- maintain insurance and other benefits available in the regular full-time position; and/or
- reduce stress and time pressures related to job and family conflicts.

From an organizational perspective, job sharing may provide a way to retain highly valued employees by accommodating their changed life situations. It also provides opportunities for more flexible staffing arrangements. However, people participating in job sharing have to work closely with their partners, communicate effectively about work projects so these are completed properly, and be flexible about making necessary adjustments to work schedules.

Telecommuting

Telecommuting, flexiplacing, or telework is an alternative way of working that appears to be growing rapidly, and it can be either for someone else or for oneself. It involves working from a site remote from the office or the employer's workplace. Home-based work is the most common arrangement (Mariani, 2000), although not all home-based workers telecommute. Telecommuting could be done wherever one has access to the Internet (e.g., in a plane, train, cab, telecenter, coffee shop, virtual office, or hotel room). This way of working has been most clearly influenced by technology (e.g., notebook computers, smartphones, the Internet, e-mail). Bureau of Labor Statistics data show that about 13.7 million people worked at home for an employer at least once a week in 2004 (Torpey, 2007). However, only about 25% had a formal arrangement to do this and many people spend less than 15 hours per week doing it. Less than 1% of wage and salary workers, about 575,000, work entirely at home.

Godinez (2003) reported that employers want independent workers who are paid by the assignment, and advances in technology make it possible for workers to have fully functioning home offices. In addition, some young professionals got their start during the technology boom in the 1990s, which makes them confident enough to telecommute. Technological innovations such as desktop videoconferencing, expanded Integrated Services Digital Network (ISDN) lines, and expanded videoconferencing sites in places like FedEx Kinko's Copy stores make it more cost effective for organizations to include more workers in telecommuting programs.

Telecommuting can ease problems in managing home and job responsibilities by providing more flexible time. Telecommuters reporting satisfying arrangements worked roughly half-office and half-home, which provides workers with opportunities for "face-time" in the office, as well as flexible control over daily schedules, particularly in meeting family needs. This new way of working places a premium on self-motivation and independence; an ability to avoid distractions in the home; the ability to effectively use, even rely on, technology; and willingness to be left out of informal office communication loops. Most telecommuters have a set of rules for the family, meaning that when they're in the office with the door shut, no one is allowed to interrupt them; otherwise, they can find it very difficult to separate work from personal life (McChristy, 2002).

However, there can be problems in communication and team building when workers seldom see each other face to face. Other problems involve liability insurance for injuries sustained from working at home. And there can be personal costs for the worker if the employer does not pay for the computer equipment, phone lines, insurance, training, and other expenses associated with maintaining a home office.

Reports indicate that some organizations do not have formal policies about telecommuting, so this is an area to explore with potential employers. An analysis of 46 studies involving 12,883 employees by Gajendran and Harrison (2007) provided some encouraging information about this way of working. They found that telecommuting had small but beneficial effects on work outcomes such as a higher sense of autonomy, lower work-family conflict, more job satisfaction, and less stress. In addition, it had no negative effect on workplace relationships unless it was more than 2.5 days per week. Effective human resource management policies would be important in minimizing any negative consequences. This is apparently a rapidly growing way to work that many college graduates will encounter.

Bringing Work Home

About 8% of workers bring work home, mostly to finish a project or catch up. Those who bring work home do work more, on average, than those who work only out of the workplace. Eldridge and Pabilonia (2010) reported that unpaid work at home is positively related to level of education, the absence of overtime rates, and being a team leader. Other studies have found that bringing work home was more common than working exclusively from home, and typically involved two hours per day in the evenings or on weekends.

Self-Employment and Independent Contracting (Including Freelancing and Consulting)

SELF-EMPLOYMENT. This is an important source of jobs in the U.S. In 2009, for example, 15.3 million people were self-employed, including both those who had incorporated their business and those who had not (Hipple, 2010). (It should be noted that the former are technically working for a wage and salary for their business and are thus employed by an organization.) This means that 10.9% of total employment was made up of self-employed people, and two thirds of them were not incorporated. Previously, self-employed workers were mostly white, older men, but in recent years there has been an increase in the number of self-employed women and minorities. According to the National Association of Women Business Owners (http://nawbo.org), women-owned businesses are the fastest growing segment of the economy.

As "traditional" full-time work options have become less available, many individuals, including recent college graduates, have considered the option of self-employment or starting a business. In addition, easier access to technology has provided a means for individuals to create Web-based businesses and take part in the e-commerce revolution. The U.S. Department of Commerce reported that from 2002 to 2009, retail e-sales increased at an average annual growth rate of 18.1%, compared with 2.2% for total retail sales (www.census.gov/econ/estats/2009/2009reportfinal.pdf).

As we noted earlier in this chapter, many of these businesses fail within a few years, so anyone who decides to pursue this path would be well advised to take advantage of the many resources available to those planning to start a business. The U.S. Government Small Business Administration (SBA; www.sba.gov) includes a wide variety of resources on its Web site, including a list of 20 important questions to ask yourself if you dream of starting a business (www.sba.gov/content/20-questions-before-starting-business). In addition to SBA's information, many states have centers designed to support individuals who want to start or own a business. One example is the Florida Small Business Development Center Network (http://floridasbdc.org/main.php). These organizations provide advice, training, help with developing a business plan, and related services. *Inc.* magazine (http://www.inc.com/), available both online and in print, has for many years been a valuable source of information to individuals who are considering self-employment. Although self-employment or small business ownership may not be for everyone, it will likely continue to provide one path to the "American dream" for a select number of individuals.

INDEPENDENT CONTRACTORS. A worker in this category is defined as someone who obtains customers on his or her own. In 2005, independent contractors accounted for more than 7% of all workers (10.3 million) (Torpey, 2007). They were also more likely to work part-time and hold managerial, professional, sales, or precision production jobs. Dan Pink further examined this trend in his book *Free Agent Nation* (2001), and he suggested that tens of millions of Americans have taken on this role. In some cases, there is confusion about whether a worker is an employee or an independent contractor. The Internal Revenue Service's Web site (www.irs.gov) has information on distinguishing between an employee and independent contractor. Some of the points of distinction are shown in Table 9.1.

Table 9.1

Distinguishing between Employees and Independent Contractors

Employee	Independent Contractor
May be trained to work in a certain way	Receives no training
Hired, supervised, paid by employer	May hire, supervise, pay others
Relationships continue beyond specific tasks	Relationships limited to completion of tasks
Hours set by employer	Hours set by the worker
Work times specified by employer	Work when and for whom they choose
Paid by the hour/week/month	Paid by the job or commission
Materials & equipment furnished by employer	Supply their own materials, equipment
Do not make profits or losses	Can make profits or incur losses
May be fired by the employer	Cannot be fired as long as contract details are met
Can quit job at any time	Cannot quit until job is satisfactorily completed or restitution provided

Source: Internal Revenue Service

Because about 7% of the workforce is self-described as independent contractors, including freelancing and consulting, and because many of these workers are in the services industry, college graduates are likely to find increasing opportunities in this way of working. Several years ago, one state social services administrator reported to a college class that independent contractors were replacing state employees for certain services (i.e., social workers and rehabilitation counselors). Thinking of oneself as a self-employed contractor is an increasingly common way to view work or one's relationship to an employer. Also, it is important when talking with employers about jobs that the nature of the work relationship is clear—will you be an employee or an independent contractor?

These new ways of working represent a complex set of arrangements for thinking about jobs, and it is important for job hunters to develop useful schema for thinking about these aspects of employment knowledge. This information helps you improve the quality of your PCT. Knowledge about these employment options can be of critical importance in your strategic career planning.

The Contingent Workforce

The Bureau of Labor Statistics categorizes the area of contingent work as the *personnel supply services industry*, which as we learned in Chapter 7 is one of the fastest growing areas of the economy.

The American Staffing Association reports that 2.5 million people are employed by staffing companies daily, and 79% work full time (the same as the rest of the workforce). Moreover, 9.7 million temporary and contract employees are hired by staffing firms each year (http://www.american staffing.net/statistics/pdf/staffing_facts.pdf). These workers once did low-level clerical work, but the demand for temporary workers in managerial, professional, and technical occupations is strongest in industries such as financial services, health care, telecommunications, and information technology. This area of labor force information is turbulent today, because new work arrangements and programs are being created on a continuing basis.

We will now discuss recent developments and the employment options that are open to you. We will also define the terms used in this area, such as *outsourcing*, *employee leasing*, *temporary services*, *interim* or *on-call workers*, *interns* and *co-ops*, and compare and contrast them where appropriate. See Table 9.2 for a sample list of terms associated with contingent workers.

Table 9.2

Employment Terms Associated with Contingent Workers

Process Terms	Job Titles
Employee leasing	Consulting workers or consultants
Temporary services	Temporary staff, temporaries, temps
Contract employment	Interns, co-ops
Self-employment	Co-employees
Freelancing	Interim staff
Flexible staffing	Short-timers, per-diem workers
Outsourcing	Subcontractors or independent contractors
Other professional services (OPS)	Flexible staff
	On-call workers

The likelihood is increasing that entry-level jobs will be contingent work. The word *contingent* refers to uncertainty, possibility, chance, unforeseen conditions, dependent, conditional, and unpredictable. When these words are added to work, a picture emerges of what is meant by *contingent workforce*. The Bureau of Labor Statistics defines contingent workers as those "who do not have an implicit or explicit contract for ongoing employment." (U.S. Department of Labor, 2001, 59).

Until recently, organizations used contingency workers primarily to fill in for employees who were absent, fired, or on maternity leave, but contingent workers are now part of the culture in many organizations. The work of contingent workers is uncertain, unplanned, and dependent on changing conditions and employer's immediate needs. It is work that is not expected to last longer than a year. This is the increasing nature of work being done in the United States and throughout the world today.

Many organizations want a specified number of workers for a specified time and project, and when that need passes the workers become an unneeded expense. In Chapter 7, we introduced the idea of "just-in-time-production," and this idea has now been transferred to "just-in-time-employment." This is the nature of the contingent workforce in the U.S. economy.

How did this situation develop? In Chapters 7 and 8 we outlined how the emerging global economy and the increased use of technology has affected organizations. As organizations have re-engineered and restructured themselves, the result has been downsizing, or a reduction in the number of employees working in the organization. There are many different terms used to describe this downsizing process (see Table 9.3). This is how organizations have become "leaner" (Rifkin, 1995). Unfortunately, it is likely that many workers in the future will be labeled with one of these terms more than once during their career.

Table 9.3

Common Terms Associated with Loss of Employment

Fired (the original term)	Outplaced
Dehired (the "cute" term)	Pink-slipped
Displaced	Reduced (in force)
Downsized	Riffed
Excessed	Right-sized
Laid-off	Terminated (sounds so permanent)
Curtailed	Surplused
Discharged	Dismissed
Redundant	Laid-off
Sacked	Canned

Outsourcing

As organizations have laid off regular, permanent employees, they have contracted with other companies to do the work previously done by those laid off. The "new" workers are hired on a contingency basis and are called contingent workers. A good example is cleaning and janitorial services, which we examined in Chapter 8. Let's say Dollar Down Securities fired its janitorial staff, then turned around and contracted with ServiceMaster to clean its buildings. It is possible that the same people would continue doing the work in the same buildings, but they would now be working for a different employer. Every kind of job is affected by growth in the contingent workforce—hourly jobs, technical jobs, and top professional positions. Organizations call this *outsourcing*.

Using our janitorial example, outsourcing cleaning and janitorial services would enable Dollar Down Securities to save money on health insurance, payroll taxes, and retirement benefits. These costs might be taken over by ServiceMaster. The trend toward outsourcing has exploded, and many other functions previously thought to be core internal elements of an organization are now contracted outside. This can include all personnel and staffing services, accounting and financial services, research and development, legal services, and marketing. In the case of personnel, for example, a firm specializing in this area would conduct employee performance reviews, health care and retirement benefits administration, training and development, and new employee recruiting and orientation, for a fee to the client.

What does this trend toward outsourcing mean for workers? The good news is that the work or job is still there, but the employer may change. The bad news is that the work or job may change more quickly, and workers will have to be flexible and change their expectations about the nature of employment arrangements—their positions are less permanent because an organization may choose to outsource. It also makes it difficult to know how to seek employment in such an organization because it is unclear exactly who is employing the workers.

Employee Leasing

In this outsourcing arrangement, an organization fires its employees and then hires a leasing firm to take over the personnel administration using the same employees. Sometimes this is called a master vendoring partnership, co-employment, or managed staffing. This administrative work includes employee records, insurance and benefits programs, payroll, government reporting, hiring/firing, taxes, and workers' compensation. The leasing company then leases the employees back to the original organization. This program can make it easier for an organization to remove ineffective workers and to avoid costly litigation and training activities. The leasing company now handles these functions.

It is unclear what benefits might come to the workers in this kind of arrangement, other than the fact that specialists handle personnel matters. Indeed, staff leasing is invisible to most workers (Miracle, 1995). Job application procedures might also be complicated because the company that you want to work for is leasing its employees from another employer, and it is unclear for whom you would actually work.

Temporary Services

One of the most common types of outsourcing or contingency work is through temporary employees, or "temps." The growing staffing services industry (discussed in Chapter 7) makes extensive use of part-time workers and temps. Temps are defined as contingent workers when they do not expect to stay with their current employer for more than one year or the job has a specified ending date.

An important distinction should be made here regarding temporary employment and working for a temp agency. If one has continuing employment with a temporary services company, then the work is permanent, not temporary or contingent (Polivka, 1996). This means that one can have permanent employment with a temp agency. This gets confusing, but it is an important point to remember when developing new schema for new ways to work.

A person doing temporary work is known as an *employee* or a *contractor*, and the temporary help organization is known as the *employer*. The organization for whom temporary employment services are being provided is known as the *client*. In our example, Dollar Down Securities is the client and ServiceMaster is the janitorial staff employer. These staffing services are provided at no charge to the employee; the client pays the employer for these services.

In contrast, it might be noted that private employment agencies, who act as your agent in helping you find employment, do not hire you as a contingent employee. In this regard they are different from temporary services. Also, private employment agencies may charge a fee to job hunters, but temp agencies do not. Public (government) employment services also do not charge job hunters a fee.

It is important to understand the schema related to temp work—to know which is the employer, the client, and the employee. Effective use of these terms is important in researching organizations, applying for jobs, and understanding the work culture of an organization.

Temp work once targeted assembly-line and clerical workers, but today lawyers, accountants, engineers, scientists, and other professionals make up the fastest growing segment of the temporary work force and a third of employees in staffing services companies. The vast majority of temp employees work about 40 hours per week. Hourly wages are higher for temps, but this may be offset by reduced benefits.

In spite of the numbers of workers involved, temporary services companies, now called staffing companies, are big business. Here are some facts:

- ManpowerGroup (formerly Manpower Inc.) is a world leader in the employment services industry. Based in Milwaukee, Wisconsin, ManpowerGroup has over 3,900 offices in 82 countries. In 2010, ManpowerGroup's total sales equaled U.S. $19 billion worldwide, with 65% of revenues coming from Europe. ManpowerGroup's customer base, which stands at approximately 400,000 companies each year, includes many multinational corporations. The number of direct staff in ManpowerGroup is estimated at more than 30,000, and the agency employs more than 4.4 million workers each year. ManpowerGroup is currently number 138 on the Fortune 500 list of American companies (http://www.manpowergroup.com).

- Manpower, like other staffing companies, is constantly training its employees to learn something new and different and to obtain more work-related experience. Such organizations are a major source of corporate training today.

- Besides ManpowerGroup, there are more than 140 national staffing companies with over 15,000 offices, including, Adecco, Interim, Kelly Services, Office Team, Spherion, and Olsten Corporation. The American Staffing Association, http://americanstaffing.net, provides information about this industry.

Many college students already have experience working with a temporary services organization, perhaps in retail or office staffing. They will want to watch the staffing services industry closely, because a temporary staffing company may become a viable method for finding professional employment in the future.

Eve Broudy (1989) offered some advantages in temping for professionals, including mobility, flexibility, and visibility. *Mobility* is a way to sustain career growth while being moved from one organization (or place) to another. It is a way to stay active, occupied, and working while looking for a more permanent position. *Flexibility*, Broudy indicated, applies to temp work in numerous ways. For example, it provides a tryout work experience without a long-term commitment. It can also provide opportunities for part-time work while a person is making a career change. Moreover, it safeguards an employee from getting stuck with a nasty boss or work situation—it puts the employee in control. *Visibility* pertains to keeping oneself exposed to potential employers and maintaining opportunities to network in one's area of interest. Being "invisible" provides a sure guarantee for career stagnation, and temping can be an antidote for this.

Temporary workers are increasingly being used by organizations as a pool for finding permanent employees. This is called a "buyout" or "temp-to-hire," meaning a change from temporary to permanent employment status. The American Staffing Association reported that 72% of temporary employees obtained permanent jobs while working for a staffing company. When organizations create new full-time jobs, they often first look inside to part-time workers or temporary staff to fill the position. This is why 75% of jobs are never advertised. An organization looking for permanent employees may first look at temps to fill the positions, even though it may have to pay a fee to the temporary services company if it hires the temp.

Staffing companies can be like a career lifeline. They promote your interests, seek to find work for you, and handle all the paperwork associated with your employment. One accepts interim jobs not intending to stay in them on a permanent basis. A staffing company determines one's interests, skills, and career goals, as well as the hours available to work, to make a good match with a client. As the employer, it is essential to the effectiveness of the staffing services business that the employee and client find the job placement a mutually beneficial one. In this way, the temp employer can expect to obtain repeat orders from the client. In Chapter 11, we will examine some of Broudy's suggestions for deciding on a temporary service company.

So what does all this information about the temporary staffing services industry mean to you?

- *First, you should realize that temporary and staffing services companies might be good organizations to use in launching a career. These organizations will represent you, coach you, and train you for various kinds of jobs. They will help you network in your field of interest and get needed initial job experience.*
- *Second, because some organizations use temps as a way to screen for regular, permanent positions, signing with a temp agency may be an avenue to full-time employment.*
- *Third, job hunters should sign up with more than one temporary service company, because these employers have staffing contracts with different clients.*
- *Finally, college students should realize that they will probably find themselves unemployed during their careers, and temporary services employers can provide a means for returning to the workforce.*

Internships and Co-ops

Internships and cooperative-education programs provide a specialized kind of contingent work for college students because the person participates in the program as a student. In an internship or co-op position, a student provides services to an organization related to the student's field of study or career goals. In this situation, the internship or cooperative education office functions like a temporary services agency, and the organization is the client. Clients have "positions" available for interns that provide their organization with an opportunity to observe the intern/employee as a potential permanent employee. Like other kinds of temporary positions, these internship positions may also provide students with career mobility, flexibility, experience, and visibility.

DEFINED. The National Association of Colleges and Employers (NACE; 2010) clarified the meaning of "internships," given that the Fair Labor Standards Act (wage and hour law) requires employers to pay at least minimum wage to employees. NACE cited U.S. Department of Labor (DOL) criteria for determining when a learner/trainee may be unpaid:

1. The training is similar to that provided in a vocational school.
2. The training is for the benefit of the student.
3. The student does not replace a regular employee but works under the close supervision of one.
4. The employer provides the training and derives no immediate benefit from the student's activities.
5. The student is not necessarily entitled to a job after the training period.
6. The employer and student understand that the student is not entitled to wages for time spent training.

Therefore, an internship should exist mostly for the benefit of the student as a learner—it is not a job.

Is an unpaid intern the same as a volunteer? DOL regulations define a "volunteer" as one who provides services to a public agency for civic, charitable, or humanitarian reasons without promise or expectation of compensation for services rendered (National Association of Colleges and Employers, 2010). Thus, private sector business internships would not be considered volunteer positions.

RECRUITING. Organizations are increasingly looking at interns when recruiting students for full-time, permanent positions. Indeed, Koc (2010) reported that the percentage of overall college hires that have internship experience has increased from 30% in 2006 to 35% in 2009. They like to "test-drive" their job candidates before offering permanent employment. Data on the conversion of interns to full-time hires has been collected by NACE for a number of years. The conversion rate in 2001 was 35.6% and reached 56.6% in 2009. This is evidence of the change in organization's recruiting college student interns for permanent jobs. More information can be obtained about cooperative education from a college career center and the Cooperative Education and Internship Association (CEIA; http://www.ceiainc.org/).

HIGH STAKES. The Collegiate Employment Research Institute (CERI, 2011) at Michigan State University suggested that the internship is increasingly replacing the first job as the place where college students begin the workplace journey. The internship, therefore, is increasingly a *high-stakes event* for both the student and the organization because of its impact on employment. However, CERI indicated that not all internships are the same; only those where the student has carefully considered his or her interests, skills, and values in light of future employment options, and managers have carefully designed internships of strategic importance to the organization, meet the high stakes criteria. Internships that required little preparation by students or employers and were primarily exploratory are not high stakes in nature, and the same applies to the typical internship where both parties have only invested a modest effort in the internship program.

CAUTIONS. Notwithstanding the allure of internships, Jean Chatzky (2011) argued that the high student demand for internships translates into a lot of free labor for organizations because nearly half the 2011 graduates were not paid for their work. In addition, an internship that carries academic credit requires a tuition payment, an additional cost for a student's free work. And there is the added cost of housing and transportation if the internship requires relocation.

Our suggestion is that students work closely with their college career center or internship office to make sure an internship is a good investment in both their education and career preparation.

What about Retirement?

We have been reviewing alternative ways of working, and they all have implications for retirement planning. In Chapter 1, we described the three boxes of life—education, work, and leisure (or retirement)—and noted that things no longer operate that way in our society because these three phases of life have merged and do not flow in that prescribed order.

In many ways, our current view of "retirement" is a new phenomenon. Generations ago, and in many parts of the world today, people just died—retirement wasn't an option. Today, millions of Americans are working at age 70, 80, and even 90 because of financial fears (Fleck, 2009). Although Social Security records indicate that, on average, Americans claim benefits at 63.9 years of age, the percentage of workers over 65 is increasing faster than any other age group, as we learned in Chapter 7.

The options for flexible work, a national health care system, and other social policy matters will shape the options that today's college students have in retirement, and current retirees will show the way. Organizations such as Encore Careers (www.encore.org/) indicate that by 2018 there will be more positions than workers to fill them. Moreover, workers over 55 will be able to pursue these jobs. Those on the leading edge of the current generation of baby boomers are pioneers in a new stage spanning the decades between middle and later life. This underscores the importance of viewing career planning as a lifelong endeavor, as we have emphasized in this text.

Problem Areas

People with alternative work arrangements have varied reactions to their situations. Some would prefer more traditional arrangements and others are quite satisfied. Among independent contractors, on-call workers, and temp agency workers, the latter are least satisfied with alternative work arrangements (Bureau of Labor Statistics, 2005).

Independent contractors may be abused by employers in several ways. For example, they may work next to permanent employees, doing the same job but not getting benefits or unemployment compensation. In effect, they are doing the same job for much less pay. A review of some of the topics in Table 9.1 can help determine whether one is truly an independent contractor or an employee. Employers may be breaking federal and state laws by categorizing workers as independent contractors when they are not.

A CIP Perspective

In this chapter, we have examined information related to the emerging new ways of working in the U.S. labor market. Along the way we have focused on alternative ways of working and the rise of the contingent labor force. Now we want to review briefly what we have learned by examining it in light of the Pyramid of Information-Processing Domains and the CASVE Cycle. *Our goal is to help you improve the relevance and quality of your PCT for solving career problems and making career decisions.*

Self-Knowledge

This chapter has focused on the enormous changes taking place in the way Americans are working today. The nature of jobs is changing. Ironically, the more some things change in the workforce, the more they stay the same. Even though these new jobs may be temporary and part-time, they can still be classified according to Holland's RIASEC codes. The bottom line is that Holland's typology applies well to these new ways of working.

These new ways of working place a premium on multiskilling, on workers being able to do a variety of things that add value to the organization's products and services. With respect to work values, it is becoming clear that the idea of job security is changing to employment security. In working with a temporary staffing company, you may actually work several jobs in one year, each in a different organization. Flexibility, mobility, and adaptability become new aspects of employability skills.

Option Knowledge

The new ways of working require the development of new schema related to employment. There is a new language associated with jobs and positions, and we learned about many of these developments in our review of the permanent and contingent workforce. We counted more than 15 different new terms used in this area, including *outsourcing, temporary staffing, contingent work force, job sharing, flextime, employee leasing,* and *outplaced.*

The development of the contingent workforce and the temporary staffing industry has made it difficult for job hunters to identify who administers the job application and employment services for many organizations. For example, few of the workers in contemporary organizations may actually work for the "client" and instead are working for a temporary staffing company or an employee-leasing firm.

Howard (1995) suggested that the whole idea of a "job" is now outdated and the new schema of "job" is still emerging; however, this chapter provided some glimpses of what it will be like:

- A job will be a loose collection of constantly changing work tasks that are both general and specific.
- A job will involve using knowledge (useful information) to solve unusual problems.
- A job will require maintaining a few core skills but primarily expanding into roles that involve interacting with others in the organization.

Howard (1995) concluded:

Post-industrial work in adaptive organizations will be cognitively demanding and complex. It will be fluid and constantly changing; in this environment, tying down stable jobs will be difficult. Uncertainty and invisibility will enhance the abstract nature of work, but interconnections to others will engender new roles and relationships. (p. 524)

In Chapter 3, we learned about occupations and the many different ways in which occupations can be packaged or a person can work. By learning more about work organizations and ways of working, we have added a necessary level of complexity to our understanding of occupations. One of the key ideas in individual career development in the future will involve piecing together part-time and temporary jobs into a coherent career tapestry. The idea of "just getting a job" includes learning about the different ways that jobs are structured and managed. *This knowledge improves the quality of your PCT and makes you a more informed career problem solver and decision maker.*

Decision Making

The process of deciding how to work, full-time or part-time, permanent or contingent, follows the same CASVE stages of decision making that we learned about earlier. Whether the gap is finding a job or choosing a way to work, a person must carefully analyze the links between self-knowledge and the available options. Synthesis elaboration, as we have learned in this chapter, means that there is an increasing array of different ways to work in jobs. The valuing phase means choosing the way of working that is best for you, your family and important friends, and your important reference groups. Work values, which we examined in Chapter 2, can be examined with respect to alternative ways of working. *This chapter should make you more aware of the rapidly changing nature of work options and the likelihood that you will have more frequent opportunities to make career decisions in the future because of the lack of stability in jobs.*

Executive Processing

In moving away from the idea of permanent full-time employment, you will probably have to develop new career metacognitions that involve flexibility, self-reliance, adaptability, teamwork, and continuous learning. The new ways of working increase employment ambiguity and complexity; therefore, you have to develop confidence in yourself as a good decision maker. You have to be psychologically comfortable in these new conditions, to develop the career identity of a self-employed person. These new metacognitions are essential for effective career planning and should become part of your PCT.

In many organizations, workers are like rented packages of skills that can be used and then discarded. The new employer might be the temporary staffing company, which acts as an agent to help the employee market job skills. More importantly, this arrangement is not related to organizational profits and success—it has become a new form of permanent employment for many people.

Summary

This chapter focused on alternative ways to work, including part-time, flextime, telecommuting, independent contracting, and the contingent workforce. We began the chapter with a brief excursion into the nature of job creation to understand why forms of employment are changing. Along the way, we examined some of the social forces that are influencing regular and contingent jobs and how this affects retirement. There are various kinds of problems associated with these new ways of working, and we examined some of these, too. Finally, we concluded this chapter with a CIP perspective of the new ways of working in America. The constant theme in the chapter was to help you improve the quality of your PCT for solving career problems and making career decisions.

References

Begala, P. (2011, November 27). Who you calling lazy? *Newsweek*, 8.

Broudy, E. (1989). *Professional temping*. New York, NY: Macmillan.

Bureau of Labor Statistics. (2005, Fall). Preferences of workers in alternative arrangements. *Occupational Outlook Quarterly*, 36.

Collegiate Employment Research Institute (2011, January). *Internships as high stakes events*. East Lansing, MI: Michigan State University. (also available at http://www.ceri.msu.edu/home/attachment/high-stakes-internships/).

Chatzky, J. (2011, November 28).The great American internship swindle. *Newsweek*, 22.

Eldridge, L. P., & Pagilona, S. W. (2010, December). Bring work home: Implications for BLS productivity measures. *Monthly Labor Review Online*. Retrieved from http://www.bls.gov/opub/milr/2010/12/art2exc.htm

Farber, H. S. (2006). *Is the company man an anachronism? Trends in long-term employment in the U.S., 1973–2005*. Princeton, NJ: Firestone Library, Princeton University.

Fleck, C. (2009, September). No rest for the weary. *AARP Bulletin*, 18–20.

Gajendran, R. S., & Harrison, D. A. (2007). The good, the bad, and the unknown about telecommuting: Meta-analysis of psychological mediators and individual consequences. *Journal of Applied Psychology, 92*, 1524–1541.

Godinez, V. (2003, November 5). Market drives workers to self-employment. *Tallahassee Democrat*, 2E–3E.

Hetrick, R. L. (2000). Analyzing the recent upward surge in overtime hours. *Monthly Labor Review*, 30–33.

Hipple, S. F. (2010, July). Multiple jobholding during the 2000s. *Monthly Labor Review, 133*(7), 21–32.

Hipple, S. F. (2010, September). Self-employment in the United States. *Monthly Labor Review, 133*(9), 17–31.

Hochschild, A. R. (1997). *The time bind: When work becomes home and home becomes work*. New York, NY: Henry Holt & Co.

Howard, A. (1995). Rethinking the psychology of work. In A. Howard (Ed.), *The changing nature of work* (pp. 513–555). San Francisco, CA: Jossey-Bass.

Kallenberg, A. L. (2009). Precarious work, insecure workers: Employment relations in transition. *American Sociological Review, 74*, 1–22.

Koc, E. W. (2010, February). Recruiting for tomorrow: Recent trends in employer internship programs. *NACE Journal*, 20–24.

Levitan, S., & Johnson, C. (1982). *Second thoughts on work*. Kalamazoo, MI: W. E. Upjohn Institute for Employment Research.

Mariani, M. (2000). Telecommuters. *Occupational Outlook Quarterly, 44*(3), 10–17.

McChristy, N. (2002, July-August). Stories from the road: Working effectively on the move. *Office Solutions, 19*(7), 16–18.

Miracle, B. (1995, June). Lease-a-worker. *Florida Trend*, 6–9.

Pink, D. H. (2001). *Free agent nation: The future of working for yourself*. New York, NY: Warner Books.

Polivka, A. E. (1996, October). Contingent and alternative work arrangements, defined. *Monthly Labor Review*, 3–9.

Presser, H. B., & Ward, B. W. (2011, July). Nonstandard work schedules over the life course: A first look. *Monthly Labor Review Online*. Retrieved from http://www.bls.gov/opub/mlr/2011/07/art1exc.htm

Rifkin, J. (1995). *The end of work*. New York, NY: Putnam.

Samuelson, R. J. (2010, October 11). The real jobs machine: Without startups, we're sunk. *Newsweek*, 26.

Thottam, J. (2004, April 26). When execs go temp. *Time*, 40–41.

Torpey, E. M. (2007, Summer). Flexible work: Adjusting the when and where of your job. *Occupational Outlook Quarterly*, 14–27.

U.S. Department of Labor, Bureau of Labor Statistics (2001, February). *Contingent and alternative work arrangements: Supplement to the Current Population Survey*, 59.

U.S. Department of Labor. (2005, Fall). Preferences of workers in alternative arrangements. *Occupational Outlook Quarterly*, 36.

Chapter Ten

Career and Family Roles

In Part Two, we learned how the increasingly competitive global economy and the use of technology have affected organizational culture and the way we work. If we were geologists, we could think about these macrolevel forces as if they were giant plates shifting on the earth's crust, creating earthquakes and tidal waves. In many ways, these social forces have produced "careerquakes" (Bolles, 2012) in the way we engage in careers.

That, however, is not the end of the story. There is another huge shift that has affected organizations and the way we work, and this is related to the movement of women into work roles outside the home. Altogether, these macrolevel forces have added complexity and change to the way we engage in career. Perhaps more than anything else, these forces have affected the Personal Career Theory (PCT) we use to solve career problems and make career decisions. This chapter explores the following topics:

- A review of changes in labor force participation among women and men and the resulting impact on organizational and family life
- Living in a dual-career relationship
- Strategies for managing work and family life, including individual and organizational responsibilities
- A case study analysis of what happened at Amerco, a family-friendly corporation
- A cognitive information processing (CIP) perspective on career/family factors related to career

As you read about these issues involving gender and ways to work, try to think about how your PCT and strategic career thinking can be improved by this information. How will this information affect the kind of work-family balance you value, and how will it affect the ways you think about family roles and relationships while working outside the home? What kind of life-career will your spouse/partner have? How will this affect the way you work?

Family Issues at Home and at Work

In this section, we will describe some of the factors affecting the way in which spouse-partner relationships can affect work and career decisions. Among the topics explored in this section are the matter of work-life balance, how men and women are working, partners sharing household and parenting duties, the idea of dual-career families, family/career issues versus women's issue, couples feeling overworked and stressed, child care and eldercare issues, and changing family systems.

What Is the Role of Relationships in Career Decisions?

Years ago, instructors asked 200 students enrolled in an undergraduate career course to indicate what information about career planning they expected to receive in the course (Gerken, Reardon, & Bash, 1988). No one checked either of the two survey items about obtaining marriage or family information related to career planning. Apparently these students' metacognitions regarding career did not encompass spouse/partner and family relationships. Many students still do not connect these personal relationships with career planning, and that can be a problem. In this chapter we will provide information and ideas to help you broaden your thinking about career (your PCT) to include family and other relationships.

Living Alone

The focus of this chapter is on relationships outside of work and their impact on the job (and vice versa). However, at the outset it is important to note that about 28% of all households today are made up of people living alone. In 1950 about four million Americans lived alone and today that number is more than 32 million (Stromberg, 2012). Eric Klinenberg (2012), a sociologist, has written about this in *Going Solo: The Extraordinary Rise and Surprising Appeal of Living Alone*. Klinenberg attributes this change, now most common in big cities, to women becoming less financially dependent on their spouses or partners, increased communication technology making work possible away from the office, longer life spans, and urban culture (one can live alone but be in the company of many people).

Where Men and Women Work

In Chapter 7, we examined how employment and income varies across Holland's (1997) six RIASEC areas. Figure 10.1 shows how the distribution of men and women varies across these six areas in the 2000 census report. Note that women are dispersed more evenly over the six areas than men, who are primarily concentrated in the Realistic (R) and Enterprising (E) areas. Women are at 15% or higher in Realistic, Social, Enterprising, and Conventional areas. This means that women, appear to be much more flexible than men regarding the RIASEC environments where they work.

figure 10.1

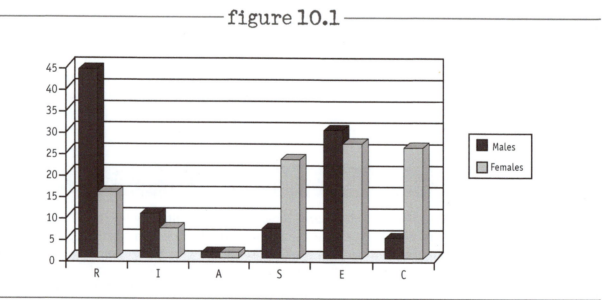

Percent of Employment Across Six Areas for Men and Women, 2000 Census

Work-Life Balance

Current college students aged 18–22 are sometimes lumped together as Generation Y or the Millennial generation, and various beliefs and values are ascribed to this group. (Other generalizations are made about Generation X, 23–37; Baby Boomers, 38–57, and Matures, 58+.) Koc (2008) observed that the Millennial generation has been characterized as looking for work-life balance in choosing a job or employer. He characterizes this as an "urban legend" because (a) there is virtually no data to support this idea, (b) most generations have subscribed to the notion of such "balance," and (c) this is a subjective judgment.

The idea that the four generational views of work and family life are very different is something that the Millennial generation may encounter in a job campaign, and it may be useful to recognize how attitudes about balancing work and family life could differ across generations, at least in the eyes of some people. Generation-Y workers need to understand that their supervisors and managers from other generations may have different values regarding working extra hours, taking care of family members, and career advancement (Galinsky, Aumann, & Bond, 2011). These differences can form the basis for supervisory discussions and mentoring.

Men and Women in the Labor Force

As we noted in Chapter 7, an average of 57% of all women and 68% of all men are projected to be employed in 2020 (Toossi, 2012). Currently, more college women are working. Koc (2010) reported that the *unemployment* rate was 6.2% for female college graduates versus 9.3% for males in November 2009. It seems that female graduates are beginning to dominate this entry-level workforce once dominated by men, which may be the result of women being more open to part-time and temporary work than men (Koc, 2011).

Dual-Career Families

Families in which both parents work are called dual-career families. The term dual-career is usually reserved for families in which both spouses hold professional, managerial, or technical jobs. Following the definition of "career" presented in Chapter 1, in a dual-career both people are engaged in the time extended working out of a purposeful life pattern through their work. Obviously, this is a much more complicated career situation, because each person is effectively seeking to manage the two careers of the people in the relationship. The issues surrounding such careers and the strategies for implementing them are the focus of this chapter.

Attitudes about Work and Family Roles

Given changes in the ways men and women work today, it is noteworthy that both disagree with the idea that men should earn the money and women should take care of the children and family (Galinsky et al., 2011). Stated another way, in 2008, only 36% of employees of all ages endorsed this attitude. Moreover, the fact that men and women now view this issue in the same way is a significant change over three decades.

This change in attitudes is especially noteworthy among men in dual-career families. In 1977, 70% of men in this situation though it better for men to earn money and women to be caregivers, but in 2008 only 36% thought this way, a change of 34% (Galinsky et al., 2011).

Travel and Relocation

Another potential problem area for dual-career couples involves travel and relocation. When one spouse or partner travels, the load of caregiving often shifts to the one remaining at home. When one person in a relationship accepts a new opportunity that requires relocation, the other individual may be negatively affected by the move, due to job loss, loss of social networks, and related factors, especially when there are not comparable work opportunities in the new location for the "trailing partner." This could result in a decreased standard of living if the job the trailing spouse has to take in the new location provides a lower salary and fewer (or more expensive) benefits. There are also changes in housing, climate, children's schools, and closeness to other extended family members that can be positive or negative. International moves significantly complicate relocation issues because laws in many countries prevent spouses from working.

When one partner accepts a promotion or transfer, or decides to pursue a new opportunity in a different geographic location, the trailing spouse or partner may be negatively affected by this decision. In the past, women appeared to be more willing than men to be the trailing spouse or partner. To make it easier for dual-career couples to relocate and to implement transfers of workers, organizations have turned to relocation-consulting firms to provide spouse relocation assistance. For example, an organization called OneSource Relocation (www.onesourcerelocation.com), based in Marietta, Georgia, offers transition consultant services that include "family assistance and spouse career counseling." These types of services are designed to help trailing dual-career partners more quickly find employment, and also to help all family members connect with the new community. Of course in some instances, couples make a decision to live apart, one individual relocating while the other remains behind. Couples may opt for "commuter marriages" or commuter partnerships (van der Klis & Mulder, 2008) to avoid disrupting family life or the stay-behind partner's paid employment.

Women and Mothers in the Labor Force

Another critical issue in the matter of work-family balance involves the movement of mothers into the workforce. This has affected work organizations, family life, and virtually every aspect of society. However, this "natural experiment," as Matthews and Rodin described it, is still ongoing, and much of the data about its impact and outcomes are conflicting and unclear.

From the time of the first colonists, women helped build America by working long, hard hours on farms and in their homes. In 1900, only about 20% of women were working outside the home, usually because they were unmarried or widowed (Matthews & Rodin, 1989). The Industrial Revolution drew men from jobs on the farm and in small stores to factories, and women were left to work at home. During World War II in the early 1940s, many women were recruited into the workforce as teachers, factory workers, and businesspeople, and some remained there after the war was over.

Despite general increases in labor force participation by women with children in the 1980s and 1990s, this upward trend has declined since 2000 (Macunovich, 2010). For example, the employment rate for married women with children rose from 40% in 1970 to 71% in 2000, but dropped to 69% in 2007. This so-called "opt-out revolution" has been especially true for professional and managerial women for two reasons. First, married women with college degrees typically have husbands with a similar education who are likely to be relatively high earners, and this provides these women with more options regarding the need for employment. Second, women with college degrees are likely to have a longer workweek (42 hours on average; 45 hours for those with professional degrees), and these heavier work hours provide an incentive to take the "off ramp" from a job.

Child Care as a Family/Career Issue—Not a Women's Issue

One of the biggest unresolved problems associated with employment for men and women is connected to child care. Women appear to be feeling the primary impact of this issue. For example, the "motherhood penalty" is associated with the lost lifetime income related to the length of time that mothers stay out of the workforce to care for children (Galinsky et al., 2011). However, this same penalty applies to men who become caregivers.

The matter of child care is a major issue in dual-career couples, but there is some good news about this. Luscombe (2010) reported a review of 50 years of research, which revealed that children whose mothers went back to work before the children were 3 years old had no worse academic or behavioral problems that those whose mothers stayed at home. Indeed, children of working mothers were rated as higher achieving by teachers and had fewer problems with depression and anxiety. (The study was by Goldberg, Prause, Lucas-Thompson, and Himsel and reported in the *Psychological Bulletin, 134*, 77–108.) Similarly, Bianchi and Milkie (2010) reported that the majority of studies on working mothers showed "no or small effects on child outcomes" (p. 710). However, despite these positive findings, the majority of new mothers in the U. S. return to work before the child's first birthday (Barnett, 2008), which points to the need for continued emphasis on finding child care solutions for dual-earner families.

Men and Women Feeling Overworked

Today's professional workers often feel that they should be somewhere else (e.g., back at the office, meeting with clients, home with the children, or at a social function) (Conley, 2009). In part this is because high-income earners are working more hours. For example, 27% of high-income men reported working 50+ hours per week in 2006 compared with 15% in 1979. Offer and Schneider (2011) noted that "employers expect high commitment to work, reward long work hours, and rely on technology that has blurred the boundaries between work and home" (p. 811). As we discussed in Chapter 9, Americans work more hours than all other industrialized countries besides Japan, and feeling overworked is one of the results. In the next section we describe how being part of the "sandwich generation" often contributes to the stress associated with work and home demands.

Sandwich Generation

Contemporary workers are sometimes described as being in the sandwich generation, the term used to describe people who have simultaneous demands of caring for aging parents and supporting dependent children. Several factors have led to increased attention to this issue: (a) more middle-aged people have living parents, (b) the parents live farther away, which complicates caregiving, (c) women are having children at a later age, so parents are older and children are still young, (d) children are supported longer than in previous generations, and (e) women are working outside the home.

A study by the Families and Work Institute (Aumann, Galinsky, Sakai, Brown, & Bond, 2010) found that 42% of employed Americans (nearly 54.6 million employees) provided eldercare in the past 5 years. Both men and women are equally likely to have provided eldercare during this period. These caregivers are in the sandwich generation—46% of women and 40% of men caregivers also have children under the age of 18 at home (Aumann et al., 2010). Another trend in recent years has been the increase of young adults living in their parents' home (U.S. Census Bureau, 2011). College students facing a difficult job market and mounting student loans may choose this option to avoid the "start-up" costs of relocating and all the expenses associated with establishing a life in a new location. The impact of these multigenerational households on how individuals balance work and family life has yet to be determined.

Changing Family Systems

In Chapter 8, we described organizations as social systems and noted that such systems have interdependent elements that have interrelated functions and share common goals. If we take a systems view of a dual-career family situation, we see each individual as separate but also interconnected with other members in pursuit of common goals. Therefore, if one member charges off on his or her own, the entire family is affected. The nuclear family in the United States is commonly thought to consist of a husband/father, wife/mother, and at least one child. The extended family includes other relatives, such as grandparents.

Family systems are changing in the United States. For example, Dr. Vernon Zunker (2012) reported that there are increased numbers of single-parent families, increased numbers of divorces, more remarriages leading to reconstituted and blended families, more people marrying later in life, more women working outside the home, and fewer children in families. A report from the Pew Research Center (2010) describes the varied family forms that have increased in number over the last 50 years, including single-parent homes and unmarried couples raising children. These new family forms have implications for work and parenting roles.

Pursuing one's career while also taking care of children requires strategic thinking and balancing several life roles. Two traditional options for parents (usually mothers) have been the *career primary option* and the *career-family primary option*. The latter group of workers is willing to change their work schedules, and perhaps their career goals, to accommodate the needs of their children. They may do this by working flexible hours, switching to part-time, changing a career path, dropping out of the workforce completely for a period of time, or starting their own business.

There is some controversy about this *career-family primary option*, but it is one way to create a family system that balances work and family alternatives. Stone (2007) provided another perspective on the phenomenon of women opting out of jobs and choosing to remain at home. In her study of high-achieving women, Stone found that the work environment (more so than family) played a key role in the woman's decision to quit, and that in many cases, what looked like a "choice" on the part of the women she interviewed was not always correctly explained that way. Although women may pursue this path most often, small numbers of men are increasingly choosing this *career-family primary option* as well. We will explore this topic later in this chapter.

Factors Affecting Women's Careers

Women's careers have been affected by a number of factors. These include low pay, stress, traditional sex-role expectations, occupational stereotypes, "glass ceilings," harassment, and becoming an entrepreneur. Current factors include becoming a mother later in life, balancing the demands of career advancement and caregiving, the glass ceiling, and higher levels of education and training. If you are a woman, think about your personal occupational and employment goals as you read about these factors. If you're a man, imagine what it would be like if some of these factors affected your career goals.

Later Mothering

More women are having children later in life because of higher education demands on time, fertility treatments, and changing attitudes toward marriage (Birnbaum, 2011). From 1990 to 2008, the number of babies born to women 35 and older rose 64%. In addition, 41% of births in 2008 occurred outside of marriage, up from 28% in 1990. Birnbaum reported that the latter trend comes largely from births to women cohabiting with the child's father. This trend for older and unmarried mothers has abundant implications for career planning and employment.

Glass Ceiling and Stereotypes

As women entered work organizations in increasing numbers in the 1980s, many of them experienced the phenomenon of the glass ceiling. The term described artificial barriers based on organizational attitudes and occupational bias that prevent qualified women from advancing into mid- and senior-level management positions (Vega, 1993). Catalyst (www.catalystwomen.org) reported that among *Fortune* 500 organizations in 2011 women held only 16% of board director seats, 14% of executive officer positions, and 7.5% of executive officer top-earner positions. Women in top positions in organizations are still the exception. Brizendine (2008) reported that one of the challenges women face in making it to the executive suite is that these advancement opportunities become available when many of them are most pressed by the multitasking demands of their varied life roles. She suggests that women might have more opportunities to move into top management if organizations would be open to "creating new patterns that work for both sexes" (p. 36), and allow women to pursue management track options later in their careers.

Higher Levels of Education

Galinsky et al. (2011) reported that since 1981 and 1982, women have been earning more bachelor's and master's degrees, respectively, than men. By 2016, women are projected to earn 60% of bachelor's, 63% of master's, and 54% of doctoral and professional degrees. Related to this, Rampell (2011) reported that younger women are dropping out of the labor force to upgrade their skills—more are in school than in the labor force. In the long term, this may mean that women will have an advantage over men in obtaining employment.

Factors Affecting Men's Careers

The movement of women into the workplace and other areas of society caused men to re-examine many of their roles, beliefs, and values. Zunker (2012) cited research indicating that many men have not had an easy time adjusting to the egalitarian movement and equal rights for women. Boys are expected to be masculine, and this includes behavioral traits such as being active, aggressive, independent, and brave. These traits are not always compatible with the new social situations at work and at home that involve teamwork, negotiating, shared power, and compromise. Let's examine some of the other changing social factors currently affecting men's careers.

Breadwinner

Perhaps the most powerful gender stereotype or schema associated with men working is the concept of "breadwinner," the "traditional male mystique" that requires men to be the primary financial provider for the family. From earliest times in food-gathering societies, men have been viewed as the hunters who came back from the forest with food that had been trapped or killed to feed the family. In the industrial society, men went to work in the factory in order to buy bread to feed the family. Males were expected to go out and obtain what was necessary for family survival. Men have perceived career success in terms of achievement, status, power, and control in their work. These schema have dominated the male idea of career for many years. However, there is a need to form a "new male mystique" in a society where gender roles have become more equal (egalitarian) and women contribute more to family economic life (Aumann, Galinsky, & Matos, 2011).

Androgyny

Although masculinity is often associated with social power, group leadership, physical toughness, lack of intimacy, logical thought, and ambition, femininity is often associated with submissiveness, frailty, emotions, nurturing, and limited physical strength (Zunker, 2012). However, these distinctions are breaking down in modern life, and androgyny, or the presence of both masculine and feminine qualities in each person, provides both men and women with opportunities to move beyond the traditional gender stereotypes. Along with androgyny, the fear of femininity creates problems for men who no longer find themselves the primary breadwinners in their families. The thought of being an androgynous male is quite unappealing to these men and makes it difficult for them to incorporate child care and housework into their life/career roles.

Traditional Male Careers

Men tend to work in traditional occupations, meaning that at least 30% or more of the workers are of the same sex. Figure 10.1 showed that men tend to work mostly in Realistic and Enterprising occupations. Some of the most segregated occupations by gender are those dominated by women (e.g., nurses, 94%). Men, unlike women, have not been as willing to move into nontraditional occupations, thus limiting their occupational alternatives. As we noted in Chapter 7, only two of the 12 occupations expected to grow most rapidly in the next decade are dominated by men (e.g., construction worker and accountant), and the others (e.g., teachers, registered nurses, home health aides) are heavily female (Romano & Dokoupil, 2010).

Stay-at-Home Dad

Fathers are spending more time with their children today than three decades ago, although the amount of time spent by mothers has not changed significantly (Galinsky et al., 2011). Mothers and fathers now spend 4 and 3.1 hours per day, respectively, with children under 13 on workdays. Galinsky et al. concluded that men today are assuming more responsibility for various aspects of family work (e.g., child care, cooking, cleaning) than three decades ago. However, the number of men who call themselves "stay-at-home dads" has stalled below 3% (Romano & Dokoupil, 2010), a very small number.

Stress

The changes in men's roles we have been discussing are associated with increased levels of work-life conflict. Stress for men has risen significantly in the past three decades and not changed significantly for women (Galinsky et al., 2011). This is especially true for fathers in dual-earner couples where 60% report some or a lot of conflict. In many ways, men are now experiencing the kinds of work-life stress that women experienced years ago when entering the workforce.

In summary, it is apparent that men, like women, are finding themselves in some uncharted areas regarding work-family balance. At the same time, there is evidence that younger men are creating new models for balancing these conflicting values, but they are also susceptible to considerable stress if they have demanding jobs working long hours, are work-centric (prioritize work over family and personal life), and are fathers in dual-career couples (Aumann et al., 2011).

Strategies for Managing Work and Family Life

In this section, we offer some additional thoughts about managing dual-career relationships at home and at work. Men and women can use some of these strategies directly in their lives, and others require organizations to change their cultures to help reduce home/work conflicts that affect working men and women and their children.

Individual Strategies

What are some of the personal and individual activities that people can use to achieve more balance in work and family life?

CLARIFYING AND LIMITING ROLES AND RELATIONSHIPS. It seems clear that problems arise when dual-career partners do not have a shared schema or vision regarding home and family life. Typically, one partner believes the other should take a secondary role in career aspirations and effort.

In the process of clarifying dual-career roles and relationships, partners might review their roles and relationships (e.g., child, student, worker, spouse/partner, homemaker, citizen) (Super, 1990) and share views about which ones are essential in their dual-career relationship. It is probably not possible to fully engage in more than several of these roles at any one time, especially without the support and role sharing of another person, members of an extended family, or contracted homemaking services (e.g., nanny, maid).

DEVELOPING SOCIAL SUPPORT SYSTEMS. Support systems for dual-career families include a variety of arrangements, ranging from carpools to help with transportation to caregivers going into the child's home. Social networks of extended family members, friends, neighbors, and associates can exchange time and caregiving services with one another.

Given all that is happening at work and at home, who will survive these changes? What kinds of individuals will be successful? Jerald Hage (1995), whose ideas were first introduced in Chapter 6, suggested that individuals who can continuously redefine their life roles by renegotiating who will do what, when, and how are most likely to succeed. The fact that so many of these negotiations end up in divorce court is evidence of how far we need to go in this area. More specifically, Hage concluded that individuals who can use higher-order cognitive processes such as the two below have the best chance to prevail.

1. People who are able to engage in highly creative problem solving using new symbols, relationships, and techniques. For example, how does one become both a father or a mother and a worker outside the home?
2. People who can use complex images of themselves—more than simply a person of one gender, race, religion, or nation—to view social problems at home or work from multiple vantage points and take into account another person's view. The capacity to do this makes it easier to negotiate new role relationships.

Judith Warner (2005), writing in her book *Mommy Madness*, observed that finding a balance in life is hard, stressful, and expensive. The harsh realities of family life in our culture, with few structures in place that allow women and men to balance work and child care or eldercare, means that career choices are nonexistent or very limited. "It almost never occurs to them that they can use the muscle of their superb education or their collective voice to change or rearrange their social support system. They simply don't have the political reflex—or the vocabulary—to think of things in this way" (Warner, 2005, p. 2). In the following section, we'll examine some organizational and governmental responses to this problem.

Our book stresses the importance of using CIP theory in solving career problems and making career decisions. College students must develop more complex PCTs in this regard, which should include strategies for social change.

Organizational and Governmental Strategies

There are limits to what individuals can do to create more positive situations for achieving work-life balance. We briefly describe some broader options in this section.

FAMILY-FRIENDLY ORGANIZATIONS. These organizations provide various kinds of child-care arrangements for workers. They have been motivated to do this to retain valued employees. These programs include the following elements provided by the employing organization (Zunker, 2012):

- *Emergency care.* Provides temporary care for children when the employee's regular arrangement fails or when the child or elder is sick.
- *Discounts.* Arranges for a discount on regular child-care fees.
- *Vouchers.* Pays some portion of the charges or offers special assistance to help employees pay for child care.
- *Referral service.* Offers a list of approved daycare and elder-care centers to employees.
- *Onsite daycare.* Provides child daycare centers that are located at the work site, often in the same building.
- *Flexible benefits.* Fees for daycare are deducted from employees' salary and are not considered part of taxable income; benefits for domestic partners.
- *Alternate work arrangements.* Flextime, job sharing, telecommuting, work from home, compressed workweeks, sabbaticals.
- *Leisure support.* Vacation child care, vacation banks, fitness club memberships.

In researching organizations for possible employment, and in considering job offers, you can use this kind of information about family-friendly organizations in assessing how supportive the employer might be in helping you manage a dual-career relationship.

OBTAINING LISTS OF FAMILY-FRIENDLY COMPANIES. Organizations that have developed good family-friendly programs are available on the Internet. For example, WFC Resources (formerly the Work-Family Connection, www.workfamily.com/), which helps organizations develop policies and programs that promote work/life balance for workers, identifies the 100 Best Companies for Working Mothers and rates companies in terms of several family-friendly categories. Magazines such as *Working Mother* (www.workingmother.com) and *Career Woman* (www.careerwomen. com) also provide lists of companies with family-friendly benefits and descriptions of their programs. Job hunters can examine the programs of organizations on these lists to learn what kinds of services and accommodations are available from employers. This might be a factor in deciding to accept or reject a job offer.

INCREASING WOMEN AND FAMILY-FRIENDLY PEOPLE ON CORPORATE BOARDS. Catalyst, an organization based in New York City, has long sought to increase the number of women on corporate boards of directors. They consider this the only long-lasting solution to making private companies adopt policies that are more supportive of family needs. Catalyst (www.catalystwomen.org) reported that among Fortune 500 organizations in 2011, women held only 16% of board director seats and 14% of executive officer positions. Given these numbers, it is no wonder that organizations have difficulty adopting policies and programs supportive of people in dual careers and/or seeking to solve work-family problems.

DEVELOPING NATIONAL POLICIES REGARDING LEAVE AND CHILD CARE. The United States has been slow to develop national policies on child care and maternal leave. A recent report by Human Rights Watch, *Failing Its Families* (Crary, 2011), noted that 178 countries have national laws guaranteeing paid leave for new mothers, whereas the U.S., Swaziland, and Papua New Guinea do not. More than 50 nations, including most Western countries, also guarantee paid leave for new fathers. In 1994, the federal government did pass the Family and Medical Leave Act, which allows workers to take up to 12 weeks of *unpaid* leave during any 12-month period for the birth or adoption of a child, the employee's serious health condition that limits the ability to work, or serious illness of a family member. This law *excludes* organizations with fewer than 50 employees, so it covers only half of the workforce.

In Sweden, a law passed in 1995 and revised in 2002 provides that couples lose one month of child care leave unless the father takes it. As a result, 80% of fathers now take four months off for the birth of a child. Germany, Britain, and Australia have adopted similar policies (Romano & Dokoupil, 2010).

Our review of individual and group strategies for achieving more balance in work and family can be informed further by examining the case of Amerco, which we describe in the next section.

Amerco: Case Study of a Family-Friendly Company

To find out what really goes on regarding work-family issues in a large, family-friendly company, Dr. Arlie Hochschild (1997), a sociologist, spent three years living and working with employees at all levels in this organization. In order to protect the workers and the company, she gave it a fictitious name of "Amerco." Here is what she discovered.

Amerco, a Fortune 500 company with over 21,000 employees, competed globally for markets. Like many modern organizations, Amerco instituted a team-based approach to management and became a "leaner" organization. It was also very profitable. Even though Amerco had won awards for its family-friendly programs, such as flextime and telecommuting, it was losing many of its most highly trained women faster than it was losing men. Top management felt that the work-family balance was not right and wanted to find out why women were leaving.

Hochschild discovered many things about the Work-Family Balance program at Amerco:

- Despite available options, 99% of Amerco employees worked full-time, which was 47 hours per week.
- Flextime was the most popular family-friendly program—25% of all workers used it, including 33% of working parents.
- Less than 1% shared a job, and only 3% of parents with young children took advantage of part-time work options.
- Workers with young children actually put in more hours at work than those without children.

These findings were *not* expected. Hochschild wondered why Amerco's workers were not taking advantage of these family-friendly programs, and she came to *the conclusion that the family-friendly programs were not being used at Amerco because working families were not asking to use them.* So, why weren't they asking?

The answers that Hochschild began to uncover at Amerco are somewhat disturbing, because they do not fit with many of our preferred ways of thinking about this matter.

- The declining quality of home life led many people to find "pink slips" at home, whereas harmony and orderliness were found at work. Poor marriages, lack of friendliness, child-care needs, and other problems at home made work a better place to spend time, according to 50% of Amerco workers. Work was a refuge from family problems.
- Workers felt more "at home" at work because they were more appreciated and competent there.
- The crush on time led to increased efficiencies in home life, including the outsourcing of many home services (e.g., child care, cleaning). Ironically, the workplace had become less hurried and more relaxed than the home.
- Amerco's corporate culture believed that time at work (face time) was a sign of commitment to the company, and this belief undercut participation in the family-friendly programs.
- The idea of a "family man" at Amerco had come to mean a worker who was not a serious player, and men avoided using family-friendly programs because it was understood that participation in such programs would sabotage their careers.
- Amerco had far more power over families' time than families had over Amerco; consequently, parents stole time from their children, not the company, to get things done. The higher the parents' income, the more time the children spent in child care.
- Although parents were spending more time at work (first shift), and the time at home was more rushed (second shift), parents were then forced to spend additional time (third shift) coping with their children's negative emotional reactions to the compressed time at home. This third shift contributed to making work at home more difficult.

Unfortunately, Hochschild did not uncover any easy solutions to the career time binds at Amerco. She found parents using three strategies. *First,* some just minimized the problem and made do with less time, less fun, less support, and less understanding. *Second,* some readjusted their ideas about being a good parent or spouse and paid others to take care of the children, clean the house, or mow the lawn. *Third,* some divided themselves into the real self with little time to get things done and the potential self who was always available to do things. To illustrate this last point, Hochschild told of a man who had purchased thousands of dollars of fishing equipment years ago that had never been used.

Readers should know that Amerco stopped the Work-Life Balance program after Hochschild completed her study. The company decided to put greater focus on flextime and flexplace so workers were offered a chance to work long hours at different times of days and locations, but nothing was done to help them work shorter hours (A. R. Hochschild, personal communication, May 6, 2005).

We can learn a great deal from the workers' experiences at Amerco. First, we realize that finding a balance in work-family life is complex and difficult. Second, it is apparent that some segments of society still adhere to traditional gender models of work and family. Moreover, there may be gaps between policies (what is said) and practices (what is done) in this regard. Third, work at Amerco provided compelling social attractors for both men and women. People felt better at work, and it is apparent that making family life attractive can be difficult. Fourth, providing sufficient time for child care and nurturing was a source of considerable stress in finding an optimum life-work balance.

Now we will analyze the matter of career and family issues from a CIP perspective.

A CIP Perspective

In this chapter, we have examined information related to gender and work-family roles. We believe this topic is important relative to successful career planning and employment. Let's examine what we've learned in light of the Pyramid of Information-Processing Domains and the CASVE Cycle. *Our goal is to help you develop a more useful PCT for solving complex career problems and making career decisions.*

Self-Knowledge

This chapter focused on the impact of work on family life and vice versa. Both women and men are increasingly recognizing the importance of fully clarifying personal and career values in solving career problems and making career decisions.

Throughout this book we have used Holland's (1997) RIASEC theory to help us think about ourselves and our options. For example, the Holland code for homemaker is SEC, and family members who have these three letters in their code might find child care or elder care and managing a household to be a good option for them, at least for some period of time.

Option Knowledge

The schema regarding women and men at work, separately and in dual-career situations, presents new ways of thinking about careers. The option of a dual career is relatively new in contemporary careers, and it affects both men and women. However, the nine roles that Super (1990) identified (see Chapter 1)—child (son or daughter), student, worker, spouse or partner, homemaker, leisurite, parent or grandparent, annuitant/pensioner, and citizen—remain the basic roles for any life/career, including people in dual-career situations.

Thinking about career options in relation to gender would not be complete without mentioning the role of organizations and public policy. The United States has been slow to develop national policies regarding work and family life; indeed, it is unique in this regard among industrialized nations. The lack of public policy has not served citizens—or organizations—well. There is evidence that more organizations want to become family-friendly, because it gives them some advantages in retaining good employees. At the same time, there is some evidence that the culture of many organizations does not reward women (or men) who make substantial commitments to family life. In exploring career and work options, you need to examine closely the culture and history of organizations in this regard.

Decision Making

The values and priorities that men and women attach to family and career are played out in decisions about having children, how the children will be cared for, how employment relocation options are handled, and how time for independence and leisure is created within work-family roles and relationships. These would typically occur in the Valuing phase of the CASVE Cycle.

In dual-career situations, decision making is ideally carried out on the basis of negotiated agreements, assuming both individuals have equity in the decision. This is a more complex kind of decision making because two people and a relationship are involved. However, the CASVE Cycle can still be used as a guide to help a dual-career couple go through the process of making decisions about issues such as child care, eldercare, or relocation. For example, the process of agreeing on the nature of the gap in the Communication phase could help clarify the issues associated with a possible relocation: How are we feeling about our present circumstances? Do we need more income? Do we need a bigger house? Do we need to live farther from (or closer to) our parents? Does one of us need a better job? A couple could have the same discussions about topics in the Analysis, Synthesis, Valuing, and Execution phases of the CASVE Cycle.

Throughout this chapter, we have emphasized the idea of making career decisions in order to achieve balance in life roles. However, we noted that the Work-Life Balance program at Amerco was not continued. Perhaps a new understanding of balance is needed. Elizabeth McKenna (1997), a former top publishing executive, suggested that there is something very wrong with our work culture, which requires men and women to make choices that are not congruent with their personal values or needs. Workers sometimes feel that they are at fault for not "fitting in," but in reality it is the organization that obsessively wants more work from them.

Executive Processing

Negative thinking makes it more difficult to cope effectively with the dual-career issues discussed in this chapter. There is also evidence that college students have not developed metacognitions that will enable them to effectively grapple with complex dual-career issues. For example, at the beginning of this chapter, we noted a study of college students who failed to see connections between "career" and family or spouse/partner relationships. The reality, of course, in today's economy, is that a significant number of men and women are working outside the home in dual-career situations. These data reinforce the need for college students to develop new metacognitions for addressing work-family issues.

Perhaps most important, however, is the need to be prepared to deal with the challenges and uncertainties associated with work-family roles and relationships. We have attempted to provide a brief overview in this chapter of key issues, and these topics continue to be a significant focus of research and discussion across a variety of disciplines in the days ahead (Korabik, Lero, & Whitehead, 2008).

Summary

This chapter examined issues associated with the movement of women into the workplace outside the home and the impact of this change on men and social organizations. We looked at factors affecting the ways men and women work in contemporary America, and we examined issues associated with dual-career couples. Issues associated with the time binds brought on by work and family needs were explored in the case study of Amerco, a family-friendly company. The chapter concluded with a CIP perspective on gender and work and offered suggestions for building a more effective PCT for solving career problems and making career decisions.

References

Aumann, K., Galinsky, E., & Matos, K. (2011). *The new male mystique.* New York, NY: Families & Work Institute.

Aumann, K., Galinsky, E., Sakai, K., Brown, M., & Bond, J. T. (2010). *The elder care study: Everyday realities and wishes for change.* New York, NY: Families & Work Institute.

Barnett, R. C. (2008). On multiple roles: Past, present, and future. In K. Korabik, D. Lero, & D. Whitehead (Eds.), *Handbook of work-family integration* (pp. 75–93). London: Academic Press.

Bianchi, S. M., & Milkie, M. A. (2010). Work and family research in the first decade of the 21st century. *Journal of Marriage and Family, 72*, 705–725.

Birnbaum, C. (2011, January). Modern mothering. *National Geographic*, 24.

Bolles, R. (2012). *A practical manual for job hunters and career changers: What color is your parachute?* Berkeley, CA: Ten Speed Press.

Brizendine, L. (2008). One reason women don't make it to the c-suite. *Harvard Business Review, 86*, 36.

Crary, D. (2011, February, 22). Paid parental leave lacking in the U.S. *Huffpost Healthy Living*. Retrieved from www.huffingtonpost.com

Conley, D. (2009, January). Welcome to elsewhere. *Newsweek, 59*.

Galinsky, E., Aumann, K., & Bond, J. T. (2011, August). *Times are changing: Gender and Generation at work and at home (revised)*. New York, NY: Families & Work Institute.

Gerken, D., Reardon, R., & Bash, R. (1988). Revitalizing a career course: The gender roles infusion. *Journal of Career Development, 14*, 269–278.

Hage, J. (1995). Post-industrial lives: New demands, new prescriptions. In A. Howard (Ed.), *The changing nature of work* (pp. 485–512). San Francisco, CA: Jossey-Bass.

Hochschild, A. R. (1997). *The time bind: When work becomes home and home becomes work*. New York, NY: Metropolitan Books.

Holland, J. L. (1997). *Making vocational choices*. Odessa, FL: Psychological Assessment Resources, Inc.

Klinenberg, E. (2012). *Going solo: The extraordinary rise and surprising appeal of living alone*. New York, NY: Penguin Press.

Koc, E. W. (2010, April). The evolution of the college labor market. *NACE Journal*, 16–20.

Koc, E. W. (2011, April). Gender and college recruiting. *NACE Journal*, 18–24.

Koc, E. W. (2008, March). The myth of the millennials: Is there really a millennial generation? *NACE Journal*, 14–17.

Korabik, K., Lero, D. S., & Whitehead, D. L. (2008). *Handbook of work-family integration*. London: Academic Press.

Luscombe, B. (2010, October 16). Working moms' kids turn out fine, 50 years of research says. *Time Healthland*. Also available at http://healthland.time.com/2010/10/18/working-moms-kids-turn-out-fine-50-years-of-research-says

Macunovich, D. J. (2010, November). Reversals in the patterns of women's labor supply in the United States, 1977–2009). *Monthly Labor Review*, 1634.

Matthews, K. A., & Rodin, J. (1989). Women's changing work roles. *American Psychologist, 44*, 1389–1393.

McKenna, E. P. (1997). *When work doesn't work anymore: Women, work, and identity*. New York, NY: Delacorte Press.

Offer, S., & Schneider, B. (2011). Revisiting the gender gap in time-use patterns: Multitasking and well-being among mothers and fathers in dual-earner families. *American Sociological Review, 76*, 809–833.

Pew Research Center. (2010, November 18). *The decline of marriage and rise of new families*. Retrieved from http://www.pewsocialtrends.org/2010/11/18/the-decline-of-marriage-and-rise-of-new-families

Rampell, C. (2011, December 28). Instead of work, younger women head to school. *The New York Times*. Retrieved from www.nytimes.com

Romano, A., & Dokoupil, T. (2010, September 27). Men's lib. *Newsweek*, 43–49.

Stone, P. (2007). *Opting out: Why women really quit careers and head home*. Berkley, CA: University of California Press.

Stromberg, J. (2012, February). Solitary refinement. *Smithsonian*, 37.

Super, D. (1990). A life-span, life-space approach to career development. In D. Brown & L. Brooks (Eds.), *Career choice and development* (2nd ed., pp. 197–261). San Francisco, CA: Jossey-Bass.

Toossi, M. (2012, January). Labor force projections to 2020: A more slowly growing workforce. *Monthly Labor Review*, 43–64.

U.S. Census Bureau. (2011). *America's families and living arrangements: 2011*. Washington, DC: Author. Retrieved from http://www.census.gov/population/www/socdemo/hh-fam.html

van der Klis, M. & Mulder, C. H. (2008). Beyond the trailing spouse: The commuter partnership as an alternative to family migration. *Journal of Housing and the Built Environment, 23*, 1–19.

Vega, J. (1993, Spring). Crack in the glass ceiling? *Career Woman*, 43–45.

Warner, J. (2005). *Mommy madness*. Retrieved from http://www.manbc.msn.com/id/6959880/site/newsweek

Zunker, V. (2012). *Career counseling* (8th ed.). Pacific Grove, CA: Brooks/Cole.

Chapter Eleven

Launching an Employment Campaign

This chapter deals with how to prepare and execute a job campaign and introduces the five chapters in Unit III. We view a job campaign as involving a series of activities. In Chapter 12, we examine how written communications, including resumes, letter writing, record keeping, and use of the Internet, contribute to a successful campaign. Chapter 13 explores topics related to verbal communication, including information interviews, social networking, and job interviews. Chapter 14 examines a critical phase of the employment campaign that is sometimes overlooked: the process of negotiating with prospective employers and deciding between or among job offers. Finally, Chapter 15 explores the transition from college to full-time professional employment, which requires careful planning with respect to budgets, time management, networking, relationships with supervisors, and related matters.

In this chapter, we begin by discussing the basic idea of a job campaign and briefly review how job-hunting methods have changed over time. Next we examine the ways current social and economic conditions affect the employment of college graduates. We share information that recruiters from employing organizations have provided about your job campaign, along with some general suggestions for managing this process. Finally, we conclude with a cognitive information processing (CIP) perspective on job hunting.

What Is a Job Campaign?

Why do we use the word *campaign*? The word is often connected to military, political, or business terms, as in a "political campaign" or "sales campaign." When we combine job with campaign, we're thinking about a similar operation. For example, it involves:

- doing a personal assessment;
- identifying goals and job objectives;
- targeting potential employers;
- considering alternative work settings and ways of working;
- preparing letters and resume(s);
- contacting employers;
- interviewing with employers;
- making onsite visits;
- maintaining a record-keeping system; and
- evaluating employment offers and choosing the best offer

Perhaps the most important idea associated with a job campaign is the need for an *active approach*—being passive will not produce the desired results. Active approaches include:

1. starting your job campaign in your first semester on campus and not waiting until a month (or week!) before graduation;
2. using multiple sources for job leads or listings and not being overreliant on the Internet;
3. not assuming that the "good jobs" will be advertised;
4. using unique, targeted resumes and cover letters for every application;
5. actively researching information about all prospective employers;
6. applying for jobs even if you don't meet all the listed qualifications; and
7. using the resources in your college career center (Connelly, 2007).

In Chapter 1, a "problem" was defined as a gap between an existing and a desired state of affairs. Stated more simply, it is the difference between *where you are* and *where you want to be*. Here are some examples of gap statements about employment that could lead to a job campaign:

- "I'm about to finish school and I need to get a job."
- "This job is going nowhere. I need to find an employer who will give me the opportunity to get into management."
- "With a new baby, I don't want to work full time, but I need to earn some money. I really want to find a part-time job and good child care."

For each of these employment problems, a person needs to figure out how to remove the gap between the existing and desired state of affairs—to move from a present condition to a more desired situation. A job campaign has been equated with actually having a job; it takes time, preparation, commitment, teamwork, and skill. People engaged in a job campaign often report how much time it takes—up to eight hours every day for weeks and months at a time. Moreover, some job campaigns are anticipated (graduation from college), whereas others are not (just laid off from a job).

A Brief History of Job-Hunting Methods

Job-hunting, by its very nature, is a very inefficient process with opportunities for discouragement. Nevertheless, a great deal of time, effort, and money is expended by employers and applicants in trying to make it work effectively. And there are many experts with advice, sometimes for a fee. Job campaigns have changed over the years, but some of the strategies developed in the past are still effective. It is important to remember that job hunting is a relatively recent social invention, and there is a great deal remaining to be studied about this process. Richard Bolles described some of these historic job-hunting methods in his newsletter (Bolles, 1994).

EARLY 1900S. Frank Parsons, one of the founders of vocational guidance whom we introduced in Chapter 1, described how he would stop at each shopkeeper's store on his way to the Vocations Bureau (career center) in Boston to pick up the day's job notices. He then took them to the Bureau, where they were made available to job seekers. This idea of collecting job notices in a central place was new. Parsons also introduced the idea of matching people to jobs.

1929. Groups of job hunters first began to meet during the Great Depression to share stories about job hunting with professional counselors. These job-hunting groups had names like Thursday Night Club, Man Marketing Group, and later, Job Club. This was a new idea at the time but is a common practice today.

1960. Bernard Haldane, an executive recruiter, studied the success rates for various job-hunting methods and reported that fewer than 5% of openings are filled by employment agencies, 15% are filled by applications or responses to "help wanted" newspaper ads, and 80% are filled through recommendations of friends already employed by the organization, by "tips," or other contacts. This laid the foundation for the concept of the "hidden job market."

1966. Networking—using friends, relatives, or other workers to learn about jobs—as an effective job-hunting technique was introduced. Networking proved to be 11 times as effective as using newspaper ads (Bolles, 1994). (This is covered in Chapter 13.)

1970. *What Color Is Your Parachute?* was first published by Richard Bolles. This book is one of the 100 top-selling books in this country, with over 10 million copies sold (Bolles, 2012), and is described as the best-selling job search book of all time. The book is rich with useful job search strategies and frames the "what do you want to do with your life?" question by encouraging readers to figure out *what* their transferable skills are, *where* they want to use them, what organizations have relevant job targets, and *who* are the people with hiring authority.

1973. New variations of job clubs were created through the work of Nathan Azrin (Azrin & Besalel, 1980), a behavioral psychologist. These groups were highly successful in helping people find jobs; they became a national network to help the unemployed. The groups emphasized that job hunting was a learnable skill.

1979. Robert Wegmann, a sociologist at the University of Houston, conducted research and found scientific evidence to support many of our beliefs about job hunting: (a) self-esteem is crucial to a successful job campaign; (b) job hunting is inherently discouraging and almost everyone needs some kind of social support; (c) there are facts to be learned about job hunting; (d) telephone and interviewing skills can be practiced before they are used; (e) the more time spent attempting to get interviews, the more interviews are obtained; and (f) the more interviews obtained, the greater the likelihood of getting a job offer (Wegmann, Chapman, & Johnson, 1985).

1996. The Internet becomes an increasingly popular resource for job hunters, and job search resources are now one of the most frequent search options among Internet users. Typing the word "employment" in any of the popular Internet search engines produces a listing of thousands of sites with employment-related resources.

1998–PRESENT. The National Association of Colleges and Employers revealed that 70% of employers hiring college graduates were using internships and/or cooperative education programs to create a pool of quality job candidates.

This brief historical review helps us understand that some of what we know and believe about job campaigns is based on relatively recent ideas and scientific knowledge.

Employment for College Graduates

This section introduces the topic of job hunting for college graduates as the economy moves out of the Grand Recession of 2007–2009. We discuss the general matter of employment for college students in terms of (a) jobs and well-being, (b) where jobs are found, (c) the job creation process, (d) the relationship between majors and jobs, (e) employer hiring strategies, (f) the importance of social/emotional competence in hiring, (g) jobs in the staffing services industry, and (h) jobs vacancies at the top. We believe this information can help you improve your thinking about this process and formulate a strategic job campaign that will help you to reach your employment goals.

Jobs and Well-Being

In Chapter 1 we noted that *work* is an important driver for most people as they assess the quality of their lives. Jim Clifton (2011), who we introduced in Chapter 1 as the CEO of the Gallup Organization, reported that 150 million of the 300+ million Americans wanted a job outside the home, but 30 million of them didn't have one and 18 million had no hope of finding one. He concluded that "joblessness is the strongest core driver of national hopelessness" (Clifton, 2011, p. 20). For Clifton, whose career has focused on learning what people worldwide think and feel, this is a very important observation. Every person has the opportunity to reduce this "national hopelessness" as they seek to enter the job market, and one of our goals in writing this book is to empower college students to be hopeful and positive about their job campaigns. Our personal and national well-being is at stake.

Where Jobs Are Found

Clifton (2011) reminded us that small and medium-sized businesses are responsible for most of the jobs in the U.S. Although big businesses are familiar and employ lots of people, they do not create significant numbers of jobs. This is a bit of an irony but is very important information for college graduates seeking employment. Statistics released by the U.S. Census Bureau in fall 2011 (http://www.census.gov/econ/susb/) indicated that there were slightly fewer than six million U.S. businesses in 2009, and those with 500 or fewer employees represented 99% of those six million. Stated another way, there were more than 80,000 companies with 100–499 employees, and about 18,000 with 500 or more workers. One characteristic of the *"hidden job market"* pertains to all of the small businesses that create most of the jobs but do not have large reputations in the national media.

To build upon Clifton's idea about the impact of small business organizations and jobs, Giordani (2009) reported how an "unglamorous" business (Mattress Firm; http://www.mattressfirm.com/) focused on career development and continuing education to attract the employment interest of college graduates. Mattress Firm is a national retailer with 530 stores in 23 states that decided to actively recruit college students by promoting its corporate university and a 180-day training program, a career ladder for promotions, a corporate culture emphasizing "fun," an internship program that converts to permanent positions, holding on-campus events, and using alumni in recruiting. The lesson here for college students is to broaden a job campaign to include organizations with limited national visibility. Students seeking employment opportunities would do well not to overlook smaller or less "glamorous" organizations that may offer suitable options for their job search.

Job Creation Process

The Grand Recession of 2007–2009 appears to be ending for college students, but it is important to remember that labor market recoveries, especially from deep recessions like this last one, are a slow process. Gross (2009) describes the recovery as a four-step process. First, as organizations stabilize, they fire fewer people, and that process appears to be underway. Second, the demand for products and services begins to increase and organizations prod existing workers to "work harder." That also seems to be happening as productivity in the economy increases. Third, as demand increases employers increase the hours of part-time workers or hire temporary workers. The number of jobs for temps in the staffing services industry has risen sharply in recent months, and this is another sign of an economic recovery. Fourth, the number of full-time, permanent positions in the organization is increased as the recovery continues to take hold. For college graduates, this four-step process can be instructive in terms of moderating employment expectations and reducing the levels of frustration and stress in a job campaign.

Majors and Jobs

Students sometimes worry that no employer will be interested in hiring their "major," but it is important to understand that employers hire people and not "majors." The Collegiate Employment Research Institute (CERI; 2012) surveyed over 4,200 employers and found that almost 40% would consider *any major* to fill positions in their organization. The emphasis is on "fit," meaning the array of skills, flexibility, and creativity that an applicant brings to the organization. Nevertheless, the most requested majors (in order) are accounting, finance, marketing, computer science, electrical engineering, economics, human resources, information systems, communications, public relations, and mathematics (CERI, 2011).

In another report on this topic, The Center on Education and the Workforce at Georgetown University examined the value of 171 college majors in terms of earnings and employment rate (Carnevale, Cheah, & Strohl, 2012). They reported that, on average, a bachelor's degree pays off with respect to earnings and employment, but some majors pay much more than others. For example, though all majors are "worth it," the median annual earnings for engineering majors was $55,000 and $33,000 for education majors (median indicates half were above and half below these numbers). However, the unemployment rate for engineering and education majors was 7.5% and 5.4%, respectively. The National Association of Colleges and Employers (NACE) collects salary survey data each quarter. Although the full report is available only to members, they provide free executive summaries that highlight differences in salary by major (http://www.naceweb.org/salary-survey-data/).

The fact that there are differences in pay for different majors has implications for career planning and job hunting. It is not always the case, as one career book notes, that by "doing what you love, the money will follow." Students need to know how their major is viewed in the marketplace by employers and what this might mean in terms of income and job security, but students also need to consider future income in relation to potential debt acquired while attending college.

Employer Hiring Strategies

As college students enter the job market they would be wise to arm themselves with knowledge about what employers are doing as they try to fill positions with the best possible people. (As an aside, it is important to note that *all* employers want to hire the best people and sometimes end up going after the same people.) As we write this book in the spring of 2012, the job market for college graduates appears to be improving and hiring is up, but there is still a gap between the number of positions available and the supply of applicants—the competition is keen for jobs. Weber (2012) reported that the cost of hiring a new employee now averages $3,479, and the best single source of new hires are referrals from people already working in the organization.

As a result, internship programs are the top strategy used by most employers (71%) to fill positions (review relevant information in Chapter 9), and social media is used by 36%. In addition, alumni working for an organization are an effective method for identifying and recruiting talent from their alma mater (CERI, 2012), along with arranged events such as career fairs, campus information sessions, faculty referrals, and interviews. CERI reported that most employers use a combination of these methods.

In summary, it is obvious that college students, whose goal it is to successfully transition to employment after graduation, need to start early, as a lower-division student, to understand and use the resources and services provided by the campus career center; indeed, the quality of the career center can be one of the criteria in selecting a college.

Social and Emotional Competence (SEC) in Hiring

Studies of how employers evaluate applicants increasingly show that interpersonal or intrapersonal skills are as important as technical skills in the hiring process (Crane & Seal, 2011). SEC skills include "a set of interrelated behaviors involving the recognition, regulation, and impact of one's emotions and the emotions of others that lead to differentiating social outcomes when used in the requisite context, manner, and purpose" (p. 26). This means that many of the competencies linked to high performance in jobs are social and emotional in nature. Examples include (a) personal traits (e.g., work ethic, integrity, self-management); (b) personal skills (e.g., problem solving, smiles, eye contact, communication); and (c) preparation (e.g., researched the organization, dressed appropriately). (In reviewing these SEC skills we are reminded of the portfolio skills identified in Chapter 2 of this text.)

Sounding a similar theme, *Counseling Today* reported the survey results of 2,662 hiring managers by CareerBuilder regarding *emotional intelligence* (EI) or SEC, and 71% valued EI more than IQ in hiring decisions. The reasons? Employees were more likely to stay calm under pressure, knew how to resolve conflict effectively, led by example, and were empathetic to team members.

Staffing Services Industry

In Chapter 9 we discussed the contingent workforce and how the staffing services industry is a source for jobs. For many college students, temporary staffing organizations are another "hidden" source of employment. Luo, Mann, and Holden (2010) reported that this area of employment grew from 1.1 to 2.3 million jobs between 1990 and 2008, or almost 2% of total U.S. employment. Employment in this industry is volatile because these workers are usually the first let go in a recession and the first hired in a recovery.

The person actually doing the work is known as an employee or a contractor, and the temporary help organization is known as the employer. The organization for which temporary employment services are being provided is known as the *client*. The client pays any fees for this employment service, which means that the services are provided at no charge to you (the employee).

For college students engaged in job campaigns, it is important to note that organizations create more temporary than permanent jobs, about 20% of employers (clients) use temp jobs to screen for permanent employees, which can lead to a "buyout" or "temp-to-hire" situation where an employee moves from temporary to permanent employment status. Finally, almost every worker can expect to be unemployed at some time in his or her life, and temporary staffing companies can help to fill in these employment gaps. Table 11.1 provides some examples of personal criteria that might be used to inform a decision about seeking employment in the staffing services industry.

The Yellow Pages (www.yellowpages.com/) has listings of temporary staffing organizations under the heading of Employment Contractors or Temporary Help. There are hundreds of such companies, and more are created every year. Here are some examples of national companies: Adecco, Fidelity Staffing, Service, Interim Personnel, Kelly Services, Aquent, Manpower, Olsten Staffing Services, Professional Staffing Group, Spherion, and Temporary Solutions. In addition to national

Table 11.1

Fourteen Personal Criteria for Deciding to Work in the Staffing Services Industry

1. You do not need a lot of job security right now.
2. You are willing to start at lower-level positions in an organization to develop inside information about permanent positions.
3. You are willing to work for different organizations (clients) in different locations in a short period of time.
4. You want to make yourself visible to employers who might be looking for someone with your skills.
5. You are relocating to another city and don't want to accept permanent employment right away.
6. You want a decent income and secure health benefits.
7. You desire a more flexible work and lifestyle.
8. You would benefit from having an "agent" who can help you market your skills in the community.
9. You want to maintain a stable work history without getting stuck in jobs you don't like.
10. You are interested in a more relaxed hiring process with an organization as a temp.
11. You would like to get training in new job skills areas, such as word processing or database creation.
12. You would like to try out new occupations or industries at less career risk.
13. You have skills—consulting, information processing, technical, professional—that would enable you to function as an independent contractor.
14. You do not want to make long-term commitments to a permanent employer.

companies, there are regional and local staffing companies, as well as those that cater to specific jobs, i.e., technical, creative, managerial. The American Staffing Association (www.american staffing.net/index.cfm) can provide additional information about this industry.

Table 11.2 provides six tips for job hunting in the temporary staffing services industry. It is important to remember that this is a different kind of employer than many students know about, and the rules of engagement are slightly different. These are temporary jobs in the contingent workforce because they have a fixed ending date (they are not permanent), but they can be long term and continuing over a long period of time.

Table 11.2

Six Tips for Job Hunting in the Staffing Services Industry

1. Be clear and honest about the kind of work you want because the temp agency will use your preferences to develop a successful match with a potential client. It is in the agency's interest for you to succeed in the job.
2. Apply to and be on the roster with several different temp agencies instead of just one. In this way you have several employers pursuing your job interests. Different agencies have contracts with different clients.
3. Be aware that you might start in low-level jobs with an employer but keep negotiating and working collaboratively with the temp agency to get you into higher-level positions.
4. Try to get all the leadership, teamwork, computer, and training experiences that you can with a temporary employment agency.
5. In reporting this kind of work experience on your resume, remember that the temp agency is your employer and that your job description should describe your duties and name of the client and the location.
6. In researching client organizations, try to find out which temporary staffing agency has the hiring contract for that organization (e.g., Spherion could have the staffing contract for Verizon, Manpower might have General Motors).

Job Vacancies at the Top

Despite high unemployment and the competition for jobs among college graduates, Margolis (2010) reminded us that organizations throughout the world are facing a massive shortage of top-tier management talent. How did this happen? In the process of shedding workers during the recession, some business organizations let go of workers that could have moved into key leadership positions when the economy recovered. In addition, the emerging global economy means that organizations throughout the world are searching for people who have soft skills to work in varied cultures leading work teams and selling services and products. Margolis found that 50,000 multinationals open for business in China annually and the Asia-Pacific region will account for 45% of global domestic product compared to 20% for the U.S. and 17% for Western Europe in the future. Organizations search for managers who can provide leadership worldwide, and the pool of top applicants is small.

An Employer's View of Your Job Campaign

CERI (2010–2011) at Michigan State University regularly polls thousands of employers who recruit on college campuses. In this section, we share some of the findings from the most recent survey results.

Employers' Tips for a Winning Job Campaign

CERI asked 2,300 employers what college students could do to prepare for their job search; the respondents shared seven ideas.

GAIN EXPERIENCE. Besides internships and co-ops, the employers emphasized civic engagement, volunteer work, leadership, study abroad, and research with faculty. They said "Get involved and get noticed."

CREATE CONNECTIONS. Respondents indicated that it is never too early to begin building professional relationships with college faculty, student services staff, friends, civic leaders, mentors, and career center staff. Networking through these relationships is among the most important job search strategies, and the quality of the relationships matters in this process.

FIRST IMPRESSIONS COUNT. Employers noted that the first minute of an interview or the greeting is of critical importance. We sometimes describe this as "impression management" and we'll discuss it more in Chapter 13.

BE A PROFESSIONAL. Employers stressed that students need to understand that transitioning from student to worker is part of the job campaign. Even in this age of technology, simple things such as proper attire, respectful demeanor, and courtesy play an important role in "sealing the deal" with a hiring organization.

BE PREPARED. The most essential idea here is thorough research and knowledge of the organization conducting the interview. Recruiters noted that preparation is the most preventive measure for reducing interview anxiety. We will say more about this in Chapter 13.

BE PERSISTENT. Employers noted that the job market is competitive and that the worst thing students can do is give up on the process. They noted that nothing is given and students must be willing to compete. In terms of CIP theory, employers suggested that the metacognition needed is "Stay positive; maintain an upbeat attitude at every interview." We discuss this more at the end of this chapter.

BE REALISTIC (MOST IMPORTANT), OPEN-MINDED, AND FLEXIBLE. Employers cautioned students to reduce expectations regarding salary and position title or rank as the economy rebounds from the recession. In other words, students need to realize that they will be competing with more experienced and credentialed people for the same jobs, be willing to try different things, and be committed to excellence and continual improvement. As one recruiter said, "Forget the career ladder. Be willing and eager to do ANYTHING and do it to the very best of your ability. The world has changed. It's not fair, but it is reality."

In summary, this section has enabled us to examine what recruiters visiting college campuses have said about the design of a college student's successful job campaign. We believe this information is important to consider as you enter the professional workplace. In the following section, we'll briefly examine some common job-hunting myths and then review some general job-hunting tips for developing your job campaign.

Four Job-Hunting Myths

Lazy or passive job hunting can be described in terms of four myths, and in this section we'll analyze these mistaken ideas before moving to more positive and active job-hunting approaches.

Wallflower Syndrome

One of the assumptions or myths associated with ineffective job hunting is the *wallflower syndrome*. This job-hunting myth is drawn from the metaphor of a party situation where some people sit and wait for other people to ask them to dance. In CIP terms, the negative self-talk includes "I'm not a good dancer," "I'm not popular," or "Nobody likes me," and the result is the wallflower syndrome. Sure enough, they don't dance. The alternative positive self-talk, "I want to dance, and I'll ask someone to dance with me," is likely to produce different outcomes. The wallflower syndrome is equally ineffective in a job campaign. Assuming that others will do the work—for example, you must wait to be chosen by an employer, an employment agency will find you a position, employers will find your resume on the Internet, the career center will send your resume to employers who will hire you—in most cases is not likely to produce the desired outcome.

Lone Ranger Syndrome

Another assumption or myth associated with ineffective job hunting is the *Lone Ranger syndrome*. This job-hunting myth comes from the television character that rides off and solves all kinds of problems by himself. As we have noted, a successful job campaign involves other people. (We'll talk about this more in Chapter 13.) A successful job campaign is not a one-person operation but rather requires the assistance of friends, family, mentors, supervisors, and current and former colleagues. Although it is important to consider input from significant others, not all input may be helpful. Be aware of the extent to which this input may be negatively influencing your thoughts related to job-search activities. Review the information in Chapter 5 about ways to improve your self-awareness of the impact of career thoughts on feelings and behavior.

Looking under the Light

The *looking under the light* myth involves looking for jobs in limited or restricted ways. There is the story of the person frantically looking for a mailbox key on the street corner under the light. A passerby offers to be of assistance and asks how and where the keys were lost. The searcher thinks the keys were lost in the driveway, but it is easier to look for them under the bright streetlight. Looking for jobs can be like looking for a lost key. They are posted in the career center, on the Internet, and in newspapers, and they are easier to find there, but many jobs are "hidden," as we have indicated earlier in this chapter, and may not be posted in places where they are easy to find.

I'll Do Anything

I'll do anything sounds like a good schema to use in a job campaign, but in reality it is highly ineffective for several reasons. Neither employers nor supporters involved in your job campaign know what you want or how to assist you, which reduces their positive impact on your campaign. The lack of a job target or goal results in confusion and wasted time and energy, and you may end up applying for all kinds of unrelated jobs. Also, you are unable to specify precisely how your interests, skills, and values match up with job requirements in your resume or cover letters and this will have a negative impact on the success of your campaign. As we discussed in Chapter 4, having a manageable number of options, in this case, five to seven job targets, enables you to more effectively focus your efforts. You can always add additional positions, organizations, or locations as you go, but adding numerous alternatives in each of these at one time can make the job search process seem overwhelming.

Focusing on these four myths or mistaken beliefs about job hunting sets the stage for an examination of a more positive, proactive way to approach this task. We'll examine some of those ideas in the next section in terms of the CIP model used in this text.

Job-Hunting Tips: A CIP Perspective

The reality of a job campaign is the presence of repeated failure. No matter how carefully one may approach this process there is always uncertainty of the outcome. Having selected several potentially appropriate employers, researched the organizations, and prepared a resume and appropriate cover letters, there is no guarantee that an applicant will get a position with any of the targeted organizations. *Several authors have described job hunting as the process of "seeking rejection," not a task that most of us would choose to engage in on a regular basis.*

The job search process can easily be placed in the context of the Pyramid of Information-Processing Domains and the CASVE Cycle phases. As with other career choices, job hunters need knowledge about themselves and their employment options, the base of the Pyramid. Next, they need to follow certain steps in using that knowledge to obtain employment. This relates to the middle of the pyramid—the CASVE Cycle—a process for solving important problems. Finally, the top of the pyramid is concerned with positive thinking about job hunting.

Self-Knowledge

The self-knowledge necessary to make an appropriate employment choice is similar to the knowledge necessary to make other career choices. *Knowledge of your values, interests, and skills can help you clarify what type of organization, industry, or position offers you the most of what you want in a job.* As a result of completing the activities in the first part of this book, you have begun to compile this type of knowledge. However, it is important to remember that this knowledge will continue to evolve and be revised as you gain experience and learn more about jobs. In addition, your search for employment may also be influenced by external factors, such as family, geographic location, and related issues that are discussed in the next section.

A person's family situation may influence an employment choice. Family situations include the desire to live close to family members; the employment opportunities for a spouse or partner; the preferences (or bias) of family members; family employment contacts; or the existence of a family business. For example, before accepting a promotion that would involve relocation, you may consider the potential impact of such a decision on significant others in your life, whether that be parents, your partner or spouse, your children, or others who are close to you. For some cultural groups, it is important to include family members in the employment problem-solving and decision-making process.

Specifying a job target is an important aspect of the job campaign. Your self-knowledge and your knowledge of options enable you to answer the question "What do I want to do?" Here is a brief summary of what is involved:

1. Consider and specify (a) job families, (b) work settings, and (c) occupational titles of interest to you. These topics were reviewed in Chapters 3 and 7. Examples for each of these areas might be (a) public relations, (b) advertising agency, and (c) account executive.
2. Consider and specify geographic locations where you want to do the work.
3. Consider and specify who employs people who do what you want to do. This involves researching potential employers in print materials, on the Internet, and through networking contacts.

Although no position is likely to be an exact match for your values, interests, skills, employment preferences, and family situation, the job offer you accept should provide the best opportunity available to match the factors that are most important to you.

Knowledge of Employment Options

Information about specific employment options was presented in Chapters 6 through 10 in terms of the "real" world of work, and this is vital in launching an employment campaign.

Knowledge about employment options is different from more general occupational knowledge in several ways. First, employment information includes specific data about an organizational structure and culture. Second, jobs across different industries can vary widely. Being a biologist and working for a timber company, a state park service, or a forest preservation association can represent very different kinds of work. Third, employment information typically includes information about geographic location, the place where the job will be done. While some occupations can lead to jobs in almost any location (e.g., accountant), others are more restricted (e.g., dogsled trainer). Finally, as noted in Chapter 10, various family issues, including child care and leave policy, may be an important aspect of your employment decisions.

KNOWLEDGE OF SPECIFIC JOBS. Similarities and differences exist between occupational knowledge and employment knowledge. In general, employment knowledge is more specific than occupational knowledge. For example, work tasks for accountants (occupational knowledge) are described broadly to reflect a range of typical employers, whereas the work tasks for a specific accounting position (employment knowledge) may be much narrower to reflect the needs of a specific organization.

KNOWLEDGE OF EMPLOYERS. In researching employers, the classification systems described in Chapter 3 can be especially helpful. For example, you can use the O*NET to obtain a "definition" of an advertised position (http://www.onetonline.org/). Employers sometimes review these definitions when they create a new position. Similarly, employers can be grouped into manageable groups via the 20 major industrial categories of the *North American Industry Classification System* (NAICS, http://www.census.gov/eos/www/naics/; see Table 3.4). Using the *Dictionary of Holland Occupational Codes* (Gottfredson & Holland, 1996), it is possible for an individual to identify potential employers by linking their Holland codes with NAICS codes. Since many print and Internet resources reference these codes, familiarity with these classifications can help individuals to more quickly find and organize the information they need.

LOCATION. What is the relevance of geographic location in designing a job campaign? Many groups and publications (e.g., *Kiplinger, Fast Company*) publish lists of "best" places to work and live, but an article by Leah Konen (2012) in *The Fiscal Times* was noteworthy. Her list of the 10 best cities for young people to find jobs included Jacksonville, Florida (military complex, filmmaking); Tulsa, Oklahoma (oil, low business costs); Fort Worth, Texas (corporate relocations); Boston, Massachusetts (technology, education); Washington, D.C. (government, tourism, lobbying); San Francisco, California (start-up culture, IT); New Orleans, Louisiana (tourism, private companies, cruise lines); Honolulu, Hawaii (tourism, business); Portland, Oregon (startups, creativity); and San Antonio, Texas (oil, aircraft). All 10 cities featured low unemployment rates.

Although jobs exist almost anywhere, it is clear that economic activity is sometimes concentrated in particular regions of the nation, which means more employment opportunities than ordinary are typically available there. In a similar vein, job hunters should also be aware of regional industry trends that point to a loss of opportunities and significant competition for employment. A stark example of this is the devastating economic and employment loss caused by the end of the National Aeronautics and Space Administration (NASA) Space Shuttle program. As we noted in Chapter 6, it is important to think strategically about your career, and this includes consideration of geographic locations.

EDUCATION AND TRAINING. In most technically oriented occupations, further education and training are essential. Employers differ in the amount and type of education and training opportunities they offer their employees. In researching employers, you may want to find out the type and amount of education and training opportunities typically provided to employees. When education and training benefits are considered, a lower salary offered by one employer may actually be "worth more" than a higher salary offered by an employer with limited education and training benefits. Typical education and training benefits include tuition reimbursement, onsite training, off-site training, and distance-learning programs.

LEISURE. Chapter 3 described the interaction between work and leisure in career planning, and Chapter 8 discussed organizational culture and the quality of the match between a person and a job. Students may want to know what kind of work/life balance can be obtained in a job. We should add that the line between work and leisure can become blurred. For example, learning to play golf or tennis may be a good strategy for enhancing opportunities for networking within an organization or with customers.

FAMILY. As we noted in Chapter 10, work has a major influence on family life. The problems in balancing work and family life vary depending on the organizational culture. Two important factors are child care and parental leave policy. In an effort to enhance productivity, some employers offer child care at the work site, making it easier for workers with children to locate child care and manage transportation.

Knowledge about Employment Decision Making—the CASVE Cycle

This is a good place to stop and review the CASVE Cycle as a tool for helping students obtain and use the right information at the right time in the job campaign.

In the Communication phase of a job campaign, you become aware that an employment decision needs to be made. Internal cues, such as anxiety, or external cues, such as statements from trusted friends or the completion of a training program or degree, signal that employment decision making needs to begin.

In the Analysis phase, you use self-knowledge and knowledge of employment options to better understand the gap between where you are and where you want to be. You begin the Analysis phase by reflecting on what you know about yourself and you obtain information and reflect on what you have learned. Generally, a more accurate understanding of yourself and your employment options leads to a more effective job campaign.

In the Synthesis phase, you first expand and then narrow the employment options you are considering. The goal is to avoid missing potentially appropriate options (Synthesis Elaboration) while reducing the number of options to a small enough list to avoid being overwhelmed when you finally choose (Synthesis Crystallization). There are two primary methods of expanding your employment options:

1. Generate a list of potential employers and positions that you have considered in the past—your aspirations.
2. Use information resources to generate options, such as print or electronic directories, databases, or job banks. When considering potential employers and positions, remember that self-employment is an increasingly viable option for some individuals.

After generating a manageable list of potential positions, narrow your options by considering what you learned in the Analysis phase. What was most important to you? Keep only those employers and positions that offer a reasonable chance of helping you to narrow your gap in employment.

In the Valuing phase, a small number of potential employment positions are prioritized based on your values, interests, skills, and other factors, and a first option is identified for real-world exploration and focused activity. There may also be good second and third employment targets to consider. Your task is to consider the costs and benefits of each targeted position for yourself and your significant others. Some individuals also consider the costs and benefits relative to their cultural group, community, and society at large.

If you are successful in your job campaign, one or more of your targeted positions will become a reality and you will receive a job offer or offers. After considering the costs and benefits of each one, the job offers are prioritized, and ultimately one position is accepted. (The Employment Decision-Making Exercise in Appendix L can be used as a tool when considering job offers.)

In the Execution phase of your job campaign, actions are taken to make the transition to employment. The first step in Execution involves developing your job search tools, including the resume(s), cover letter(s), and interviewing skills. It is also important to set up a record-keeping system to help you keep track of everything going on in your job campaign. Initially, Execution involves an active campaign to go after your selected job targets that were identified in the Valuing phase. A key reminder here is "leave no stone unturned" when seeking the types of positions you think fit you best.

You will likely revisit Execution when offers are received. At this stage of the job hunt, it is important to inform an employer in writing (by e-mail, fax, or letter) that you will accept the position that has been offered. If multiple employment offers exist, it is important to communicate with other employers in a timely manner, let them know you are withdrawing from the applicant pool; any concrete offers should be declined in writing. These activities will be discussed in more detail in Chapters 12, 13, and 14.

The final phase of the CASVE Cycle involves a return to Communication to determine if internal and external cues indicate whether or not the original employment gap has been successfully closed.

Understanding How Thoughts Influence a Job Campaign

Throughout this chapter, we have indicated how important it is to be persistent and positive in conducting a job campaign. In CIP theory, the executive processing domain is at the top of the Pyramid of Information-Processing Domains. As we saw in Chapter 5, the metacognitive skills in this domain influence how we think and subsequently act in conducting a job campaign, and they include the following components: (a) self-talk, (b) self-awareness, and (c) control and monitoring.

SELF-TALK. Self-talk is the conversation that we have with ourselves about our past, present, and future capability to conduct a job campaign. Table 11.3 shows some of the practical outcomes of positive and negative self-talk. Negative self-talk generally makes it more difficult to do the following:

- Clearly write a career objective for a resume.
- Accurately identify skills on a resume.
- Be motivated to identify potential employers and position openings.
- Follow through with networking opportunities.
- Be motivated to research an employer.
- Positively articulate your potential contributions in an employment interview.
- Respond with clarity and enthusiasm to questions posed by an employment interviewer.

Table 11.3

Practical Outcomes of Positive and Negative Self-Talk

Positive self-talk can help you do this:
- Stay motivated even when no job offers are coming
- Overcome shyness and lack of confidence in job hunting
- Actively seek job offers even when rejections are received
- Think clearly and realistically about the good and bad points of job targets and offers
- Make better use of the opinions of important people in your life
- Get outside help in your job campaign when needed

Negative self-talk often leads to this:
- Fear of rejection by employers
- Failure to get the information needed to sustain your job campaign
- Spending more time with other frustrated job hunters, which carries the risk of keeping you focused on frustrations and negative feelings
- Procrastination or not getting started in your job campaign
- Confusion about the good and bad points of job targets and offers
- Despair from the negative opinions of people in your life
- Discouragement when quick responses to job applications don't come through

For some individuals, a job campaign may provoke more anxiety than an occupational choice or college major choice. A job campaign involves specific and immediate rejection from potential employers. As a result, failure is concrete and easily perceived.

Job applicants are often aware that they are likely to receive many rejections before actually receiving a job offer. As noted in the section on the Communication phase of the CASVE Cycle, a little anxiety may be motivational, but too much anxiety may lead to self-defeating coping behaviors, such as procrastination. In dealing with rejections, we sometimes advise job hunters that the ratio of employment rejections to offers can be more than 20 to 1. A positive reframing statement would be "I need to get my 20 rejections in order to get an offer," or "I'm thankful for 'no's,' because they probably signal a poor person-environment fit."

Tom Jackson (1992, p. 50) described the job hunting process as a series of "no's." A typical job search looks something like this:

No, No, No, No, No, No, No, No, No, No, Yes!!

You have to be willing to encounter a series of "no's" before you get to the employer who will say "yes." The faster you get through the "no's," the sooner you'll get to the "yes!"

SELF-AWARENESS. Effective problem solvers are aware of themselves as they are doing a task (in this case processing employment information). Self-awareness includes an awareness of the interaction among thoughts, feelings, and behaviors, especially the debilitating impact of negative self-talk on a job campaign. Examples of being self-aware could include recognizing the need for emotional support from a friend or a mentor, negative emotions such as depression or anxiety, or the lack of energy to persist in the campaign.

Self-awareness also includes being aware of the positive and/or negative comments from friends or family members that might distract you or affect your energy in conducting your job campaign.

CONTROL AND MONITORING. Effective career decision makers know when to stop and get more information and when to continue with the next step in the process. *Control* refers to an individual's ability to purposefully engage in the next appropriate decision-making task in a job campaign. *Monitoring* refers to an individual's ability to judge when a task has been successfully completed and when to move on to the next task or when additional assistance with a task is needed. Effective decision makers are aware of what they know and what they need to know, and they are aware of the sequence of steps that must be completed in a successful job campaign.

Good control and monitoring in executive processing enable you to use schema that lead to a successful job campaign. Reframing the four syndromes (i.e., wallflower, Lone Ranger, I'll do anything, and looking under the light) is one strategy that can be used to achieve this.

In concluding this section on using a CIP approach in conducting an effective job campaign, we offer some suggestions:

1. Get positive support from friends and career services professionals, especially those who can help you reframe negative metacognitions into more positive thoughts.
2. Reward yourself when you make progress in your job campaign; for example, do something you enjoy when you successfully complete research on eight possible employing organizations.
3. Take care of yourself physically, because job hunting takes energy; get plenty of sleep, eat well, and exercise.
4. Avoid negative people, especially those who have been unsuccessful in protracted job campaigns.
5. Keep good records of everything happening in your job campaign—costs, people, and dates.
6. Consider part-time or temporary work as a way to stay involved and continue networking while you continue your job campaign.

7. Join a job hunters' club provided by an employment services agency, church, school, or community organization.

We close Chapter 11 with this thought: *The best jobs don't always go to the best qualified but to the best job hunters.* In other words, jobs go to those who can sell an employer on a match between the applicant and the job. Employers want the best person for the job, and this might not be the most talented, highly trained person. They are looking for the best match, a competent, dependable employee who can do what the position requires now.

Summary

This chapter introduced the idea of the employment campaign, explored perceptions of employers regarding the employment process, and applied the basic elements of CIP theory to employment problem solving and decision making. We expanded on ideas introduced in Chapters 1 through 10 and connected them to specific aspects of the job campaign. The chapter introduced employment campaign strategies that can be used in the temporary staffing services industry, a sometimes hidden source of employment in the contemporary economy. The Pyramid of Information-Processing Domains was reviewed in relation to conducting a job campaign, and the CASVE Cycle was applied to the steps involved in making employment choices. The goal was to help you to improve the quality of your PCT related to employment issues.

References

Azrin, N., & Besalel, V. (1980). *Job club counselor's manual: A behavioral approach to vocational counseling.* Baltimore, MD: University Park Press.

Bolles, R. (1994, December). A history of ideas and events in the job-hunting field during the twentieth century. *Newsletter about life/work planning,* 1–12.

Bolles, R. (2012). *What color is your parachute? A practical manual for job hunters and career changers.* Berkeley, CA: Ten Speed Press.

Carnevale, A. P., Cheah, B., & Srohl, J. (2012). *College majors, unemployment, and earnings: Not all college degrees are created equal.* Washington, DC: Georgetown University, Center on Education and the Workforce.

Clifton, J. (2011). *The coming jobs war.* New York, NY: Gallup Press.

Collegiate Employment Research Institute (CERI, 2012). *Recruiting trends, 2011–2012.* East Lansing, MI: CERI. Also available at http://www.ceri.msu.edu/wp-content/uploads/2010/11/Recruiting-Trends-2011-2012.pdf

Collegiate Employment Research Institute (2010–2011). What employers want you to know about winning in your job search. *Recruiting trends note 2010–2011:2.1,* 1–4.

Collegiate Employment Research Institute (2010–2011). *Recruiting trends 2010–2011.* East Lansing, MI: Michigan State University (also available at http://www.ceri.msu.edu/ceri-publications/).

Connelly, A. R. (2007, December). How not to find a job. *Counseling Today,* 29.

American Counseling Association (2011, November). Employment and emotional intelligence. *Counseling Today,* 4.

Crane, D. D., & Seal, C. R. (2011, April). Student social and emotional competence in the hiring process. *NACE Journal,* 26–30.

Girodani, P. (2009, September). Recruiting for unglamorous industries. *NACE Journal,* 29–31.

Gottfredson, G., & Holland, J. (1996). *Dictionary of Holland occupation codes.* Odessa, FL: Psychological Assessment Resources.

Gross, D. (2009, December 21). Jobs are on the way! *Newsweek,* 50–51.

Jackson, T. (1992). *The perfect job search.* New York, NY: Doubleday.

Kaihia, P. (2005, March). Features/what you're worth. *Business 2.0,* 6(2), 99. Retrieved from http://proquest.umi.com/pqdweb

Konen, L. (2012, January 12). The 10 best cities for young people to find jobs. *The Fiscal Times.* Retrieved from www.thefiscaltimes.com/media/slideshow/2012/01/12/10

Luo, T., Mann, A., & Holden, R. (2010, August). The expanding role of temporary help services from 1990–2008. *Monthly Labor Review, 133*(8), 3–16.

Margolis, M. (2010, June 14). Executives wanted: Despite record unemployment, recruiters are desperate for top-tier talent. *Newsweek*, 40–41.

Weber, L. (2012, January 24). Your resume vs. oblivion. *The Wall Street Journal online*. Retrieved from http://wsj.com/article

Wegmann, R., Chapman, R., & Johnson, M. (1985). *Looking for work in the new economy*. Salt Lake City, UT: Olympus.

Chapter Twelve

Written Communications in Job Hunting

As we have emphasized many times, the process of career decision making and job hunting is grounded in information processing. Although technology has affected the way we communicate with prospective employers, it has not eliminated the need for various forms of written communication. How you present your qualifications in cover letters, e-mails, and in your resume should take into account your self-knowledge—your skills, interests, and values—and your knowledge of the job options you are pursuing. For example, if your job or internship target is a position in pharmaceutical sales, it is important to know how your personal qualities match up with this type of position and to be able to describe that effectively.

We begin with a review of the following:

- The various types of letters used in the employment-search process
- Resumes
- Strategies for creating career objectives
- The distinction between resumes and vitae
- The role of references in the job-search process
- Methods for effective record keeping
- Job and internship searching on the Internet.

As you read about how written communications are used in a job campaign, concentrate on how your Personal Career Theory (PCT) and strategic career thinking can be improved by this information. How will this information affect the kind of job campaign activities you will pursue, and how much time will you devote to these activities? How and when will you begin preparing these materials? Our goal is to provide information and knowledge that will help you to improve your PCT and the skills needed in solving employment problems.

Letters in the Job Search Process

The most common written communication used in the job-search process is a cover or application letter. This is often the first piece of information the employer sees, and it is generally accompanied by a resume. A letter that precedes the cover letter is called a letter of inquiry or a "prospecting" letter.

Letter of Inquiry

One type of letter that is less well known is the letter of inquiry. Many times in the job-search process, you may not know if opportunities are actually available with a prospective employer. Some writers suggest that you begin by sending a letter of inquiry, or information-seeking letter, before you formally apply to the organization. After preparing a list of organizations that might have the position you are seeking, you send a letter of inquiry which you approach the employer requesting employment information. It is important to research the organization as much as possible so as to lend credibility to your inquiry letter.

A sample letter of inquiry is included in Figure 12.1. In these days of instant communication, this type of letter is probably used less frequently. Much of what you might hope to learn through such a written inquiry can be learned through an e-mail, Web site, or phone call. The main advantages of this type of job-search correspondence are that it has the potential to help you learn useful information and it gives employers a chance to see your written communication skills. What you learn from these types of inquiries can improve what you include in your job application, or it can let you know that it may not be worth your time to apply (for example, you may learn that the employer recently merged with a multinational corporation and is laying off 3,000 employees).

---

figure 12.1

Ronald B. Carter
P. O. Box 1056
Tallahassee, FL 32303

April 10, 2012

Rita Monroe
Jackson Communications Company
1010 Western Drive
Denver, CO 79036

Dear Ms. Monroe:

I read with interest your profile in the Executive Suite section of *Business Week*. I am very much impressed with the rapid growth of Jackson Communications in the telecommunications field.

During my senior year I have received advice from several people here in Tallahassee about the direction my career might take, and have decided that an organization like Jackson Communications is where I would like to start. I feel my education and experience fit well with the kinds of entry-level opportunities that are potentially available with your company.

During the semester break, I expect to be in Denver and would appreciate meeting with you to explore opportunities with your organization. I know your schedule is busy, but I would appreciate 30 minutes of your time, any day between May 5 and May 10th. I will accommodate my schedule to yours. I appreciate your willingness to consider this request.

Sincerely,

Ronald B. Carter

Enclosure

Sample Inquiry Letter

Cover Letter Format

As we noted, the most common type of job- or internship-search correspondence is the traditional cover letter. This basic form of communication has remained essentially the same over the years, despite all the changes in the workplace and the new methods available for communicating with employers. Although there are a variety of styles, formats, and content elements, there are two basic formats that may help you in writing your letter of application. These are often referred to as the "broadcast" and the "targeted" approach.

BROADCAST APPROACH. In this type of cover letter, job hunters announce their availability to many employers in their field without composing a separate letter for each one. Job hunters who are seeking employment across a fairly wide geographic range and who have numerous job targets often find themselves using this approach. In using this format, you're essentially playing the numbers game—that is, if I send out many letters, I can hopefully count on at least a few positive responses.

Although the broadcast letter is not typically used to pursue a specific job lead, it is wise to personalize the letter. Some examples include: "I am writing to present you with my qualifications for a position as a sales representative at . . ." or "I am aware of the changing role of the nurse in today's (hospital, clinic, etc.)." By inserting the appropriate word or phrase, you can tailor each correspondence with less effort than would be required in composing individual, company-specific letters. Determine and state your exact interest in the organization and explain why it, in turn, should be interested in you. The more you know about the organization, the easier it will be for you to tailor your letter to the organization's needs and interests.

Emphasize your positive assets and skills in your letter. Be as specific as possible about the type of position you are seeking, and tie this to your knowledge of the organization and its business, product, or service.

TARGETED APPROACH. This type of cover letter is typically used to investigate a specific job lead. You may be answering a newspaper ad, responding to an Internet listing, or following up on a suggestion offered by your career center or a relative, friend, or faculty member. Because you are aware of the opening, you construct the letter to show how your abilities and qualifications can be applied to meet the employer's needs. In this letter you are constructing a match between your career goals and background and the employer's needs. You are literally *selling* yourself to the employer.

You can also refer to specific information you discovered through conversations or by doing research on the organization. You can include this type of information with statements such as:

"My academic background, together with my work experience, have prepared me to perform well as an Account Executive for American Express" or "I am impressed by your continual growth through grant-funded activities."

When writing your letter, it is always important to first identify the correct contact person in the organization, although in some cases this is not possible. For example, you may find yourself replying to a box number from a newspaper listing. Directing your letter to the key executive or department manager who oversees the position to which you are applying is advisable, but in some larger organizations, you are required to apply through the human resources or personnel department.

Here are some more tips on preparing your letters:

- Thoroughly read and reread job ads to determine what potential employers are seeking in applicants. Try to speak to the organization's "needs" as outlined in the ad because the managers who wrote the position announcement carefully considered every word in it. Check the organization's Web site to get a general sense of what type of applicants they are seeking.
- Answer the ad as soon as possible after it appears. However, make sure that you allow yourself enough time to prepare a tailored response.
- To make your letter stand out from the mass of applications the organization is likely to receive, be as innovative and creative as possible in describing how your skills and interests match up with the organization's needs.
- Follow instructions in the job listing carefully; note where the response should be directed and what to include (e.g., resume, statement of geographic preference). Answer all questions, with the exception of responding to a request for salary requirements. Our best advice is to avoid the question and simply indicate that it is open or negotiable.

- State when you would be available to meet for an interview and include a phone number and e-mail address where you can most easily be reached.
- Be brief! Letters should be individualized, concise, truthful, and factual.
- Always consider the employer's perspective by putting yourself in the recipient's place. Try to determine what accomplishments and skills would be most attractive to a particular employer.
- Be straightforward, professional, and businesslike—remember you are selling yourself. As with the resume, stick to the facts.
- Remember that the cover letter's primary purpose is to get you in the door for the interview—make sure the letter has impact!

In today's electronic age, you may find that you are doing all of your employer correspondence via e-mail or social media, especially if you learn that this is the employer's preferred mode of communication. However, be sure that you follow all the guidelines related to professionalism in business communications, even when communicating via e-mail. Avoid e-mail slang, abbreviations, and similar phrases that are typically used for more casual, social exchanges.

Figure 12.2 provides a sample cover letter outline that you can use in drafting your letter. Although most letters written for your job campaign will be cover letters for specific jobs, there are additional forms of written communication that are important; these are described below.

---

figure 12.2

Your Name
Contact Information
Tallahassee, FL 32303

Today's Date

Ms. Jane Blank, Title
Organization
Street Address
City, State, Zip Code

Dear Ms. Blank:

1st Paragraph • Tell why you are writing; name the position, or field, or general career area about which you are asking. Tell how you heard of the opening or organization.

2nd Paragraph • Mention one or two of your qualifications you think would be of greatest interest to the organization, slanting your remarks to the employer's point of view. Tell why you are particularly interested in the employer, location, or type of work. If you have had related experience or specialized training, be sure to point it out. Refer the reader to the enclosed application form or resume. If appropriate, mention that the career center has or will send full credentials to provide additional information concerning your background and interests.

3rd Paragraph • Close by making a request for an opportunity to visit the employer, suggesting a possible date and time. Indicate that you will follow up with a phone call (when you reach the city, for instance) for a confirmation of the appointment unless you hear beforehand that the reader does not wish to meet with you. If, instead of wanting an interview, your request is for further information concerning the opening, you can ask them to reply via e-mail or enclose a self-addressed, stamped envelope. Make sure your closing is not vague, but makes a specific action from the reader likely.

Sincerely,

(Your Handwritten Signature)

Type Your Name

Enclosure (if provided)

Sample Cover Letter Outline

Interview Appreciation Letter

Interviews should always be followed up with a thank-you letter expressing appreciation for the interviewer's time. Thank-you notes are one of the most powerful and overlooked job-search tools (Farr, 2009). Not only is this an accepted courtesy, the letter's content can re-emphasize your continued interest in the position and provide additional information to support your qualifications. When an onsite visit to the organization is involved, the appreciation letter may accompany your visit expense receipts.

FORMAT SUGGESTIONS. The items below can be helpful in structuring the content of your appreciation letter.

- Express appreciation to the search committee chair or the employer representative for inviting you to interview.
- State the date of the interview and the name of the interviewer.
- Reiterate your interest in the employer and the position by mentioning new points or assets you may have forgotten to address in the original interview or become aware of afterwards.
- Ask any questions you may have that were not answered in the original interview.
- Express your anticipation of receiving word regarding the employer's decision.

Letter of Acknowledgment

Once you have received an offer from an employer or institution, it is important to respond as soon as possible. An immediate "yes" or "no" is not essential, but prompt acknowledgment of the offer is expected. This process may occur over the telephone or via e-mail, but in the event that you need to respond in writing, the following information is generally included in this type of job search communication:

- An acknowledgment that you received the offer.
- Expression of appreciation for the offer.
- A date by which you will respond to the employer with your decision.

Letter of Acceptance

Once you have decided to accept an offer, the employer should be notified immediately. You don't need to wait until the job offer expiration date before contacting the organization's recruiter or other individual who extended the offer (e.g., department head, vice president). Employers appreciate promptness, as it allows them to know in a timely manner how to proceed with the next steps in their personnel selection processes. You may acknowledge acceptance of an offer by phone, but it is always important to follow up with a written confirmation that includes the following information:

- Acknowledge the letter, verbal offer, or telephone call of the dated offer.
- Be as specific as possible, mentioning starting salary and supervisor's name. Be sure to list and detail all items (e.g., benefits, performance reviews, moving expenses) agreed to in the offer.
- State when you will be able to report to work. Acknowledge if the offer is contingent on any events, such as award of a degree, certification, medical requirements (e.g., drug test), background checks, or certification.
- Express appreciation to the contact person and anyone else who has been particularly helpful in the recruiting process.
- Ask if any other information is required or if additional details should be attended to prior to reporting for work.

Job Offer Rejection Letter

As a matter of courtesy, a letter declining a job offer is due to organizations whose offers you are rejecting. Despite the possibly negative nature of the correspondence, it is vital that other employers know your decisions. A letter declining an offer often includes a telephone call, but the letter makes your decision a matter of record and helps to avoid any later confusion arising from verbal communication.

A letter in which a job offer is declined should

- express appreciation for the offer;
- mention name of potential supervisor;
- state the exact position for which you were being considered;
- decline graciously; and
- briefly explain the reason for your decision, sticking to the facts.

No profuse apology is necessary; simply re-express your appreciation of the offer.
Here are some more "do's" related to job-search communication:

- Follow rules of layout and format for a standard business letter.
- Address your letter, whenever possible, to an individual, along with his or her correct title.
- Spell, punctuate, and paragraph your letter correctly.
- Write in your own words and in conversational language.
- Hand-sign rather than type your signature (unless you're sending electronically).
- Print on good-quality paper.
- Be brief, concise, and to the point.
- Take advantage of any link to the employer that can put your foot in the door or give you an edge over the competition (e.g., "My former internship supervisor suggested I contact you regarding possible openings").

The appearance and tone of your letter and resume can say more about you than you can gracefully say about yourself. For further assistance in the development of your letter(s), review career center or campus library resources, check local bookstores for publications on letter writing, and explore Internet sites devoted to this topic. Finally, we suggest you have drafts of your letter(s) critiqued by a career services professional, mentor, or friend with relevant skills.

Resume Writing

The most widely recognized form of written communication used in a job campaign is the resume. We will examine the purpose of a resume; the style of a resume, including length and format; alternative forms of resumes; organizational approaches and resume categories; sample resumes; issues regarding resume critiques and reproduction; and resume posting on the Internet. As you learn about resume preparation, remember that writing a resume requires time and effort.

Purpose of a Resume

Many years ago, resumes were actually called "qualifications briefs." As a self-marketing tool, a resume should be unique in both content and format to highlight facts about an individual as they relate to a job or position. A resume is a summary of one's educational preparation, experience, work-relevant skills, and personal qualifications. The purpose of a resume is to grab the employer's attention and help secure an interview. It should not be a complete life history. The resume should show how you can be an asset and bring value to the organization (Beecher, 2011).

Resumes can be used by candidates applying for full- and part-time jobs, internships, graduate schools, or scholarships/fellowships. Sometimes they are even used to apply for mortgage loans.

Resume Styles

Although it is true that there is no absolutely correct way to design a resume, there are certain resume writing traditions that have become standard. The descriptions presented here are intended to help you create a resume that will serve your individual needs and present your qualifications to others making decisions about you.

The style in which you choose to write your resume will give it tone and a personal flavor. The style can either enhance your resume or detract from it. Don't forget: a resume is a sales device and must present a positive image. Keep in mind that although a resume is an essential tool in the job campaign, it is not meant as a substitute for the interview (even though it usually precedes the interview). Because of this, and because the resume is a summary, you may (and most people do) use incomplete sentences (e.g., "analyzed survey data," "led small group recreation activities," "supervised staff"). Some people feel that the resume should be action oriented and reflect an assertive and confident job seeker. Others are more comfortable with a neutral tone, showing qualifications and interests without much attention to assertiveness or self-promotion.

LENGTH. Most resumes are usually one to three pages in length. The resume should be as long as necessary to present your qualifications concisely. One-page resumes are typically used by traditional age (18 to 23) college students applying for entry-level positions, whereas two- to three-page resumes are appropriate for individuals with more education and work experience applying for executive-level positions. A variation on the resume—a "vita"—is generally much longer. Vitae are discussed later in this chapter.

FORMAT. The format of your resume should attract attention and create interest. In constructing a resume, choose appropriate categories for your information and order them from most to least relevant to your objective. Use capital letters, underlining, boldface, indentations, and white space to emphasize important information. However, once you've selected a format, be consistent within categories. The resume should be easy to follow and pleasing to the eye. Other factors that may affect your choice of resume format are whether the targeted employer(s) use resume-scanning systems and/or online systems for resume posting.

Alternative Resumes

POSTING RESUMES ONLINE. A common form of job hunting involves posting your resume on various Web sites. Distributing your resume via the Internet may or may not increase your chances of securing an interview, but it may be one base you want to cover in your job campaign. The *Riley Guide* (www.rileyguide.com) is a useful resource on this topic because it maintains quality and currency. There are two recommendations to consider before posting your resume on the Internet:

1. Pay close attention to your choice of words throughout your resume. Employers who search online resumes typically use keyword-search programs to find resumes of interest. If your resume does not include these keywords, it may not be retrieved during the search process. To select keywords, consider the specific skills and qualifications necessary for success in the position you're seeking.
2. Keep in mind that the information you place in your resume will likely be available to anyone in the world with access to the Internet, so avoid including information that you wish to keep confidential, such as your mailing address and phone numbers. Use your e-mail address as a point of contact.

SCANNABLE RESUMES. Some employers use scanning technology to handle the large number of resumes they receive. Weber (2012) noted that only 19% of hiring managers in small companies examine all the resumes they receive, and 47% examine only a few of them. As a result, some organizations use a system that scans the resume into computer memory. Employers can then search the resume for specific keywords or skills that match those necessary for a particular job.

Weber (2012) reported that 50% of online applicants do not meet the basic qualifications for positions, so large companies use applicant-tracking systems to search resumes for the right skills and experience. These systems can screen out half the applicants and they are used to get hundreds or thousands of applicants down to a manageable number that an employer can review.

When constructing a scannable resume, remember the following tips:

1. Specify skills you have obtained, using nouns as opposed to verbs—for example, "responsible for training" should be worded "trainer for new employees."
2. Use lots of white space to aid the computer in recognizing the information. One suggestion is to put the names of the organizations, the positions, and the dates worked on separate lines.
3. Avoid creative formatting that might affect how the scanning program reads the text.
4. Use words that everyone will be able to recognize. Scanning programs may not be designed with a thesaurus, so some words may be overlooked.
5. Examine employers' Web sites to see if there are certain words that describe their culture and values, because these words may be programmed into the screening software.
6. Do not fold or staple a resume that will be scanned. If you are concerned about whether an employer included in your job campaign scans resumes, you may wish to call in advance to check.

Organization of a Resume

In organizing the information in your resume, there are two basic approaches: chronological (also called general) and functional.

CHRONOLOGICAL OR GENERAL. A chronological resume lists, describes, and dates the details of each job and educational experience separately. Figure 12.3 shows an example. Listings under each category are placed in reverse chronological order, starting with the most recent schooling or job. This approach is most appropriate if you have extensive uninterrupted work experience in the area in which you seek employment. It is also the most common approach. Employers are generally more familiar with this format.

One variation on the chronological format, which has become popular, leads off with a summary statement of relevant skills and qualifications. This section is then followed by the more traditional chronological arrangement of information. An example of this format is shown in Figure 12.4. By including this type of section, you quickly call an employer's attention to qualifications that relate most directly to the type of position you are seeking.

FUNCTIONAL. A functional resume consists of selections from your total experience that best relate to the job you seek. Under each category, you list qualifications, skills, and experiences that logically support your job objectives in functional areas such as management, research, writing, teaching, sales, or human relations. This approach is more difficult to construct, but it may be more effective in documenting the skills or functions you want to perform, especially if your background is varied. This approach may also be more appropriate if you have significant time gaps in employment and education.

figure 12.3

ALICE HARRIS

AliceHarris@hotmail.com

Present Address	**Permanent Address**
FSU Box 3035	1305 Iroquois Dr.
Tallahassee, FL 32313	Ft. Pierce, FL 34946
(904) 644-XXXX	(305) 465-XXXX

CAREER OBJECTIVE

To utilize my strong interpersonal and organizational skills in a competitive sales program and eventually advance to a management position.

EDUCATION

Bachelor of Science, April 2012, Florida State University, Tallahassee, FL
Major: Advertising   **Minor:** Business
      Overall G.P.A.: 3.5

EXPERIENCE

Securities Agent Trainee, A. L. Williams Co., Boca Raton, FL, 05/2011–05/11

   Learned the securities industry by co-managing accounts and compiling research on investment opportunities for clients.

Undergraduate Student Assistant, FSU College of Communication, Tallahassee, FL, 09/10–12/11

   Advised undergraduates on course selection and assisted the dean in carrying out administrative duties.

Sales Associate, Circuit City Department Store, Atlanta, GA, 05/10–08/10

   Assisted customers with product selection & provided product information; received award for monthly sales totals; managed departmental inventory.

Account Executive, Advice Advertising Agency, Tallahassee, FL, 01/10–04/10

   Developed marketing strategies for local businesses, supervised media and market research; managed local accounts.

HONORS/ACTIVITIES

- President/Founder, Association of Black Communicators
- Sigma Chi Iota, Minority Honor Society
- Golden Key National Honor Society
- Dean's List, Spring/Fall 2007
- Advertising Club

Sample Resume—Alice Harris

Categories of a Resume

As stated earlier, certain traditions in resume writing have become standard. The following categories have come to be regarded as typical in resume writing.

IDENTIFICATION. Your name (generally in all capital letters or in bold), e-mail address, full mailing address, and phone number(s) with the area code should be the first items on your resume. If you are at a temporary address, you can include this in addition to or in place of your permanent address, depending on the circumstances. You may also include your fax number if you wish to be contacted in this manner. The main purpose of the information in this section is to make it easy for employers to get in touch with you at any time.

figure 12.4

JACK CARTER
JackCarter45@hotmail.com
1311 Canopy Road
Tallahassee, FL 32312
(904) 531-XXXX

QUALIFICATIONS

- Strong written and oral communication skills
- Dependable and enthusiastic worker
- Familiar with database and spreadsheet applications

EDUCATION

Bachelor of Science, **Multinational Business Operations & Finance**, August 2012
Florida State University, Tallahassee, FL   **Overall GPA:** 3.8

EXPERIENCE

Coordinator, USTA Under 16 National Tennis Tournament, Tallahassee, FL, November 2011
- Helped the organization and coordination of the tournament
- Responsible for tournament financial accounts and concessions

Assistant Coach, Florida State University Summer Tennis Camp, Tallahassee, FL, June 2011
- Trained and supervised participants
- Prepared and coordinated activities

Receptionist, Marquee Sports Facility, Saint-Raphael, France, July–August 2010
- Answered the phone and helped manage financial records
- Coordinated recreation activities for members

HONORS

2011, 2010, 2009 ACC Spring Honor Roll
2011, 2010, 2009 FSU Dean's List
2011, 2010, 2009 Winner of the Golden Torch Award for best team GPA
Phi Eta Sigma National Honor Society, 2009–Present
Beta Gamma Sigma Honor Society for Accredited Business Programs, 2010–Present

ACTIVITIES

FSU Tennis Team, 8/09–Present
Camp I AM SPECIAL—Camp counselor to help children with disabilities; served as head counselor & tennis coach for 3 years
Play golf in free time

REFERENCES AVAILABLE UPON REQUEST

Sample Resume—Jack Carter

CAREER OBJECTIVE. The career objective section of a resume is probably the most controversial and most difficult to prepare. Employers, career counselors, and job-hunting books often have different opinions about how to handle this part of the resume, including some that suggest you omit it. Furthermore, although other resume sections are easy to put into words—they are part of your personal history—writing a career objective involves projecting into the future, putting down on paper in a concise form what you want to do with your life! Some individuals get to the end of their education and training without giving much thought to this topic. The following paragraphs clarify some of what you may have heard about career objectives.

A career objective is designed to state as concisely as possible the type of position or opportunity you are seeking. It should be broad enough to cover any suitable employment and to interest a wide array of employers, yet specific enough to give an element of sound career direction to your resume. Your career objective should be guided by the self-knowledge you developed through the earlier activities and exercises in this class. What skills, interests, and values are reflected in the type of position you might be seeking? If you are a skilled writer with an interest in travel who values variety, your objective might be something like this:

Seeking a position where I can use my writing skills as a features editor for a travel magazine.

Another strategy for developing your career objective involves focusing on things like the following:

- Position title
- Occupational or functional area
- Kind of organization
- Specific population to serve or manage

An example of this type of objective might be:

Seeking a counselor position in a rehabilitation hospital, specializing in eldercare.

In writing your objective, you may also combine your self-knowledge with your knowledge of specific options or types of organizations:

To work for an environmental organization using my planning and technical skills.

If you are planning to seek employment in several different areas where the same objective would not be appropriate, consider writing a resume for each area. Do not try to mix diverse objectives in one statement. It will make employers think you don't know what you really want to do. Likewise, don't write a statement that is so vague that you aren't telling the employer anything of value, for example:

Seeking a challenging position where I can apply my skills and knowledge and advance to my full potential.

An objective like this is basically a waste of space. The best objectives are action-oriented and specific. They communicate what you have to offer the employer, and they show that you've done your homework on the field you want to enter. They are generally no more than one to two lines in length.

If you are having trouble writing your career objective, several activities might be helpful. Review your self-assessment exercises. What skills, interests, and values do you want reflected in your objective? Review your knowledge of options by examining occupational literature for fields you're interested in and employer literature for organizations you're interested in. Read job announcements for positions in your field. Review sample objectives in various job hunting and resume publications found in the career center, campus library, online, or in a local bookstore.

As an alternative to putting the objective on the resume, you could omit it and use your cover letters to specify an objective targeted at a particular employer or position. This approach allows you to use language that matches the type of position you are seeking. The main disadvantage of this approach is that cover letters and resumes can get separated, creating a void for employers when it comes to information about your job interests and objectives.

Remember, whether you put the objective on the resume or leave it off, it is still important to give it some thought. When those in your circle of job-hunting contacts or prospective employers ask you "What are you interested in doing?" or "What type of position are you seeking?" you should have some fairly concrete ideas in mind. It never works to your advantage to say, "I'll do anything." The problem with that statement (as we learned in Chapter 11) is that most job hunters really don't mean it (there are some jobs they wouldn't do!), and it makes narrowing down their job targets almost impossible. The Valuing stage of your job campaign should leave you with three to five well-focused job targets. You may add to these at any time, but it helps to have a manageable number to start your job search.

EDUCATION. This section should begin with the highest level of training (even if your graduation date is some months in the future) and continue with all other schools attended, degrees earned, or training received. It is not necessary to include high school. However, if some items in the high school background show high honors or generally reinforce the career objective, that data should be included. You should list the names of schools, dates attended or graduation date, degrees earned, and major/minor subjects. If your G.P.A. is good (3.0 or higher), you may wish to list it. You could include your G.P.A. in your major if that is higher. If your G.P.A. is not your strong suit, leave it off, but be prepared to talk about it. Employers may still ask!

The possibilities for expansion in this category are unlimited, and you may decide to list selected courses you have taken, study abroad experiences, as well as special projects, academic honors you have received, academic specializations, and activities in which you have participated. If you have a long list of these items, it might be wise to select only the most important and omit the others or include them in separate resume categories, such as "Honors/Awards," "Activities." Including all of these items under the "Education" category might distract from your degree and give your resume a cluttered appearance.

EXPERIENCE. This category reflects your contact with specific organizations in paid and unpaid work experience. It is permissible to include internships, volunteer work, summer jobs, special projects, or military experience under this category. If you have several experiences directly related to your objective, you may want to list those under "Related Experience" and your other experiences under "Other" or "Additional Experience."

List position titles, names of organizations, locations (city and state), dates, and duties for each entry under "Experience." Again, in presenting this information, choose a format where the material most relevant to your objective comes first in the resume. Here are two different examples:

Holiday Inn: Atlanta, GA

Desk Clerk (01/11–present) or

Desk Clerk—Holiday Inn; Atlanta, GA, January 2011 to present

Employers are mainly interested in the degree of responsibility you held and the skills you demonstrated. Try to outline your duties in such a way that the information about that experience is presented in the most positive way, and at the same time relate the experience to your professional objective. Here is an example:

McDuffy's Restaurant; Orlando, FL

Crew Chief, 09/10–12/11

- Managed daily food preparation and other operations
- Supervised five staff members
- Compiled inventory data and maintained stock
- Assisted in selecting, hiring, and training new employees

POSITIVE-QUALITY/ACTION WORD LISTS. Use the positive-quality word list and positive-action word list in Table 12.1 to help you specify skills and accomplishments connected to your work experiences. Remember, any experiences, including those gained through student activities and volunteer work, can demonstrate your dependability, resourcefulness, and responsibility. Choose whatever shows your qualifications and experience to your best advantage. In describing your experience and identifying your skills, action verbs are an indispensable tool. When selecting action verbs for your resume, make sure that you can provide detailed examples in an interview of when, how, and where you applied these skills in your previous experience.

Table 12.1

Positive-Quality and Positive-Action Word Lists

Positive-Quality Word List

ability	effectiveness	original	significant
academic	efficient	particularly	significantly
accuracy	enlarging	pertinent	sound
administrative	executive	positive	special
building	expanding	potential	stable
capability	experienced	preference	substantially
capable	extensive	productive	successful
capacity	increasing	professional	technical
competence	judicious	proficient	thorough
competent	knowledgeable	proven	thoroughly
completely	major	qualified	versatile
consistent	management	record	vigorous
developing	mature	resourceful	well-rounded
effective	maturity	responsible	

Positive-Action Word List

accomplish	budget	counsel	edit
account	build	create	engineer
achieve	calculate	dance	entertain
act	catalogue	delegate	establish
administer	chart	demonstrate	estimate
advertise	clarify	decrease	evaluate
advise	collect	decide	exercise
analyze	communicate	design	exhibit
appraise	compete	determine	experiment
appeal	complete	develop	explain
arrange	compile	devise	facilitate
assemble	compose	diagnose	formulate
assign	conduct	direct	furnish
assist	contribute	discover	guide
attend	control	document	handle
audit	coordinate	draft	hire
authorize	correct	draw	
implement	market	preside	serve
improve	measure	produce	solve
increase	meet	program	speak
initiate	mobilize	promote	start
influence	model	propose	structure
inspect	motivate	provide	submit
install	negotiate	publish	supervise
instruct	operate	purchase	supply
interpret	order	qualify	synthesize
interview	originate	raise	talk
invent	organize	read	teach
investigate	paint	recommend	test
judge	perform	recruit	train
landscape	persuade	repair	translate
lead	photograph	report	travel
learn	plan	research	tutor
listen	play	review	type
make	predict	schedule	understand
manage	prepare	select	verify
manufacture	present	sell	write

PERSONAL. Experts once varied in their recommendations on whether or not to include personal information on your resume, or on what to include if you do have this category. However, because such personal information (e.g., birth date, marital status, physical characteristics, health, religion) has been ruled a basis for discrimination in hiring, employers do not like to see it in job application materials. Moreover, such personal information can be used by cyberthieves "phishing" for information that will compromise your identity. For these reasons, we advise against including personal information, especially related to your social security or driver's license numbers, in any of your job campaign materials.

OTHER CATEGORIES. Education and Experience are standard resume categories. However, there are many more possible categories that might be included. Create other categories that you feel are important to best highlight your skills and qualifications. Here are some possibilities:

- Activities
- Awards/Honors
- Background
- Certifications
- Computer Skills

- Languages
- Memberships
- Special Skills
- Workshops/Seminars

Besides the two sample resume formats in Figures 12.3 and 12.4, additional samples can be found in career center libraries, online, and in the resume-writing books in most college and commercial bookstores. Don't get hung up on the search for the perfect format. You may find that none of the samples seem appropriate for the presentation of your unique qualifications. You may also, however, discover that all the samples seem like the best way for you to proceed. Confused? Choose whatever is useful and consistent with your individual needs and objectives and whatever presents your qualifications well to prospective employers—then create your own original resume. The final document should be one you're proud of and about which you're comfortable talking to prospective employers.

Critiquing Your Resume

We recommend that you have several people whose opinion you respect critique your best draft copy. You can also bring your resume to the campus career center campus, and a staff member can provide you with some useful feedback on how to produce a final version that is polished and professional. Career center staff members are in regular contact with employers who provide suggestions on what they are looking for in resumes. Use the Resume Critiquing sheet in Appendix K as you review your resume.

Reproducing Your Resume

Your resume is only good if many people see it, and this means that you will need to make many copies, perhaps hundreds (this goes back to the cost issue we brought up earlier). There are several considerations in reproducing your resume in quantity.

PREPARING THE ORIGINAL. To reproduce your resume, you will need a good, clean, high-contrast original copy. Most people use word-processing software on their computer to create the original copy. In some locations, you will find people who advertise resume-writing services. We believe that most individuals can create an attractive and professional resume with the help of some good resume writing-resources and career center staff members. Check on free resources that are available to help you do this before you pay someone to create your resume.

Another development in the preparation of resumes is the fairly widespread availability of resume-writing software packages or templates. These usually provide several preset formats to guide you through the resume preparation process, as well as other helpful tips on preparing your resume. Some people like having the resume sections already laid out in the template so all they have to do is fill in the blanks. In some cases, career centers purchase these systems for students and alumni to use. Examples include ResumeBuilder and Optimal Resume. The downside of using templates is that your resume tends to look like everyone else's and the preset format may restrict your options for arranging and highlighting information in a way that best presents your qualifications. We discourage the use of preset formats in resume development, but you can decide what approach to resume development works best for you.

MAKING COPIES. Once you've got a high-quality electronic version of your resume, use the best printer available (high-quality laser printers are recommended) to make extra copies. You may opt to purchase higher quality paper from a local print shop, office supply store, or similar source to use in making copies. Consider getting some extra blank sheets for any cover letters that you ending up mailing or handing directly to employers.

Resume Tips

Before you begin the task of actually writing your rough draft, thoroughly familiarize yourself with the "Do's and Don'ts" outlined here. By following these tips, you should increase the probability of producing a clear and readable account of your unique qualifications. Use the self-knowledge gained in Part One as you think about how you want to market yourself to prospective employers.

1. *Be brief, clear, and concise.* A resume stands a much better chance of getting attention if it is easy to read and well organized.
2. *Be consistent.* Experiment with the arrangement of headlines, captions, indentations, blocks of text, and the use of capital letters, bolding, and other formatting techniques. Then choose a layout that is readable and appealing to the eye, and stick with it.
3. *Be positive.* Start statements or phrases with verbs denoting positive activity, such as "designed," "initiated," and so on. (See the Table 12.1 Positive-Quality/Action Word Lists for ideas. Avoid the use of the personal pronoun "I").
4. *Be honest.* Many organizations consider your resume to be part of a job application, and false information on an application or resume is grounds for immediate dismissal. Besides reflecting a lack of personal integrity, false resume information is just bad practice in a job campaign.
5. *Be careful.* Double-check for typographical errors and mistakes in grammar, spelling, or punctuation. Do not hesitate to consult a dictionary or use the computer's spell-check feature. Errors in copy editing may suggest careless and shoddy workmanship, and most employers immediately eliminate any resumes with errors.
6. *Be neat.* Create your resume on 8.5 × 11 inch paper, then print it or make copies on a high-quality copier. Use text arrangement and margin formatting to avoid a cluttered look and make key items stand out. You want the paper resume to present you in the most positive light possible, both in appearance and content.

In addition to the six resume writing tips above, do not state salary requirements, give reasons for changing past employers, limit yourself geographically unless absolutely necessary, expound on your philosophy or values, or offer any negative information.

You will find that there are many different ideas among experts and in the literature about the best things to do in writing a resume. Everyone seems to have an opinion. A recent search on Amazon.com of educational and reference books on resume writing produced almost 3,000 results. This is an indication of the numerous and varied points of view on this topic. The information in this chapter is a distillation of what we think is most important, especially for a college student seeking employment after graduation.

Resume versus Vita

For typical college graduates completing bachelor's degrees, the accepted format for resumes is a one- to two-page document that focuses primarily on education and experience and, second, on any additional activities and honors that enhance qualifications and skills in the eyes of prospective employers.

A resume should be brief and concise. Its purpose is to get you an interview. A vita or curriculum vita (CV), on the other hand, is a complete, cumulative record or history of your academic and professional accomplishments. The word vita is Latin and literally means "life."

Occasionally, on some position announcements (especially in Europe), you may see at the bottom a request to send a copy of your vita or CV. Vitae have their origin in the academic job search process. They are primarily used by people with advanced degrees who are seeking positions in colleges, universities, or similar organizations. They may also be used by people applying to graduate school.

The focus of a vita is on areas of accomplishment that are traditionally valued by academic institutions, such as:

- Teaching
- Research
- Publications
- Presentations
- Consultations
- Grant writing
- Fundraising
- Certifications or licenses
- Professional development activities
- Professional leadership activities
- Service to the profession, institution, and community

The length of a vita may be anywhere from two to as many as 100 pages—as is the case with some college faculty! It is unlikely that a recent undergraduate would need a vita. Books devoted to the academic job search include sample vitae. If you're in doubt about whether to send a resume or a vita when applying for a particular position or seeking admission to graduate school, check with a career services professional or someone in the field to ensure that you follow the most appropriate format in your application.

References and Letters of Recommendation

In the process of making a decision about whether or not to hire you, employers may ask for a list of references or for letters of recommendation. This is another aspect of written communications in job hunting.

You may use both your letters to employers and your resume to communicate information about the availability of references. References in the job-search process usually consist of three to four individuals who can speak to prospective employers about your qualifications and personal characteristics, particularly as they relate to a specific position. Reeves (2009) suggests that a job candidate should be strategic in selecting references and identify "people who have openly admired you and your work" (p. 104).

For recent graduates, references are usually some combination of current and former employers, as well as campus individuals such as faculty, student organization advisors, or other staff that know you fairly well. For more experienced job hunters with a lengthy work history, references are usually drawn from their most recent employers. Personal references such as neighbors, close friends, and similar types of individuals are rarely requested. The exception to this is some positions, particularly in government settings, that may require various security clearances.

Employers are generally more interested in references who will speak honestly and accurately about your qualifications as a prospective employee. They are interested in your work habits, and they may want to verify information on your resume. The most important thing for you to do is to ask your references if they're willing to serve in this capacity *before* you put them on a list and give it to prospective employers.

Some references might be willing to write specific letters for each position you apply for (this is the ideal option), and others may prefer to simply write "To whom it may concern" letters that are more generic in nature. In the latter instance, you would keep these letters yourself and send copies of them when requested by employers. Another alternative is to submit reference letters to your career center's credentials service (this is described in more detail later). You can also opt to use one of the commercial services that offers electronic storage of letters and related documents (e.g., www. interfolio.com).

When presenting reference information on your resume, several formats can be used:

1. One option is to simply include "References available upon request" at the bottom of the resume. This is the most common practice.
2. Another alternative is to state "Credentials available from Career Services, State University, Anytown, FL 32306-2490." If you choose this option, contact the appropriate office to get more information on how to create a credentials file. A credential service allows you to keep reference letters on "file" with the career center. Most centers that still offer credential file services have switched to various Web-based storage systems. These may be tied to the center's job listing and on-campus interviewing system, thus providing seamless services for job candidates and employers. For a small fee, the career center can send your reference letters to potential employers or graduate schools upon your request.
3. A third alternative is to list on a separate page the names, titles, addresses, phone numbers, and e-mail addresses of people (three to five) who can attest to your experience or knowledge of subject matter.

A sample reference page is shown in Figure 12.5. As a courtesy, remember to send copies of your resume to your references so they are informed about the materials you are using in your job campaign and can address any questions raised by potential employers. Make the task of providing a reference as easy as possible on the individuals you've asked to write letters (Reeves, 2009).

--- figure 12.5 ---

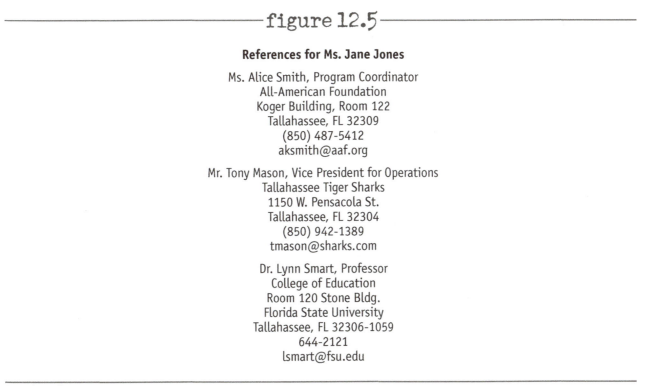

References for Ms. Jane Jones

Ms. Alice Smith, Program Coordinator
All-American Foundation
Koger Building, Room 122
Tallahassee, FL 32309
(850) 487-5412
aksmith@aaf.org

Mr. Tony Mason, Vice President for Operations
Tallahassee Tiger Sharks
1150 W. Pensacola St.
Tallahassee, FL 32304
(850) 942-1389
tmason@sharks.com

Dr. Lynn Smart, Professor
College of Education
Room 120 Stone Bldg.
Florida State University
Tallahassee, FL 32306-1059
644-2121
lsmart@fsu.edu

Sample Reference Page

Record Keeping in the Job Campaign

It should be apparent by now that the job campaign is an information-intensive process. For example, if you are working with five prospective employers and you have 10 bits of information about each of them, that's 50 pieces of information to catalog and file. You will be keeping up with many documents in the job-campaign process, including the following:

- Your own letters of inquiry, application, thank you, acceptance
- Resume(s) and career objective statements
- Lists of job contacts and referrals (information interviews and social network contacts)
- Business cards
- Notes from telephone and personal conversations
- Past and future dates of contacts with employers
- Copies of job announcements and position descriptions
- Employer literature
- Printouts from Internet sites
- Receipts, invoices, and costs associated with your job campaign
- Return correspondence, e-mails, and phone messages from employers

The most successful job hunters develop some kind of system that helps them maintain this information in a usable and easily retrievable form. As you make contacts through your networking and information interviewing, you need a record of whom you spoke with (name, title, phone, e-mail, etc.), what was discussed, and what follow up is needed (by whom and by when). Similarly, if your contacts give you additional referrals, you need to repeat this process with those individuals. For employers you contacted regarding specific vacancies, you need to note when letters or e-mails were sent, when to follow up, and what action is needed next on your part or the employers' part.

Before you begin sending any written correspondence as part of your job search, it is important that you devise some way of keeping track of when and what you have sent. For instance, if you contact Mr. Jones asking for an interview and offer to call him during the week of June 6, you need to have that date on record so you can be sure to meet that commitment. Also, if you are targeting 25 or more different employers, it is critical to know what you said in your initial communication with a particular employer to make an appropriate follow up at a later date.

The format used and the type of information included in any record-keeping system may vary slightly from one job hunter to another, but it's critical that you develop such a system One example of a record-keeping form is shown in Figure 12.6. Copy this for your own use, or adapt it in a manner that fits your system.

figure 12.6

Organization	Position	Location	Contact Person	Contact Person Phone, Email	Applied for Job	Close Date	References Requested	Interview Date	2nd Interview Accepted/ Rejected	Job Offer Received	Rejections Letter Received
Widgits, Inc.	account executive	Denver	Jane Mills	303-413-1121; jmills@widgits.com	7/12/2012	7/15/2012				7/26/2012	

Sample Record-Keeping Chart

We have now outlined the standard ways that written communications are used in a job campaign. We have seen several different kinds of letters used in job campaigns, an analysis of resume types and content, a discussion of career objectives, the use of references, and the need for establishing a record-keeping system. Now we'll examine methods for job hunting on the Internet.

Using the Internet in a Job Campaign

Any discussion of job-search strategies in today's marketplace would be incomplete without a discussion of the expanded role of the Internet. A recent search of the keyword "employment" using one of the more popular search tools on the Internet resulted in over 813 million hits related to this topic! (It was 240 million in 2008.) This section will:

1. examine books, Web sites, and other resources describing how the Internet can be used in career planning and job hunting,
2. review how the Internet can be used to research organizations and identify jobs,
3. discuss social media in the job campaign,
4. review research on use of the Internet in a job campaign, and
5. analyze the pros and cons of using the Internet.

Internet Resources

You can find career and job search information in one of several ways using the Internet or other sources:

- Use online indexing systems (search engines), such as Bing, Google, or Yahoo!.
- Identify special topic Web pages that may link to useful sites.
- Check your career center's Web site for links related to career planning and job hunting (e.g., www.career.fsu.edu/library/links.cfm).
- Look in publications or directories of specialty Internet sites.
- Ask professionals in your career area for the electronic addresses of helpful sites.

BOOKS. Information related to career planning and job hunting on the Internet has been published since 1995. These books provide detailed information about using the Internet for a job search, such as locating specific sites and services and developing helpful strategies for different career development and job-search activities. In using any resource materials, always consider the qualifications of the authors or presenters and the date of publication. Remember that the Internet and the job-hunting process are changing continuously!

Here are some sample titles:

- *Career Planning and the Internet* (Osborn, Dikel, & Sampson, 2011)
- *Internet Your Way to a New Job* (Doyle, 2011, e-book)
- *Guide to Internet Job Searching 2008–2009* (Dikel & Roehm, 2008)
- *Guide to Job Hunting Online* (Bolles & Bolles, 2011)
- *The Panic-Free Job Search: Unleash the Power of the Web and Social Networking to Get Hired* (Hill, 2012)

WEB SITES. There are thousands of Web pages related to job campaigns and careers, but we provide a sampling of seven Internet categories of such information. (Note that URL addresses and the quality of information on these Web sites may have changed since the publication of this text.)

1. Occupational information—useful to review prior to researching specific job titles and employers.
   - *Occupational Outlook Handbook* (OOH) <www.bls.gov/oco/>
   - O*NET <http://online.onetcenter.org/>
   - State Occupational Projections <www.projectionscentral.com/>

2. Employer research—needed to identify possible employers and do research prior to interviews.
   - SEC Edgar Company Filings Search <www.sec.gov/>
   - GuideStar National Database of Non-Profit Organizations <www.guidestar.org>
   - Researching Companies Online <www.learnwebskills.com/company/>

3. Job boards—post open positions; often offer applicant resume database services, and related job search support resources.
   - Career One Stop <www.careeronestop.org>
   - Career Builder <www.careerbuilder.com>
   - Indeed <www.indeed.com>
   - Monster <www.monster.com>
   - Jobster <www.jobster.com>
   - Employment Spot <www.employmentspot.com>

4. Government employment/jobs—focus on openings at federal, state, or local levels
   - State Government Jobs <www.50statejobs.com/gov.html>
   - Federal government jobs <www.usajobs.gov>

5. Job search process—contain articles, guides, lists of resources, etc. to guide the job seeker
   - America's Career InfoNet . . . links to state job banks <www.jobbankinfo.org/>
   - CareerJournal.com . . . executive career site <www.careerjournal.com/>
   - JobWeb . . . advice for new college graduates <www.jobweb.com>
   - The Riley Guide . . . career and employment information <www.rileyguide.com>

6. Salary and relocation—helpful for salary negotiations and making decisions on job offers
   - Bureau of Labor Statistics Wage Estimates <http://stats.bls.gov/oes/2000/oessrcma.htm>
   - Homefair.com <www.homefair.com/>
   - Salary.com <www.salary.com>

OTHER RESOURCES. In addition to books and Web sites, additional information resources and tools can increase your Internet career skills. Relevant articles about finding jobs and other career information on the Internet can be found in career center resource materials and in other print and electronic collections, including the campus library. In many campus and public library settings, you will find guides or information sheets with specific or generalized instructions for using and finding information on the Internet. Finally, consider attending a workshop for detailed instruction, in-depth assistance, and hands-on practice on how to effectively use the Internet in a job search.

Now that we have reviewed some of the basic sources of information about using the Internet in career planning and employment, we focus on how the Internet can help a job hunter learn more about an organization or a job target.

Employer and Job Information

By using effective online research strategies, you can locate specific, detailed industrial and employer data on the Internet. The more you develop skills in keyword and advanced searching techniques, the more effectively you can communicate your research objectives and obtain the information you need. Directory Web sites maintain databases of public and private enterprises, where you can identify employers by location, industry, occupation, or employer name. For example, you can locate the Chamber of Commerce directory for many towns in the U.S. at www.chamberof commerce.com.

Another useful Web site, www.learnwebskills.com/company/index.html, provides a way for you to search for companies online. Don't forget that your campus library may have other tools to help you research employers. Articles from newspapers, magazines, and other media sources, available through online databases, can give you an organization's history, its current position in the industry, new products or services, major competitors, and general financial status. Employer Web sites often contain mission statements, annual reports, employee benefits information, and press releases. Information on employer sites typically favors the employer, so you may want to use other resources in your research to get a complete picture of the organization. For example, Glassdoor (www.glassdoor. com) describes its site as an "inside look at jobs and companies," that includes information provided by current employees and job seekers who have interviewed with various organizations.

The Internet is also a place to search job openings. As noted in our earlier discussion of Web sites, job database services contain job listings that may be searched by criteria such as location, industry, occupation, salary level, position, etc. The more you know about the type, level, and location of the job you want, the more efficient your search will be. Specialty sites focus on certain geographic regions (local, state or international), type of work (industry or occupation), or targeted populations (e.g., people with disabilities, LGBT people, career changers, veterans), and usually include both job openings and career information.

In addition to some of the Web sites listed below, check newspapers in cities where you are seeking employment (e.g., www.orlandosentinel.com) or specialty sites (e.g., www.overseasjobs.com). Employers may ask you to submit your resume electronically. However, many organizations want you to do things the "old-fashioned way" and send your resume and related application materials through the (snail) mail. Read the instructions carefully when following up on any job listing to see which communication methods the employer prefers.

RSS FEEDS. With so many job listing sites on the Internet, it is easy to become overwhelmed and frustrated with regard to where you should focus your time and energy. One way to be more efficient in gathering job listings is to use what is called an RSS feed. An RSS (Rich Site Summary or Really Simple Syndication) feed helps you collect job listings and related information from constantly changing Web sites that include blogs, job search databases, professional association job lists, and more. An RSS feed allows you to receive new information the moment it is posted, and have it sent to one specified location or folder designated by you.

You can choose from various applications (e.g., Google, Bloglines, Live Bookmarks) to create your RSS feed. For example, if you use Google, you can access recent job postings with your Google reader (found under the "More" tab). Or if you use Live Bookmarks, you can access recent job postings on the toolbar in your Web browser. Simply choose Web sites that may be relevant to your job search and look for this symbol or the words "RSS feed." Make sure that you type in the details for your job search before looking for the RSS feed. For example, if you decide to use Indeed.com, type in the position title and the location, and then connect to the RSS feed. You can usually find the RSS feed link or symbol at the top of the webpage, but it may also be on the side bar or at the bottom of the site. This tool can be a helpful resource for keeping up on the latest job postings and organizing your job search on the Internet.

Online Social Networking

In Chapter 11 we noted the importance of social networking with other people in a job campaign because it provides a way to enter the "hidden" job market and get recommendations and support from friends or associates. The Internet makes it possible to do networking in an easy and expanded way. The purpose of social networking sites is to connect people to one another and to share as much personal and professional information as they wish. With social media, people can create Web logs or blogs to report about their lives and invite others to share similar information. In the following section we briefly describe four of the more common social networking tools that might be used in a job campaign: Blogs, Facebook, Twitter, and LinkedIn (McEvoy, 2010).

BLOGS. Blogs are a way to build your personal, online "brand" or reputation, and they provide a home base for networking. Given that you have total control of your blog contents and you are using it in your job campaign, stick to ideas, trends, and issues in your field of career interests. It might help to think of your blog as a personal portfolio or a detailed resume that includes accomplishments, work history, goals, and photos. A recruiter for a major sports media organization who recently visited the authors' career center described how he used his pro football sports blog to get the attention of his prospective employers and finally land his dream job after four years of trying.

FACEBOOK. Facebook's history is with personal and social networking, but because of its massive size employers have taken an interest by advertising positions and screening applicants. Facebook offers an extensive array of applications that can become overwhelming and challenging to manage. For example, the U.S. Department of Labor and Facebook have now launched a Social Jobs Partnership (www.facebook.com/socialjobs), which will provide a one-stop shop for both employers and job-seekers directly from Facebook. It will also provide information about education and training (Tsukayama, 2011).

It is important to remember that Facebook is built on a model that packages your personal information and shares it with advertisers—the more information you provide about yourself the more you are worth to the company (Lyons, 2010). For these reasons, it is important to regularly update your privacy settings on Facebook and avoid posting information about your job or your employer.

TWITTER. This microblogging tool limits posts to 140 characters. McEvoy (2010) describes quick tweets as comparable to conference chatter with questions, ideas, and insights about work passed around. Also like a conference, regular communication once or twice a day is important in order to be perceived as an active member. A successful Twitter campaign means finding people and getting others to follow you, starting with 50 people and working up to hundreds. "Networking on steroids" is the way one person described Twitter in a job campaign (McEvoy, 2010). Many organizations are using Twitter to highlight current activities and events, as well as to recruit new employees. In addition, Twitter has launched its own job search engine, www.twitjobsearch.com.

LINKEDIN. LinkedIn (www.linkedin.com) is a professional social networking site with over 150 million users globally. It is growing by two million members each month, including executives from all Fortune 500 companies and over 170 industries (Pollak, 2009). It provides social networking for you through "connections" when you ask co-workers and friends to join your professional network. These connections provide a special access to members where contacts must know one another or be introduced from a common contact. Members can participate in groups and write recommendations for other contacts that may be seen by employers. Members can also use search functions to find contacts in a specific organization or browse employer profiles. Organizations post jobs on LinkedIn and you can choose to "follow" a particular company to stay current with corporate trends and hiring needs.

To network online with LinkedIn, you have to develop a profile, a page of information that gives a brief introduction about your personal history, interests, goals, and accomplishments. Pollak (2009) provided some tips about profile development:

- Include keywords from our bio that a search engine might pick up
- Post a friendly photo
- Write for the screen with bullets and short sentences
- List all your experiences

- Collect diverse recommendations with one for each of your past jobs
- Share your news by updating your status or current projects.

After creating a profile, you can search for friends, colleagues (former and present), classmates, using the tools available in the system. Build connections through existing groups such as university alumni, student professional groups, specific companies and organizations, and by asking questions. Some have described LinkedIn as "the Rolodex of the business world" because it notifies users when someone's information (e.g., job title, work address), have been updated (McEvoy, 2010). An employer could review this profile information to identify a potential recruit from a rival company or identify someone with professional interests and goals that match the organization's needs.

Issues With Social Networking

A major issue is the extent to which a person wants to use a social media site for posting personal versus professional information. Some social networking sites blur the distinction between the two by having "friends" who are both family members and co-workers or mentors. When employers or potential employers begin to examine "personal" information posted in Facebook, for example, the distinction between personal and professional information is further blurred.

"Digital dirt," which includes one's rants and raves, photos, hobbies, and other unflattering personal information drifting around the Internet on blogs and social networking sites, can become a liability in a job campaign. It has reportedly doomed some candidates' job searches before they got going because employers checked out these sites regarding prospective hires and decided not to pursue the applicant further.

Employers, aware of the expanding use of social media, have started conducting searches of potential employees as they appear on social networking sites. Experts remind students and others in the job market to carefully edit the information they post about themselves, especially photographs, political and religious statements, group memberships, or humor. Social media has emerged as a recruiting tool because it is a cost-effective, targeted way for employers to find talent without making a large investment in travel and on-campus appearances.

Employers have conducted background checks for a long time (e.g., credit reports, driving record, criminal history), but now they can examine information in social media to see information about one's personal interests, hobbies, and political views. More than 90% of employers are using social media to check on more than posted photographs (Rainey, 2012). For example, they could check LinkedIn to see if a candidate's background matches up with the resume.

In some instances, employers have asked a candidate to "friend" them (a forced friend) so that personal Facebook information could be reviewed before making a final hiring decision. A more recent controversy has involved employers asking candidates to log in to their Facebook site so employers can access the information directly. Issues about the legality of this are yet to be resolved. Lory (2010) noted that the law tends to lag behind the use of technology, and the use of Facebook to screen applicants is unregulated. The National Association of Colleges and Employers has not taken a position on this matter, but Lory (2010) concluded that students should be aware that their personal image becomes transferred to an employer if they are hired and employers have a right, at least currently, to screen applicants using social media tools.

Internet Networking Resources

The Internet can be a great way to network with professionals in different fields and organizations, even though you do not generally interact face-to-face. In fact, a great deal of your networking communications will be written e-mails or postings and should follow good "netiquette" (an appropriate level of formality). Developing relationships, building up your contacts, sharing information, getting advice, and establishing a credible presence in your field can be done in various ways, including professional association listservs, social networking site forums, chat groups (e.g., http://groups.google.com/, http://groups.yahoo.com/), and related entities. Association Web sites, in addition to providing career information and education resources, may offer online mentoring programs, sponsor chat forums (in some cases these are hosted on LinkedIn), and/or provide access to membership directories.

An example of an association Web site for public relations majors is http://www.prssa.org/. The Florida chapter of this group also has a LinkedIn group. Another is the American Society for Association Executives, which provides directories to people in various professional groups (www.asae center.org). Listservs allow members to send and automatically receive messages via e-mail; thus, professionals use listservs for their particular career area to discuss significant industry topics and trends and to post an occasional job opening. Discussion forums or groups can provide you with current job openings in your field and/or professional networking opportunities, as users ask and answer questions of interest to the group and post job openings, career fair announcements, and resumes.

Although e-mail is common and flexible, it is important to remember that in a job campaign your messages communicate an image of you as a professional. Besides being detailed and concise, here are some other pointers: (a) use spell check; (b) provide an informative title in the subject line; (c) never use "hey" as a greeting instead of Mr., Ms., or Dr.; (d) reply in a timely fashion; (e) sign off courteously; and (f) limit the graphics in your signature card because it may be blocked by the recipient's computer (Primm, 2004).

Research Reports

The use of the Internet in job campaigns has created considerable interest and controversy. However, there is little published research about this topic and even less of it is refereed (evaluated by independent reviewers before publication). Given this situation, we can share some of what we have found.

The traditional way of using the Internet in a job campaign was through job boards such as Monster and CareerBuilder, but organizations may be increasingly moving to social media such as Facebook and LinkedIn. In part this is happening because Facebook has a 750-million user base and LinkedIn has dominated the professional networking area (Light, 2011). This means that organizations using job boards and social networks have different views of what is happening.

For example, http://monster.com, the online job board, reported that only 42% of companies indicated social networks were useful in recruiting college students. However, Adams (2011) reported that almost 90% of companies are *planning* to use social networks to find job candidates, compared to 83% a year earlier. These findings came from Jobvite, a company that helps organizations find candidates using social networks. Adams also reported that LinkedIn was the top site for hiring and was used by nearly 87% of companies, contrasted with Facebook, which was used for recruiting by 55%. In terms of actual hires, Facebook users reported 43%, LinkedIn 41%, and Twitter 16%.

In contrast to these industry reports, a survey by the Collegiate Employment Research Institute (CERI; 2012) at Michigan State University indicated that social media was used by only 36% of employers respondents in that survey. Leonard (2011) reported the results of a recent survey conducted by the Society for Human Resource Management that asked employers about Web-based recruitment and the use of social networking sites. Twenty-six percent of respondents said that their organization used search engines to screen applicants, and 18% said their companies used social networking sites. Finally, Light (2011) noted that hires through Facebook accounted for less than 1% of total company hires according to Jobs2Web, which helps companies track the sources of candidates and hires. These numbers reveal some of the conflicting information on this topic.

Pros and Cons of Using the Internet in a Job Search

Most authorities agree that the Internet should supplement, not replace, other information sources and job-search methods. Continue to utilize all contacts, information resources, and services available to you for the most effective and efficient search for employment. Like other job-search tasks, using the Internet requires you to use good research and critical evaluation skills.

Using the Internet for your job search lets you do the following:

1. Access timely (and often free) employment resources and data both day and night.
2. Locate unusual or difficult-to-find career information.
3. Communicate with many people or resource groups in specialized areas.
4. Research potential employers and organizations.
5. Identify position openings by occupation and state.
6. Post your resume and apply online on various networks.

Margaret Dikel, creator of the Web-based Riley Guide, provides additional tips on how to use the Internet in your job search (www.rileyguide.com/jobsrch.html).

Some drawbacks of using the Internet for your job search include:

1. Vast, unwieldy amounts of career and job search information (sometimes it's like looking for a needle in a haystack).
2. Privacy issues related to posting your resume and other personal information online.
3. Overuse of the Internet and underuse of traditional job-hunting resources (print, people, etc.)
4. Disappearance or relocation of useful sites without notice.
5. Dated or inaccurate information found on some Web sites.
6. Fees for access to some resources and job listings (it may be hard to determine if it is worth paying the fee!)

Despite these drawbacks, the Internet can still play a key role as one tool in your job-search kit. Three job search activities—networking, researching employers, and identifying job openings—take advantage of the Internet's capabilities.

This is a brief overview on using the Internet as part of your job search strategy—to locate job listings, research employers, network with professionals, and learn about specific job search topics such as salary negotiation, interviewing, or starting your first job. Understanding how to use the Internet effectively may give you an edge in your job campaign. As can be seen from all the activities described above, job searching involves considerable information processing, storage, and retrieval. This is part of the reason why we believe a cognitive information processing (CIP) approach to career decision making is appropriate.

A CIP Perspective

We have discussed written communications associated with a job campaign, including letters, resumes, and the Internet. Now we'll review what we have learned about this topic from a CIP perspective.

Self-Knowledge

In developing various forms of written communication in the job-search process, your self-knowledge is extremely important. Both the cover letter and the resume are marketing tools that communicate to prospective employers how you see yourself and what you have to offer. Using the results of your self-assessment, you can better describe the skills you want to use, the types of interests you want to incorporate into your work, and what's important to you about the type of work you do. If your self-knowledge is vague or disorganized, it makes it hard to focus your job search and communicate to employers what it is you want to do for and with them.

Option Knowledge

Being effective in written communication in your job campaign means knowing enough about prospective employers, job targets, and industries to express effectively why you want to be considered for a particular position and why your qualifications make you a good candidate for the position. There's an old saying in the job-hunting process: "You can't go looking until you know what you're searching for." A job campaign means knowing what's out there, and that involves learning about the various environments where you might find employment.

Decision Making

The information gathered in the Analysis phase of the CASVE Cycle helps you move to the Synthesis phase, where you may expand your thinking about job search options and then narrow that list to those three to five options with the most potential for you. When you move into the Execution phase and begin writing resumes and cover letters, these tasks become a little easier when you're working with accurate and well-focused information about what your want in a job and which employers have the potential to meet your objective.

Targeting employers and implementing a plan to reach them using various communication methods requires you to give attention to each aspect of the CASVE Cycle. Most experts agree that a job hunter who goes right to the Execution phase, sending out dozens of resumes, applying for anything, anywhere, is doomed to failure, either because that person will fail to turn up any serious offers or will accept a position that is a poor fit with his or her longer-term personal requirements. In developing your PCT for solving employment problems, you will want to avoid this trap.

Executive Processing

Some job hunters sabotage themselves early on in a job campaign with the poor quality metacognitions embedded in their PCT. For example, we often hear job hunters saying things such as "I don't have anything to put on a resume." "What employer would be interested in me?" "I don't have any work experience in my field." "I've searched online for jobs in my major and there aren't any." These job hunters allow themselves to be intimidated by thoughts of rejection, and they engage in negative thinking when they put themselves on paper or use Internet resources in the job search. They only have vague notions of what they want to communicate, and their lack of confidence comes through in their job-search documents.

If you don't think you're someone worth hiring, employers probably won't either. We suggest that you use the techniques described earlier in this text to learn how to think more positively about what you have to offer, and make sure this is clearly communicated in all your written correspondence with prospective employers.

Summary

This chapter highlighted and contrasted basic forms of written communication used in the employment campaign. Despite many advances in electronic communication, much of the job-search process still relies on standard forms of written and verbal communication. In fact, you may see employers noting in their position announcements "Do not send e-mails." Demonstrating effective written communication skills can greatly increase your chances of gaining access to employers and achieving the ultimate goal of a job offer that matches your personal goals and preferences. We concluded this chapter with an analysis of how CIP concepts can help you think through the information you need to communicate in written forms to prospective employers and avoid the tendency to let negative thinking interfere with your ability to successfully present your paper "credentials." The goal was to enable you to improve the quality of your PCT related to written communications and the employment process.

References

Adams, S. (2011, July 13). More employers using social media to hunt for talent. Retrieved from www.forbes.com/sites/susanadams

Beecher, M. (2011, November). Only assets need apply. *HR Magazine, 56*, 84–85.

Bolles, M. E., & Bolles, R. N. (2011). *Guide to job hunting online* (6th ed.). Berkeley, CA: Ten Speed Press.

Collegiate Employment Research Institute (CERI, 2012). *Recruiting trends, 2011–2012*. East Lansing, MI: CERI. Also available at http://www.ceri.msu.edu/wp-content/uploads/2010/11/Recruiting-Trends-2011-2012.pdf

Dikel, M., & Roehm, F. (2008). *The guide to Internet job searching 2008–2009*. Columbus, OH: McGraw-Hill.

Farr, J. M. (2009). *The very quick job search*. (3rd ed.). Indianapolis, IN: JISTWorks, Inc.

Hill, P. (2012). *The panic free job search: Unleash the power of the web and social networking to get hired*. Pompton Plains, NJ: The Career Press, Inc.

Leonard, B. (2011, October). Few employers use social media networks to screen candidates. *HR Magazine, 56*(10), 16.

Light, J. (2011, August 8). Recruiters troll Facebook for candidates they like. *Wall Street Journal online*. Retrieved from http://online.wsj.com

Lyons, D. (2010, June 7). Facebook's false contrition: A business built on your data. *Newsweek*, 20.

McEvoy, C. (2010). Let's get digital. *ADVANCE for Healthcare Careers*, 29–33.

Osborn, D., Riley-Dikel, M., Sampson, J. P., Jr., & Harris-Bowlsbey, J. (2011). *Career planning and the Internet* (3rd ed.). Broken Arrow, OK: NCDA.

Pollak, L. (2009, November). Everything you always wanted to know about LinkedIn. *NACE Journal*, 24–26.

Primm, C. (2004). E-mail etiquette. *KForce professional staffing*. Retrieved from http://www.kfroce.com/kforce/corporate/me.get?WEB.entities.show&Kforce_00548

Rainey, M. (2012, March). Social media background checks: How your Facebook and Twitter accounts can cost you a job. *Insight Diversity*, 6–7.

Reeves, E. G. (2009). *Can I wear my nose ring to the interview?* New York, NY: Workman Publishing.

Tsukayama, H. (2011, October 20). Facebook, Labor launch "Social Jobs Partnership." *The Washington Post*. Retrieved from www.washingtonpost.com/blots/

Weber, L. (2012, January 24. Your resume vs. oblivion. *The Wall Street Journal online*. Retrieved from http://wsj.com/article/

Chapter Thirteen

Interpersonal Communications in Job Hunting

In addition to the written communications presented in Chapter 12, job hunters also need skills in verbal and interpersonal communication. A person might get a job offer without submitting a resume or completing an application, but it is almost inconceivable that a person would get a job offer without being interviewed. Job hunting is basically a social process that involves meeting and talking with different people. There is no way to escape this reality.

The interpersonal communication skills needed in job hunting take many different forms, including information interviews, networking, initial interviews, and second interviews or site visits. Mastering the skills associated with these different kinds of interview situations can significantly increase your success as a job hunter. There are entire books, Web sites, and seminars devoted to helping job hunters improve their skills in these forms of verbal communication, and this chapter will provide a basic overview. We will include distinctions between the terms listed above and suggest strategies for effectively using these communication techniques in the job-search process. (Note: Although our focus is on job hunting, effective interpersonal communication is also associated with applications for job-training programs, internships, co-op positions, and graduate school.)

As you read about how verbal communications are used in a job campaign, think about how your Personal Career Theory (PCT) and strategic career thinking can be improved by this information. How will this information affect the kind of job campaign activities you will pursue, how will you go about preparing and improving your interviewing skills, and how much time will you devote to these activities? How and when will you begin preparing for the interpersonal aspects of a job campaign? Our goal in this chapter is to help you improve your PCT and the interpersonal skills needed for solving employment problems.

Information Interviews

One way to research a potential employer or career field is through "informal" sources of information. Information interviews involve direct meetings set up with selected people to obtain "insider" information about an industry, occupation, organization, or training program, which may provide answers to your questions that print or electronic resources do not cover. An information interview can help you learn about special problems or needs associated with a work area and how you might fit into a job situation.

Information interviews can often be arranged regardless of an existing job vacancy. In contrast, an employer may not grant a job interview because vacancies do not exist.

Unlike job interviews, information interviews require you to initiate contact with an employer and schedule the appointment. If you already have a referral through friends, family, former employers, or associates, you can call or e-mail the interviewee directly to set up an appointment at his or her convenience. If you don't have a referral, you may seek contacts from your campus career services staff, faculty, or other university personnel, alumni organizations, individuals, and groups on social networking sites, members of professional organizations and trade associations, or local newspapers and magazines, or you can contact the employer directly and ask for suggestions. In setting up an information interview, a possible lead-in might be to explain that you are conducting personal research on occupations in areas of interest to you.

Preparing for the information interview and conducting yourself well during the 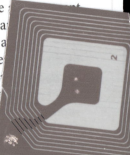 are very important. You must truly desire to obtain information from the interviewee a prepared questions related to the occupation or work area you're trying to learn more a

Information interviews should not be used in a dishonest way to obtain a job inte employer. For example, don't pretend to need information about a position or organiz cuse for an interview when you already have the information. People who do this ha mation interviewing a bad name in some places, and organizations have adopted po ing staff from participating in information interviews.

Information interviews should not be used to obtain information that is readily where else, such as in employer literature, Web sites, or other media sources. Also, do your home work on the field you're seeking to enter by reading career information before you call to set up the interview. You can then use the information interview to verify the impressions you've gained from other sources.

Preparing for the Information Interview

Here are some possible questions you might want to ask in an information interview. Remember, you are using this technique in personal research related to your career options, and you want to select questions that will provide information to help you move through the CASVE Cycle.

1. *Background.* Tell me how you got started in this field. What was your education? What educational background or related experience are helpful in entering this field?
2. *Work environment.* What are the daily job duties? What are the working conditions?
3. What *skills/abilities* are utilized in this work?
4. *Problems.* What are the toughest problems you deal with? What challenges does the organization as a whole face? What is being done to meet these challenges?
5. *Lifestyle.* What, if any, work obligations do you have outside the workweek? How much flexibility do you have in terms of dress? Work hours? Vacations?
6. *Rewards.* What do you find most rewarding about this work?
7. *Salary.* What are typical salary ranges for people entering this field? What are some typical fringe benefits? What are other forms of compensation (bonuses, commissions, securities)?
8. *Potential.* Where do you see yourself going in a few years? What are your short- and long-term goals?
9. *Promotional.* What are the opportunities for advancement in this organization? How does one move from position to position? How are employees evaluated? What types of training are typically available to help employees maintain and diversify their skills?
10. *Industry.* What trends do you see for this industry in the next three to five years? What kind of future do you see for this organization? How much of your business is tied to the economy, government spending, weather, and global marketplace conditions?
11. *Demand.* What types of employers hire people in this line of work? Where are they located?
12. *Networking.* Whom might you contact to obtain further useful information? Request the names, phone numbers, and/or e-mail addresses of people in similar positions at other organizations.

Answers to these and related questions should provide you with supplemental information beyond what is available in print resources, on Web sites, and in recruiting materials.

Arranging an Information Interview

To arrange an information interview, e-mail or phone people you wish to interview and request a brief meeting (20 to 30 minutes) at their convenience. Given that the person doesn't really owe you the time and information, it is important to be respectful and courteous. It's preferable if you can introduce yourself by using a personal referral, for example, "Ms. Jones in the New Products Division suggested I contact you to get more information on opportunities in the Web-based marketing field." If the person you contact is busy, ask when would be a better time in the future to speak to you, or ask if he or she could suggest someone else in the organization that might be able to answer your questions.

Be prepared to encounter staff members who may not let you through. Be persistent. Be aware that, having been abused by other job hunters, some employers may be suspicious, and they may question you rather directly about your motives and purpose in seeking to meet with them. Be ready to answer questions from people you call about why you want the meeting. Some people only hear the word "interview" and immediately try to put you off by saying, "we don't have openings" or something similar. You need to be clear in your purpose—that you're seeking some "real world" information about a field or industry you're interested in, information not available through print sources. Anticipate these types of questions by employers so that you're not intimidated or flustered, and politely but firmly explain your purpose in seeking a face-to-face meeting with them.

Sometimes when you make your phone call to set up the interview, the person will say, "I have some time now—what would you like to know?" Be ready for this! This means that you need to be prepared for the interview before you call and have the questions in front of you, so you will not be thrown by the interviewee's willingness to talk on the spur of the moment.

The following are more tips for handling an information interview:

- Practice with a friend or career advisor who can help you become comfortable asking questions if information interviewing is a new skill for you.
- Dress as if it were an actual job interview. First impressions are always important, and it is possible that the interviewee might be impressed with the way you conduct the interview and offer you an internship or an opportunity to interview for a job later.
- Get to your appointment a few minutes early, and be courteous to every staff member that you meet, regardless of their position in the organization.
- Take the initiative in conducting the interview. You ask the questions; you interview the person. Ask open-ended questions that promote a discussion and cannot be answered with one-word responses. Make it a conversation—ask follow-up questions about things that interest you.
- Once inside the organization, look around. What kind of work environment do you find? What are the dress styles? The communication patterns? The office arrangements? The organizational culture? Is this a place you would want to be trained or work?
- Do not exceed your requested time for the interview, but be prepared to stay longer in case the interviewee is willing to continue the conversation beyond the allotted time.

After the Information Interview

After the information interview, follow up immediately and send a note thanking the person for taking the time to meet with you. This can be done via e-mail, but remember, as noted in Chapter 12, to communicate in a professional manner regardless of the method. If, as a result of the meeting, you want to pursue further employment with the organization, you may follow up later with a cover letter, resume, or application. Record the information you obtained in the interview (e.g., names, comments, new referrals). Make appointments to conduct follow-up interviews with the referrals you were given. Every information interview contact will hopefully produce the names of additional individuals to add to your networking circle.

EVALUATE YOUR EXPERIENCE. Were you pleased with how the process went? Did you get the information you sought? What information do you still lack? What do you need to do next? Sometimes people come away from information interviews saying, "That was a waste of my time. They didn't have any openings." That kind of statement reflects a lack of understanding of the many uses of the information interview. Although it would be ideal if every information interview uncovered "hidden" openings, you need to go in with the understanding that in most cases all you will be getting is a unique source of information to help you in exploring options and employers, and possibly referrals to other useful contacts. Any information about specific openings is a bonus. Getting job leads should not be the primary goal in conducting information interviews.

Information interviews have the potential to make you a more informed job hunter and enable you to make better decisions about your future options, including internships, training programs, and organizational preferences. Many job-hunting books (e.g., Bolles, 2012) have additional tips devoted to information interviewing. If you're unsure about how to best use information interviews in your job-search process, or are hesitant about getting started, read additional information about this technique in these books or talk with a career advisor about how you can incorporate this useful tool into your job-hunting kit.

Social Networking

Much like information interviews, social networking can be a valuable asset in the job-search process. It is another example of the interpersonal processes of job hunting. Networking can provide the following information:

- Inside knowledge about job opportunities, especially the "hidden" job market within an organization,
- Means for making a valuable contact within an organization, which employers indicate is the most important thing in considering an applicant, and
- General knowledge about career fields and industry trends.

Numerous sources stress the importance of networking as one of the keys to an effective job-hunting strategy. Much useful information about occupations, job openings, what's happening in organizations, and industry trends can be learned by researching more than print materials. The people contacts in your network are just as important (and sometimes more important) as print-based resources, especially given the rapidly changing nature of the workplace. People sources are more likely to have up-to-the-minute information about what's happening in a particular field or organization, and they may be able to provide direct access to the people making hiring decisions.

The power of networking was apparent at one professional meeting several years ago. A workshop leader asked 75 participants if anyone needed help in his or her job campaign. A woman raised her hand and indicated that she was being transferred and that her spouse was looking for a job in the private security field in the Seattle area. By asking a series of questions of the group, such as did anyone have a family member or friend working in the investigative and security fields or did anyone know people working in that career field in the northwestern United States, the leader quickly found three people who could provide the woman with information about jobs for her spouse in Seattle. In two minutes, the woman went from zero potential job contacts to several, and more were probably reported to her after the session ended. Farr (2004) likens this to the idea behind the movie *Six Degrees of Separation*, in that it is possible to "connect to anyone on the planet through the personal contacts in a chain of just six or fewer people" (p. 44). With the explosion in the number of social media sites, this same networking strategy can be implemented many times over and reach an even wider audience in a matter of seconds.

There are several important factors related to networking that are useful to keep in mind:

- Networking is a transferable skill that can be learned and polished.
- Join a professional group (even as a student member) and volunteer to serve on a committee or in a leadership role to begin to develop your network early on.
- Network with alumni from your school who majored in your field; many career centers have Web-based resources for this purpose and many alumni have created major and department-specific groups on social media sites.
- Social media reviewed in Chapter 12 provide powerful tools to assist in professional networking for a job campaign.

Although *networking* may seem like a simple and familiar term, there are several factors to consider when including this as part of your job-search strategy. First, networking is an activity that draws upon your self-knowledge. Whom you choose to network with may be based on your ideas about people who share your interests or values or work in organizations that reflect your interests or the skills you would like to use. For example, do you enjoy being outdoors (interest) and believe it's important to protect the environment (value)?

Second, self-knowledge can be used to narrow the list of organizations or employers that you will focus on in your research. In the case of the person who likes the outdoors, he or she might seek employment with nonprofit environmental organizations and might find it helpful to network with members of the Sierra Club or Audubon Society. This knowledge about yourself and the options you're considering can help guide your networking activity.

Third, networking is like a web of interconnected people and can be the basis of lifelong relationships. A network is not something to be used for short-term gain and discarded.

Job Interviews

The ultimate aim in a job-search strategy is a job offer. However, the gateway to offers is generally through the face-to-face interviewing process. The initial job interview may occur in a college or university setting (often called "on-campus interviews"), at conventions, on location at the work setting, or even in hotel rooms. As with other forms of interpersonal communication used in the job search process, job interviewing is a skill that can be learned and polished. At this point, we discuss what must happen before the initial job interview, what to expect during the job interview, and how to follow up after an interview. *In all of this review of job campaign and interview procedures, just remember that hiring is a people-intensive process where one person or persons make a choice to hire another person.*

Interview Questions

Students preparing for a job interview are typically focused on the questions they will be asked. Bradt (2011) suggested that every interview question is intended to focus on three critical areas: (a) strengths, (b) motivation, and (c) fit. More specifically, the three questions in the interviewer's mind are: (a) Can you do the job? (b) Will you love the job? (c) Can we tolerate working with you? If you can reassure the interviewer about your qualities in these three areas with examples and insights, you will probably have a successful interview

Sounding a similar theme, Bolles (2012) suggested that an employer wants to know five things about you, and your self-knowledge provides the basis for responding to these questions: (a) Why are you here? (b) What can you do for us? (c) What kind of person are you? (d) What distinguishes you from the others? (e) Can we afford you? In effect, you as a job hunter are selling yourself as a solution to the problem facing an organization.

To help you prepare for a job interview, study the 50 sample questions in Table 13.1. It is almost a guarantee that interviewers will ask some of these questions.

Table 13.1

Sample Interview Questions

Career Goals

- What are your long- and short-range career goals and objectives, when and why did you establish them, and how are you preparing yourself to achieve them?
- What specific goals (other than occupation) do you have for the next 10 years?
- What do you see yourself doing five years from now?
- How will this position assist in achieving your career goals?
- What are the most important rewards you expect in your career?
- What do you expect to be earning in five years?

Self-Knowledge

- Why did you choose the career for which you are preparing?
- What do you consider to be your greatest strengths and weaknesses?
- How would you describe yourself?
- How do you think a friend or professor who knows you well would describe you?
- What motivates you to put forth your greatest effort?
- How do you determine or evaluate success?
- What qualifications do you have that make you think that you will be successful in this field?
- We have all accomplished things in our lives that we are proud of. What do you consider to be your greatest accomplishment at this point in your life?

Experiential Knowledge (College, Internships, & Jobs)

- What have you learned from participation in extracurricular activities?
- What have you learned from your previous jobs or internships?
- In what kind of work environment are you most comfortable?
- In what part-time or summer jobs have you been most interested? Why?
- How would you describe the ideal job for you following graduation?
- How have your previous experiences prepared you to be successful in this position?

Industry & Occupational Knowledge

- Why did you decide to seek a position with this organization?
- What do you know about our organization?
- What two or three things are most important to you in your job?
- Are you seeking employment in an organization of a certain size? Why?
- What criteria are you using to evaluate the organization for which you hope to work?
- Do you have a geographical preference? Why?
- Will you relocate? Does relocation bother you?
- Are you willing to travel?
- Are you willing to spend at least six months as a trainee?

Decision-Making Abilities

- Give me a specific example of a time when you used good judgment and logic in solving a problem.
- Give me an example of a time when you had to make a split-second decision.
- Tell me about a difficult decision you've made in the last year.
- How did you decide on the school you wanted to attend?

Situational & Behavior-Based

- Talk about a time you didn't meet a deadline, and what did you do about it?
- Tell me about a time when you realized that you made a mistake. What did you do?
- Describe a time in school or work when you adapted quickly to a change of plans.
- Give me an example of when you showed initiative and took the lead.
- Describe a major problem you have encountered and how you handled it.
- How do you juggle all of your responsibilities to set priorities and stay organized? Give an example.

Closing

- Why should I hire you over another qualified candidate?
- Is there anything else that you want me to know about you and your abilities?
- What questions do you have for me?

Preparing for the Interview

When you make an appointment for an interview, you need to be fully prepared for it. You don't get a second chance to make a first impression! Think of the interview as a conversation with a person who shares mutual interests with you—you need a job, the employer has a job to fill. There are two critical areas of knowledge that come into play in this process: self-knowledge and employer knowledge. Your knowledge in each of these two areas is an important part of your pre-interview preparation.

KNOW YOURSELF. You need to know many facts about the employer, and the interviewer needs to know many facts about you to make a fair evaluation. Both of you are looking for a good match of interests, skills, and values. Before an interview, it's important to know what you have to offer a potential employer. Evaluate yourself in terms of your strengths and how you could translate these strengths into skills your prospective employer can use. It is also helpful to know your weaknesses, because no one is perfect. If you state a weakness, do not elaborate on it. Instead, try to turn it around into a potential strength for the organization.

Think about how your interests, skills, and values fit with the type of organization and position for which you are being interviewed. You may have to prioritize these in some fashion. For example, if one of your values is to make money, will this be more important than other work values you've rated highly, such as job security, having leisure time, helping others? Review the list of values in Chapter 2. Think about these in relation to each interview situation.

Be ready to talk about your career objectives, your long- and short-range goals, and your interests. Study your resume and be familiar with your educational and work background. Practice illustrating how your extracurricular activities are examples of skills in leadership and responsibility. The most important point to remember when preparing for an interview is that the prospective employer is primarily concerned with hiring someone who will make a valuable contribution to the organization.

In Chapter 9, we described jobs as being "gaps" between what the employer wants and the present situation. You as an employee are a potential "gap remover." Be prepared to present several key points that summarize your skills related to the job, and prepare questions to ask the employer about the position. With many applicants for the same job, it will be up to you to convince the interviewer that of all those interviewed, you are the best choice.

KNOW YOUR EMPLOYER. Once you've done the research on yourself, you need to use your best research skills in understanding your potential employer. Although researching employers is a process that should be continuous throughout one's job hunt, it becomes even more important prior to an actual interview. Researching potential employers is useful for a number of reasons.

1. Employers are looking for someone with a real interest in their organization, and your personal research reflects your interest, thoroughness, and enthusiasm. This is your first opportunity to show how you prepare for completing important tasks.
2. When you know something about an organization, you can describe in more relevant terms how you could work within that culture or how your skills could help the organization be successful. Being familiar with an organization can also help you answer questions such as "Why are you interested in our organization?" "Will my personality fit in this environment?" "Do my goals correspond to the promotional structure?"
3. There is more to many organizations than meets the eye. When you assume that you know enough about a potential employer without researching it, you could be overlooking important information. For example, most of us know that ESPN is a sports media company, but its divisions include over 50 business entities that span the globe.
4. Researching employers and asking informed questions will strengthen your position and help you make a positive first impression in an interview. Targeted questions resulting from research will also provide you with answers that can help you decide whether to accept an employment offer.

Your task in the interview is to discover what kinds of workers employers need and are looking for (Farr, 2004). It is important for you to find out as much as you can about the organizational history and culture where you are interviewing. Areas you may want to focus on in your research include knowledge of the industry, specific employer, occupation, and position. Ask yourself the following questions:

1. What does the organization make or what type of service does it provide?
2. What is the size of the organization? What is its organizational structure? How much potential for advancement is there within this structure?
3. Who are the organization's officers, administrators, and leaders? What about their background, recent achievements?

4. What are the employer's personnel policies? What employee benefits are typically provided?

In your research, try to find out how a position of interest to you is structured in relation to the whole organization. Review the contents of Chapter 8 on organizational culture and Chapter 9 on ways of working to obtain ideas about things to investigate. Try to pinpoint some problems, policies, or philosophies of the organization, and plan to focus on these during the interview.

You can find some of this information on the Internet, in your career center or library, or at the local public library. Your career center will likely have a Web-based job-listing and recruiting system that includes basic employer profiles with a link to the employer's "careers" Web site (e.g., www.espncareers.com). It is essential to start early when researching a specific employer. You may find a lot of information that you will need to sort through to find the important facts. If print or Web information is limited, you may need to make phone calls or set up information interviews. Additional career center materials that might be helpful are employer literature resources (e.g., brochures, DVDs), as well as various employer directories (e.g., *The Almanac of American Employers*).

Table 13.2 provides a checklist that may be used as a guide for gathering data on potential employers. The earlier you start researching, the more categories you will be able to cover. Remember, not all facts may be relevant; it depends on the type of organization you are researching.

Table 13.2

Checklist of Employer Facts to Know

Basic Facts
- Name, address, telephone of organization
- Complete product line or services provided
- Number of plants, stores, outlets, divisions, branches, and employees
- Geographical locations
- Location of corporate headquarters
- Parent or subsidiary company information

Employer History/Image
- Position of organization in the industry (leader, newcomer?)
- Organization's national and local reputation, awards, other recognition
- Associations in which the employer is an active member
- Major competitors (How can you help the employer gain a competitive edge?)
- Stock prices and history (if relevant)

Financial Information
- Size of organization and industry
- Potential growth
- Annual sales and budget growth for past five years

Philosophy/Goals
- Mission statement—should reflect current strategies and long-term goals
- Biographical information on top executives—salaries, age, education, history
- Political, research or social interests and financial support

Professional/Work Environment Concerns
- Organizational structure and processes, including teamwork
- Position descriptions, including part-time and permanent
- Types and quality of training programs
- Salary and benefits
- Typical career paths
- Employer's review or evaluation process of workers
- Background of entry-level positions and managers

Your research on prospective employers will not only increase your self-confidence, it will also impress interviewers. They will regard you as a person who has sincere interest in the organization because you took the time to find out something about it. However, simply being informed about an employer does not guarantee a successful interview unless you use that information effectively. Knowledge of products and opportunities is only helpful if you know how to tactfully weave that knowledge into the interview. Spouting out facts or prefacing a question with a lot of memorized details will not convince the employer of your interest and/or knowledge. In a later section, we will discuss how to use your research in developing questions to ask the employer during the interview. Although your personal and employer research are critical aspects of pre-interview preparation, the key to using this knowledge well is to practice what you'll say before the real thing.

Practice, Practice, Practice

The best way to improve your communication skills in this area is to practice role-playing before the interview. Ask a friend, your spouse, or roommate to help simulate an interview using the 50 sample questions in Table 13.1 as a guide. Make sure you are critiqued on the strength of your voice, posture, and eye contact.

Another suggestion for role-playing might be to get together with people who are also preparing for interviews. You could learn a lot by critiquing different approaches, and this might also be a good way to boost each other's morale. Consider recording your practice interviews and reviewing the results with someone whose opinion you respect and trust. Many career centers offer mock interview programs, which can be a great way to improve your interview skills.

A critical point to remember while practicing is to avoid memorizing what you want to say. Whether you are talking about yourself or the organization with which you are interviewing, let your words flow naturally. If you come across like you have a speech prepared, your interview will be less effective. Job interviews are, in essence, social interactions, so try to make the interview a positive social experience. Bolles (2012) suggests a 50-50 rule and a 20 second-2 minute rule. With the former, try to share "air time" equally with the interviewer. With the latter, keep your responses to questions between 20 seconds and no more than 2 minutes.

You probably will be nervous during the interview. Concentrate on what is being asked and respond appropriately and in a normal tone. After giving your response, avoid the temptation of saying to the recruiter: "did I answer your question?" If you have prepared well, your answer will fit the question. Allow the recruiter to follow up if she or he wants more detail.

Appearance and Clothes

Although there are a number of things you can't control in the interview process, it is important to use to your best advantage the things over which you do have control. One of these is the impression you make on employers with your attire. If you are seeking a professional position, you must look like a professional. A good guideline to follow is to dress as others do in the position. For some organizations, you can often take your cues from the organization's literature and Web site by observing how staff members are pictured.

Remember: Employers are evaluating you as soon as you walk in the door, and clothes make a critical first impression. Make sure it's a positive one! As Sinberg (2010) noted, individuals who appear polished and pulled together are more likely to get the job offer than those who pay less attention to appearance. Reeves (2009) suggested that the safest look for both men and women at interviews is traditional and conservative. "The idea is to give the interviewer the impression that you are already part of their organization" (Sinberg, 2010, p. 1). Although certain workplaces may tolerate more relaxed styles of dress, don't dress the part until you have the part. Here are some other general guidelines:

WOMEN. Wear a simple tailored pants suit or skirt suit. Wear conservative nail polish and lipstick. Have a neat hairdo. Keep accessories to a bare minimum (e.g., small watch and maybe small earrings). Make sure the bag or briefcase is not large (Colista, 2002). Be especially moderate in use of perfume and makeup.

MEN. Wear a clean, pressed, conservative suit with a shirt and tie. Have your shoes shined and wear plain socks. Have your hair neat and trimmed. Clean and trim your nails. Avoid flashy jewelry. Limit the use of fragrances. Neatly trimmed facial hair may or may not be OK, but it is probably best to cover tattoos until you have a better sense of the organizational culture.

Many of the general job-search sites we listed in Chapter 12 provide more detail on how to dress for an interview (e.g., http://career-advice.monster.com/job-interview/interview-appearance/jobs. aspx), including how to handle "business casual" situations. Be sure to give your outfit a "test run" before the day of the actual interview. While some research suggests that there is still discrimination on the basis of physical attributes, your choice of dress for the interview can set a positive tone and speak volumes about you before you answer the first question. If your career center offers workshops on "dress for success" or employer panels on proper interview behavior and attire, take advantage of these resources. Research has shown that "students who participate in interview preparation activities are more likely to advance in the hiring process" (Gaw, 2012, p. 1).

Being on Time

It is better to be a few minutes early than even one minute late for your interview. Interviewers have a busy schedule, and if you are late, it will cut down the amount of time allotted to you. Most important, if you are late, you will make a bad impression. As we noted earlier in the chapter, you don't get a second chance to make a first impression. If your interview is in an unfamiliar location, make sure you allow enough time for any problems with traffic or for locating the specific building or office. It is a good idea to make a test drive to the interview location at the time of day you will actually be interviewing so you can account for traffic. Ask about the best place to park. Check your appearance in the restroom beforehand.

The Initial Interview

Interviews can take many different forms. They can vary from a one-to-one contact between you and an employee of the organization, such as a human resource specialist, campus recruiter, or department manager, to a panel composed of several different employees representing various levels, functions, or teams. The situation also can vary from a single interview with an organization representative to a sequence of several interviews on a given day.

Some recruiters may conduct a highly structured interview as prescribed by the organization's human resources policies, whereas others may have a more free-flowing style. Although the specific questions asked can vary greatly, based on the type of position and the specific organization, interviewer questions tend to fall in four areas: (a) the candidate's academic background, (b) experience, (c) strengths and weaknesses, and (d) personal characteristics.

With this caution in mind, we will proceed to discuss what various authorities have indicated might happen in initial recruiting interviews and other employment interactions. Our goal is to inform you about this process and help you more effectively plan your job campaign. Many students seeking employment experience a "typical" on-campus interview, which generally lasts about 30 minutes. Although recruiters or interviewers may have a slightly different routine, the process generally proceeds as follows:

- Initial review of position requirements and applicant's resume.
- Opportunity for small talk to put the applicant at ease and review the interview structure.
- A series of questions to assess how well the candidate matches with the position.
- Sharing of information by the recruiter to explain the position in more detail and share additional information on the organization, job environment, etc. (this may occur sooner if the position and/or the organization is less well known).
- Opportunity for the candidate to ask the recruiter questions.
- A summary of what has been covered and explanation of next steps and timeline for second interview (if needed) or hiring decision.
- Recruiter completes candidate evaluation, making any notes about follow up.

TELEPHONE INTERVIEWS. Although face-to-face interviews continue to be the most common method used in hiring, organizations also use telephone interviews (we will discuss Skype in a later section) as their initial screening method. When you're actively engaged in a job hunt, you should be prepared at any time to pick up the phone and converse with an employer who calls. Telephone interviews are just as important as face-to-face interviews.

This leads us to make a point about a related issue: When you're expecting calls from employers, don't have cute, weird, or long and drawn-out messages (including music clips!) on your phone. At best, some employers will question whether you're really a candidate they want; at worse, they'll be so put off that they'll hang up and move on to the next candidate on their list.

In any case, most formal telephone interviews are set up by employers in advance. They will arrange a day and time to call you. It is probably best to take the call on a landline phone rather than your cell phone to reduce the possibility of a disconnection. They should also tell you the format for the call, such as how long the interview will last, what other staff will be sitting in, whether they will call you or whether you are to call them at a set time. Like other types of interviews, phone interviews require you to do your homework on both yourself and the organization.

One advantage of telephone interviews is that you can have some "cheat sheets" or notes in front of you to help you in responding to questions. Rosen (2011) suggests having a list of key points you want to cover in the interview. In phone interviews, you can also more easily take notes because you don't have to worry about maintaining eye contact. However, don't let your note-taking distract you from listening carefully to what is said. Some job hunters have reported that they dress for the phone interview and remember to smile because it helps them be both professional and relaxed during the interview.

Make sure you understand who's sitting in on the call, if there is more than one person present, and what their position is in the organization. You may want to sketch out a little diagram or chart of the participants in the group. If you take the call at home or in an office setting, make sure there are no distractions—hang out your "Do Not Disturb" sign. If the telephone interview goes well, you should expect a face-to-face interview at some point and certainly before a job offer is extended.

VIDEO AND SKYPE INTERVIEWS. In some cases, candidates and recruiters are not in the same location and some form of video connection is used as part of the interview process. With the availability of webcams, Skype, and other video technology, employers are able to do screening interviews without having to pay candidates' travel expenses. One of the challenges with these types of interviews is the quality of the technology on both ends. It is extremely important to check this in advance of the actual interview! If you can arrange it, be in a location where you have some technology support if things go wrong.

Interviewees need to remember to speak slowly and clearly, because there might be a delay in the sound transmission. It is also important to look at the camera and not the monitor so your face will be visible on the interviewer's monitor. Kiviat (2009) reported on a story about a candidate who leaned in too closely and gave the interviewer a close up view of his nose! Also be aware of the surrounding space and any background noises. Avoid having a messy room, barking dog, crying child, etc., as distractions during the interview (Kiviat, 2009). Check with your career center to see if their interview preparation includes practice with telephone and/or webcam interviews.

BEHAVIORAL-BASED INTERVIEWING (BBI). Behavioral-based interviewing continues to be popular with employers. Employers use this form of interviewing as a means of predicting future behavior by examining past behavior. Questions tend to focus on success experiences in your past and specific behaviors you engaged in to achieve that success. For example, students must be able to intelligently discuss how an international experience has helped them develop skills that can be used in a work setting. Keever (2008) reported that BBI was used by 70% of training managers and recruiters for Fortune 500 companies. Students should realize that BBI does not ask for opinions or pose hypothetical questions, but starts with "Tell me about a time that . . ." or "Can you think of a situation where . . .?"

In training interviewers to use BBI, Keever provided this example of how the interviewer would persist in questioning to get a more meaningful answer. If the interviewer said, "Tell me about a time you had to deliver difficult information to your intern supervisor," the student would need to focus on four areas in responding and provide more detailed information:

1. *Situation*—provide a detailed account of the situation, what was happening, and who was involved.
2. *Action*—what exactly did you do in this situation and what did others do.
3. *Outcome*—explain what happened and whether the issue was resolved, if further action was needed, and whether the supervisor was pleased.
4. *Learning*—summarize what you learned in this situation and how your behavior changed as a result.

This example illustrates why BBI takes longer than a typical 30-minute initial interview, and may run 60–90 minutes. A similar approach, called the STAR technique, is described below.

Keever (2008) also suggested that interviewers using BBI seek contrary evidence about an interviewee's behavior. For example, "Tell me about a time when your confidence served you well during your internship" will provide positive information, but contrary information can be provided if the interviewer asks, "tell me about a time when your confidence hampered your success." Students providing information about a negative experience should be prepared to explain what they learned from the experience and how that affected their subsequent behavior.

Students can prepare for behavior interviews by identifying concrete examples that specifically illustrate what they can do to solve a job problem. The examples should draw attention to specific job skills by explaining a problem and the student's solution. Ideally, the examples might also provide quantitative measures, such as percentages, and students should be prepared to explain unexpected results or provide more details in response to interviewer questions (e.g., "When the funding for our student organization was cut, I prepared a proposal for the student government fee allocation board that resulted in a $10,000 grant being given to our group in support of future projects.").

Another way to prepare for a BBI is to use the four steps in the STAR technique: Situation (S), Task (T), Action (A), and Result (R) or outcome. For example, you might recall a situation (S) when communication in a group had broken down. To resolve the problem (T), you organized informal meetings at lunch and other times (A) where members discussed issues related to the situation. As a result of these meetings and discussions, communication improved and productivity increased (R).

STRESS INTERVIEWS. Although some job hunters consider all interviews to be stress interviews, there really is a more high-pressure type of interview beyond the ordinary. According to one author (Yate, 2004), this type of interview is widespread in the professional world. These may be characterized by a barrage of unusual questions (e.g., what animal would you be if you could be any type? Why?), and the questions may be flung by many different people in a rapid-fire manner. What may seem like a simple question posed by the interviewer initially may be immediately followed by a series of why, when, who, what, how, and where questions. In this type of interview, the interviewer(s) may be intentionally trying to upset you or see how you react under pressure. Often the key to handling this type of interview is to refuse to be intimidated, keep your emotions in check, and rely on your pre-interview preparation. Don't be afraid to ask for time to think about a question or ask for clarification. If you have a really bad experience with this type of interview, you may ask yourself whether you really want to work for a place that screens prospective employees in this way.

TRICK OR "CREATIVE" QUESTIONS. Students sometimes worry about trick or creative questions being used in a job interview. Although there is no evidence that these are used often, there is some indication that puzzles and riddles may be posed by interviewers in an effort to gauge the intelligence, resourcefulness, or "outside-the-box" thinking of applicants. Pachter (2003) offered several examples: "If you could remove any of the 50 states, which would it be?" "Why are beer cans tapered on the ends?" "How long would it take to move Mt. Fuji?" "Why does a mirror reverse right and left instead of up and down?" Poundstone (2004; 2012) described several organizations (e.g., Microsoft, Google) where it is highly likely that candidates will encounter these types of questions and provides a variety of helpful suggestions on how to prepare for those situations. The verdict is still out on whether these types of questions truly identify the best candidates, but because the organizations that use them are most admired and innovative, some suggest that they must be doing something right (Poundstone, 2012).

PERFORMANCE, OR IN-BASKET, INTERVIEWING. In this type of interview you will be asked to perform tasks associated with a job in a limited amount of time. Mistakes are expected; the employer is looking for the way you handle yourself. In some cases, you will be given a particular organizational problem or situation to analyze, and you will be allowed to go into another room and formulate a response or plan for dealing with the problem. You may be given access to a computer to write your response, or you may be asked to make an oral presentation.

Although the literature provides conflicting information about the prevalence of each of these "types" of interviews, the bottom line is that candidates need to demonstrate how they can contribute value to the organization (Schuele, Madison, & Gourniak, 2010).

Katz (2007) suggested that applicants should prepare for seven general questions:

1. What do you know about us?
2. What do I need to know about you?
3. How do you work with others?
4. What are your skills relevant to this position?
5. What are your personal goals?
6. How much do you know about your area of specialization?
7. How have you handled specific situations?

Although we have presented some general guidelines related to preparing for interviews and what to expect, it is important to remember that interviews are often unpredictable and no two interviews are alike. A lot depends on the interviewer, who has control and will take the lead in conducting the interview. Try and pick up cues from the interviewer regarding when and how to respond.

Social/Emotional Competence (SEC)

In Chapters 2 and 11 we reported that skills in the area of social and emotional competence may be the most important to prospective employers. These skills include communication, problem-solving adaptability, responsibility, positive demeanor, and teamwork involving a set of interrelated behaviors that involve recognition, regulation, and impact of one's emotions and the emotions of others (Crane & Seal, 2011). Cherniss (2000) indicated that two thirds of competencies linked to superior performance in the workplace are emotional or social in nature.

How is SEC communicated in an interview? Strauss, Miles, and Levesque (2001) indicated that nonverbal cues, such as eye contact and smiling, are important indicators of positive interpersonal evaluations in an interview. Crane and Seal (2011) reported that SEC, especially self-management and relationship management, is important in getting a second interview, whereas self-management and social awareness are the dominant factors in receiving a job offer. Self-management includes demonstrated composure in the interview and relationship management includes building rapport with the interviewer, whereas social awareness includes demonstrating active listening skills. Students can gain experiences to improve their SEC through volunteering, group memberships, and mock interview experiences. In addition to your resume, you can document these types of skills through an e-portfolio and/or your profile on LinkedIn or similar social networking sites.

Salary

One question you should be ready to answer is about the expected salary. You should not mention salary on your resume. If you are completing an application form, you can write "negotiable" or "will discuss." This is preferable to leaving the item blank since the interviewer might think you overlooked it. In an interview, however, you may be asked to state a figure. Know what others with your general qualifications are being offered as starting salaries in positions similar to the one for which you are interviewing. More detail on salary issues in interviewing and negotiating job offers is presented in Chapter 14.

Candidates whose salary demands are too high may price themselves out of a job offer, especially if they appear locked in. If you are too low, interviewers might not consider you an ambitious person, and there is a chance you will be removed from further consideration for employment. Another possibility is that they might hire you at a lower rate, and then there will be no chance for negotiating a higher salary figure. One way to handle salary questions is to give a salary range. Be prepared to back up your salary request with specific information about your education and experience, as well as the research you have conducted on this question that informs your response.

"Sticky" Interview Topics

Despite the progress that's been made in the area of equal employment opportunity and the efforts that have been made to eliminate discrimination in the workplace, there are still interview situations where improper questions are asked. A discriminatory question differentiates people on a basis other than merit. Illegal questions vary among cities, counties, and states. The U.S. Equal Employment Opportunity Commission (www.eoc.gov) provides more detailed information about prohibited employment policies and practices. Employers can be held liable for discriminatory questions even if the questions were not meant to intentionally discriminate against an applicant.

In certain situations, employers may appropriately ask questions in these areas if they are asked of all candidates, if the information is clearly relevant to success on the job, and if the information obtained does not lead to employment discrimination on the basis of age, sex, gender, ethnic heritage, race, national origin, marital status, religion, or disability. For example, some government agencies or contractors are required by law to hire only U.S. citizens. Religious organizations are permitted to discriminate on the basis of religion when hiring. Some position advertisements can legitimately request gender-specific applicants, for example, for acting roles or modeling jobs.

Here are some examples of "illegal" questions:

- Are you a U.S. citizen?
- How old are you?
- What is your marital status?
- What social organizations do you belong to?
- Do you have any disabilities?
- Have you ever been arrested?

There is no one right answer regarding how to deal with these types of situations or so-called "problem" interview questions. Conrad and Salgado (2007), writing in the *NACE Journal* (National Association of Colleges and Employers), noted that you have several options:

1. Answer the question. Although you are free to do this, remember that you are answering a question that is not related to the job, and if you do not answer it satisfactorily it could hurt your chances of getting an offer.
2. Refuse to answer the question. Depending on how you frame the answer you might be perceived as challenging or abrupt. This probably would not make you an ideal candidate for receiving an offer.
3. Examine the intent of the question in relation to the job and respond accordingly. For example, if the interviewer asks, "Do you plan to get married?" You might answer, "I can meet the travel and work schedule required for this job."

Most sources suggest that you try to understand interviewers' motives in asking these types of questions. Do they want to know about your commitment to the job? Your ability to travel? Your willingness to relocate or work long hours? Getting angry or offended at the employer is unlikely to win you any points, so it is best to avoid this reaction, no matter how much you are put off by the questions. In a positive nondefensive manner, reassure the employer about your interest in the job and why you believe the position is a good fit with your skills and qualifications. Having a plan for these questions and training yourself to respond in a professional, but calm manner is likely the best strategy (Reeves, 2009).

Conrad and Salgado (2007) provided numerous examples of improper and proper questions in relation to all of the sensitive topics listed at the outset (e.g., race, gender, and others). Criminal history or arrest record can be especially problematic. Although some states have laws regulating criminal history information in the context of hiring, others do not. Even in the case of a conviction, employers must show that criminal history is related to the job. Off-the-job conduct (e.g., smoking) is another legal grey area, and employers must demonstrate that such inquiries are job related. Employers may obtain an applicant's credit report.

If you experience this type of questioning in the interview, you may decide that this is not the organization for you. However, don't always assume that the interviewer is representative of the organization. This person may only do preliminary screening, and your supervisor may question differently. Don't prematurely remove yourself from the job application process until you are certain that the organization is not a good fit, based on contact with several individuals, particularly those who would be your colleagues.

During the interview, the most important thing to remember is to be honest. Interviewers will not be able to evaluate you fairly if you attempt to mislead them. Telling interviewers what you think they want to hear is not the purpose of the interview. If you try to con interviewers, and they catch on, your chance of being invited for a second interview is slim.

Your Turn to Ask Questions

Following the interviewer's questions, you should have an opportunity to ask some questions of your own. Do your pre-interview research and prepare some relevant questions in advance. These questions should truly reflect your interest in the position and the organization and not come off as an attempt to impress the recruiter or convey a sense that you are asking simply because it is expected.

Ask questions that encourage the employer to expand on information from the organizational information you have reviewed. If you have uncovered negative information about the organization, this is not the place to discuss those findings. For example, you could ask the interviewer about corporate policy regarding government regulations (rather than a local environmental scandal), future marketing strategies for specific products (rather than a recent drop in stock prices), or descriptions of the organizational structure and culture (rather than recent store closings). Some examples of other questions include the following:

1. What kind of training do you provide? How long is the training period?
2. Where does this position fit in the organizational structure?
3. What is the normal progression of a trainee over the first few years?
4. What qualities do you see as essential for someone seeking to fill this position?
5. How much travel is involved in this position?
6. What is the nature of the supervisory and evaluation process for people in this type of position?
7. What options do I have in selecting (or accepting) assignments?
8. Will I have the opportunity to work on special projects?
9. What staff development programs are available after the initial training?
10. Is this a new position? If not a new position, what happened to the last person who held this position?

Never ask about vacation time, benefits, or similar topics. These are not work-related activities. You must talk opportunity, not security. Make sure your questions are not just focused on what's in it for you, but show that you'd like to know more about the organization and its future plans and goals. Interviewers will be impressed by your interest and preparation.

Closing

During the interview, be sensitive to signals that the interview is coming to a close. Campus interviews are usually scheduled for 20 or 30 minutes. Interviews end in different ways. Some interviewers might look at their watch, which is a cue for you that the interview is nearing an end; other interviewers are blunt—they stand up, hold out their hand, and thank you for coming in. Most employer representatives, however, expect you to sense the proper time to leave on the basis of subtle indications that your time is up.

When the interview is over, thank the interviewer for taking time to talk with you. Ask the interviewer for his or her business card. You can use this information for writing your follow-up letters. Re-emphasize your interest in the position (e.g., you want the job) and your appreciation for being considered. This is important, since many candidates mistakenly assume that interviewers sense their interest. Employers don't want to be rejected either, and believing that you are genuinely interested gives them confidence in making a job offer to you.

If the interviewer does not definitely offer you a job (this is very rarely done in the initial interview) or indicate when you will hear from him/her, ask for an estimate of a date when a decision might be made about making a job offer. Ask the interviewer if it is appropriate for you to contact him or her in the future via e-mail or phone if you want to check the status of your application.

After the Interview

Following up after an interview is a critical part of the whole interviewing process and one that is often overlooked by job hunters. It is important to send the interviewer a thank-you letter after the interview. Bolles (2012) described not sending a thank-you note right after the interview as the most overlooked step in the entire job-hunting process. You can use post-interview follow-up letters in several ways. Tell the interviewer that you are still interested in the position, and go over some of your qualifications discussed in the interview so that the interviewer's memory will be refreshed. You might include in your note a couple of pertinent questions that you did not ask in the interview.

It is important for you to be tenacious in this process, to "sell" yourself. Keep the communication going without harassing the employer. Some employers have noted that those receiving an offer have most likely asked for it. It shows initiative and commitment. If the interviewer answers you quickly, this might be an indication that you are still under active consideration for an offer. However, employers vary greatly in the length of time they take to make hiring decisions. For some it may be a matter of days, for others it may take several weeks or months to fill a position (Reeves, 2009). If you determine, based on the interview, that you would not accept the position if it were offered, use the letter-writing guidelines presented in Chapter 12 to halt the selection process. For most interview situations, these letters are considered business correspondence. As we've noted previously, regardless of whether you send your response via e-mail or regular mail, it is still important to maintain your professionalism and not burn any bridges. For further hints, see the section in Chapter 12 on job offer rejection letters.

As soon as possible after the interview, write down what you have learned. Ask yourself these questions:

- What points did I make that seemed to interest the employer?
- Did I present my qualifications well?
- Did I talk too much? Too little?
- Was I too tense? Was I too assertive? Not assertive enough?
- What questions were difficult for me? How can I improve my answers?

By reviewing your performance, you can make plans to improve your skills. You may want to discuss your experience with someone whose opinion you respect and trust. Remember, the more you interview, the sharper your skills become and the sooner you will receive an offer! A next step before the offer, however, is often the second interview or site visit. We will now look at how these might differ from the initial interview.

Second Interviews/Site Visits

The second or onsite interview is usually the final step in obtaining a job offer. You probably have a 50% chance of receiving an offer at this point, although this probability varies according to industries and organizations. Both the employer and you as the interviewee should have specific goals during the second interview. What might some of these be? In initial interviews, employers typically focus on many general qualities that are important in their organization. In the second interview, employers are more likely to be trying to determine if you have the specific qualities they are seeking in a new employee. Employers also want to see how others in the organization respond to you and if you fit into the organizational culture.

As an interviewee, this is an additional opportunity to decide if this is an organization from which you would accept a job offer. It is important to remember that the second interview allows you the opportunity to view the facilities, get answers to questions not addressed in the first interview, meet other employees of the organization besides the initial interviewer, possibly tour the local community, and generally determine whether or not this organization is a good fit for you.

Second interviews can take several different forms. Two broad categories used to describe them are structured and unstructured interviews. A second interview is considered structured if each interviewer has specific criteria they use to assess you. For example, one person may ask questions to determine your work ethic or your sales ability. Another person may only ask you about your educational background or your work experience. The key to doing well in this type of interview is identifying the specific quality being assessed and then directing all your answers to information about that area.

In the case of unstructured interviews, interviewers are making a broad evaluation. You may get similar questions from all the interviewers. Treat each interviewer with equal importance. Answering the same question over and over again can become boring, but try not to let it show. Indeed, it is important that each interviewer gets the same message from you, otherwise your truthfulness and trustworthiness may be questioned. Remember, interviewers often compare notes about an applicant.

Preparing for Second Interviews

If possible, obtain an itinerary and interview schedule in advance. It is important to know the schedule of the day's activities, including names and titles of the interviewers. Knowing who will be interviewing you can help you anticipate the questions they may ask, because these may be tied in with their particular area of responsibility. For example, you may be interviewing for an advertising position, but the person from budget and finance may want to see if you understand the economic realities of putting together an ad campaign. Can you produce a budget? Manage the funds allotted to a project?

You will want to continue your employer research in preparing for the second interview. Ask the first-round interviewer to send you any additional information that you should know about the job, organization, department, or team you would work in, or anything else they think is important to review before your visit. Check various sources for timely articles or information about the organization or industry. Use your social network as discussed earlier to learn more about what it might be like working for this particular employer.

Interviewees who are prepared for the upcoming schedule, who understand what to expect and have knowledge of the workings of the organization and its related industry, stand a greater chance of success than candidates who do not care enough to do the necessary research.

Prior to the second interview, you should understand from your contact person how the costs for travel, lodging, car rental, and other expenses will be handled. You may be asked to make your own arrangements, or the organization will handle them for you. Ask your contact person what expenses will be prepaid and what expenses you will need to request reimbursement for (pay attention to the receipts you will need to collect while traveling). With some organizations, you may be asked to pay all the travel expenses, whereas others will reimburse you only if they extend a job offer and you accept.

As with other types of interviews discussed earlier, it is also important to send a follow-up letter or letters after the second interview. You may want to thank the person who coordinated your visit and/or the person who chaired the search committee or other key people who were involved in the interview process. These letters can be used to once again restate your interest in the position and why you think you're the best candidate for the job.

Other Sources

The job-hunting literature includes thousands of books and related resources on interviewing. Amazon.com lists over 35,000 on the topics of job interviews. Major bookstores have many of these books in the careers or business section. Several recent and helpful books on the topic are *Can I Wear My Nose Ring to the Interview?* (Reeves, 2009), *Job Interviews for Dummies* (4th ed.) (Kennedy, 2011), *Just Give Me the Damn Job!: How to Get Hired After the First Interview* (Smith, 2011), and *101 Great Answers to the Toughest Interview Questions* (6th ed.) (Fry, 2009).

A CIP Perspective

In this chapter, we learned about the social interactions associated with job interviewing, including information interviews, networking, initial interviews, and second interviews or site visits. Now we'll review what we have learned from a cognitive information processing (CIP) perspective.

Self-Knowledge

This chapter focused on the interpersonal relationship aspects of job campaigns, particularly social networking and interviewing. With respect to self-knowledge, it is important to note that job-interview skills can be learned. We emphasized that through drill and practice of the standard interview questions included in Table 13.1, you can improve your interviewing performance.

We also determined that good interviews and networking behavior requires knowledge of personal interests, skills, and values, because these are a focal point of interest in interviews and other job-search interactions. Employers want to know about your self-knowledge in these three areas. In addition, a thorough understanding of your priorities—geographic location, job title, salary, and training opportunities—will enable you to respond to interviewer questions with confidence and consistency. You will not have to worry about what you told one interviewer in one situation when speaking with another interviewer, because your answers will be consistent and based on your self-knowledge. *Self-knowledge, we believe, is the cornerstone of your PCT and strategic career planning, and it will be reflected in your interpersonal communications related to employment.*

Option Knowledge

This chapter emphasized that information interviews and social networks provide an important way for a job hunter to get insider information about an industry, training program, occupation, organization, or position. Table 13.2 provided examples of the kinds of information that would help you in researching an employer. Interpersonal communications, both formal and informal, are powerful tools for improving the facts and data in the knowledge domain about options. With better knowledge in this area, you can make better decisions about employment and job offers.

Decision Making

The social interactions inherent in interview behavior can influence each phase of the CASVE Cycle. Through social interactions, such as information interviewing and networking, you can develop information useful in the Analysis phase to fine-tune matches between your preferences and an employer's needs. Social interactions enable you to make judgments about the organizational culture or the personal characteristics of team members with whom you might be working. Regarding the Valuing phase, conversations with your possible supervisor or coworkers can provide the information that can help you prioritize your employment options and think more concretely about whether you would accept an offer. Finally, social interactions are essential in the Execution phase of decision making because this is where you develop the information that will enable you to take the next steps to start a new job.

Executive Processing

Throughout this chapter, we have repeatedly noted the importance of positive self-talk, self-awareness, and control and monitoring. When seeking employment, you must build these metacognitions into your PCT. Initiating information interviews and creating social networks in your job campaign will not happen if your self-talk is negative. We have often encountered job hunters that don't make good use of these tools because they allow themselves to be derailed by negative thinking. They say things such as "What if I can't think of what to say?" "Won't employers think I'm bothering them if I call?" "The employer didn't return my phone call; she must be trying to avoid me."

Effective interpersonal communication in the job search requires you to be aware of the tendency for this type of negative thinking to creep in and the need to use appropriate reframing techniques such as those described in Chapter 5 to learn how to think differently. Successful face-to-face interviewing depends on your ability to effectively and quickly process information coming from an interviewer about your behavior. Positive self-talk is also associated with handling the stress of rejections following interviews (e.g., "Although this job opportunity didn't work out, I learned some valuable things that will help me improve my next interview.").

As we stressed throughout this chapter, job-search communication skills can be learned and improved upon over time. If you find yourself trapped in a cycle of negative thinking based on your interpersonal interactions during the job search, talk with a career services professional or a trusted friend or mentor about how to frame these experiences in a different and more positive light.

Summary

This chapter reviewed various forms of interpersonal communication that are important in the job-search process. In the early stages of job hunting, job seekers can use information interviews and networking skills to make valuable contacts and gain useful information about positions, employers, and organizations. This information continues to be useful in the interview process, both in preparation for the interview and for communicating with employers during the actual interview. By successfully completing initial interviews, one will hopefully have the opportunity for second interviews or site visits with prospective employers. We concluded with an analysis of how CIP concepts can help you think about what you need to communicate with prospective employers, as well as avoiding the tendency to let negative thinking interfere with your ability to effectively present your credentials in an interview.

References

Bolles, R. N. (2012). *What color is your parachute?* Berkeley, CA: Ten Speed Press.
Bradt, G. (2011, April 27). Top executive recruiters agree there are only three true job interview questions. *Forbes online.* Available at www.forbes.com/sites/georgebradt/t2011/04/27

Cherniss, C. (2000). Social and emotional competence in the workplace. In R. Bar-On & J. Parker (Eds.), *The handbook of emotional intelligence: Theory, development, assessment, and application at home, school, and the workplace* (pp. 433–458). San Francisco, CA: Jossey-Bass.

Colista, C. (2002). Dressed for interview success. *Graduating Engineer & Computer Careers*, 48–51.

Conrad, N., & Salgado, T. (2007, December). Legal Q & A. *NACE Journal*, 8–13.

Crane, D. D., & Seal, C. R. (2011). Student social and emotional competence in the hiring process. *NACE Journal*, 26–30.

Farr, J. M. (2004). *The very quick job search: Get a better job in half the time* (3rd ed.). Indianapolis, IN: JIST Works, Inc.

Fry, R. (2009). *101 great answers to the toughest interview questions* (6th ed.). Boston, MA: Cengage Learning.

Gaw, K. (2012, January 4). Measuring SLOs: Effective on-campus interviewing. *Spotlight for Career Services Professionals*, 1.

Holland, J. L. (1997). *Making vocational choices*. Odessa, FL: Psychological Assessment Resources, Inc.

Katz, S. M. (2007, October). The job interview: Is career services giving students a realistic picture of what to expect. *NACE Journal*, 38–44.

Keever, S. (2008, October). Behavioral-based interviewing: Taking the guesswork out of interviewing. *NACE Journal*, 31–36.

Kennedy, J. L. (2011). *Job interviews for dummies* (4th ed.). Hoboken, NJ: John Wiley.

Kiviat, B. (2009, October 20). How Skype is changing the job interview. *Time*. Retrieved from http://www.time.com/time/magazine/article/0,9171,1933214,00.html

Pachter, R. (2003, May 12). Author explains perverse logic behind trick questions. *The Herald*, 5D.

Poundstone, W. (2004). *How would you move Mount Fuji?: Microsoft's cult of the puzzle*. New York, NY: Little, Brown, & Co.

Poundstone, W. (2012). *Are you smart enough to work at Google?* New York, NY: Little, Brown, & Co.

Reeves, E. G. (2009). *Can I wear my nose ring to the interview?* New York, NY: Workman.

Rosen, A. G. (2011, June 14). 17 tips to ace your next phone interview. *U.S. News & World Report*. Retrieved from http://money.usnews.com/money/blogs/outside-voices-careers/2011/06/14/17-tips-to-ace-your-next-phone-interview

Schuele, K., Madison, R., & Gourniak, A. (2010). Navigating the 21st century job search. *Strategic Finance, 91*, 49–53.

Sinberg, L. (2010, February). Dress for interview success. *Forbes.com*. Retrieved from http://www.forbes.com/2010/02/16/job-interview-fashion-forbes-woman-style-meetings-10-mistakes_2.html

Smith, A. D. (2011). *Just give me the damn job!: How to get hired after the first interview*. Parker, CO: Outskirts Press.

Straus, S. G., Miles, J. A., & Levesque, L. L. (2001). The effects of videoconference, telephone, and face-to-face media on interviewer and applicant judgments in employment interviews. *Journal of Management, 27*, 363–381.

Yate, M. (2004). *Knock 'em dead 2005: The ultimate job-seeker's guide* (6th ed.). Holbrook, MA: Adams Media Corporation.

Chapter Fourteen

Negotiating and Evaluating Job Offers

The job-search activities discussed in Part Three are designed to help you obtain job offers from prospective employers. Offers mean opportunities! However, opportunities really don't mean much until negotiations have occurred, agreements are finalized, and an offer is accepted. As we will learn in this chapter, job offers are not the end of an employment campaign. There is more important work to be done after a job hunter receives an offer.

Some students fail to successfully negotiate an offer or accept the best job. It is like running a good race and then crossing the wrong finish line or shooting a great round of golf but failing to sign the score card. How does this happen? After doing everything right, how does a person mess up at the end? To find some answers, let's look at the case of Anna.

Anna completed a bachelor's degree in childhood education, and she received two job offers. She was happy and relieved to receive the offers because she believed that there was little demand for someone with her degree and skills. She was afraid to ask many questions about the two offers because she feared the employers might view this in a negative way. In other words, there were many aspects about the actual jobs that she did not really understand due to her failure to ask questions and learn more about the positions.

Both jobs would have enabled her to stay in the same town as the university from which she had graduated. One position involved teaching at a local elementary school and the other involved working for a child welfare agency to investigate child abuse cases. The second position paid about $5,000 more than the first, but the teaching job provided two months of summer break. Anna's friends and her mother told her to "go for the money," so she accepted the second job in child welfare.

What happened? Anna quit her new job after six weeks, and she was unhappy about the stress and disappointment associated with the job. Why? She never understood that the second job required almost two weeks of travel per month, that she might be out of town three to five days at a time, and that she would be returning from most trips in the evening. Anna had pets that needed care when she was away, she did not like the amount of travel, and she disliked returning to her apartment after dark. Anna's lack of skill in negotiating her job offers, together with her failure to act on the basis of her values and personal preferences, led her to make a poor employment decision. Even worse, after all this she found herself unemployed again.

The concepts in this book can help you avoid an experience like Anna's. Evaluating and negotiating job offers are activities that draw upon many of the ideas discussed in previous chapters. They are activities that require you to process information about yourself (see Chapters 2 and 5) and prospective employers (see Chapter 3 and Part Two), and it requires application of the CASVE decision-making skills discussed in Chapter 4.

211

This chapter will discuss the following:

- The importance of negotiating job offers
- The skills needed to negotiate effectively
- A process you can use in evaluating offers
- The proper steps to follow in accepting and declining job offers
- A cognitive information processing (CIP) perspective on negotiating and accepting job offers

Before we begin, it might be useful to reflect on this part of the job campaign in CIP terms and to explore several important metacognitions. First, if you are not confident of your job skills, it is probably difficult to imagine how you could be strong and confident enough to tell an employer what you want in a job. This lack of self-confidence is a gap that needs to be removed if you are to be successful in an employment campaign. We talked about this in Chapters 5 and 11.

Second, if you are not sure of your goals and values—what you want to obtain from a job—it is difficult to imagine how you could evaluate two or more offers and choose the best one for yourself. For you to fully understand and appreciate the material in this chapter, it is essential that you be confident of your value to an employer and for you to be clear about what is important to you in a job. These are essential metacognitions in negotiating, evaluating, and accepting offers.

The Context for Negotiating

Employers and job hunters enter the recruiting and employment process with different needs. In this section, we'll define some terms, describe some of the "rules of engagement" in employment negotiations, and examine some of the basic things that employers and students are seeing in a job campaign.

In Chapter 13, we said that it is almost impossible to imagine a situation where you could obtain a job without being interviewed, without talking to the person who will make the hiring decision. This can also be said about negotiating. From the very beginning of the first interview, it is important to realize that you have begun to negotiate an employment offer. A National Association of Colleges and Employers (NACE) survey revealed that employers extend job offers, on average, to 35% of new college graduates they interview, and about 74% accept these offers. On average, employers take about 22.5 days after the interview to extend an offer to job candidates (National Association of Colleges & Employers, 2011).

Negotiating Defined

What exactly do we mean by negotiating? The *Merriam-Webster Dictionary* defines *negotiating* as "conferring with another so as to arrive at the settlement of some matter." In this chapter, negotiating refers to an interpersonal process that involves reaching an agreement about employment. Think of negotiating as a way of reaching a common goal: your agreement to work for the employer. Both you and the employer should end up "winning." If one person wins and the other person loses, the agreement is not likely to last, either the employee will be dissatisfied and quit or the employer will be dissatisfied and will not promote the employee and in some cases may terminate the employee!

What Employers Are Seeking

First, we'll look at employers' needs. The Collegiate Employment Research Institute (CERI; 2010, February) surveyed 950 employers to determine what they were seeking in new college hires. Their list of employers' most desirable abilities is shown in Table 14.1, including those deemed essential and those rated important to highly important. Building and sustaining professional relationships was rated the most important skill that new hires would be asked to demonstrate initially.

Table 14.1

Employer Ratings of Importance of Selected Abilities for New Hires (N = 897)

Ability	Essential (percent)	Important to Highly Important (percent)
1. building working relationships	40	57
2. analyze, evaluate and interpret data	34	58
3. engaging in continuous learning	30	61
4. oral persuasion and justification	20	61
5. plan and manage a project	15	57
6. create new knowledge	12	63
7. global understanding	12	54
8. build a successful team	12	43
9. mentor others	11	36

Using these data, students can begin to assess their personal qualities and skills and how they might be used in applying for jobs and negotiating offers. The more effectively students can communicate their personal characteristics and document their skills, the more likely it is that employers will evaluate their employment applications positively. As we noted in Chapter 2, a portfolio can be useful in this process.

What Students Are Seeking

To determine what students are looking for in a job campaign, NACE asked over 19,000 students nationwide to rate the importance of 15 attributes of employers in selecting a job (Koc, 2008). These rankings are shown in Table 14.2. Students wanted employers and/or the job to provide some measure of financial security and they appear to be looking for long-term relationships with employers.

Table 14.2

Student Ratings of Employer Characteristics in Selecting a Job (N = 19,000)

Rank	Job/Employer Attributes	Mean Score
1	Provides opportunity for advancement	9.74
2	Offers job security	9.26
3	Has a good insurance package	9.20
4	Friendly co-workers	8.93
5	Location	8.90
6	Opportunity for personal development	8.88
7	Offers a high starting salary	8.85
8	Recognition for good performance	8.54
9	Opportunity for self-expression and creativity	7.69
10	Clearly defined assignments	7.47
11	Casual atmosphere (noncompetitive environment)	7.25
12	Embraces diversity	7.15
13	Takes active role in the community	6.77
14	Offers a signing bonus	6.21
15	Has a recognized name	6.18

Another national survey (Universum, 2011; www.universumglobal.com/) of over 60,000 students revealed that respondents valued such things as good work/life balance, secure employment, creative and dynamic work environments, and opportunities for training and development. Examination of the factors that students rated highly suggests that these are not likely to be fulfilled by an employer because most current employers are simply not able to meet these priorities.

Inspection of the items on these two tables reveals how far apart employers and students might be in their perceptions of the important things to consider in jobs and hiring decisions, and it provides some idea about what things might be negotiated in a job campaign to reach a satisfactory agreement about a hiring situation.

Social Power in Negotiating Job Offers

Negotiating is a social process between two or more people—you and the employer (or the person in the organization with hiring authority for your position). As in any social relationship, the idea of social power or influence applies to this situation. Social power comes from perceptions of leadership, expertise, ability, integrity, desirability, and authority. In employment negotiations, the social power changes over time (see Figure 14.1). In Figure 14.1, the applicant is represented by the solid line and the employer by the dotted line.

── **figure 14.1** ──

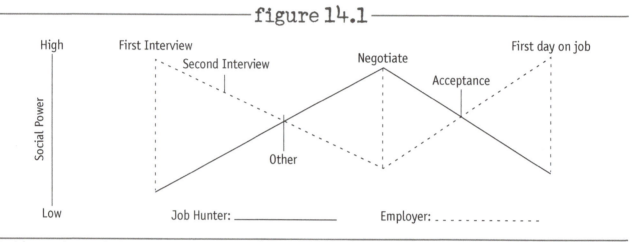

Social Power in Negotiating

At the time of the initial interview, the employer has the most social power. However, as the process moves along, the applicant gains more power in the relationship. As Figure 14.1 shows, the best time for the applicant to negotiate is *after* the job is offered and *before* it is accepted. That is when the job hunter is at the highest level of social power in negotiating. Once you have received a job offer, you immediately have more power than at any other point in the interviewing and negotiating process. As the author of one job-search book noted, this is most likely the only time where you will have even a slight edge in the negotiations (Yate, 2012).

Before the offer is made and after the offer has been accepted, the employer is relatively higher in power. This is true because as the interview process moves along, the employer is making more and more commitments to an applicant, showing an interest, and spending money to recruit the applicant for the position. Recruiting is an expensive process—NACE (2010) reported that employers' average cost per hire in 2010 was $8,947, an increase of 57% from the previous year. An organization's success greatly depends on getting the right people into the right positions. The stakes are really higher for an employer than many applicants realize.

When an employer makes an offer, there is a public indication that the applicant is the one wanted for the position. In effect, the employer is saying, "Forget about the rest. We want you." At this point, employers have usually invested considerable financial and emotional energy in recruiting and picking the best people to work in their organization, and they don't want to lose them. Bringing new workers into the organization once they have been selected is important to the managers in most organizations. It is a matter of successfully finishing the recruiting process at this point—egos are on the line.

On the other hand, in the current job market there are fewer available jobs than candidates, so employers have the upper hand. In fact, a NACE (2010) survey of over 20,000 graduating college students revealed that of those students who applied for jobs, only 38% received at least one job offer.

What this does mean for the 38% of students with offers, however, is that they are the best and most qualified for the job. For each offer given, hiring managers must comb through hundreds of resumes from many job seekers, so negotiating with you and finalizing their hard work in finding you will be much easier for them than going back to the beginning of the process (Weiss, 2009). Therefore, negotiating, even in a tough job market, is still a good idea.

Maximizing Your Bargaining Power

Job hunters can increase their bargaining power in negotiating job offers by paying attention to the eight items listed below. If you happen to be six months or more away from launching your employment campaign, this list might help you focus your efforts on building your resume or taking other actions that will increase your negotiating power later.

1. **Knowledge increases power.** The research that you do on the industry, organization, and job will provide information that will be invaluable in negotiating. The more you know about the job and organization, the less likely you will be "sold" a position that you will not like, will not be qualified for, or will not perform well in. Be prepared to explain why you are better than other candidates. Knowing the average salaries for positions such as the one you seek, the cost of living in different areas, or new types of training associated with jobs can strengthen your negotiating position with an employer.

2. **Solid recommendations.** Your reputation and prior work record, including internships, volunteer work, part-time employment, summer jobs, and campus activities, can provide you with documented references that increase your bargaining power. Get letters from former supervisors and professors who can provide recommendations based on your personal work habits and work standards.

3. **Poise and confidence.** Your negotiating style can be very helpful in increasing your success in this process. Negotiating provides the employer an opportunity to learn more about you. It is important for you to be clear about your goals, be respectful of the other people involved in the process, and avoid becoming intimidated by the social power of the interviewers (don't be rushed into making decisions). Remember, negotiating is a process where friendliness, listening and speaking clearly, and personal presentation (e.g., dressing appropriately) are important. If you handle the negotiating process well, the employer is able to learn more about how you might handle other delicate work situations that involve negotiating.

4. **Inside recommendations.** If you have some contact with one or more persons already working in the organization, this can increase your negotiating power. In effect, this is a special kind of recommendation, focusing on how and why you should become a member of the organizational team. Unlike other recommendations, this one focuses on you as a potential match as a new member of the "organizational family."

5. **Supply and demand.** If the job is currently "hot" and there is a shortage of qualified workers in this field, your bargaining power increases. Your research should provide you with information about the current labor market demand relative to this job or the particular skills needed for a position. A low unemployment rate in the geographic area will also work in your favor.

6. **Other offers.** If you are already considering other job offers, then your bargaining power is increased. If employers know that someone else wants you, this may raise their competitive fires to beat the competition. However, you need to be careful and honest with this informa-

tion, because misleading someone (not bargaining in good faith) can seriously damage your reputation among employers. Don't imply that you have another offer, when you don't have something firm, preferably in writing, from other employers that you have had contact with through the interviewing process. This type of "gamesmanship" runs contrary to the win-win process we described earlier in this chapter and could cost you future opportunities if other employers learn that you've handled negotiations in this way.

7. **Persuasion.** Give the employer reasons to negotiate a better offer to you. Explain your qualifications clearly. List your accomplishments related to the job, explain how it matches your goals, and compare and contrast yourself with others who may have held this position. Your purpose is to demonstrate your potential value to an employer, how your contributions could exceed the employer's expectations for the typical person in the position. One technique for doing this is to summarize your understanding of the position's duties and responsibilities: "I understand that I would be responsible for a budget of $1 million, would cover a three-state territory, would report to the regional manager, and would lead a staff of five."

8. **Silent on salary.** Your bargaining power in negotiating can be enhanced if you can successfully sell your credentials and yourself to an employer without having to discuss the topic of salary. By keeping the focus on your goals, the organization's mission, the high quality of the match between you and the organization/job, you are reassuring the employer that you are interested in more than money. If you are asked about salary early in the interview process, try to buy time by indicating "open" or "willing to negotiate." We'll say much more about salary later in this chapter.

In summary, these eight factors can strengthen your position in negotiating a job offer. However, if you are unable to negotiate from a position of strength and power, don't try to "fake" it. The employer probably has more experience in negotiating job offers than you do, so you don't want to lie about other offers, your recommendations, your prior experience, or the results of your research regarding the supply and demand of workers for position.

Receiving a Job Offer

Several matters are important to consider when you receive a job offer. These include timing of offers, personal impressions, clarifying the offer, and deciding when to make a decision.

Timing of an Offer

Job hunters often wonder, "When can I expect to receive an offer?" Generally, an offer can arrive anywhere from one day to six weeks after your second or third interview. Occasionally employers give you the offer after the final interview.

Impressions Still Count

Don't assume you can "let your hair down" once you have an offer in hand. You will want to continue to make a good impression when the offer arrives, because the employer is still collecting data about you. This requires a delicate balancing act. It is important to let employers know that you are pleased to receive an offer, but do not let them hear you announce to your roommate or significant other, "Yahoo! I got the job!" On the other hand, you do not want to make a negative impression with employers by telling them how sought after you are and how many other offers you have already received.

While we are focusing mostly on the impression you are making on the employer, remember that you are also still in a position to collect data on the employer. If you feel that the employer is not respecting you in the negotiating process or not listening to your concerns, think about what it might be like if you accept the offer and the employer still has such an attitude. Remember, you are in your strongest position in the relationship after the employer has extended an offer (review Figure 14.1).

Clarify the Offer

In the excitement of receiving an offer, job hunters may overlook certain details that are important to clarify before they sign or verbally agree to an offer. Be clear on all the factors that make up the offer, including the position title and description, general and specific responsibilities, salary and frequency of payment, location, reporting date, travel or relocation expenses, signing bonus, other forms of compensation (e.g., stock options), benefits (e.g., medical, vacation, insurance, tuition reimbursement, car allowance), and the deadline for an answer. Other important information related to acceptance of an offer will be discussed later in this chapter.

Hlavac and Easterly (2008) described several aspects of employment agreements that prospective employees should understand because they can affect employment security.

"AT-WILL" VERSUS TERM EMPLOYMENT. These concepts are similar to the idea of contingent and permanent jobs introduced in Chapter 9. At-will employment simply means that the employee relationship can be terminated at any time by either party (with or without notice) for any reason (with or without cause). At-will employees are usually not eligible for any kind of severance pay.

WITH OR WITHOUT CAUSE. Employee job termination can be for cause, but this can include disloyalty, insubordination, or failure to perform duties to the employer's satisfaction. "Cause" is an aspect of a job offer that should be clarified before it is signed.

"EVERGREEN CLAUSE OR CONTRACT PROVISION." Employees in a permanent position or employed for a specific term (i.e., an end date is specified) may have a provision in the agreement that provides for an automatic renewal for another term unless one of the parties provides written notice that they do not wish for this to happen.

RESTRICTIVE COVENANTS. The employment offer may include noncompetition, nonsolicitation, and nondisclosure covenants that protect the business and the intellectual property of the employer. These provisions in the agreement could affect the work of an employee who leaves the organization and seeks employment with another organization in the same field.

EXEMPT AND NONEXEMPT. Finally, the Fair Labor Standards Act (FLSA; www.dol.gov/whd/flsa/) provides that nonexempt employees are eligible for overtime pay if they work more than 40 hours per week. Exempt employees do not receive overtime regardless of how many hours they work per week.

Job hunters need to understand these provisions and others described by Hlavac and Easterly (2008) so that they are very clear about the employment relationship and can thus make it a positive and enduring one.

Negotiate Time of a Decision

Most job hunting sources suggest that you should never accept a job offer on the spot. Although you may have already been considering the possibility of an offer, you need time to evaluate all the factors in this decision. Have a date in mind when you can give the employer your decision prior to receiving an offer—this will help you negotiate more effectively. Remember not to be "starstruck" by the excitement of the offer. Be prepared to negotiate when you can give the employer your decision about an offer. Employers should not be surprised that you are interviewing with other organizations, and they will appreciate your being honest and careful about your decision. Employers give candidates 14 days on average to accept or reject offers (National Association of Colleges & Employers, 2011).

Next, we'll take a look at some of the things that might be negotiated by a new college graduate.

Things That May Be Negotiated

Remember you have nothing to negotiate until you have an offer. However, once you receive an offer it is important that you consider all the possible factors that could be negotiated. In this section, we review 15 things that might be negotiated, depending on the organization's policies and your employment needs.

1. Salary

The salary offered may or may not be negotiable, and it may or may not be a fair one. You should research the salaries offered in your field by geographic location, experience, and education or training prior to negotiating this factor. You will often find that the salary an employee receives varies greatly from job to job, employer to employer, and from one region of the country to another. Some consultants suggest that you come up with three figures: (a) your minimum or bottom-line figure, (b) a realistic midpoint desired salary, and (c) a "dream salary" (Yate, 2012).

It is much easier to negotiate down from your upper range than it is to negotiate up from your bottom-line figure; therefore, your salary range will be from your realistic midpoint salary to your dream salary. You do not want to give a figure that is too low because you will undervalue yourself and give the employer a reason to think less of you. One author suggested that when developing a counter offer to an employer's original offer, you should ask for 10 to 15% more than the average salary (Skelton, 2011). Below are some resources that are useful in researching salary. The first one is available in most college career center libraries.

- *NACE Salary Survey* (available at SS_January_exsummary_4web.pdf)
- *Occupational Outlook Handbook* (also available at http://www.bls.gov/ooh/)
- www.salary.com
- www.glassdoor.com/Salaries/index.htm
- www.homefair.com/calc/salcalc.html (helps you compare salary levels in different geographic locations)

In negotiating salary, try to avoid mentioning a specific salary—talk about ranges. Indicate that you want to be flexible and consider options. If you have researched the organization and job carefully, then you have some ideas about an appropriate salary. Ask for the top of the range, for more than what you expect the employer to offer.

2. Timing of Appraisal Reviews

Some employers may give bonuses for the quality of your job performance, which are determined as a result of your appraisal reviews. If the organization uses this type of appraisal system, it might be possible to ask for an earlier performance review. Sometimes you might consider accepting a lower salary with the understanding that your first salary review will be sooner than originally stipulated. For example, if the first review typically takes place at six months and involves a 15% salary increase, you might want to negotiate a review after four months.

3. Signing Bonus

The relocation package may also be in the form of a signing bonus, which is simply an agreed upon amount of money given to you at the time of your acceptance of the offer. If an employer does not offer a signing bonus or a relocation package, you might want to consider negotiating for one. According to the National Association of Colleges and Employers (2011b), 46% of employers offered signing bonuses to students graduating from college in 2011.

4. Sales Commissions, Profit Sharing, Stock Options

If the job is in the private sector, the employer might offer you a package of base salary and other financial incentives. These might be based on sales and meeting quotas. Some (Reed-Woodard & Alleyne, 2011) suggest that in these times of uncertain job markets, negotiating for benefits like stock options may contribute more to your long-term security than initial salary offerings. Your research into the field will help you know what kind of salary package is typically offered in the industry, and you can then evaluate what might be good for you.

5. Location of the Job

There are many differences between working in one city or another. Take the time to check out the geographic area of your new position. Here are some possible questions to consider:

- Does the community offer the lifestyle you are looking for?
- What other community factors are important to you; for example, family, schools, churches, and so forth?
- How long a commute would you likely have?
- Can you choose the location of the job?
- What is the cost of living compared to where you live now?

The location of the job directly affects the cost of living. Sperling's Best Places is a free reference that can be used to measure this factor (http://www.bestplaces.net/). This site provides information about various places, as well as an opportunity to compare cities in terms of costs, taxes, health, and growth, among other factors. As noted earlier, you can find information on salaries and other job matters at www.salary.com. We suggest you do the "salary wizard" first and then check different locations to see how your net worth will change if you live in one place or another. Another site, sponsored by NACE (http://www.jobsearchintelligence.com/NACE/jobseekers/salary-calculator.php), has a salary and negotiation program that might be helpful in relocation.

6. Insurance, Pension Plans, and Other Benefits

An organization's benefit package might be as much as 30% of a salary offer. It is important to convert the benefit package from percentages into salary or expense dollars so you have a more complete measure of the financial terms of an offer. For example, if the employer provides complete health coverage, what is the equivalent in premium costs if you had to go into the market and purchase all or part of this yourself?

Organizations vary in terms of exactly what is included in employment benefits, the flexibility of building a benefit package to meet your special needs, tax liabilities of benefits, who can be covered by the benefits, and the transferability of the benefit programs. Items in an optional benefits package could include incentive savings, 401(k) savings plan, maternity/paternity leave, dental/optical insurance, frequent flyer/travel clubs, disability insurance, sick leave, life insurance, assistance with interest on loans, tuition reimbursement, wellness program, and child-care expenses. These may be points of negotiation for you. Many employer benefit plans are managed by independent groups (e.g., FBMC), and their Web sites provide educational resources that help job hunters and employees learn more about these various options (www.fbmclearningcenter.com/). These can be helpful for you to review before you sign a final offer letter or contract.

7. Relocation Expenses

Many employers provide relocation benefits to help you move to the community where the job is located. A NACE (2007) report revealed that 80% of the employers planned to offer relocation assistance to hires. This may include travel to the community to look for a place to live, mortgage assistance, cost of moving your possessions or car, and living expenses until you are settled. Other compensations might include the cost of temporary lodging, moving expenses, home mortgage rate differential, closing costs, and real estate broker fees. You might want to negotiate for a short-term interest-free loan to help you cover the costs for relocating to the new job.

8. Expense Account, Car, Mileage, Fuel Allowance

Another part of a financial package offered by an employer could include reimbursement or advances for expenses associated with the job. These items might include a mobile phone or pager, a public transportation reimbursement, expenses for commuting or parking. There may be tax advantages to having this income as a business expense, or perhaps you want it as a benefit.

9. Club Memberships

If the job involves entertaining customers, or if it is stress-producing, you might want to negotiate paid memberships at a private club, tennis club, or fitness center. Does the employer have a recreational facility that you can use? Can any fees be waived or reduced?

10. Consumer Product Discounts

The organization may have options for employees to participate in discount buying programs of various kinds. You might be able to negotiate your participation in such programs.

11. Office Furnishings

Another aspect of "location" that you might want to negotiate involves the location of your work space or the physical arrangements of your office. Do you want to work from a home office? What types of communication and office equipment might you need in a home office that the employer might provide? Do you have a disability that requires reasonable accommodations? If having an office with a window is going to affect the quality of your work, negotiate for it. Perhaps new office furniture, a new computer, or a tablet computer might be tied to improving the location of your work.

12. Reporting Date

Depending on the organization and the job, some employers might be able to offer a flexible starting date. If you have ever dreamed of backpacking or cycling through Europe, now may be the time, or maybe you just want to take some time off to relax. Remember, it's probably too late to negotiate the reporting date after you accept the offer.

13. Vacations

Vacation time may vary in terms of the actual amount (days, hours), whether it is paid, and when it can be taken. If taking time off at a particular season or time of year is important to you and will make you a happier, more satisfied employee, then it might be something you want to negotiate. Some individuals are content with a lower salary in exchange for three or four weeks of vacation time.

14. Division, Department, Title, or Classification of Position

In general, not all jobs are created equal within an organization. If you decide that certain divisions or departments appeal to you more than others, let it be known during your interview and before you sign. The division or department responsible for your specific work assignment might be a factor that can be negotiated. Related to this, you might be able to negotiate a different title or classification for your job.

15. Fulfillment and Fun

"Gold-collar" workers who are in very high demand expect to be well paid and fed, but they also seek a job that's fun and offers fulfillment. Some companies resist the idea of catering to what might appear to be fanciful whims in negotiating, fearful that once the precedent has been set there's no going back. But if you have unique skills that add value to an organization and if a competitor lets employees keep a fish tank in the office, your prospective employer may be willing to let you have one if it leads to your acceptance of an offer. If the corporate goal is to hire and retain the most talented people available, then letting you have what you want may be the best way to do that.

Not all of these 15 factors will be negotiable in your situation, but it is prudent and reasonable to explore them if they are important to you and will affect your ability to be a successful and satisfied employee in the organization.

Some Additional Words about Salary

The matter of salary is especially important and critical in negotiating job offers, and we should say a few more words about it. The basic strategy in salary negotiation is to be informed (NACE, 2011a), know what a job pays and what you're worth, and wait until it's clear the employer has targeted you as the top choice for the job.

In negotiating salary, as well as other aspects of an offer, you should assume that the employer is seeking to take steps to make you a happy, satisfied employee. As a result, you must be clear with employers about what will make you a happy, satisfied employee. Indeed, you can even use this kind of language as you discuss the details of an offer.

In discussing salary, employers sometimes talk about salary in terms of rates of time, hour, week, month, or year. Do your homework, and be prepared to think about salary in these terms. Employers may also talk about percentage increases, never using actual dollar amounts, so be prepared to know what these percentages really mean. If you are unsure, ask for time, clarification, or assistance in understanding all aspects of an offer before you begin negotiating. Most employers have had much more experience than you in discussing and thinking about these matters, so you want to take the necessary steps to keep the negotiating field somewhat equal among all parties involved in the process.

The salary for your first professional position is of special importance. In some organizations, you cannot negotiate the beginning salary offer. Nevertheless, this salary is important because your future positions will probably be based in part on what you were making in your last job. Your next employer will typically offer you at least 10 to 15% more, so your starting salary is important for this reason. In addition, salary increments are usually based on a percentage of your current salary, for example, a 10% New Year's bonus. Future salary negotiations often are based on a percentage of your current or base salary. Benefits may also be calculated in terms of the base salary.

Salaries are typically set for positions in the organization. Because of this, explain what added value you can bring to the position if you have the job. This means that any special qualities you bring to the position, such as international experience, language skills, leadership, community service, or technical expertise, can increase the salary you might receive.

What if an employer asks, "What are your salary needs?" How should you answer? Rather than blurt out some numbers, you could ask, "What is the typical pay range in your organization for this position?" This puts the ball back into the employer's court. Let's say the employer cites a pay range of $32,000 to $36,000 for a position. You could then apply Skelton's (2011) 10–15% rule. As in, you know that the average going rate for this particular job is $32,000, so you should respond asking for 10 to 15% more than $32,000. You could respond that you were hoping to earn a salary in the range of $35,200–$36,800. Remember, Yate (2012) suggests that your range should begin at the realistic, midpoint number and end at your dream salary number.

Never accept a job until you know the salary and are sure that it is acceptable to you. Once you have accepted, be certain to get a letter detailing all aspects of the offer. Never, never leave a job for another one unless you have a written offer in hand. Write a formal letter of acceptance expressing appreciation for the time and energy of those involved in the recruiting process and reiterating all details of the offer, including position title, starting date and place, starting salary, and special arrangements. Remember, the person you are negotiating with might not be there when you arrive later, so it is important to have everything in writing.

The Process of Negotiating

In closing this section, we want to mention several matters that are important in successfully negotiating job offers. These have to do with using your positive metacognitions to guide the process.

Decide Your Conditions

It is important to determine what you want from the offer, but it is also important to know the minimum you will take from an offer. Create a plan that will allow flexibility. You want to be consistent in communicating to the employer what is important to you in a job. Typically, there will not be many surprises in negotiations.

Remain Positive

The person you are negotiating with may be your future supervisor or at the very least your colleague. If you are truly interested in the job, don't put the employer on the defensive when negotiating. The key ingredient is to stay positive about the other person, the offer, and the organization. Restate that you are really interested in working for the organization and say, "Is there some way we can work this out?" or "I really want to try and make this happen."

Make a Decision

Be prepared to make a decision once the organization has stated its final offer. Know when to stop negotiating and either accept or decline an offer. Try not to focus too much on the salary; consider all aspects of the offer in making a decision. It might be possible to convert some of the factors identified earlier in this chapter into dollars or a percentage of your salary. After negotiations are completed, the next task is to evaluate the outcomes and make the best employment choice available to you.

Be Honest with Employers

Now we will examine the sometimes difficult process of evaluating offers. Negotiating is not really a "game" where deceit or lack of integrity work well. Indeed, it is in your interest to be as honest, polite, and forthright in negotiations with employers as possible. *Spotlight Online for Career Services Professionals* (NACE, 2008) quoted Jennifer Gillilan, a senior corporate recruiter/campus programs for Manhattan Associates, "As a general rule, I do not think attempting to negotiate is inappropriate, provided the student is polite, appreciative of the initial offer and opportunity, and has done his/her research on the 'market rate' for the position and is able to substantiate that" (p. 1). At the same time, it is important to note that employers may not always be as forthcoming as they should regarding the amount of flexibility they have to negotiate salary and other aspects of a job offer.

Evaluating Offers: Making the Best Choice

*W*e presented the story of Anna and her difficulties in successfully negotiating and evaluating two job offers at the beginning of this chapter. Now we will examine in more detail the matter of deciding between, or among, offers. Let's look at some other scenarios.

Sara Feng, majoring in Chinese and management information systems, had 25 interviews in the fall semester and expected multiple offers. Her biggest challenge was organizing her priorities to make the best choice. Her priorities were a challenging work environment and room to advance, and she wasn't planning to stick around if the first employer did not measure up.

Jose Esposito left his job after eight weeks. A state university graduate, he wanted a position that emphasized teamwork and training, and would pay enough to finance a graduate degree. Feeling pressure from the employer to decide, he accepted a sales position in advertising with a small firm. After joining the firm, he quickly learned that the culture was not what he had expected. The company atmosphere was competitive, impersonal, and unfriendly, and in spite of an impressive salary, he quit and found himself unemployed.

What does all of this mean for a college student engaged in an employment campaign? We think it means that students need to take an active approach and be clear about their goals and ready to take specific steps to develop information that will enable them to make wise employment decisions.

Waiting on Other Offers

Evaluating two or more offers and deciding which one to accept is likely to involve a host of factors. It is entirely appropriate to tell Employer A that you need more time because you are waiting to hear from Employer B and Employer C. There is nothing wrong in talking with several organizations at the same time about your employment situation. Indeed, it probably increases your value. Employers are each trying to hire the best people for the job, and knowing that you are being considered elsewhere makes you more attractive to all three organizations. The key in sharing this type of information with employers is to do so in a nondemanding way, continuing to express appreciation for their offers, and stressing that your goal is to be respectful of all parties involved, and make the most informed decision possible.

The Sales Pitch

Remember that the recruiter's job is to bring you into the organization, to get you to say "yes." During the negotiating process, you may be "wined and dined" by organizations—provided first-rate meals, lodging, and entertainment. You may be told about many perquisites ("perks") that the organization offers new employees. However, you have to gauge all of this information and experience during the recruiting and negotiating process against your values—what you really want and need in a job.

Ethical Dilemmas: Can You Renege on an Accepted Offer?

Once you have negotiated with a prospective employer, several scenarios are possible. In the event that you only have one offer and have negotiated your best conditions, you must decide whether to take the employer's offer or decline it and continue searching. You may put yourself in a very awkward position if you have been demanding with the employer during the negotiations, the employer has met all your demands, and then you turn down the offer. If you decline the offer, you should have very legitimate reasons for doing so and share them as appropriate. Otherwise, the employer may not believe that you were negotiating in good faith, and this can damage your reputation in the profession or industry.

You may also encounter intense pressure from an employer to make a decision about an offer. For example, if you accept the offer in 24 hours you get a $3,000 bonus. According to NACE's (2008) *Reasonable Offer Deadlines Guidelines,* recruiters should refrain from any policy or practice that would unfairly influence or affect whether a candidate accepts a job. These practices could include excessive time pressure for accepting the offer or encouraging a candidate to revoke an offer from another company. If you have been unable to negotiate more time to evaluate other offers or to consider acceptance of the offer, there are some things to reflect upon. The pressure you feel from your employer may give you an idea of how you will be treated as an employee. If this is how you are made to feel at a time when you have some social power in the relationship, imagine what you can expect from the employer after you accept an offer and your power decreases.

Another situation involves turning down a job after accepting it—this is called *reneging* on an offer. When an employer offers a job and a candidate accepts it, a contract for employment has been created, and this is especially true for a position that has a specified end date. However, per the earlier discussion about offers in this chapter, if the job is an "at-will" position, then either party can terminate the employment at any time. Leaving a job after only a few weeks or months can be taken as a sign of impulsiveness or impatience.

Students are expected to accept offers in good faith, but there may be circumstances that force one to renege (e.g., an unexpected family responsibility to care for a critically ill parent). If this case arises, the student should immediately contact the employer and notify him or her of the circumstance then withdraw the acceptance (NACE, 2009).

Being Sure about the Job

In helping you think about an offer, we have drawn upon an article by Humphrey, Nahrgang, and Morgenson (2007), who used a meta-analytic research procedure to examine factors contributing to good working situations. Here are some factors they identified that you might use in deciding whether or not to accept an offer:

1. *Autonomy*—the freedom to carry out tasks and activities of the job.
2. *Skill variety*—the extent to which different skills are used in performing the job.
3. *Task identity*—the extent to which one can complete a whole project.
4. *Task significance*—the extent to which the job affects the lives of others.
5. *Feedback from the job*—the extent to which the job provides information about your work performance.
6. *Social support*—the extent to which the job provides opportunities for getting assistance and advice from supervisors or coworkers. Considering that you may spend 25% of your week at work, make sure it is a place where you are comfortable and can grow.
7. *Outside interactions*—the extent you can connect with others and gain insight and feedback on specific job tasks.
8. *Compensation*—the extent to which the job provides satisfactory monetary rewards.
9. *Meaningfulness*—the extent to which cherished goals can be pursued in work.
10. *Location*—the extent to which the job is close to home. We have found that many recent college graduates prefer employers close to home when looking for a first full-time job, especially if students have significant debt from attending college (Winograd & Hais, 2011). Location might also involve the commuting time, which could involve transportation costs and stress. Just a 25-minute commute each way means 200 hours per year.

Bottom line? The feeling you have when you ask yourself: "Do I really want to work here?" Consideration of these factors may help you verify what you know what is important about the job you have been offered and are trying to make a decision about accepting.

The Matching Process

In making a decision about accepting a job offer, it may be useful to think about the things that are important to you. Table 14.3 provides a list of 46 factors that you might consider in four categories: (a) lifestyle, (b) nature of the employer or job, (c) pay and benefits, and (d) work activities. These 46 factors are similar to the topics introduced earlier in Table 14.2 regarding what students are seeking in an employer or job. A careful, thoughtful review of these factors can help you make sure that an offer you accept will be a good match for you. Moreover, identifying your most important factors in considering jobs as you engage in the research, interviewing, and negotiating phases of a job campaign will ensure that you develop the information you need to make an informed job choice.

Table 14.3

Forty-Six Factors to Consider in Evaluating Job Offers

Lifestyle	Nature of Employer or Job	Pay and Benefits	Work Activities
Flexible benefits	Reputation	Cost of living	Creativity
Community size	Product/service offered	Education assistance	Independence
Further formal education required	Advancement opportunities	Professional development opportunities	Intellectual stimulation
Geographic location	Compatibility with fellow workers	Salary/income present	Opportunities to help others
Flextime available	Compatibility with supervisor	Salary/income potential	Opportunities for leadership
Impact on spouse/child	Organization size	Moving expenses	Prestige
Social expectations outside of work	Pleasant surroundings at work	Home computer, telecommunications	Variety
Shift work required	Job security	Association memberships	Work in your field of interest
Work-related travel required	Job duties	Vacation	
Closeness to home	Job title	Insurance programs	
Cultural/recreational opportunities	Stability of the organization	Health club	
	Support staff	Child care	
	System for performance evaluation		
	Type and amount of on-the-job training		
	Opportunities for mentorship		

Appendix L, An Employment Decision-Making Case Study, provides a case study and worksheet that enables a job hunter to rate the importance of selected factors and then determine the extent to which a job offer matches the factor (no match, poor match, close match, exact match). Employers and candidates are both looking for good employment matches because better matches mean happy employees, productive workers, and organizational success.

Final Steps before You Start

Once you have accepted an offer, the next step is reporting on the first day, right? Well, not quite. There are several other important things that will probably happen before you actually start to work. Your contract or signed appointment papers will probably hinge on the employer obtaining some final pieces of information. These might include a physical, a drug test, civil and criminal background checks, loyalty oath, driving record, nondisclosure agreement, and even checks of your references and credit rating.

Madden (2011) reported that 73% of employers conduct criminal background checks and 81% check employment references. Only 13% of employers conducted credit checks. If a third party is used to check your background, the employer needs to obtain your permission. Regarding the drug test, most organizations test employees and job applicants for drug use. In fact, many local and state laws require post-offer testing (Chin, 2010).

Using CIP to Negotiate and Decide on an Offer

In this chapter, we have been discussing the process of negotiating and deciding on employment offers. Now we'll review what we have learned about these topics from a CIP perspective. *Our goal is to help you improve key elements in your PCT for solving employment problems.*

Self-Knowledge

Just as self-knowledge is important in exploring occupational and educational alternatives, it also has a role to play in helping you evaluate job offers and selecting the best one. Clear knowledge of what you seek in a job will give you a yardstick by which to measure the opportunities that come your way.

Knowledge of Options

In researching occupational alternatives, you have learned something about what you want in a job you might hold now or in the future. Knowledge about options includes knowledge about specific positions with various employing organizations. Many job hunters create problems for themselves by accepting positions where their knowledge about the specific job was incomplete, as in the case of Anna.

Applying the CASVE Model

We suggest that you evaluate each offer based on the same set of factors. The CASVE Cycle model presented in Chapter 4 can be applied to the decision-making process associated with evaluating job offers.

COMMUNICATION. An employer extending a job offer is an example of an external event that would cause you to begin the decision-making process. Your own emotions are likely to be at work during this time as well. You may be excited at having received an offer, but at the same time anxious about committing to a particular employer or turning down an offer that is not an ideal fit with your preferences. You may also be getting input from significant others who are pressuring you to take any job offer that comes along.

ANALYSIS. Having accurate and complete knowledge about yourself and your options is a critical aspect of choosing among offers. In analyzing a job offer, you will want to determine the extent to which the offer meets the skills, values, interests, and goals you have identified as important. The 46 factors to consider in analyzing employment offers and the matches provided by different jobs will facilitate this process. You also need to be aware of your decision-making style and how that influences the process, along with any thoughts you may be having about any job offers on the table.

SYNTHESIS. With respect to evaluating job offers, the Synthesis phase of the CASVE Cycle involves both Elaborating and Crystallizing offers. In Elaboration, you may choose to negotiate more features into the job being offered that meet some of the important factors and issues identified in Analysis.

The process of evaluating offers is more likely to be focused on narrowing your options, or Synthesis Crystallization. The number of job offers you may have to consider at any one time is likely to be small. However, when the offers are equally attractive or they satisfy different sets of criteria you've identified in the Analysis phase, the process of deciding may be harder. You may also find that the structured exercise in Appendix L can help you weigh various factors in making a job choice.

VALUING. As noted previously, this phase of the CASVE Cycle includes considering the costs and benefits of each option, not only to yourself but also to significant others, your cultural group, community, and society, now and in the future.

- Does this job accommodate your needs and lifestyle preference with regard to your immediate and extended family? Would you accept a job offer that makes it more difficult for your spouse or partner to find appropriate employment?
- What about issues that may relate to your cultural group (Has this employer typically discriminated against members of my cultural group?) or community (Would I work for a chemical company that has been cited for polluting the drinking water in my neighborhood?), and society (What is the employer's reputation across the country?)?
- Finally, if you were considering more than one offer, the outcome of this process would be a ranking of your offers. You would identify the employer that is your first choice, followed by your other priority rankings. In general, you would not want to eliminate any options until you had accepted an offer, received written confirmation, and signed an agreement letter or contract.

EXECUTION. Once you have made a decision, there are several key steps related to the Execution phase of the CASVE Cycle. The first of those is communicating with the employers who have extended offers. Once you have decided to accept an offer, it is extremely important to communicate with other prospective employers who extended offers to you. This includes declining both verbally and in writing any offers you did not accept. This is an important step because you may have contact with these employers at a later time—never burn your bridges.

After you have made a verbal commitment to an employer who has extended you an offer, the next step is to confirm your acceptance in writing. Remember to include the position title, salary, starting date and time, location, any perks or signing bonuses that were negotiated, and any other factors that you feel were vague or were not included in the offer.

Executive Processing

Your ability to think strategically and effectively is a critical aspect of the process of negotiating and evaluating offers. In addition, you're required to consider a great deal of information about yourself and your options at a time of great pressure. There may also be significant others involved who are providing their input.

Negative thinking is likely to occur when you only have one offer on the table. There may be a tendency to jump at the first offer that comes along. You hear yourself saying, "I'd better take a sure thing." "What if I don't get another offer?" "This is a very good opportunity—I'd be stupid to turn it down." You are the only person who can decide the level of risk you are willing to take in turning down offers in hopes that something better will come along. Challenging your thinking in this area might involve saying, "If one employer thought I was good enough to extend an offer to me, chances are another employer will as well." Negotiating job offers is a process that requires your highest levels of self-confidence and positive self-talk.

figure 14.2

P.O. Box 334
State University
Anywhere, FL 32301-4708

March 30, 2012
Ms. Alice Murphy
Recruiting Coordinator
Information Systems Technologies, Inc.
100 Broadband Ave.
Denver, CO 80207

Dear Ms. Murphy:

Thank you very much for your letter dated March 17, 2012. I am pleased to accept your offer for the account executive position within the Customer Support division. I understand that my initial assignment will be working with Mr. Bruce Allen in the Network Support group at a salary of $40,000 per year.

As we agreed, I will start work on Monday, June 4, 2012, and I will report to Human Resources that morning at 8:00 a.m. to complete the necessary paperwork. As you noted in the offer letter, I will be reimbursed for my moving expenses up to, but not exceeding, $3,500.

I appreciate all your efforts on my behalf. If additional information related to my appointment is needed prior to June 4, please let me know. I look forward to joining the team at Information Systems Technologies, Inc.

Sincerely,

Joan Roberts

Joan Roberts

Sample Offer Acceptance Letter

Summary

This chapter reviewed the factors associated with negotiating job offers, including what items you may wish to negotiate and the steps to follow in the negotiation process. The chapter also discussed the steps that job hunters might follow in evaluating offers and making an employment choice. We noted that metacognitions, the quality of one's thinking, can influence the process of negotiating and evaluating offers. The goal was to enable you to improve the quality of your PCT for negotiating, evaluating, and finally accepting job offers.

References

Chin, J. (2010, April). Legal Q & A: Updates for career services and recruiting professionals. *NACE Journal.* 8–14. Retrieved from http://naceweb.org/Publications/Journal/2010April/Legal_Q___A_Updates_for_Career_Services_and_Recruiting_Professionals.aspx

Collegiate Employment Research Institute. (2010, February). Under the economic turmoil a skills gap simmers. *CERI Research Brief 1-2010,* 1–18.

Hlavac, G. C., & Easterly, E. J. (2008, May). Legal Q & A. *NACE Journal,* 8–12.

Humphrey, S. E., Nahrang, J. D., & Morgenson, F. P. (2007). Integrating motivational, social, and contextual work design features: A meta-analytic summary and theoretical extension of the work design literature. *Journal of Applied Psychology, 92,* 1332–1356.

Koc, E. L. (2008, May). NACE research: The oldest young generation—a report from the 2008 NACE graduating student survey. *NACE Journal,* 23–28.

Madden, K. (2011, February 11). Be ready for a background check. *Tallahassee Democrat,* 11.

National Association of Colleges and Employers. (2007, July). *Moving on: Student approaches and attitudes toward the job market for the college class of 2007* (executive summary). Bethlehem, PA: Author.

National Association of Colleges and Employers. (2007, June). *NACE 2007 recruiting benchmarks survey: A report on key measures for college recruiting & experiential education* (executive summary). Bethlehem, PA: Author.

National Association of Colleges and Employers. (2008, June). *Reasonable offer deadlines guidelines*. Retrieved from http://naceweb.org/legal/offer_deadlines

National Association of Colleges and Employers. (2008, December 10). To negotiate or not to negotiate: Should the economy dictate how students respond to salary offers? *Spotlight Online for Career Services Professionals*. Retrieved from http://naceweb.org/printerFriendly.aspx?printpage=/spotlight/2008/december/negotiating_salary_offers

National Association of Colleges and Employers. (2010, September.) *2010 Student survey: Key findings. NACE research brief*. Bethlehem, PA: Author.

National Association of Colleges and Employers. (2010, October.) *2010 recruiting benchmarks survey: Key findings. NACE research brief*. Bethlehem, PA: Author.

National Association of Colleges and Employers. (2011a, November.). *Job outlook 2012 survey*. Bethlehem, PA: Author.

National Association of Colleges and Employers. (2011b, November). *NACE 2011 recruiting benchmarks survey*. Bethlehem, PA: Author.

National Association of Colleges and Employers. (2011). Reality check: Salaries for new graduates. *Job Choices 2012: Diversity edition*. Bethlehem, PA: Author.

Reed-Woodard, M. A., & Alleyne, S. (2011, September). Negotiating beyond the salary. *Black Enterprise, 42*, 50.

Skelton, A. (2011, September 16). You got the job offer. Now, about that salary offer . . . *USA Today College*. Retrieved from http://www.usatodayeducate.com/staging/index.php/career/you-got-the-job-offer-now-about-that-salary-offer

Universum. (2011). *Universum student survey 2011: US undergraduate edition*. New York: Author.

Weiss, T. (2009, June 23). How to negotiate for a better salary, even now. *Forbes.com*. Retrieved from http://www.forbes.com/2009/06/23/jobs-salary-negotiating-leadership-careers-basics.html

Winograd, M., & Hais, M. D. (2011). *Millennial momentum: How a new generation is remaking America*. Piscataway, NJ: Rutgers University Press.

Yate, M. (2012). *Knock 'em dead 2012: The ultimate job-search guide*. Avon, MA: Adams Media.

Chapter Fifteen

The First Job and Early Career Moves

Many career books do not include this chapter because they focus on career preparation and job hunting rather than the job itself. Ironically, employment is viewed as something separate from career development and planning. We actually think that this last chapter might serve equally well as the first chapter in this text. Therefore, it is appropriate to end this book with the job hunter on the job and anticipating those first days at work.

A recent college graduate shared her story about the first day on the job. Traci was an English major who had put together an excellent job campaign, been recruited by a dozen organizations, successfully negotiated an outstanding offer, and reported for her first day on the job. Upon arriving, she was surprised to learn that the person with whom she had negotiated the offer, and had expected would be her supervisor, had left the organization. Things were rather disorganized; indeed, it seemed like they weren't expecting her at all. The appointment papers were not ready, and neither was her office. She wondered if she had made a mistake. Fortunately, people at the work site quickly rallied, and Traci was soon feeling better about her career situation. This story illustrates the unexpected things that can happen in a new job and why it is important to be prepared.

This chapter is about transitions. First-year employees are no longer college students but they are not really professionals yet either. They are in a unique transition period. Some hang on to their student attitudes and behaviors for too long, and they fail to realize that it takes time to earn the rights of a full-fledged professional. There are different rules to follow during this initial entry stage, and those are the focus of this chapter:

- Getting a good start in the new job
- College and work compared
- Adjusting to professional work
- A career strategy for the first year
- A career center director's suggestions for a successful transition
- Moving up or out
- A cognitive information processing (CIP) perspective on transitioning to the first job

Along the way we will provide suggestions for helping you develop appropriate meta-cognitions for making career decisions during this transition period. *Your Personal Career Theory (PCT) will serve you more effectively if it extends beyond initial career choices into lifelong career transition management.* Finally, we will offer a CIP perspective on starting a new job. As we said in Chapter 1, "career" is a process where solving one career problem leads to subsequent problems and career decisions. This will become evident as we proceed through Chapter 15.

Getting a Good Start in the New Job

The Collegiate Employment Research Institute (Render, 2010–2011) asked 1,850 employers what college students should do as new employees to successfully secure a position and launch their career. Although high-level skills were important and discussed in Chapter 11, employers also emphasized basic skills and competencies in three categories, along with other skills mentioned less frequently. What did they say?

1. **Basic skills.** This area was most frequently mentioned by respondents (26%) and it includes writing (spelling, grammar, sentence structure, etc.), oral and visual communication, preparing reports, and summarizing ideas clearly and succinctly. Some employers indicated that poor writing was a "huge" problem and projected a negative image of the person and the organization.
2. **Professionalism and maturity.** This area included being realistic about salary expectations, acting professionally with managers and clients, managing time and priorities, and accepting feedback. This area was mentioned by 24% of respondents. Specific comments included poor e-mail communications, resistance to feedback, and lack of initiative.
3. **Interpersonal skills.** This area was noted by 23% of respondents and included the inability to conduct a one-on-one conversation with another adult, to engage in teamwork, and establish rapport with clients, coworkers, and supervisors. Specific comments included using more direct, personal communication and less reliance on social media.

The good news is that these three basic skill areas are familiar and within the reach of college students; the bad news is that these areas were frequently mentioned by employers as deficient.

Some of the other areas mentioned by employers were *work ethic* (11%; coming to the job prepared, on time, not distracted); *research and preparation* (8%; knowing important information about the organization and having a sense of personal career direction); *initiative* (7%; showing interest in the position and seeking higher roles in the organization); *software skills* (7%; Excel and Word skills); *experience* (6%; internship and professional training upon starting the job); and *leadership/project management* (5%) and *time management* (5%; keeping others informed on project deadlines and completion).

College and Work Compared

College students may experience some "entry shock" as they move into jobs as new professionals, because the job and college environments can be quite different. Holton (2011) suggested that many students "just haven't learned how to go to work" (p. 40). Table 15.1 elaborates upon these views and shows some points of comparison between the (a) college and job cultures, (b) attitudes and behavior of your professor and your boss, and (c) nature of the learning process at college and on the job.

This table also illustrates why some college graduates may have problems adjusting to their first professional job given differences in the use of time, environmental structures, organizational cultures, effort required over time, and more complex interpersonal relationships. In the following sections, we'll focus on these topics in more detail and make suggestions to ease your transition into the professional workplace. But first, let's examine some bottom-line realities.

Adjusting to Professional Work

Even if you have had part-time jobs, internships, summer jobs, or volunteered in an organization, when you become a full-time working professional some adjustments will be required. In this section, we review some of the things that can affect this transition process.

Table 15.1

College versus Work Environments

Job Culture	College Culture
More rigid time schedule	Flexible time schedule
You can't skip work	You can skip class
Feedback is irregular and infrequent	Feedback is more regular and specific
No summer vacations and few holiday breaks	Long vacations and frequent holiday breaks
Very few right answers to problems	There are correct answers to problems
Assignments may be vague and unclear	Syllabus provides clear assignments
Team performance is evaluated	Individual performance is evaluated
Longer work cycles (months, years)	Short work cycles (class meets 1–3 times weekly), 17-week semester
Rewards based more on subjective criteria and personal judgments	Rewards based on objective criteria and merit
Your Boss	**Your Professor**
Not often interested in discussion	Encourages discussion
Assigns rush jobs with short lead time	Schedules lead time for completion of assignments
Is sometimes arbitrary; not always fair	Is expected to be fair
Is outcome (e.g., profit) oriented	Is knowledge oriented
The Learning Process	**The Learning Process**
Concrete problem solving and decision making	Abstract, theoretical principles
Based on incidents happening on the job; concrete, real life	Formal, instructional, symbolic learning
Socialized, shared learning	Individualized learning

Employer Suggestions for Your First Job

The Collegiate Employment Research Institute (CERI; 2010–2011) at Michigan State University asked 2,300 employers for suggestions they would give to college graduates on the first job. Recruiters visiting college campuses shared their ideas, and we believe this information is important to consider as you enter the professional workplace. Here is what they said.

BE A 24/7 LEARNER. Respondents indicated that the first priority for students should be to seize any opportunity to learn and grow, and to take on every task as a new learning experience. Students should position themselves as coachable and open to change, realizing that learning outside the classroom will require initiative and new approaches.

SHELVE THE TECHNOLOGY AND BUILD PEOPLE SUPPORT. Employers were clear that good interpersonal skills are essential for building relationships with coworkers and managers. This may mean less reliance on e-mail, Twitter, or texting and more time in direct personal interactions. One respondent noted that "Young adults have developed an extreme overreliance on technology and are losing interpersonal communications and human relations skills that are sadly decreasing and nonexistent."

ACT WITH INTEGRITY. Employers indicated that students' character will determine how well they do from the outset. Honesty, building trust with others, and honoring commitments make one a valued employee according to the respondents.

TAKE THE INITIATIVE THROUGH HARD WORK. Some of the comments in the survey included "Treat every day like an audition" and "Ask not what a company can do for you, but what you can do for a company." These survey respondents were reflecting the realities of the contemporary workplace in these comments. They indicated that demonstrating initiative and commitment to success of the organization are keys to success in most cases.

BE POSITIVE, YET HUMBLE. Finally, respondents to the CERI survey suggested students understand that they have been labeled as Generation Y or the "entitlement generation," and this perception can be corrected by being willing to learn, asking questions, and helping others when possible. The key is to balance self-confidence with humility. You've left your student role but you're not a fully formed professional simply because you've started a new job (Holton, 2011).

The On-Boarding Program

Some employers call the orientation program "on-boarding" because it is designed to keep you on the "ship" for as long as possible. Giordani (2009) indicated that the five-year turnover rate for new-graduate hires has been consistently about 20–23%, but the first year rate could be less than 5% with a good orientation program. What can you expect from a program like this?

ORIENTATION. This could range from some brief welcome sessions to several months of sessions that orient you to every aspect of the history, services, mission, culture, products, policies and procedures, along with tours and introductions to coworkers.

ASSIMILATION PERIOD. This part of an on-boarding program could last for months or a year, and typically includes *rotations* for "trying on" different jobs in the organization and interviews with workers; *feedback* from managers on new employee progress and expectations; *structured mentorship* where the new employee is matched with a long-term worker for support and guidance; *socialization* including social events, dinners, breaks, and mingling outside normal working relationships; and *use of technology* including access to the organization's intranet site for networking and learning about the culture.

Adjusting as a New Professional

Numerous publications and articles have been written to help graduating students ease the transition from college to employment. We categorized these ideas into four areas of adjustment: (a) the job culture, (b) personal life after graduation, (c) first-year financial management, and (d) assessing the culture. In the next section, we will elaborate on these ideas, which remain practical and useful for college students a generation later.

Job Culture

Suggestions for adjusting to the culture of the work organization include skills in managing the clock, your boss, and your coworkers, as well as skills in handling supervisor feedback in a positive way.

CLOCK AND CALENDAR MANAGEMENT. Consistent punctuality is one of the easiest ways to make a good initial impression at the job. Moreover, it is essential to be alert and ready to start early each day. Good clock-management skills might also require some evening and weekend hours to get projects completed. In addition, make it a point to be early or on time, and do not leave every day exactly at the closing hour.

As a professional, you are expected to be more committed to your job than nonexempt employees. This could mean staying longer to finish a project on some days. Make sure that your supervisor and office assistants know where you are during the day and when you travel. Calendar management involves not asking for holidays or vacations until you have been on the job six months, unless you successfully negotiated otherwise before you accepted the job offer.

It is important for new hires to take control of their schedule on the job. If you are assigned a project, set clear goals for it and specify exactly who is responsible for what. Set timelines for when activities need to be completed and develop a written plan for the project. If you have not had special training on project development, management, and evaluation, seek it out at your first job even if you have to learn it on your own and in your free time.

IMPRESSION MANAGEMENT. Image is very important in a job, much more important than in college. Most college students will have to make an investment in clothing and grooming in preparing for their first day on the job. Impression management is too important in most organizations to risk an initial bad impression. "A key to making a good impression is figuring out what you need to do to earn credibility and respect" (Holton, 2011, p. 40).

Besides dress, it is important to make sure that you do not use office equipment or supplies for personal or social reasons. Make sure you're clear on policies regarding use of office e-mail because mistakes here create a negative impression. Practice good workplace e-Etiquette (Langland, 2011). Take the time to learn how others in the office want to be addressed, both in private or public, and clarify their titles. It might also be wise to go slow in decorating your office or work area and observe how others at your level have done this. Also, you probably want to be sensitive about the display of religious or political symbols, be careful about posters and cartoons that might be offensive to co-workers or customers.

Impression management, however, also includes your work performance. On work products, form most often precedes substance in the workplace. Coworkers will sometimes not read what you write unless it is in the proper form—appropriately formatted with no typos or spelling errors. Sloppy work is generally not tolerated in the workplace, even though your colleagues may say otherwise. Unlike when you were in school submitting assignments, you may not get a "do over" or an option to resubmit a corrected version.

If you act like a college student rather than a new professional, you'll be labeled "green" or "wet behind the ears." Accept the fact that you are in a kind of fishbowl where much of what you do will be observed, and supervisors and coworkers will be evaluating your potential to succeed. The fact that you have no track record tends to magnify what you do.

Avoid any behavior that reminds coworkers of college student behavior. Having the reputation as someone who "parties hard" might have been acceptable in college, but in the work organization, it could be considered a lack of maturity and limit your potential for promotions. Be aware that your private behavior (drinking, drugs, complaining about work) can reflect poorly on you as an employee and affect your job evaluations or continued employment. This caution also applies to any part of your online "identity" that reflects poorly on you as an employee, especially if your online postings or tweets have included criticism of your workplace (Barnett, 2012).

MANAGING YOUR BOSS. From the very beginning, you want your boss or immediate supervisor to become an ally in your career development. As Holton (2011) noted: "The single most important person in your first year of work is your new boss" (p. 42). As you get settled in during your first week of work, ask your supervisor to suggest particular people who might help with getting oriented, including learning any procedures or policies, or getting access to various resources and materials. In some settings you may be following a formal orientation process, whereas in others it may be learn as you go, and you will have to figure out more things on your own. The best rule of thumb is, "when in doubt, ask!"

To make your boss look good, you will need to complete projects of high quality on time, act like a professional, and maintain a positive attitude. You'll want to cultivate a reputation as someone who knows how to maintain confidential information and who is honest. If you make a mistake, it is better to inform your boss immediately and take the necessary steps to learn from the error and avoid it in the future. Typically, your boss will be more upset about being surprised and caught off guard or learning about the mistake from someone else.

Making the boss look good could mean sacrificing personal weekend time during your first year to complete unscheduled, emergency projects that your boss needs to have done. This kind of flexibility, cooperation, and willingness to sacrifice for the organization usually earns "career advancement points" from higher management in the organization.

Sometimes you will encounter a supervisor who is unfair, overly demanding, or even deceitful. Rather than immediately quitting a job in situations where you have a difficult boss, you may want to first try to get promoted or transferred away from this person. Above all, don't let these types of supervisors contribute to a negative work attitude (metacognitions) or weak performance on your part. Responding in this way will likely cause trouble for you before they cause trouble for the boss.

COWORKER RELATIONSHIPS. Developing peer, coworker relationships is another critical area of adjustment. On the one hand, you will likely be asked to collaborate with colleagues in completing projects as a team. On the other hand, you will probably be competing with these colleagues for recognition and advancement. The best advice is to go slowly in forming relationships. As we discuss later in this chapter, people with negative attitudes and gripes may befriend you but they are usually going nowhere in the organization. Take your time in developing permanent lunch or social hour associates. Be friendly to everyone initially, and when you have determined who is positive and engaged in the organization, consider forming friendships with those people.

Be cautious about using coworkers as confidants. Over time you may develop supervisor/supervisee relationships or other kinds of dual relationships with these people, and this can create ethical problems. However, as we noted in Chapter 10 when discussing the Amerco case study, employees tend to form very close relationships with coworkers. This is a difficult area that requires your good judgment over an extended period of time.

You will be an outsider until you prove otherwise to your colleagues. Holton (2011) advised new employees to not rush through the transition period but to embrace the role of newcomer, be willing to "pay your dues." You'll want to demonstrate that you are part of this new organization *by not trying to change it at the outset*. In other words, learn the business and understand the culture (before you try to change it). For example, find out what shift workers in production are doing and how that affects marketing. As a faculty colleague once remarked, "you never really understand how an organization works until you try to change it" so go slow.

As a new professional, you may find yourself doing many of the same tasks as hourly nonexempt employees, those who are not salaried. You may also have supervisory responsibility over several such employees, such as office assistants, salespeople, or production workers. From your first day on the job, it is important for you to treat these lower-level coworkers with respect. Indeed, although many of them may not have bachelor's degrees, they may have worked in the organization for many years, have earned considerable good will from other managers in the organization, and have seen other novice professionals move into your position. The key is to treat these workers with respect and learn from them about how the organization functions.

Don't complain about doing low-level tasks. Given that most people don't start at the top, you might find yourself beginning as a "go-for" doing "grunt work." This can include getting coffee and lunch, running errands, and stuffing envelopes. Such activities might be especially important if you start your work through a temporary staffing company or you do not have technical skills needed for the job. Don't complain about these low-level tasks, but use them as an opportunity to learn about the organization and the other people who work there. Almost every job has some duties that are boring or apparently pointless. This is part of managing your expectations and being realistic about all aspects of the job. The rosy picture of the job painted by the person who recruited you may not match your day-to-day reality, especially starting out (Holton, 2011).

Your most valued trait in your relationship with coworkers might be your ability to listen and give undivided attention to others when needed. Coworkers appreciate those who are genuinely interested in their stories and opinions. At the same time, you don't want to reinforce griping or get involved in office gossip.

OFFICE ROMANCES. With so many people working closely together in organizations, in constant contact and often on their best behavior, office relationships are inevitable. One study found that more than 59% of employees reported being involved with a coworker in an office romance (Vault. com, 2011). More recent polls suggest that involvement in and attitudes towards these types of relationships can vary by generation (Tuggle, 2012). Opinions differ about the level of "risk" associated with office relationships.

In some cases, office romances can be disruptive at a work site. The blurring of boundaries between personal life and job by a couple can lead to gossip among coworkers and awkward moments in the office. Even more problematic are relationships between supervisors and supervisees and between employees and clients or customers. In the former situation, coworkers may believe that their colleague is getting favored treatment and special information from the boss. In the latter situation, the boss may question the loyalty of the employee.

These romantic relationships can threaten your job or lead to a transfer. Some young people believe they can just quit if the relationship becomes problematic, but in reality, this type of short-term thinking may have longer-term implications for future employment in other organizations (Tuggle, 2012). It is important to check out company policies regarding employee relationships and to inform your supervisor about such matters if they can affect other employees in the organization in any way.

YOUR EVALUATIONS. Your performance evaluations are likely to be informal, continuous, ambiguous, critical, and very important. Your boss is usually your principal evaluator, and the evaluation may include some negative comments about your work. Avoid becoming defensive and take the feedback as a challenge to improve job performance. It is important to recognize that even informal comments (e.g., "That phone call was long" or "This report is very short at the beginning") point to behaviors that need to be corrected. Such observations and feedback are often shared among supervisors, and their cumulative memories are long, so it is important to avoid a reputation as one who does not respond positively to supervisory feedback.

To minimize surprises in your evaluation, consider the following tips:

1. Pay attention to sometimes subtle, even nonverbal, cues about the quality of your work; it's late, it's inaccurate, it doesn't follow policy, it's messy.
2. Read your job description carefully and clarify what you don't understand; preview the rating form that will be used for your evaluation and make sure your supervisors know about your activities and accomplishments related to categories used in the rating form.
3. Ask your supervisor and coworkers whom you trust for frequent feedback on your work.
4. Read the organization's personnel policies regarding tardiness, ethics, drugs, dress, deadlines, absence, and other matters. Don't allow your behavior to break policy because of ignorance on your part.
5. Realize that the evaluation will be made in the context of a social relationship. The evaluation may say more about your boss's evaluation of you as a person than your job performance. Pay attention to the human factor every day in your interpersonal relationships at work.

A negative first evaluation is not the end of the world. Because organizations do not want to spend the money and time to replace workers, you can obtain a second chance if you don't become defensive and if you let the employer know that you want to improve your performance.

Personal Life

This section is written with the assumption that you are still single as you begin your first job. If you are married or living with a significant other, some of it might be less relevant for you.

Finding social relationships away from work may be difficult. Unlike college, people in your new surroundings may be more varied in age, social status, and affiliations. However, although situations in college change every semester or year, life in the workplace and elsewhere may operate on a longer calendar. It might be good to look for friends in places away from work, including the apartment or neighborhood, sports and fitness activities, religious groups, volunteer activities, alumni groups, continuing education courses, service organizations, and professional associations.

Related to personal life issues, the first six months in a new job can be very stressful. There is a high probability that you will be on probation, make mistakes, have much to learn, and be physically tired. In this situation, you will want to learn as much as you can about stress-reduction activities and developing a healthy lifestyle. For some, this will be one of the most significant areas of adjustment.

Managing Finances

This section is also written with the assumption that you are single and living alone. We would focus on things a little differently with the assumption that you are married or jointly managing your finances with another person.

Some college graduates find that managing finances during the first year on the job is a challenging area of adjustment. Indeed, as college students find themselves graduating with increasing debt, entire books have been written to address the topic of managing personal finances after college (Blumenthal, 2009; Koblinger, 2009), For some graduates, the problem stems from overestimating the spending power of the new salary in relation to the start-up costs of beginning a new job, often in a new community. It may be important for you to live *beneath* your means and concentrate on saving some money.

Some have reported that recent college graduates had to borrow money from their parents or borrow additional money during the first year to make ends meet. What areas might be included in a first-year budget? We categorize them in terms of living arrangements, wardrobe development, transportation, food, and loans, credit, and savings.

LIVING ARRANGEMENTS. If you have been living in an apartment, you already know something about the deposits and advances that are required in renting. In addition, you will need furniture, a good bed, kitchen items, and other basic furnishings. One problem faced by many new job holders involves spending too much money on furniture and home entertainment while skimping on a good bed and food. Chances are that you'll be working harder, longer hours than in college, and you don't want to cheat on items that will affect your health. Another possible adjustment difficulty has to do with maintaining a pet, especially if your job requires even a small amount of travel.

WARDROBE DEVELOPMENT. Depending on the culture of the organization in which you are working, you might find that you will need to spend several thousand dollars on an appropriate wardrobe. Although you may need to make some purchases immediately, it may be wise to take some time in buying most of these new clothes. Consult with people who have worked in the organization successfully regarding a priority list of items to purchase; buy good-quality durable items that will last; and consult with knowledgeable salespeople about wardrobe trends as you make purchases.

TRANSPORTATION. Be cautious in purchasing an expensive automobile until all the other budget items have been settled. Safe and reliable transportation might be sufficient for the first year. It is also important to remember that insurance, fuel, parking, and tolls will need to be factored into transportation costs. If public transportation will be used, then fares will need to be included in your budget.

FOOD. It is likely that you will be eating and drinking differently as an employed professional than as a college student. Depending on the type of job, you may be going out to eat with coworkers on a regular basis. These types of meals may affect your budget more than your typical student dining (no more meal plan!), and could easily add $75 a week or more to your expenses. If you do any entertaining, this will affect your budget situation as well. Of course, if you are able to cover these items with an expense account, that will help. In general, however, you will probably be spending more of your money on better-quality food and in the preparation and care of that food now that you are employed.

LOANS, CREDIT, AND SAVINGS. Finally, financial management adjustments in your first job will involve issues surrounding loans, credit, and savings. Chances are good that you will be making more money in this first job than you have ever made before. This can be a heady experience. However, there can be some sobering realities to consider. Let's say you are making $34,000 a year, or approximately $2,800 a month. With taxes and other payroll deductions, your actual take-home pay may be less than $2,000 per month. Payroll deductions for life insurance, long-term disability insurance, health insurance, annuities, stock options, and savings plans are often valuable, but they further limit your take-home pay. When signing all the appointment papers for your new job, be sure and clarify exactly what your take-home pay will be each month.

There are two other financial pitfalls. Two thirds of college graduates are entering the job market owing an average of $25,500, of which $3,500 could be credit card debt (AFT on Campus, 2010). With an average starting salary of $35,000, this level of debt affects home purchases, vacations, starting a business, and credit ratings. In addition to credit cards, penalties for late payments on bills, rent, utilities, and checking overdrafts can also sap your financial resources.

You will probably need some start-up funds to pay deposits and buy clothes. If family members cannot provide assistance, look for a loan through your employer's credit union or use some mechanism that will pay back the loan through payroll deductions.

Finally, it is absolutely essential to save something out of each paycheck. Think of it as "paying yourself first." Putting some money into an interest-bearing equity account will provide the funds you need for big-ticket purchases in the future, such as a house. Many sites (e.g., http://www.finaid. org/; http://moneymix.cuna.org/13856/easy_budget.php) and guides (Blumenthal, 2009) are available that can help you increase your financial IQ. Take advantage of these before you start your new job and make long-term financial planning as essential part of your career planning.

Sizing Up the Culture

Throughout this chapter, we have referred to the culture of the organization and how important it is to learn about it during the first year on the job. As we noted in Chapter 8, organizational culture is much like the personality of an individual; it captures what is unique, persistent, and noteworthy about the organization. In general, organizations want new employees to embrace their culture, to fit in, and to understand how things are done. How do you do this as a new hire?

Just providing outstanding performance on the basic tasks in your job description will not result in an outstanding rating, because this is reserved for employees who have a positive attitude, get along well with coworkers, and have learned the culture of the organization—who "fit in." Perhaps the most critical skills in learning an organization's culture have to do with listening to and watching more experienced members of the organization. Read about the founders of the organization, and ask for information about how and why they started it. Watch for evidence of the work ethic in the behavior of experienced and successful colleagues; observe how they spend their time, address others; and dress.

Clifton (2011) reported Gallup survey findings that 28% of the American workforce is actively *engaged* in their work, but 53% are *not engaged* and 19% are *actively disengaged*. The 28% of engaged employees will be your best colleagues because they are cooperatively building the organization and creating good things in the environment, including new customers. In sizing up the culture of the organization, these are the people you need to identify.

The workers *not engaged* are not hostile or disruptive, but they have essentially checked out and have little or no concern for customers, productivity, safety, or organizational mission. Those employees *actively disengaged* involve themselves in creating problems for the organization in terms of theft, sickness, accidents, and absenteeism. These people may seek you as a new ally in dismantling the organization, so be wary of them.

But what about those who are actively engaged? How can you recognize them? Clifton (2011, p. 104) described 12 behaviors or characteristics of these engaged employees, which are listed in Table 15.2. As you read these 12 items, be aware of how the behaviors of the employee and the manager (representing the organization) are interrelated in these items, and think about how you can use these indicators of engaged employees to monitor your work behavior and that of others.

Table 15.2

Twelve Characteristics of Engaged Employees

Number	Description of Characteristic
1	I know what is expected of me at work.
2	I have the materials and equipment I need to do my work right.
3	At work, I have the opportunity to do what I do best every day.
4	In the last seven days, I have received recognition or praise for doing good work.
5	My supervisor, or someone at work, seems to care about me as a person.
6	There is someone at work who encourages my development.
7	At work, my opinions seem to count.
8	The mission or purpose of my organization makes me feel my job is important.
9	My associates or fellow employees are committed to doing quality work.
10	I have the best friend at work.
11	In the last six months, someone at work has talked to me about my progress.
12	This last year, I have had opportunities at work to learn and grow.

In Chapter 8, we described Schein's (1985) six practical ways to observe organizational culture, including its regular behaviors, norms, dominant values, philosophy, rules, and feeling or climate. We also identified some common ways organizational culture affects individual career development and behavior. As you prepare to begin a new job in a new organization, we think it might be especially useful to reread Chapter 8 to help you prepare for this new life situation.

In summarizing this section on culture and adjusting to the new job, we are reminded of Holland's (1997) RIASEC theory, which we introduced in Chapters 1 and 2. You will recall that Holland identified six kinds of occupational personalities and six corresponding work environments: Realistic, Investigative, Artistic, Social, Enterprising, and Conventional. We believe that these six types provide a useful framework for you in thinking about your personality and the expectations and rewards of a particular work environment. The differences in culture among RIASEC types are often significant and help us understand the culture of an organization or work group.

Developing a Career Strategy for the First Year

This section provides some thoughts on strategies college graduates might adopt to increase the likelihood of positive evaluations at the end of their first year on the job. These were collected from management experts and young workers.

In-Service Training

Carliner (2010) reported that U.S. organizations spent $56.2 billion for training in 2008. In comparison, $29 billion was spent in 1986. This report revealed that the amount budgeted by organizations for training is affected by the overall state of the economy, but even in lean times companies are willing to spend on things like learning technologies. As a college graduate, you might think that your education and training will be over when you enter the workforce, but nothing could be further from the truth.

Besides what the organization offers in training, you can join professional associations or trade groups to keep abreast of changes in the field, maintain contacts, and receive job offers. Association directories, available online and in most libraries and career centers, can be invaluable in this regard. (Review Chapter 12 for details.)

As a new employee at your first job, these data suggest that it would be important for you to expect to spend considerable time in training. Indeed, you should embrace these training opportunities with a positive attitude and enthusiasm. Some authorities suggest that the only thing workers might reasonably expect from an organization is ongoing training to enable the worker to become more productive and competitive in the marketplace.

Communications Skills

Throughout this chapter we have suggested that improving your communications skills is especially important. This includes the development of presentation skills and taking special speech courses or joining organizations like Toastmasters International. Your ability to present ideas in face-to-face discussions, staff meetings, or large group presentations will depend on your ability to make effective presentations.

A second area for communications skills improvement is the telephone. Although you have probably spent a great deal of time on the phone, it was probably not for professional purposes. To improve your professional skills in this area, consider using a preplanned agenda to help make calls as brief and productive as possible, to create an outline and take notes on important information or decisions made during the call, and to use a clock to time your calls. We might add that it is important for you to seek training to learn how to use all the features of the telecommunications system in your office, such as parking calls, call waiting, conference calls, and forwarding messages. Learn workplace e-Etiquette (Langland, 2011) and realize that organizations vary greatly with regard to guidelines and policies related to professional and personal communication by employees.

Be Your Own PR Machine

Doing good work is essential, but if it isn't noticed it will not be rewarded. One suggestion is to trade your free time for face time to let people know what you are doing. Keep others informed of your progress with projects. Share interesting work-relevant articles with colleagues, but avoid bombarding them with e-mails and links or creating the impression that you spend most of your time surfing the Web! Volunteer to make presentations about your work. Share your ideas on listservs and through e-mail as appropriate. Directories for mailing lists and newsgroups are at http://www.lsoft.com/catalist.html and http://groups.google.com. Keep your resume updated, especially after you obtain new certificates, complete important projects, or gain new skills. Maintain and update your personal Web page or portfolio.

Moving Up or Out

In Chapter 14 (Tables 14.1 and 14.2) we listed expectations of employers and students regarding a job. The quality of the match between the two parties can result in (a) successful transition to employment or (b) termination. We'll provide some details about getting promotions, getting fired, and quitting in the following paragraphs.

Getting Promoted

Gardner (2007) surveyed a national sample of employers to discover what characteristics of new hires led to promotions and new assignments in the organization. Respondents listed about 1,500 positive characteristics, which Gardner and his associates clustered into seven categories.

1. *Taking initiative.* Accepting responsibility beyond the job description; self-motivated; volunteering for extra work; promoting new ideas.

2. *Self-management.* Setting priorities; time management; handle change; completing work on time; understanding quality indicators for work.
3. *Personal attributes.* Being friendly, dependable, patient, flexible, reliable; respecting diversity.
4. *Commitment.* Working with a positive attitude; enthusiasm and dedication.
5. *Leadership.* Formulating, stating, and building consensus on common goals; recognizing the need to develop people; developing management skills.
6. *Show and tell.* Presenting ideas persuasively in written and oral forms.
7. *Technical competencies.* Possessing core knowledge in an area of study; demonstrating technical skills appropriate for the job; obtaining mastery of position.

Getting Fired

This same survey of employers revealed the factors that most frequently led to disciplinary action and the termination of new employees (Gardner, 2007). New employees get into trouble by displaying a bad attitude or poor work ethic and engaging in unethical behaviors. The seven most noted reasons are listed below, followed by the percentage of respondents indicating that the occurrence of the poor behavior was fairly or very often.

1. *Lack of work ethic/commitment* (52%). Acting as if the position is temporary until something better comes along; lack of enthusiasm about the job.
2. *Unethical behavior* (46%). Improper use of technology (e.g., hacking into the organization's computer system).
3. *Failure to follow instructions* (41%).
4. *Ineffective team member* (41%).
5. *Failure to take initiative* (26%).
6. *Missing assignments/deadlines* (33%).
7. *Unable to communicate effectively* (32%).

It should be noted that although these behaviors might not lead to a dismissal, they could result in a poor performance rating or some kind of disciplinary action. Unethical behavior, closely tied to inappropriate use of technology, would most likely lead to firing. Petrecca (2010) reported that 26% of employers in an American Management Association survey reported firing someone for either e-mail or Internet misuse. These same behaviors are sometimes evident in the classroom, so it is important for students to overcome these weaknesses in their career behavior. It appears that lack of self-management and poor relationship skills are at the heart of career transition problems.

Quitting

Previous data indicated that people in their 20s change jobs every 18 months, and 75% of workers in this age range indicate that they are looking for a new job (Loeb, 2007). A recent Bureau of Labor Statistics (BLS; 2010) report showed that the median job tenure for wage and salary workers ages 25–34 for women and men was 3.0 years for women and 3.2 years for men. Employee tenure is not stable for many college students. In this section, we examine the decision to remain with an employer and some of the factors that appear to be relevant to this issue.

The general consensus in the literature on this topic indicates the importance of negotiating a solution to job problems rather than quitting. For example, a worker might try negotiating with the boss for better conditions in the current position. It is probably best to arrange a separate meeting for this discussion rather than doing it during a performance review or a job evaluation meeting because the boss's agenda is most important in that situation. As we explained in Chapter 14, negotiating is a matter of reaching an agreement, and you need to be fully prepared before engaging in this process.

Discussing a decision to quit with the boss is directly related to the quality of the relationship with the boss and the boss's management style. Some bosses are supportive of career changes; others are not. If you do not have a good relationship with your current boss, it is probably best to not say anything about quitting until you have a firm, written offer from your next employer. Your current employer might suggest that you leave immediately, because quitting is seen as a sign of disloyalty and the manager doesn't want a "rotten apple spoiling the barrel." If your relationship is good and supportive, let your boss know that you have accepted another position and ask for assistance in completing your current projects and setting priorities. In general, the poorer the relationship, the longer you wait to say anything.

Some companies such as Deloitte & Touche (Coster, 2007) have gone so far as to hire career coaches as independent contractors to help employees explore career opportunities within the organization rather than going outside. This company reported that 23% of its employees (9,700 people) have been through this process.

In any case, leaving your job will probably place your employer in a bind. Various sources report that the cost of replacing an employee can range from 30% to more than 200% of the person's salary. Of course, these costs vary greatly by position type and level. In high-demand fields, the costs are at the upper end of this range. It typically takes weeks or months to fill a position and involves many hours of work by the remaining employees.

Here are some practical suggestions regarding quitting: (a) give at least a two-week notice—more if you hold a high-level position or the employer handbook specifies a longer time; (b) write a resignation letter; (c) finish outstanding projects and leave directions for completing the others; (d) offer to help in filling the position; (e) know what severance benefits you have; (f) don't criticize your former employer; (g) stay in contact with your former boss and colleagues; (h) say thank you to your former associates in writing and highlight the positive aspects of your job; and (i) honor any confidentiality agreements you signed when you started the job.

The bottom line: don't burn any bridges, especially if you plan to remain in the same field, because your reputation will follow you into other work organizations and you may become colleagues again with your former associates.

From Career Planning to Career Management

In your new job situation, career planning will shift slightly in focus because you now have supervisors and managers who can help you develop and manage your career journey. As we noted in Chapter 8, an organizational career development program could include such things as individual and group career counseling, assessment, job vacancy postings, training and development, organizational career planning, and special programs for targeted groups (e.g., outplaced, younger workers, preretirees). One of your early tasks will be to study the career program offered by your employer and find one or more mentors who can advise you about managing the career process in this new organizational context. This is an important issue, so take some time and make it an effective part of your ongoing career development.

A CIP Perspective for Your New Job

In this chapter, we have been learning about the process of beginning a new professional job and working through issues that may occur during the first year. In this next section, we'll review what we have learned about these topics from a CIP perspective. We want to focus on the new metacognitions that have been created and added to your PCT and strategic career thinking.

Self-Knowledge

In Chapter 2, we emphasized the importance of interests and values in solving career problems and making career decisions. These are also important in helping you set your priorities and preferences in the way you will perform in the new job. This new job will provide opportunities for you to clarify your interests and values and to validate and advance your job skills. Self-knowledge will help you determine how you are adjusting to your new job, because it will provide the criteria you will use to determine whether you are satisfied and happy in the job or want to begin planning your next career move.

Knowledge of Options

Knowledge about options includes knowledge about occupations, specific positions, and the culture of an employing organization. To effectively assess a new job situation, you need to learn everything possible about the organization, your boss and coworkers, and how you will be evaluated in your first performance review. This is essential to making an optimal adjustment to your new job and to make progress during the first year. Understand how your new job relates to other positions within the organization. You may use this information in the years ahead and as you think about your own career advancement.

Applying the CASVE Model

We suggest that you evaluate your new job and the first year based on the same set of factors that we have used throughout this text: the CASVE Cycle.

COMMUNICATION. In a new job situation, you might find yourself feeling alone, lost, uncertain, or overwhelmed. Some of the difficulties might stem from the differences between college and workplace cultures. These kinds of feelings may signal that a career problem exists or that decisions need to be made.

On the other hand, you may be excited at all of the opportunities available to you in your new position but unsure of how to choose from among them. A focal point of your feelings about the new job will come from the quality of the relationship with your new boss, and/or the coworkers with whom you spend most of your time. In either case, it is essential to properly frame the "gap."

In CIP terms, the gap is not simply surviving the first few days or weeks, it is developing an ongoing awareness of yourself in your work environment, your feelings, your impressions, and your comfort with work and your colleagues. If discomfort arises, don't deny it or think it will go away but try to learn from it.

ANALYSIS. As noted in the previous section, having accurate and complete knowledge about yourself and your new job is a critical part in adjusting to the new work situation. Many of the cultural behaviors and values acquired and used in college will be counterproductive in employment. In analyzing a gap, you will want to determine the extent to which the job meets the skills, values, interests, and goals you have identified as important in your employment. These personal characteristics are examined in terms of the relationship with your boss and coworkers, the organizational culture, the results of your first performance evaluation, trends in the industry, and other environmental matters.

Analysis also involves having a complete knowledge and understanding of the position you are in and all the policies and rules that apply to it in the organization. Other key aspects of Analysis involve understanding how you can best accommodate yourself to your supervisor's expectations, deciding when to ask for help, and developing a strategic plan for your advancement in the job, organization, or industry. As noted earlier, be aware of negative cognitions that may be affecting how you think about your job (e.g., "I'm not sure how to get all my work done," "I feel overwhelmed by the details of this assignment").

If you find yourself having difficulty trying to analyze a gap related to adjustments in your first job, find a trusted friend or mentor to serve as a confidant for exploring causes of a gap and possible options for removing it.

SYNTHESIS. With respect to evaluating your options in the new job, the Synthesis phase of the CASVE Cycle involves both Elaborating and Crystallizing offers inside and outside your organization. In Synthesis Elaboration, you try to generate more options for ways you can work in the job or in the organization to increase the quality of your career, including the possibility of leaving.

The process of evaluating your adjustment in your new job is more likely to be focused on narrowing your options, or Synthesis Crystallization. This might involve decreasing your expectations, concentrating on the most important parts of your job, and meeting the expectations of your supervisor.

After you master your first position in the organization, your knowledge of options may expand to include how you can advance in the organization or what types of lateral transfers would provide some level of job enrichment or career development for you.

VALUING. This phase of the CASVE Cycle includes considering the costs and benefits of each job adjustment option, not only to yourself but also to significant others, your cultural group, community, and society, now and in the future.

You are the only one who can decide whether to adjust to the organizational culture. The "Employment-Decision Making Exercise" in Appendix L is one method that you can use to compare and evaluate options by weighting factors that you rank more highly both personally and in a job.

EXECUTION. Once you make the decision to stay at your job, there are several key steps related to the Execution phase of the CASVE Cycle. The first of those is communicating to your boss that you are committed to the organization and want to make a positive contribution. The second involves improving your personal performance, such as clock management, impression management, and personal financial management. The third pertains to developing effective, collaborative relationships with coworkers within the context of the organizational culture. This will lead to your success in managing projects and providing leadership on the job.

If you choose to leave the job, cut your ties and don't look back. Have no regrets or second thoughts about your choice. You are already on the way to the next place in your career path.

Executive Processing

Executive processing is thinking about how you identify problems and how you solve problems. Your goal is to think about yourself as a problem solver, not only of work tasks but life and career tasks as well.

Negative thinking is most likely to occur when you enter a new job and the realities of life in the organization affect your expectations. You are the only person who can decide if you are happy and satisfied enough to remain in the job. Challenging your thinking in this area might involve saying, "If one employer thought I was good enough to extend an offer to me, chances are another employer will as well. I can make something positive happen in this job situation." This process requires your highest levels of self-confidence and positive self-talk.

Adjusting to the new job means taking responsibility for yourself and your future—for taking action to create situations and environments that will foster your career development. You are not a passive observer in this process, but an active designer and creator of your career within the jobs that you hold in the organization. Finally, your career metacognitions at the executive-processing level will enable you to set standards for your work ethics and values, for establishing an effective balance between the job in relation to your other life roles and the level of excellence that you will seek to achieve in your life and work.

Summary

This chapter examined the topics relevant to beginning a new professional position and setting goals for the first year on the job. The chapter included research findings regarding new college graduates and job adjustments, fundamental differences between college and work environments, economic realities of contemporary work life, strategies for adjusting to a new professional job and the first year, thoughts about quitting or staying at the first job, and moving from career planning to career management. The chapter concluded with a CIP perspective of issues associated with starting a new job and moving through the first year of professional employment. Finally, a particularly relevant Web site regarding career development and career management can be found at http://careers.wsj.com/. This site includes materials from the *Wall Street Journal Interactive Edition* and the *National Business Employment Weekly*.

References

AFT on Campus. (2012, January/February). Climbing student debt worsened by high unemployment. *AFT on Campus*, 2.

Barnett, E. (2012, February 18). Tweeting about a bad day could lose you your job. *The Telegraph*. Retrieved from http://www.telegraph.co.uk/technology/social-media/9089826/Tweeting-about-a-bad-day-could-lose-you-your-job.html

Blumenthal, K. (2009). *The Wall Street Journal. Guide to starting your financial life*. New York, NY: Three Rivers Press.

Bureau of Labor Statistics. (2010, September 14). *Employee tenure in 2010*. Retrieved from http://www.bls.gov/news.release/pdf/tenure.pdf

Carliner, S., & Bakir, I. (2010). Trends in spending on training: An analysis of the 1982 through 2008 training annual industry reports. *Performance Improvement Quarterly, 23*, 77–105.

Collegiate Employment Research Institute (2010–2011). What employers want you to know about winning in your job search. *Recruiting trends note 2010–2011:2.1*, 1–4.

Coster, H. (2007, October 15). Baby please don't go. *Forbes*, 86–87.

Gardner, P. D. (2007). Moving up or moving out of the company? Factors that influence the promoting or firing of new college hires. *CERI research brief 1-2007*. East Lansing, MI: Collegiate Employment Research Institute, Michigan State University.

Giordani, P. (2009, May). Elements of a top-notch on-boarding program. *NACE Journal*, 36–41.

Holland, J. (1997). *Making vocational choices* (3rd ed.). Odessa, FL: Psychological Assessment Resources.

Holton, E. (2011). The critical first year on the job. *Job choices for business & liberal arts students: 2012*. Retrieved from www.jobchoicesonline.com

Koblinger, B. (2009). *Get a financial life: Personal finance in your twenties and thirties*. New York, NY: Fireside.

Langland, M. (2011). Workplace e-Etiquette. *Job choices for business & liberal arts students: 2012*. Retrieved from www.jobchoicesonline.com

Loeb, M. (2007). How to make a graceful job exit. *MarketWatch*. Retrieved from http://www.cbsnews.com/stories.2007/04/25/business/printable2724936.shtml

Petrecca, L. 2010, March 17. Feel like someone's watching you? You're right. *USA Today*, 1B–2B.

Render, I. (2010–2011). What employers want you to know about winning in your first job. *Recruiting trends note 2010-2011:1*. East Lansing, MI: Collegiate Employment Research Institute, Michigan State University. Also available at http://www.ceri.msu.edu/ceri-publications

Schein, E. (1985). *Organizational culture and leadership*. San Francisco, CA: Jossey-Bass.

Tuggle, K. (2012, April 16). *Office romances on the rise among young employees*. Retrieved from http://www.foxbusiness.com/personal-finance/2012/04/18/office-romances-on-rise-among-young-employees

Vault.com. (2011, February 7). *2011 office romance survey results*. Retrieved from http://blogs.vault.com/blog/workplace-issues/2011-office-romance-survey-results

Appendix A

Glossary

Analysis. A phase of the career problem-solving and decision-making (CASVE cycle) process marked by career thoughts associated with identifying the causes and relationships among components of a career problem; a period of reflection to more fully understand all aspects of the problem.

Career. The time extended working out of a purposeful life pattern through work undertaken by the person. The combination of a person's multiple life roles, including worker, student, parent, child, spouse/partner, citizen, and retiree. Occupation is an important part of one's life and career, as well as educational field of study, leisure pursuits, and family roles.

Career Development. The total constellation of economic, sociological, psychological, educational, physical, and chance factors that combine to shape one's career.

Career Problem. A gap between an existing state of career indecision and a more desired state of decidedness; may be multifaceted in nature, involving feelings, beliefs, behavior, family, community, leisure, and spiritual dimensions.

Career Thought. An outcome of one's mental activity (thinking) about behaviors, beliefs, feelings, plans, and/or strategies related to career problem solving and decision making.

CASVE Cycle (pronounced Ca SA, Veh). A career problem-solving and decision-making process using a series of logical, rational steps to enhance decision making that also recognizes the role that feelings and behavior play in this process. The simplest way to think about the CASVE Cycle is as the means by which clients recognize and solve a career problem—they need to resolve the "gap" between where they are now and where they'd like to be. The CASVE Cycle includes the phases of Communication, Analysis, Synthesis, Valuing, and Execution.

Code (also Holland or SDS Code). One to three RIASEC letters that indicate which types a person, occupation, field of study, or leisure area most resembles.

Cognition. The memory and thought process that a person engages in to perform a task or attain a goal; it is the thinking process.

Commitment Anxiety. The inability to make a commitment to a specific career choice, accompanied by generalized anxiety about the outcome of the decision-making process, with anxiety perpetuating the indecision; a scale on the CTI.

Communication. A phase of career problem solving and decision making (CASVE cycle) marked by career thoughts related to becoming fully "in touch" with all aspects of a career problem, or the gap between the present and an ideal career situation. Cues about

247

a gap may come from external sources (e.g., a parent's remark), or internal sources (e.g., negative emotions, avoidance behavior). The awareness of a gap motivates one to seek a solution to the career problem.

Congruence. The degree of matches between two codes (e.g., a person and an occupation) in the Holland RIASEC model; e.g., a Realistic person in a Realistic occupation is very congruent, whereas a Realistic person in a Social occupation is incongruent.

Consistency. The degree of consistency in an SDS code is determined by the distance between the first two code letters on the Holland hexagon: High, first two letters are adjacent on the hexagon (e.g., RI); Average, first two letters are alternate on the hexagon (e.g., RA); Low, first two letters are opposite on the hexagon (e.g., RS).

Contingent Work. Employment that is uncertain, unplanned, somewhat accidental, dependent on changing conditions and the employer's immediate needs; work that is not permanent and is time limited.

Control and Monitoring. Control alludes to regulation of thought process, whereas monitoring refers to observing one's self in the act of problem solving. Control and monitoring allows one to know when to move forward in the CASVE Cycle and when to stop and get more information.

Decision Making. It includes the four steps in the problem solving cycle (CASV), but it adds the development of a plan or strategy for implementing the chosen solution and the adoption of a risk-taking attitude and commitment to carry the plan to completion (E). Decision making, then, adds our feelings and behaviors to the problem solving process, and includes the implementation of a choice.

Decision-Making Confusion. The inability to initiate or sustain the career decision-making process as a result of disabling emotions and/or a lack of understanding about the decision-making process itself; a scale in the Career Thoughts Inventory (CTI).

Decision-Making Skills Domain. Middle-level region in the Pyramid of Information Processing that includes the five phases of the CASVE Cycle, which comprises Communication, Analysis, Synthesis, Valuing, and Execution.

Diamond-Shaped Organization. An organizational structure where the top of the diamond is reserved for the top executives and managers (5–10% of the workers); the bottom portion of the diamond has 15–40% of the workers that might be employed as contract workers or temporary employees; the remaining middle portion of core workers (50–80% of the organization's workforce) are involved in leading teams, supervising coworkers, monitoring quality control; these workers may enjoy higher earnings and more job security because of their contributions to the success of the organization.

Differentiation. The level of definition or distinctness of a personality profile. A person is highly differentiated who demonstrates a profile with large differences between scales, whereas a person who is undifferentiated demonstrates a "flat" profile with small differences between scales.

Dual-Career Family. Usually reserved for families in which both partners hold professional, managerial, or technical jobs and are seeking to manage both careers and family relationships concurrently.

Enterprise Web. High-value business enterprises that are complex, flexible work organizations, which also may be very temporary; may be best understood in terms of a spider's web where each connecting point is a place where information is exchanged by the workers.

Execution. A phase in career problem solving and decision making (CASVE Cycle) marked by career thoughts that involve the planning and implementation of steps to carry out the solution to a career problem; may involve a tryout or reality testing of a first choice solution to a gap.

Executive Processing Domain. The cognitions associated with the apex of the Pyramid of Information Processing. The cognitions associated with monitoring, controlling, regulating, and evaluating lower-order information processing, including an awareness of one's self as a career problem solver via self-talk, with the complementary cognitions about one's ability to solve career problems.

External Conflict. The inability to balance the importance of one's own self-perceptions with the importance of input from significant others, resulting in a reluctance to assume responsibility for decision making; a scale on the CTI.

Hexagon. A six-sided figure showing the order and symmetry of the RIASEC types according to Holland's theory; can also be used to show the degree of agreement between a person's type and alternative occupational environments; persons can use a Personal Career Theory to think about careers in terms of personal typologies and matching jobs (e.g., "Where is she on the hexagon?").

Independent Contractors. Self-employed workers who obtain customers on their own to provide a product or service; also consider themselves to be consultants or freelance workers.

Job. A paid position held by one or more persons requiring some similar attributes in a specific organization; persons lose or gain jobs; organizations lose or gain positions.

Job Campaign (or employment campaign). Involves thinking and planning about the many aspects of a job search, including identifying goals and objectives, finding resources for identifying potential employers, specifying employers and/or job targets, considering alternative work settings and ways of working, preparing letters and resume(s), contacting employers, interviewing with employers, making onsite visits, maintaining a record-keeping system, and choosing from among job offers.

Knowledge Workers. Those who know how to acquire and use knowledge and information to produce marketable goods and services; they produce something of intrinsic value; see also symbolic analysts.

Leisure. Relatively self-determined nonpaid activities and experiences that are available due to discretionary income, time, and social behavior; the activity may be physical, intellectual, volunteer, creative, or some combination of all four.

Mailing Lists/Listservs. Topical discussion groups that allow one subscriber to e-mail messages to all other subscribers; it may or may not be moderated.

Metacognitions or Metacognitive Skills. The skills that govern how we think about career problem solving and decision making, that is "thinking about thinking." The prefix "meta" simply means "beyond" or "higher," such as "higher-order thinking skills."

Netiquette (Internet etiquette). Preferred conduct for communicating with professionals and employers via discussion groups, e-mails, and chat sessions on the Internet; use of the appropriate level of formality for various types of communications, such as thank-you letters, requests for information, or online forums.

New Social Contract. Based on the employee's opportunities for training and development in an organization; loyalty may be more to the occupational group or profession than the organization.

Occupation. A group of similar positions found in different industries or organizations.

Occupational Level. The relative prestige, status, education required, usual income, or substantive complexity of an occupation compared to other occupations.

Occupational Knowledge. One of the knowledge domains in the lower tier of the Pyramid of Information Processing; includes cognitions related to the acquisition, storage, and retrieval of information about individual occupations, fields of study, training programs, and the structure of the world of work.

Office Work. Part of the services industry; employs large numbers of all workers, pays the highest salaries, is growing the fastest, employs over half of college graduates, and captures about half of all earnings; includes accountants, managers, sales representatives, and brokers.

Old Social Contract. Now generally outdated tradeoff that if workers were loyal to the organization and dedicated their working lives to producing its products and services, the organization would maintain the worker as an employee and pay them benefits in retirement.

Organization. Special-purpose institution that concentrates on one task and functions best when it has a clear purpose and the people working in the organization know exactly how to align themselves with this larger purpose.

Organizational Culture. Characteristic of a stable social group that has a history and in which members have shared important experiences in solving group problems; these common experiences have led the group members to have a shared view of the world and their place in it; this shared view has worked successfully long enough to be taken for granted by the group and has now dropped out of the group members' awareness; they take this shared view for granted as members of the group; "culture" may be viewed as a learned product of group experience, and it is found in a group or organization with a significant history.

Permutation. Alternative orderings of letters in a 3-point Holland code: RIE, IRE, IER, etc.

Personal Career Theory (PCT). Personal views and ideas about careers and work, which may include a typology of work personalities and environments, as well as a variety of career thoughts about educational and career decision making, job hunting, and life roles. A weak PCT may lead to career problems. PCTs may be related to the hexagon and the pyramid.

Personality Pattern. The profile of scores unique to individuals earned on interest and personality inventories; the SDS and MBTI are examples of instruments that provide personality profiles.

Position. A group of tasks performed in an organization; a unit of work with a recurring or continuous set of tasks; a task is a unit of job behavior with a beginning point and an ending point performed in a matter of hours rather than days.

Problem Solving. Thinking or processing information that will lead to a course of action to remove the gap between a state of indecision and decidedness. In other words, problem solving is "gap removal," and it can occur with respect to any aspect of our lives. This thinking process involves (a) recognizing the gap, (b) analyzing its causes, (c) coming up with different ways to remove the gap, and (d) choosing one of these ways to remove the gap. Thus, problem solving involves arriving at a choice among plausible alternative courses of action.

Profile. A pattern of scores earned on interest and personality inventories or other tests.

Pyramid of Information Processing. Based on cognitive information processing theory, a figure showing the three domains of knowledge (self and occupational) at the base, decision skills in the middle (CASVE Cycle), and executive processing at the top. Career thoughts operate at all three levels to inform, guide, and control career decision making. A person's career situation can be understood in terms of the quality and content of his/her status within the domains of the pyramid (e.g., "Where is she in the CASVE Cycle?" "How well developed is her occupational knowledge?").

Reframing. The process of changing or restating a metacognition or thought as it is reflected in a sentence or statement; for example, one might reframe a negative thought into a more positive one by rewriting a sentence or statement that alters a negative thought into one that is more positive.

Self-Awareness. A state of self-detachment that enables an individual to perceive oneself as a doer of a task; a state of self-consciousness.

Self-Knowledge. One of the knowledge domains at the bottom tier of the Pyramid of Information Processing. It includes cognitions related to the acquisition, storage, or recall of information about one's personal characteristics (e.g., interests, skills, values).

Self-Talk. The verbalization one uses to talk to oneself as if from the perspective of an observer. Self-talk may be kind or punitive. For example, you can make a positive statement about yourself, such as "I am a good decision maker," or a punitive statement, such as "I could never trust myself to make good decisions that are best for me."

Services Industry. Occupations that provide or assist individuals in having certain experiences or in acquiring certain kinds of information (e.g., an airplane ride or telephone call); includes low paid burger flippers and floor sweepers, as well as highly paid brain surgeons, defense lawyers, movie stars, and accountants.

Social Economy. See Third Sector.

Strategic Career Thinking. Planning your career according to a vision or mission by setting your career direction in light of the internal forces (e.g., your interests, values, skills) in relation to the external forces existing in society (e.g., global economy, new ways of working).

Subtype. The second or third letter in a 3-part Holland code. For example, saying that a person is identified with the RI subtype means that the person resembles the R type most, followed by the I type.

Success. With respect to career, it is a personal standard of achievement and satisfaction; an individual matter that has much to do with life satisfaction; is based more on internal factors and one's state of mind rather than external factors over which one may have little control; involves trade-offs among personal values.

Synthesis. A phase of career decision making (CASVE Cycle) marked by career thoughts related to the formulation of a plausible set of alternatives for resolving a career problem; Synthesis Elaboration involves brainstorming a wide variety of possible solutions, and Synthesis Crystallization involves narrowing the potential solutions to the best 3–5 options to bring forward into the valuing phase of the CASVE Cycle.

Temporary Work. Individuals employed as contingent workers ("temps") who do not expect to stay with their current employer more than a year or who hold a job that has a specified ending date; however, if one has continuing employment with a temporary services company, the work is permanent, not temporary or contingent; this means that one can have permanent employment with a temp agency.

Third Sector or Social Economy. Known as the independent or volunteer sector, in contrast to the Public Sector (government) and the Market Sector (business); includes volunteer and community organizations that feed the poor, protect the environment, teach reading, and build churches.

Type. Holland's theory makes use of six personality types (e.g., RIASEC) and six environmental models in explaining behavior in environments; no person or environment is a true, perfect type, but the extent to which one resembles a type helps in describing the person or environment.

Valuing. A phase of career problem solving and decision making (CASVE Cycle) marked by career thoughts related to the prioritizing of possible solutions in terms of what is best for the individual, significant others, community, and society; a tentative best choice emerges from this phase of decision making.

Vocational Aspiration. A person's desired occupational or career aim; similar terms include vocational expectation, occupational aspiration, occupational daydream, and occupational expectation; classified aspirations or expectations can be used to derive a person's Holland code; aspirations are a measure of expressed interests.

Vocational History. A work history of a person's positions, occupations, or vocational aspirations can be used to derive his/her Holland code.

Work. Activity that produces something of value for oneself or others; work is not limited to activity for which we get paid; it can include unpaid, volunteer activity, if it produces something valuable for us or another person (e.g., coaching youth baseball, leading the church choir, providing care for older persons or children).

Appendix B

Chapter Study Guide (CSG)

Directions: This guide is designed to help you process the information in each chapter. You can duplicate and use this form for note taking on the materials you read in the chapters. Concentrate on new words and concepts. Focus on (a) what you already know and (b) what you're unsure about.

1. **Definitions of terms/concepts.** List all the terms that were new or difficult. Define new terms in your own words. Do you agree with the definitions being used?

   _____

   _____

   _____

   _____

2. **Author's message.** Briefly summarize the author's major ideas.

   _____

   _____

   _____

   _____

3. **Analysis of major ideas.** Do you understand the author's major themes and methods? Are they important now and in the future? Headings and subheadings in the reading are cues to finding the author's major ideas.

   _____

   _____

   _____

   _____

4. **Connecting other knowledge.** How useful are these ideas in relation to things you know and have experienced? Have the ideas been covered in your other classes?

_____

_____

_____

_____

5. **Applying the information.** How do these ideas affect you personally? Are there implications for your educational and career planning? Do the ideas affect your educational and career planning?

_____

_____

_____

_____

6. **Evaluating the author's ideas.** Will the author's ideas be useful to you in the future? Which ones?

_____

_____

_____

_____

7. **Write down in your notebook one important learning you can take away from this chapter.**

_____

_____

_____

_____

Appendix C

A Guide to Writing Your Autobiography

Imagine you are preparing for an interview about a job or graduate school application. You can be sure the interviewer will ask you about your background and how it has influenced your goals. The purpose of this assignment is to help you prepare for the interviewer's questions. The time you spend on this assignment will probably pay off in numerous ways in the future.

Directions

In reviewing your history, concentrate on three areas of your life that have influenced your present life/career goals. Your autobiography will include four sections each with the following subheadings:

1. Family Experience
2. Educational Experience
3. Work Experience
4. Current Life/Career Goals

Each section will include about 250–300 words; begin each with a left margin subhead as shown on this page. Use your best writing skills in producing this paper. Try not to simply report activities in each section, but analyze or review your experiences to uncover deeper meanings affecting your life/career. It might help to think about how a special person or event influenced your life in each section.

Only your instructor will read the information in your autobiography. This paper and all other course materials can be reclaimed at the end of the course. Completed autobiographies may range from four to six pages (printed, double-spaced, 1-inch margins all around, 12-point font, Times New Roman).

Family Experience

Consider experiences and activities from childhood and how they have affected your life/career choices. How have work roles of your family members influenced your thinking about career? You might want to focus on where you lived, immediate and extended family member relationships, ethnic heritage, your gender, and family activities.

Educational Experience

You might want to focus on favorite subjects or activities in school from kindergarten up to the present, as well as important teachers, organizations, and achievements that have influenced your life/career.

Work Experience

Recall aspects of your working experiences that have had the most impact on you. Remember that the definition of "work" includes unpaid, volunteer experiences. You might want to focus on relationships with supervisors or peers, the nature of the work organization, the work activities (what you did and did not like about them), or trends in your work experiences. Are you seeking new work experiences?

Current Life/Career Goals

Identify three of your current life/career goals or aspirations. Explain how your family, education, and work experiences are related to each of your goals. If your goals about education and occupation are currently uncertain, try to project 5–10 years into the future and focus on what you will have accomplished, what matters to you, and how you want to be viewed by others.

Appendix D

RIASEC Hexagon

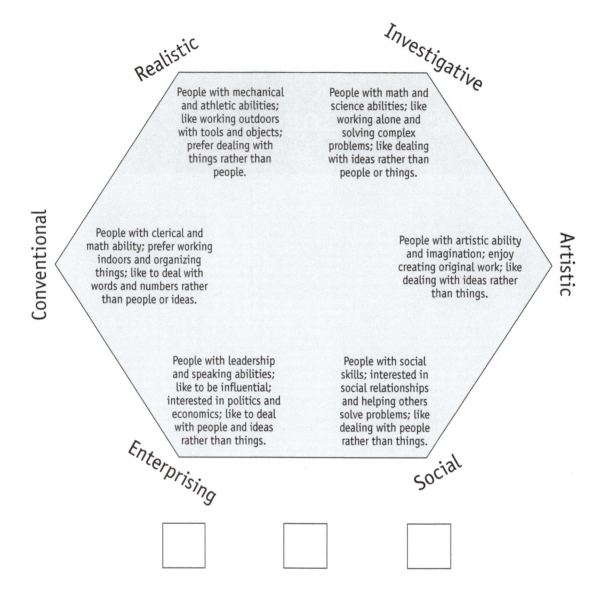

Appendix E

Career Field Analysis (CFA)

Purpose
This project is designed to help you learn about sources for occupational and educational information and give you an opportunity to either explore several alternatives in occupations or majors or conduct more in-depth research on one occupation.

Objectives
1. Become more informed about either **one** occupation or **three** occupations or majors.
2. Write a research paper, including proper **in-text** and **end reference citations**, to improve and demonstrate personal research skills. (*Note*: A personal, subjective writing style is *not* appropriate for this assignment.)
3. Learn how to more effectively use career information resources in the Career Center Library, on the Internet, or other resource sites.
4. Demonstrate project management skills in executing a work assignment effectively and on time.

Two Options for CFA Contents
1. Choose **one** occupation to learn about in-depth by including **16** topics. You must use **at least 5** of the **12** different **types** of information sources shown below. This means your reference page, at a minimum, will have five entries, *or*
2. Choose **three** different occupations **or** majors to learn about by including **six** topics for **EACH** occupation or major chosen. For this option, you must use **at least 3** of the **12** different **types** of information sources shown below for **EACH** occupation or major chosen. This means your reference page, at a minimum, will have nine entries.

Procedures
1. Confer with your instructor and decide if it will be most helpful for you to study one occupation or three occupations/majors.
2. Decide on the name(s) of the occupations/majors you will study.
3. Learn how to use the *various types* of information sources including the 12 numbered items shown below and on the following page:
   (1) **books** published on occupations, career fields, or majors
   (2) **information interviews** (e.g., resource persons, networking)
   (3) **employer literature** (e.g., annual reports, employer websites)
   (4) **computer-assisted career guidance systems** (e.g., Choices™ Planner, e-Discover®, SIGI³)

259

(5) **university or college-produced publications**

(6) **government documents** (e.g., U.S. Dept. of Labor publications, *Occupational Outlook Handbook*)

(7) **professional association materials** (e.g., reports, newsletters, pamphlets, websites, or bulletins)

(8) **news reports/magazines** (e.g., newspapers, *Black Collegian*, *Job Choices*)

(9) **occupational briefs** (e.g., Chronicle Guidance Publications)

(10) **multimedia materials** (e.g., DVDs, videos)

(11) **directory information** (e.g., Chamber of Commerce Directory, industry-specific directories)

(12) **job announcements**

4. Select the *types* of information sources you will use to research the occupation(s) and/or major(s) in your report, using *at least **five*** different *types* of the 12 sources for option 1, and **three** different *types* of the 12 sources for each occupation/major in option 2. Examples of 12 types of information sources are shown in the numbered items above.

5. Prepare a **6–8-page** (excluding references, table of contents) typed, double-spaced research paper using the topics described below to format your paper.

6. Format your paper:
    a. Staple the pages in the upper left corner
    b. Number each page
    c. Use a left margin subheading for **EACH** topic used in your paper
    d. Do not use a binder

7. Use proper **in-text** reference citation procedures for **all** facts and data included in your paper. This means that every time you use a fact or figure in your paper, you must reference the source after stating the fact or figure. Except for the introduction and conclusion, all topics in the paper should have a **minimum** of one in-text reference citation. To reference sources, you should use the American Psychological Association (APA) style. Examples of the preferred APA style for reference citation are shown in later sections of this Appendix. **APA style is used also in your text—look there for examples of reference formats.**

8. The research paper will be evaluated using the *CFA Evaluation Form* shown at the end of this document, with 25% of the points allocated for the technical aspects of the assignment, which includes formatting and grammar, and 75% allocated for the substantive aspects, which includes the content.

9. Attach the CFA Evaluation Form to your paper when it is turned in.

10. CFA options 1 and 2 should include the 3 elements listed below:
    a. *Title Page*, including your name, instructor's name, title of research paper, and date;
    b. *Table of Contents*, including page numbers of each topic used in the paper; see the topic lists for options 1 and 2 in the next section below;
    c. *References*, including proper in-text references for those sources used in your paper *and* a reference list at the end; only sources cited in the text of the paper should be included in the reference list at the end.

OPTION 1: Research **one occupation** by using the **16 topic subheadings** below:

1. **Introduction.** Provide a brief, basic description of the occupation, such as typical work settings and kind of work done.

2. **Typical Career Path.** Describe the typical career path for someone in this occupation from entry to the highest level position.

3. **Trends.** Describe how technology, new organizational structures, diversified training, and other management or economic trends are affecting the occupation.

4. **Salary Information.** Provide salary range information for different types of positions in this occupation; indicate differences for entry level and experienced workers, and if there are geographic differences in salary.

✓ 5. **Skills Used.** Describe the skills or abilities typically used in this occupation.

6. **Employing Organizations.** Explain what kinds of organizations hire persons in this occupation; what industries are involved; are persons self-employed in this occupation?

7. **Multicultural Aspects.** Explain if a particular gender or ethnic group dominates employment in the occupation.

8. **Becoming Employed.** Describe how persons find employment in this occupation; are internships, volunteering, job fairs, faculty referrals, websites, and other means used?

9. **Typical Job Notices.** Review and describe a typical job notice in this occupation that is of personal interest to you.

✓ 10. **Work Conditions.** Describe the physical environment, stress level, type of supervision, customer/client contact, hours, work-related travel, etc.

11. **Education/Training.** Describe the majors or fields of study related to preparation for working in the occupation.

12. **Certificate/License.** Identify any licenses or certificates required in the occupation, if any. Are there requirements for ongoing training? Does this vary across states? What are the requirements in states where you plan to reside?

13. **Affiliations.** Specify professional or organizational memberships typically held by persons in this occupation. Are the organizations international, national, regional, state, local?

14. **Outlook.** Describe the current and projected job openings in the occupation, regional influences, industry changes, etc.

15. **Lifestyle Impact.** Discuss how working in this occupation affects family roles and relationships, leisure options, vacations.

16. **Conclusion.** Write a brief summary or review of your general findings; then state your conclusions as a result of your research.

OPTION 2: Research **three occupations or majors** by using the **six topic subheadings below for each one in your paper:**

1. **Introduction.** Provide a brief, basic description of the occupation or major field of study, such as kind of work done or courses taken; typical career or educational path.

2. **Interests/Skills Used.** Describe the interests, skills, or abilities typically used or needed by persons in this occupation or field of study.

3. **Work or Learning Conditions.** Describe the physical environment of work or classes; stress level; type of supervision or instruction; nature of customer/client/instructor contact; hours worked in class or in study; relationships with colleagues; nature of work or learning activities, etc.

4. **Training/Education/Licenses.** Describe the ways in which one prepares for this occupation or field of study (e.g., on-the-job training); majors or fields of study related to the occupation; courses taken in the major, including prerequisites; licenses or certificates required; organizational memberships typically held by workers or students.

5. **Outlook/Salary.** Describe the current and projected job openings in an occupation or those related to a major; current and future salaries; regional influences affecting outlook for the occupation or major; demand for workers or students with this training; anticipated changes in training or curriculum, etc.

6. **Conclusion.** Write a brief summary or review of your general findings and conclusions as a result of your research about **each** occupation and/or field of study.

Suggestions for Referencing

Avoid academic dishonesty and plagiarism in writing research papers for this class. Consult with your instructor if you have any questions about proper referencing of materials used in your paper.

APA Style

The preferred writing style for the CFA paper is found in the *Publication Manual of the American Psychological Association* (APA, 2010). This style was, in fact, developed for the preparation of manuscripts for publication in journals in the areas of social sciences and education. It presents an easy—almost shorthand—way of citing references within the CFA paper; long, complicated citations in the form of footnotes and endnotes are avoided. Therefore, it is also useful for academic and research projects other than this CFA.

What to Cite/Document

Your sources and how well you use them allow the reader to evaluate the quality of your research. You are, therefore, expected to document, *within* your paper, **any and all of the following**:

1. Direct quotations
2. Statistics, tables, figures
3. Words, ideas from sources other than yourself
4. Paraphrases and restatements of facts, ideas from sources other than yourself

---

If you are unsure whether or not you should acknowledge a source, document it!

How to Cite Material in the Text of the CFA Paper

APA style simply acknowledges a source within the text of the CFA paper, giving the reader only enough information to find that source in the alphabetical reference list (reference page) at the end of the document. This information usually consists of:

1. The last name(s) of the author(s) (if author's name is unavailable, use the first words given for the document/source in the reference list).
2. Year of publication (or interview). If no date is available, use "n.d." in place of the date. For example: (Kenneth, n.d.).
3. Page number(s) (if available) for all direct quotations.

This information may be worked into the words of your paper or set within parentheses. (If the in-text citation is within parentheses, this is called parenthetical format.) The text uses APA style—examine it for examples of how to reference your work for this paper. Some other examples follow in the next section. These are only intended as examples. Use the exact information from your data source in creating your reference citations.

Quotations in the CFA Narrative Text

1. The last name(s) of the author(s) (if author's name is unavailable, use the first words given for the document/source in the reference list).
2. All reference information is within the parentheses for a direct quote:

"The profession of law is becoming popular among women" (Jones, 2012, p. 7).

3. Partial information within the narrative:

   In reviewing the current literature, Jones (2012) concluded that "the profession of law is becoming popular among women" (p. 7).

4. Long quotations (40 or more words) in the CFA are indented block style, and double spaced (Note: no quotation marks are used):

   Jones (2012) noted:

   The profession of law is becoming popular among women. For the past ten years law schools have admitted more women each year; in a few law schools, women now outnumber men. Likewise, increasing numbers of women are being admitted to the bar in every state. (pp. 7–8)

5. Citing *paraphrased* material that is not a direct quote, and the author's name **is** available. In citing information sources that are not directly quoted from the original, include the author(s) and year; page references are not necessary.

   a. One author, the citation information is within the parentheses:

      Women are beginning to enter law in greater numbers (Jones, 2012).

   b. More than one author, the citation information is within the parentheses:

      Women are beginning to enter law in greater numbers (Smith & Smith, 2012).

   c. One author, the author information is out of the parentheses:

      Jones (2012) tells us that women are entering law in greater numbers.

      or

      In 2012, Jones found more women were entering law.

   d. More than one source says the same thing:

      Women are beginning to enter law in greater numbers (Jones, 2012; Smith & Smith, 2011).

6. Author's name **is not** available.

   When an author's name is not available, you simply use in the text narrative the first word or words found in the alphabetical reference list (usually the title) so that the reader can locate the full reference. This could also be used with references from the *Occupational Outlook Handbook* or computer guidance systems (e.g., Choices). If you have several sources with the same first word, make sure you use enough of the title to distinguish one source from other sources with the same first word in the title. (Note: If two or more sources begin with the same name or words [e.g., Biologist or Smith], use letters, e.g., a, b, c, after the date to distinguish between or among them.)

   a. In-text citation for a source with no known author, citation information in parentheses:

      Women are beginning to enter law in greater numbers (Women, 2012b).

   b. In the reference section at the end of the paper, list as:

      Women and Law. (2012b, December). *Working Women*, pp. 43–45.

7. Citing an interview.

   To cite an information interview in the text, cite it as a personal communication. Personal communications are not included in the reference list because they do not provide recoverable data.

How to Cite References at the End of the CFA Paper

The following are examples of specific references. They are shown in bold print. Items on the Reference List should be in *alphabetical order*, ***not*** in the order they appear in the paper.

1. Books, pamphlets, brochures (specific).
    a. Author(s) known, whole book:

    Doran, G., Willis, J., & Jones, P. (2011). *Business careers in the global economy.* Dubuque, IA: Kendall Hunt Publishing.

    b. Author unknown, whole book:

    ***Medical school admissions requirements,* 2012–2013: United States and Canada (2011). Washington, DC: Assoc. of American Medical Colleges.**

    c. Book in a numbered series (unusual type of reference, but there are often several sources like this in a library):

    ***Administration, business and office* (Career Information Center Series, No. 1). (2011). Encino, CA: Glencoe.**

    d. Pamphlet/brochure (Note: corporate author; author is publisher):

    ***National Association of Social Workers.* (undated). The point is helping people. Washington, DC: Author.**

2. Books, reference type.

    Lawyer. (2012). In *Occupational Outlook Handbook* (2012–2013 ed., pp. 263–265). Washington, DC: U.S. Department of Labor.

    a. Multivolume, edited reference:
        i. Author of selection known (Vol. I):

        Bogart, L. (2010). Chemical and drug industries. In W. E. Hopke (Ed.), *The encyclopedia of careers and vocational guidance* (15th ed., Vol. I., pp. 193–197). Chicago: J. G. Ferguson.

        ii. Author of selection unknown (Vol. II):

        Flight Attendants. (2010). In W. E. Hopke (Ed.), *The encyclopedia of careers and vocational guidance* (15th ed., Vol. II, pp. 407–470). Chicago: J. G. Ferguson.

3. Periodicals (magazines, newspapers, newsletters, journals).
    a. Magazine:

    Thompson, P. A., & Dalton, G. W. (2011, February). Balancing your expectations. *Business Week Careers,* pp. 32–35.

    b. Newspaper:

    Snelling, R. O., & Snelling, A. M. (2012, April 21). New era in marketing creates greater need for professionals. *The Atlanta Journal and Constitution,* pp. 28–30.

    c. Newsletter (author unknown):

    Entrepreneurs—who are they? (2012, April). *Career Planning & Adult Development Newsletter,* p. 5.

    d. Journal:

    Blustein, D. L. (2005). Decision-making styles and vocational maturity: An alternative perspective. *Journal of Vocational Behavior, 30,* 61–71.

4. Occupational Briefs/Biographies.

   Purchasing agents (Occupational Brief 167). (2012). Moravia, NY: Chronicle Guidance.

   Wildlife Photographer (Vocational Biography D, 6, 4). (2012). Sauk Centre, MN: Vocational Biographies.

5. Computer Guidance Systems.
   a. Specific occupational information:

      Pediatrician. (2012). *CHOICES Planner* [computer software]. Oroville, WA: Bridges Transitions, Inc.

      Market research analyst. (2012). *SIGI3* [computer software]. Tucson, AZ: Valpar International Corporation.

6. Electronic Media.

   Electronic media change rapidly, creating a need for frequently updated referencing style. Such updated information can be found at www.apastyle.org/elecref.html. However, as with other references, the goal is to credit the author and enable the reader to find the material. Electronic correspondence (i.e., e-mail messages) are cited as personal communication (see Information Interview note).

   a. Elements of references to online information:

      author   *n.d.*   *title*   *link*

      American Dental Association. (2012). *Careers in dentistry*. Retrieved from http://www.ada.org/public/careers/index.asp.

7. Others.
   a. Report:

      National Association of Colleges and Employers. (2012, March). *NACE salary survey: A study of 2010–2012 beginning offers*. Bethlehem, PA: Author.

   b. Information Interview (by you):

      H. P. Jones (personal communication, February 10, 2012).

8. Missing Information/Strange Sources.

   Career resource libraries often attempt to provide as much information as possible about each career field. Sometimes this means that there will be "clippings" or other documents (e.g., sample job notices) in the files with incomplete referencing information. Don't hesitate to use these if the information is pertinent; just do the best you can with the reference. Example:

   Glut of lawyers. (n.d.). (Clipping found in Career Center vertical file II B 211 "Lawyer").

Career Field Analysis Project Evaluation Point Distribution

Instructors will use the *Career Field Analysis Evaluation Form* to guide their evaluation of your completed paper. The final evaluation of the CFA is based on a review of both the content (75%) and format (25%) of the paper. The points assigned to the CFA by letter grade are shown in the table below.

Letter Grade	Content Points	Format Points	Total Points
A+	74–75	25	98–100
A	70–73	24	93–97
A–	68–69	23	90–92
B+	66–67	22	88–89
B	62–65	21	83–87
B–	60–61	20	80–82
C+	58–59	19	78–79
C	55–57	18	73–77
C–	53–54	17	70–72
D+	51–52	16	68–69
D	47–50	15	63–67
D–	45–46	14	60–62

Information about the *APA Style Manual* can be found at www.apastyle.org/manual/index.aspx.

Reference

American Psychological Association. (2010). *Publication manual* (6th ed.). Washington, DC: Author.

Student Name: _____ Date Due: _____

Career Field Analysis (CFA) Worksheet

Option 1: One Occupation/Major Field Researched

Name of occupation/major field to be studied: _Corrections / Criminology_____

Indicate at least *five types* of information resources to be used:

1. _____
2. _____
3. _____
4. _____
5. _____

Other possible sources for information:

1. _____
2. _____
3. _____
4. _____
5. _____
6. _____

Student Name: _____ Date Due: _____

Career Field Analysis (CFA) Worksheet

Option 2: Three Occupations/Major Fields Researched

Name of **first** occupation/major field to be studied: _____

Indicate at least *three types* of information resources:

1. _____

2. _____

3. _____

4. _____

Name of **second** occupation/major field to be studied: _____

Indicate at least *three types* of information resources:

1. _____

2. _____

3. _____

4. _____

Name of **third** occupation/major field to be studied: _____

Indicate at least *three types* of information resources:

1. _____

2. _____

3. _____

4. _____

Other possible sources for information:

_____

Appendix F

Guide to Good Decision Making (GGDM)

Note: The CASVE Cycle (see Figure 4.2) shows the phases in making a career choice.

Knowing I Need to Make a Choice

Events and things that happen to me
   "I need to choose a major by next semester."

Comments from my friends and relatives
   "My roommate said that I'll have problems if I don't make a decision soon."

The way I feel
   "I'm scared about committing myself."

Avoiding my problems
   "I'll get started next week."

Physical problems
   "I'm so upset about this, I can't eat."

Understanding Myself and My Options

Understanding myself, such as:
   My values, my interests, my skills

Understanding occupations, programs of study, or jobs
   Understanding specific occupations, programs of study, or jobs
   Understanding how specific occupations, programs of study, or jobs are organized

Understanding how I make important decisions; understanding how I think about my decisions
   Self-talk
   Self-awareness
   Being aware of and controlling my self-talk

Expanding and Narrowing My List of Occupations, Programs of Study, or Jobs

Identify occupations, programs of study, or jobs that fit my values, interests, and skills.

Pick the three to five best occupations, programs of study, or jobs using what I learned from "Understanding Myself and My Options."

Choosing an Occupation, Program of Study, or Job

Costs and benefits of each occupation, program of study, or job to:
    Myself? My family? My cultural group? My community or society?

Rank occupations, programs of study, or jobs.

Make a choice.

Make back-up choice(s) in case I have a problem with my choice.

Implementing My Choice

Plan—Make a plan for getting education or training.

Try out—Get work experience (full time, part-time, volunteer) and take courses or get training to test my choice.

Apply—Apply for and get a job.

Knowing I Made a Good Choice

Have events changed?

How did my friends and relatives react to my choice?

How do I feel now?

Am I avoiding doing what needs to be done?

Appendix G

Instructions for Completing Your Individual Action Plan (IAP)

Breaking your decisions into small concrete steps makes the process of career choice more manageable. Your small-group leader can help in developing your action plan. Refer to the sample IAP for "Jane" on the following page to help you draft your own IAP. Complete in pencil the blank IAP form to prepare for your instructor conference. Follow these steps:

1. Write your name and the date at the top of the IAP form.

2. Write down your decision-making goal in the space provided. Examples include:
   - Choose a college major or get a job related to my education.

3. In the first column, list any activities that you can think of that will help you reach your goal. Examples include:
   - Learn about entry requirements for physical therapists,
   - Talk with professionals in my field, or
   - Locate possible job openings.

4. In the second column, identify any people or information resources that can help you complete each activity. Examples include:
   - Occupational descriptions of physical therapists, or
   - Identify people who can help me locate possible job openings.

5. Review the activities you have written down and show in the third column which activities you will do first, second, third, etc. The information you get in one activity may be needed in a following activity. For example, you will need to know where job openings are before you can fill out a job application or send a resume and cover letter.

6. In the fourth column, write the date that you plan to complete the activity. This step makes your action plan more concrete.

7. As you complete each activity in the plan, place a check mark in the fifth column. This will give you feedback on your progress.

Sample Individual Action Plan (IAP)

Name: _____Jane_____ Date: _6/07/12_

Goal: __Choose a major where I can get good grades and then get a good job__

Activities to Help Me Reach My Goal	People or Information Resources Needed	Activity Order	Date	Activity Completed (✓)
Talk with career advisor	Marilyn Abbey	1	June July	
Learn how to make better decisions	Marilyn Abbey	2	7/2	
Complete decision-making activity	Career class textbook	9	July	
Identify possible majors	Computer Guidance System, Educational Opportunities Finder	3	7/8	
Learn about possible majors	Academic Program Guide	4	7/10	
Learn about occupations	Career Information Systems & Career Library Resources	5	7/8	
Talk with people in occupations	Career Center Online Network	6	7/15– 7/19	
Talk with advisors about specific majors	Dr. Ortez, Dr. Chu	7/8	7/22 7/29	
Complete change of major forms	Undergraduate Studies Office	10	by 8/26	

Appendix H

Exercise for Improving Your Career Thoughts

Directions: The following page shows an example of four negative career thoughts taken from the Career Thoughts Inventory (CTI) and corresponding new thoughts that have been reframed into more positive statements.

Examine your results on the Career Thoughts Inventory (CTI) and note the items you marked "Agree" or "Strongly Agree." Rewrite one of these items in the column marked "Old Career Thought." You might want to add some detail that makes it even more relevant and personal (e.g., use names of persons involved).

Examine your "old" career thought in light of each of the following questions.

1. What is the evidence for this thought? Looking objectively at all of your experience, what is the evidence that this is true?
2. Does this belief invariably or always hold true for you?
3. Does this belief look at the whole picture? Does it take into account both positive and negative ramifications?
4. Does this belief promote your well-being and/or peace of mind?
5. Did you choose this belief on your own or did it develop out of your experience growing up in your family?

Does the old thought still make sense? Does the old thought help you make a good decision? If you now think the old thought does not help you engage in effective career problem solving or decision making, rewrite the thought into a more positive statement in the column headed "New Career Thought."

You might find it useful to use the remaining spaces on the exercise worksheet to reframe other negative career thoughts that interfere with your effective career planning.

The CTI Workbook provides extensive materials to help you reframe many thoughts important in career problem solving and decision making. Your instructor can help you use the CTI Workbook if that might be a useful activity for you to pursue in the process of becoming a more effective career decision maker.

Sample Exercise for Improving Your Career Thoughts

Item No.	*Old* Career Thought	*New* Career Thought
6	The views of my parents make it harder to	I know my parents want me to be a success. I
	choose a new major.	will talk this over with them, but I need to think
		it through and make a good choice.

Item No.	*Old* Career Thought	*New* Career Thought
8	I get so worried when I have to make	It's OK to be worried about an important
	decisions that I can hardly think.	decision like this. Instead of getting stuck,
		I need to use the help available to make a
		good choice.

Item No.	*Old* Career Thought	*New* Career Thought
16	I've tried to find a good major three times	I can learn to make better choices, Thinking
	before, but I can't make good choices.	I'm a failure only keeps me stuck. Waiting
		until it's too late won't help either. Help is
		available.

Item No.	*Old* Career Thought	*New* Career Thought
19	If I change my major again, I will feel	I can change my mind if I make my choice on
	like a failure again.	good information. I've made some bad choices,
		but I'm NOT a bad person!

Sample Exercise for Improving Your Career Thoughts

Item No.	*Old* Career Thought	*New* Career Thought

Item No.	*Old* Career Thought	*New* Career Thought

Item No.	*Old* Career Thought	*New* Career Thought

Item No.	*Old* Career Thought	*New* Career Thought

Appendix 1

Information Interviews Assignment

Directions: This assignment involves conducting **two** information interviews with people who have special knowledge that can inform your educational and career planning. Review the section on Information Interviews in Chapter 13 and the notes below before beginning this assignment.

Some organizations have policies that limit staff participation in information interviews. You may find it helpful in gaining access to interviewees if you mention that this is part of a class assignment. Some tips for arranging and conducting information interviews include:

- Use friends, family, former employers, and career center staff to identify contacts
- Research the career field or industry where your contacts are employed
- Prepare a list of questions (use the sample questions in Chapter 13 as a starting point)
- Make arrangements by phone or e-mail for a time to interview the person
- Dress appropriately and be respectful of the person's time
- Ask the person for names of additional people who might be good information interview contacts
- Follow up with a thank-you note, and if appropriate, a cover letter and a copy of your resume

Many employers view information interviews as a professional contact. Some well-prepared students have been so impressive in information interviews that they were invited to submit applications later for internships or jobs.

In completing this assignment for the class, prepare a brief typed report for each interview that includes the following information:

1. Name of interviewee
2. Position title
3. Name or type of employing organization
4. Date of interview
5. Brief summary of interview content (**one** paragraph)
6. Your personal reactions to the interview (**one** paragraph; e.g., were you surprised by anything you learned?)

From beg. of class to End of class.

Strategic Academic/ Career Planning Project

Directions: This project is the culminating activity of the course. It is designed to help you pull together all that you learned in the course. You should use *all* of the papers, activities, and reports you have completed to prepare this paper. Think of this project as the "open-book, take-home, cumulative final exam" for the course. There are 100 possible points available for this project.

Specific Requirements

1. Use the stages of the CASVE Cycle (see following pages) as section headings to structure your paper. You may also choose to use additional subheadings if you feel they would make your presentation clearer. Use the questions in each section to stimulate your discussion. Read the material in each of the six sections below *before* you begin to write and refer to them again while preparing your paper.

2. If you are still unsure of your academic and/or career plans, discuss this situation with your instructor, advisor, or counselor and specify the processes and resources you plan to use to make your academic/career decisions. Use the CASVE Cycle model.

3. This is a formal paper and should follow appropriate academic style. It should be **typed** with a **cover page** and a **table of contents**. If you make reference to specific sources of information, those must be properly cited and a reference list included. **Staple** the pages together in the upper left corner, DO NOT USE A BINDER OR COVER. If you adequately cover the categories outlined, your paper will be at least **six typed pages**.

Summary

Remember that the purposes of this project are to help you pull together what you have learned about yourself and the academic and career options available to you, and to use that information to develop a plan for yourself. This paper should represent your highest level of academic work and career thinking. If you have any questions—or get stuck—work with your instructor.

Outline of Strategic Academic/Career Planning Project

Cover Page
Table of Contents (include page numbers for each of the six topics below)
Contents:

1. Communication
2. Analysis
3. Synthesis

4. Valuing
5. Execution
6. Communication

Evaluation Form

Your paper and table of contents should include the following **six** sections:

1. **Communication**
   a. *What was the concern that prompted you to begin the academic/career problem-solving and decision-making process at the beginning of the class? What was the gap between your situation at that time and the situation you wanted to be in?* (Example: "I began this class not having any idea about a major beyond that it should have no additional math requirements." OR "Ever since I was a small child I wanted to be a doctor, but after taking biology and chemistry courses I know that I cannot do well enough in those courses to get into medical school. I wanted to know what careers might better suit me.").
   b. *What internal (feelings, emotions, hunches) and external (family, the university, news reports, grades, letter saying you had to declare a major) cues did you experience that alerted you to this need to reduce the gap between your situation and the desired state?* (Examples: "I had just begun to realize that I will graduate in the spring and really have no idea about what I will do when school is over. My family keeps asking me about my plans and I am seeing my friends getting jobs and moving away. This made me nervous and anxious.")
   c. *What did you want to learn from this class?* (Examples: "I wanted to find out about careers that I might enjoy." OR "I wanted to decide on a major."). What were your learning goals?

2. **Analysis**
   a. *What have you learned about yourself in this class that is important in making your academic and/or career decisions?* Examine your values, interests, skills, and experiences. Refer to assignments from the first part of the class Self-Directed Search (SDS, autobiography, computer printout, skills exercise, CTI, etc.) in addressing the "Analysis" topic.
   b. *What have you learned about the world of work that will influence your decisions?* In a broad sense, what kinds of occupations/majors seem most attractive? What types of organizations? What kind of activities? What scheme did you learn about for organizing options?
   c. *What have you learned about your decision-making processes that will relate to this?* In general, which phase or phases of the CASVE Cycle are you in? What evidence can you provide to support your thinking about this? Do your CTI results apply, for example decision-making confusion? Commitment anxiety? External conflict?

3. **Synthesis**
   a. *What have you done (or what do you plan to do) to generate educational and/or occupational alternatives for yourself?* This might include getting suggestions from others, the media, online and resources in the career center (computers, inventories, books). Be specific about resources and learning activities.
   b. *Identify three to five educational, occupational, or employment alternatives that you have considered, are considering, or plan to consider.* What have you eliminated in the process of reducing this number to 3–5?

4. **Valuing**
   a. *What factors were/are/will be important to you in making this decision?* What will make this decision a good decision or a bad decision? This might include factors internal to yourself (interests, values), practical factors (you can enter the field/major from your

current preparation), or factors that relate to others (e.g., "My parents would pay for that major." OR "My friends will be working in Denver and I want to work near them.").

b. *What are the costs and benefits of **each** alternative to yourself, your significant others, and society?* How would the effort and expense (costs) of each alternative compare to the potential benefits to yourself and others?

c. *Based on these questions and your answers to them, prioritize (rank) the alternatives identified in your synthesis section.*

5. **Execution**

a. *What would you need to do to implement your first choice?* Be as specific as you can; lay your plan out step-by-step (it is okay to number the steps). Who will you talk with? Where will you go? What new behavior will you undertake? What resources will you use? How will you implement your chosen options? This is your strategic plan. It may involve educational, occupational, and employment activities. Include a time frame for accomplishing each step.

b. *How much effort do you think it will take to implement your top-ranked alternative?*

6. **Communication**

a. *Where are you now in your educational and/or career decision making and where do you want to be in a year?* By thinking about the difference between where you are now and where you would like to be in the near or far future you can better anticipate and plan for the next decision that may have to be addressed.

b. *How do you feel about your current academic and/or career situation?* What are your internal and/or external cues telling you about your current situation? Are you satisfied or not?

c. *What are the next questions or issues that you will need to address?* If you are currently satisfied, what do you think might be the next issue that you will need to address ("I'm happy with my major, now it is time to find some experiences related to possible occupations or jobs."). If you are not currently satisfied, what do you need to focus on now?

Note: Remember to attach the Evaluation Form on the following page to your paper.

Appendix K

Resume Critique Worksheet

RESUME CRITERIA	COMMENTS
1. **Heading:** Is the name, address, and phone number located at top of first page? Is the name on subsequent pages? Temporary address? For how long? E-mail?	
2. **Objective:** Does career objective appear immediately under identification? Emphasize area in which they seek employment? Indicate general level of job they want? Clearly stated? Focused?	
3. **Overall Appearance:** Does the resume look professional? Do you want to read it? Easy to follow? Correct spelling, grammar, and punctuation?	
4. **Layout:** Do key sales points stand out? Uncluttered? Uses margins, white space, headlines, bold type, capital letters, underlining, etc.	
5. **Organization:** Is key information presented to accentuate skills, abilities, and accomplishments? Appropriate categories emphasized? Specifics stand out? Avoids unnecessary captions, strongest to weakest order? Consistent format?	
6. **Action-oriented:** Do sentences begin with positive action verbs? Avoid introductory phrases? Results-oriented? No exaggerations or lush adjectives?	
7. **Concise:** Uses short, clearly written phrases and paragraphs; avoids complete sentences; summary statements? Lists of accomplishments?	
8. **Relevance:** Has extraneous material been eliminated? Focuses on specific information about experience? Provides facts? Avoids generalities?	
9. **Controversial:** Does the resume raise more questions than it answers? Avoids mentioning controversial activities? Values?	
10. **Bottom Line:** How well does the resume present a positive picture of the applicant's qualifications for obtaining an interview?	
11. **Additional Items:**	

Appendix L

Employment Decision-Making Case Study

A Profile of Suzy

Suzy is a 22-year-old college senior who is about to graduate with her bachelor's degree from State U. She majored in psychology and minored in business management. She was raised in a small town in a rural part of the state. She chose State U. because of the school's reputation in psychology and because it is located near her home.

Suzy has shown an interest in helping people. Since her sophomore year, she has been a volunteer telephone crisis counselor. In her senior year, she interned at the local community mental health halfway house for adults who were recovering from alcohol dependency. Suzy received a great deal of satisfaction when she helped one of her clients through a difficult period. She enjoyed the opportunity to help others learn new skills. She liked the constant variety and challenges presented by her clients. Once she demonstrated her ability to help others she was given the freedom to work independently, which she valued. Suzy enjoyed the family atmosphere among the staff members.

During her summers, she worked as an administrative assistant for the supervisor of a small publishing company. She liked the fast pace of the business world and the excellent salary she received. Suzy hoped to find a job that would provide her the opportunity to help others, to manage the work of others, and to make a good salary that would allow her to enjoy some of the finer things in life. Suzy has been offered two positions described below. Which job should she choose?

Suzy has identified the eight factors below for consideration in her employment decision making (see Chapter 14 for the complete list of 46 factors). Based on her profile information, use the following three ratings to indicate how important you think each of these factors is for Suzy, e.g., (**1**) Somewhat Important, (**2**) Important, (**3**) Very Important?

1. Independence
2. Opportunities to help others
3. Variety
4. Advancement opportunities
5. Compatibility with employer
6. Work-related travel required
7. Closeness to home
8. Salary/income (present)

Assessing the Match between Suzy and Two Job Offers

Suzy has received two job offers but she is having some difficulty deciding which one to take. Review the information provided below and estimate which job offer would be the best match for meeting the **eight** factors Suzy identified. Use these ratings to assess the degree of match between Suzy and the job offer:

0 = Not a Match at All; **1** = Poor Match; **2** = Close Match; **3** = Exact Match.

Job Offer #1

Suzy has been offered a full-time, live-in job at the halfway house where she interned. A dorm-type room and meals are provided. Her job title: Mental Health Technician. Starting salary: $30,000 with a raise to $32,000 after one year. Tuition reimbursement and release time is available if she pursues her master's degree. She will be a member of a five-person paraprofessional support team. Turnover in house staff is frequent due to morale problems, which stem from long hours and low pay. With hard work, Suzy could be promoted to the position of House Director within two or three years. Some of her friends and instructors in psychology have told her that this is an excellent entry-level opportunity to gain a wide range of skills and experiences in the mental health field.

Job Offer #2

Suzy has also received an offer to work as a New Employee Trainer within the Training and Development section of the Human Resources Office of a new telecommunications firm in Jacksonville. Personnel work has always sounded exciting to Suzy. She has been offered a starting salary of $40,000. She would be required to do research on how to teach others new skills, and to develop written and multimedia materials to aid in training. Her supervisor expects all decisions to be cleared by him. The job would require her to evaluate the progress of new trainees and to recommend the termination of those who failed to meet the minimum job standards. During slow periods, she would be expected to help the clerical staff with the paperwork. One of her friends works for the organization. She told Suzy that the benefits were good but there was very little turnover and the opportunities for advancement were slim. However, after two years, she would be eligible for admission to the management training program at the firm. Suzy has heard that women are being actively recruited into this program.

A form for evaluating offers is included on the next page.

Directions: Write the eight job factors that Suzy selected in the blank spaces in the left column. The names of her two potential jobs are at the top of the other columns.

Using the numbers below, **weigh** how important you think each FACTOR is to Suzy ( ) in the left column below (FACTORS & weights):

> **1**—Somewhat Important
> **2**—Important
> **3**—Very Important

Using the **match** numbers below, rate ( ) how well you think each JOB matches Suzy's factors in the remaining columns:

> **0**—Not at All
> **1**—Poor Match
> **2**—Close Match
> **3**—Exact Match

Multiply the weight for each factor times the rating for each job in matching that factor, and then total the scores for each job in the last row below. Which job should Suzy take?

FACTORS & (weight #)		JOB 1 Technician (match #)	JOB 2 Trainer (match #)
	( )	× ( ) =	× ( ) =
	( )	× ( ) =	× ( ) =
	( )	× ( ) =	× ( ) =
	( )	× ( ) =	× ( ) =
	( )	× ( ) =	× ( ) =
	( )	× ( ) =	× ( ) =
	( )	× ( ) =	× ( ) =
	( )	× ( ) =	× ( ) =
TOTAL			

Appendix M
Computer/Website System Feedback Forms

Subject Index

Author Index